Learn
&
Live™

Executive Editor: Patty Burness
Editor: William Snider
Contributing Editors: Roz Kirby, Randall Duckett,
Jane Hartford, Linda Chion-Kinney

Copies of *Learn & Live*™ are available by
calling 1-888-4RKIDS1 (toll-free)

Printed in the United States of America on Multi Web,
a recycled, acid-free paper using soy-based inks. ♻ ∞

Cover art by Kristen Funkhouser

Library of Congress Catalog Card Number: 97-70481
ISBN 0-9656326-0-1

The George Lucas
Educational Foundation

Patty Burness
Executive Editor

William Snider
Editor

Roz Kirby
Randall Duckett
Jane Hartford
Linda Chion-Kinney
Contributing Editors

The George Lucas Educational Foundation
Nicasio, California

A Letter from George Lucas

Photo by Howard Roffman

I believe public education is the cornerstone of our society. It is the foundation of our freedom and a vital building block of our democracy—a stepping stone for young and old alike to reach their full potential. And that's why people are so passionate about it. The challenge we face today is to translate this passion into action and reinvigorate public education. If we are successful, we can make a vast difference in the quality of life for our children, ourselves, and for future generations.

This will not be easy. My own experience in public school was quite frustrating; I was often bored. Occasionally, I had a teacher who engaged me, who made me curious and motivated me to learn. Those were the teachers I really loved, but they were few and far between. I was disappointed that there were not more teachers like them and wondered, "Why can't school be interesting all of the time?" College was where I finally began to enjoy school. I felt challenged by what I was learning and encouraged to pursue my dreams.

The problems I experienced in school are not dissimilar to those faced by many students today. Traditional education can be extremely isolating—the curriculum is often abstract and not relevant to real life, teachers and students don't connect with resources outside of the classroom, and schools operate as if they were separate from their communities. School is actually one of the few institutions in our society where the participants work in an isolated environment—too often, they go through intellectual exercises that aren't linked to the world outside.

Many people are wrestling with how to improve the educational system so it is more responsive to the needs of learners. All over the country educators, parents, policy makers, business and community leaders, and students are rethinking the mission of schools and adopting innovative approaches to teaching and learning.

People are also beginning to recognize that technology can be a powerful tool for change in education, just as it is in the worlds of business, science, and entertainment. Telecommunications can break down the isolation that is so prevalent in schools, connecting students and teachers to their peers and experts, and opening an electronic gateway to a universe of information. Interactive multimedia and simulation technologies offer exciting opportunities for students to explore information, pursue their interests, experiment, and demonstrate what they have learned.

There are literally hundreds of exciting programs all across the country that are providing the sparks that will energize education and propel us into the 21st century. That's why The George Lucas Educational Foundation sponsored this book and the accompanying documentary film—to show parents, educators, policy makers, and the general public how technology and other innovations are being used to help create dynamic, effective public schools, places where learning is meaningful and often fun.

Our leaders have to make difficult choices every day, dealing with issues as complex as health care, transportation, and the infrastructure. We cannot afford to let education be left out of the national debate. If we share a common love of learning throughout our lives, then the nation's enormous resources can be brought to bear in this important endeavor.

George Lucas

Contents

ix   *About This Book*

xv   *Acknowledgments*

1   Introduction

Students   7

13   Chapter 1: Learning

39   Chapter 2: Assessment

Teachers   57

63   Chapter 3: Role of the Teacher

81   Chapter 4: Learning to Teach

Communities   99

105   Chapter 5: Involving Families

123   Chapter 6: Connecting Communities

141   Chapter 7: Business Partnerships

Schools   159

165   Chapter 8: Reinventing Schools

191   Chapter 9: Places for Learning

209   Chapter 10: Technology

231   Glossary

234   Electronic Resources

253   Index

About This Book

In this modern, rapidly changing world, a solid foundation of learning is essential for successful living. Education offers people the skills and knowledge needed to lead rich, rewarding lives, to adapt and prosper in the workplace, and to be active participants in our democracy. Every child who receives a good education can be an asset to society, while each one who falls through the cracks adds to the social and economic costs we all bear.

We hope this book and accompanying documentary film serve as catalysts for conversation in communities around the nation. The images in the documentary film and descriptions in the book attempt to provide a starting point for talking about the role of public schools, about what their goals should be, and about what they could be doing differently. They also can be used as a focus of town meetings or informal gatherings in your living room.

These materials are about people who are committed to providing every child with a quality education—and who are demonstrating, day after day, that this goal is within reach. Using new technologies together with proven ideas about learning, dedicated teachers across the country are showing that it is possible to successfully educate all students.

When you visit a school like Clear View Charter School in Chula Vista, Calif., or Shorecrest High School in Shoreline, Wash., it is impossible not to be struck by what teachers and students are inspired to do. Fourth and fifth graders at Clear View work via a two-way interactive video connection with scientists at a local university to study insects under an electron microscope. Juniors at Shorecrest design sophisticated computer graphics and write programs for a leading software company.

The kids at the schools in the documentary film and this book aren't unique. They are a mixture of modern Americans, representing a range of racial and ethnic backgrounds, coming from varied family environments and structures, possessing the full spectrum of interests and abilities. The kids aren't different, but many things about these schools are.

Why We Wrote This Book

We wrote this book to share the good news about pioneering education efforts. We want a broader audience to know that programs like those just described are making a difference in the lives of children. The work of committed teachers and other school leaders deserves to be recognized and celebrated. The state of public education in this nation is not as grim as it is often painted—the accomplishments of many schools, including those portrayed here, are simply not getting enough attention. They show that creating better public schools is not a mystery—much of the knowledge and many of the skills needed already exist.

This book and documentary film are meant to help connect you with ideas that are generating excitement in schools throughout the country. They will hopefully inspire you to join the effort to improve public education and to ask "How can we make *our* schools that good?" The task of transforming the educational system into one that works for all children is immense, and it will take the efforts of every one of us, day by day and school by school. A substantial investment of time, resources, and other support will be required over the long haul.

Finally, we wrote this book as a tool for those who are ready to begin—or have already started—working to improve schools. These pages are chock full of ideas to think about, personal stories to draw inspiration from, descriptions of schools and programs to outline the range of possibilities, and hundreds of pointers to organizations, reading material, and electronic resources to turn to for information and assistance. We have made it as easy as possible to contact all of the schools, programs, organizations, and people we mention. All of the entries include a phone number, and most also include a fax number and e-mail and World Wide Web addresses.

We don't attempt to provide answers in this book. Instead, we present a wide range of possibilities because we believe there is not one way to improve schools, just as there is not one way to educate all children. Each community needs to make its own decisions about how to advance change.

How This Book Was Prepared

This book is the product of almost three years of research and writing. We started by convening meetings with several hundred people—leaders in education and technology, teachers, students, child development specialists, government officials, and business people—who shared their ideas and asked us to help get the word out about innovative, exciting programs in education.

Next, we conducted an extensive survey of the recent literature on school reform and educational technology and began hundreds of interviews to compile a list of schools, programs, organizations, and electronic resources for possible inclusion in the book. We visited a number of schools ourselves and relied on recommendations from a network of trusted sources for others. Our database of possibilities continued to grow, and we ended up with many more than we had imagined—or could possibly fit in a single volume. It is clear that committed people are working in every corner of the country to make schools better, often with little recognition or publicity.

We had to make a lot of hard choices in deciding what to include. This is not an empirical study—we did not try to identify or quantify the "best" schools and programs. Instead, we based our selections on a desire to show the broad sweep of what is going on in innovative public schools and districts. We also tried to ensure a wide geographic sampling. We decided not to include the many exciting projects that are being carried on in individual classrooms, although they are important, because we want to focus attention on broader school-wide and district-wide changes. At several points along the way, we asked a variety of experts to review the selections we had made and confirm that we were on the right track. We're confident that the schools and programs we chose to include are representative of some of the most exciting and effective things going on in education, but we're also aware that, for every school and program in this book, there are dozens more that are equally deserving of inclusion.

An important criterion throughout our work was to find examples that demonstrate intelligent and sophisticated uses of computers, telecommunications, and interactive multimedia technologies. Most of the ideas about teaching and learning in this book are not new, although research is only now revealing how and why they work. What is new today is the availability of technologies that can help make learning more engaging for everyone. The kinds of changes that must be made to the educational system can often be enhanced by technology. We want to show how it can transform teaching and learning in much the same way it has recently transformed many businesses.

We have made every effort to double-check the information and make sure it is current. But the passage of time means that inevitably names will change, staff will move on, phone numbers will be disconnected, and electronic resources will evolve. Meanwhile, new efforts will begin and better practices will be discovered. An electronic version of this book and other information are available at our World Wide Web site (http://glef.org). We will update it regularly.

How This Book Can Be Used

Every reader has a role to play in helping make the possibilities described in this book a reality. Educators cannot do the job of changing schools and teaching children alone. The more that people get involved, the faster we can reach the goal of educating all children well. And it's not just children who will benefit—all of us stand to gain if we pitch in together to make sure the next generation receives the best possible education.

A good place to start is by helping to establish a new vision for what schools should be as we approach the 21st century. This book and the accompanying documentary film are meant to question traditional assumptions about schools. What goals should our local schools have today?

What are the strategies that engage more children in learning? How can technology help students and teachers learn? These questions need to be asked and answered at each individual school, at the district level, in statehouses, and in a national conversation about education. Raise these questions with colleagues and friends— collaborating with others is an important aspect of fundamental change.

This book is also designed to be used as a launching pad for increasing your own knowledge of teaching and learning. In a book of this length, we can only scratch the surface of the many ideas and innovations that people are struggling with as they work to create effective schools. We've included pointers to resources that are intended for the general public, because we believe that the first step in improving our schools is to make sure everyone shares a common understanding and language. We've also listed resources that are targeted to educators, because sharing ideas and learning different practices are essential elements in changing a school.

Finally, we hope readers will use this book to celebrate the things that schools are already doing well. It offers ammunition to those who are working with these ideas to improve their schools. It also offers information that anyone can use to act as an advocate for public schools, reminding communities why public education is important and working to ensure that it gets the investment and support it needs. Efforts to transform schools cannot succeed without a shared understanding of the enormous importance of a long-term investment in education and of the reality that there are no quick fixes.

Navigating This Book

This book is designed to be useful even if you don't read it from cover to cover. Start in any chapter that interests you, or turn to the index to find programs and topics that you want to learn more about. As you flip though the pages of this book, the message should be clear: you are not alone. There are a lot of other people working to improve schools, people that you can learn from and with whom you can share your thoughts.

As the staff of the Foundation researched innovative ideas and practices in American education, we continually debated the best way to organize the information we uncovered. It's impossible to completely separate the interlocking issues that are important to creating effective schools. Yet, as we looked around the country and read the literature, a clear pattern emerged. Few schools, districts, or states have the luxury of planning and implementing wholesale changes in every facet of their operations. Instead, most pick one or two issues, like curriculum or technology integration, as the initial focus of their efforts. So we decided to organize material into 10 chapters built around the broad areas essential to changing schools. We don't mean to imply, however, that reforming one or two elements of the educational system is sufficient. In fact, much of the information you find in any one chapter may fit into any of the others. We firmly believe that success in any of these 10 areas requires a close look at all of the other areas, because many well-intentioned reforms fail when they are undermined by other entrenched parts of the system.

The chapters are grouped into four sections: Students, Teachers, Communities, and Schools. The first three highlight the fact that education is built on interactions among people who must alter their habits and attitudes to achieve lasting change. These three groups are the main players and stakeholders in education—the ones who stand to be most affected by and bear the most responsibility for improving schools. The fourth section, Schools, acknowledges that the institutional aspects of education also affect the ultimate success of school reform. It examines aspects of organizational and physical infrastructure that can help or hinder learning, as well as the ways computers, telecommunications networks, and other emerging technologies can transform how students and educators do their work.

Each chapter is a blend of vision, inspiration, and information. They are organized into these main elements:

Imagine the Possibilities The answers to education's problems don't lie in an idealized memory of school days past, but in a shared vision of its future. So, to start each chapter, we asked some of the nation's most well-known leaders in school reform to paint a picture of what our schools could—and should—look like. If the pieces seem idealistic, it is because they are. The writers were given free rein to assemble the best current ideas, technologies, and programs into a coherent whole—essentially reinventing schooling from the ground up. Their pieces are part essay, part fiction, and part road map for the progress we can make in the near future.

From the Front Lines The visionary essays are followed by reports from the front lines of school reform, written by people who are actively involved in education. These pieces show how, through dedication and hard work, ambitious goals and promising ideas become reality in America's classrooms. The writers share their personal struggles and successes in achieving educational change, and talk about the lessons they have learned along the way.

Snapshots When it comes to understanding the value of innovative ideas, there is no substitute for seeing them in action. Each chapter includes a number of brief profiles that describe how concepts in this book have been put into practice in a variety of schools and communities. Although it is tempting to call these places successful, all will admit they are still working hard to improve and change. Due to space limitations, the most we can offer is a slice of life in these schools and programs; they are doing far more than we have described.

Access to Information Each chapter contains a broad selection of resources that can help you learn more about the ideas and practices raised in this book. We describe hundreds of books, reports, periodicals, and organizations that can provide further information, advice, and support for school reform initiatives.

Appendices At the end of the book we provide two additional resources. The first, a glossary, defines some of the terms that are central to this vision of educational change. The second is an extensive list of electronic resources to supplement the information in the chapters.

Getting Involved

Our goal in publishing this book and funding the documentary film is that you, the reader, will be inspired and empowered to take the next step. We want to arouse your curiosity to learn more and motivate you to become involved in public education in whatever ways you think best. We urge you to view these materials as tools for getting started or for reinforcing what you are already doing. Organize a community meeting or invite some friends over to view the documentary film and talk about your goals and aspirations for your schools. Compare what other schools and districts are doing to what's happening in your community. Call or visit the schools and programs we profile. Contact the organizations and networks that seem most appropriate for your needs. Read the periodicals, books, and reports that we found most useful in trying to understand these issues ourselves. Go on-line to explore the wealth of educational resources available on the Internet. Write, call, or e-mail the Foundation and tell us what you think of our work. Above all, make a commitment to support public schools so that someday soon every child will have a quality education. ●

Acknowledgments

During the course of the past few years, scores of people have contributed their time, energy, and expertise to bring this book from conception to the printed page. It truly has been a collaborative effort. We share a deep commitment to public education and its role in our lives and the lives of our children. That commitment has been our guiding star; during the long hours, technical glitches, and philosophical disagreements, it enabled us to keep focused on the task at hand. The result is a book in which we can take great pride, a book that celebrates public education and that we hope many people will find useful as they work to improve schools.

This book owes its existence to the vision and commitment of the Board of Directors: George Lucas, Steve Arnold, Kim Meredith, Kate Nyegaard, Marshall Turner, and Sam Yamada. They brought their strong leadership and entrepreneurial spirit to bear on this challenge. Our Board of Advisors is an incredible group of people whose expertise, insight, and advice over the long haul has helped make this effort worthwhile. Our thanks to Pat Bolaños, Bonnie Bracey, James Burke, Christopher Cerf, Dee Dickinson, Judith Lanier, Shirley Malcom, Bob Peterkin, Linda Roberts, Bill Rojas, Ken Sakatani, Barbara Sampson, Karen Sheingold, and Grant Wiggins.

To complete a project of this scope required massive amounts of research on-line, in person, and over the telephone. Our researchers read what seems like every book, journal, report, and newsletter that has ever been published on education and technology. During the endless conversations we had in the office, we dissected every issue in every possible way. Thanks to Roz Kirby and her team of researchers, including Laura Bucuzzo, Kara Finnegan, Marko Fong, Daniella Phillips, and Maia Rosen.

Each chapter of this book contains essays we commissioned from some of the best-known people in education today, as well as from those who are less known, but no less important—the people on the front lines actually doing what others are talking and writing about. Thank you for the important contributions you made in helping present the issues from a variety of perspectives.

It is no small feat to edit a work like this. In a jargon-laden world like education, clear, concise language is an imperative. Without the guidance of Bill Snider and his team of Randall Duckett, Jane Hartford, and Linda Chion-Kenney, the book would not be the readable, useful resource it is today. Thanks to Roz and Sybil Ellery and Scott Hill for their editorial contributions.

A book of this nature requires checking and re-checking information, careful handling of correspondence, accurate and reliable proofreading, and attention to hundreds of details. Julie Byers, Jenny Roisman, Laurie Yusem, and Suzy Starke were patient and persevering as they coped with all of the tasks and changes that came their way.

As we reported about advances in technology, benefits of telecommunications, and the ever-expanding Web, we consistently experienced frozen computers, interrupted transmissions, and sites that never existed. In the midst of all of this, Geoff Butterfield and Rick Phelan provided the technical support and assistance that was so essential.

Every project of this magnitude receives invaluable help from interns who willingly do all kinds of things. This project was no exception, and I want to recognize the contributions of Laura Century, Scott Donnelly, David Goldstein, Denise Howald, Beth McCullough, and Mike Widener.

This resource book would not have been possible if there weren't so many schools, districts, programs, and organizations around the country that are dedicated to helping all children learn and reach their true potential. We applaud their efforts. Thanks to the teachers, parents, students, principals, superintendents and other district staff, educational technology coordinators, chief state school officers, business people, program directors and coordinators, community members, policy makers, researchers, and others who graciously answered phone and e-mail requests for information. They remained eager to help no matter how many times we came back for more information or for verification of the facts and figures they had given us. Many spoke with us and gave of their time yet do not appear in the book—our thanks for helping us to understand the issues and for what you are doing for children.

In 1993, the Foundation held a series of meetings intended to inform us and shape our thinking about education and technology and the changes that were likely to occur during the next 25 years. They were attended by experts in education, multimedia and telecommunications technologies, child development, and psychology as well as policy makers, researchers, teachers, principals, students, parents, program directors, and business and community leaders. We certainly benefited from their wisdom, but the great thing about those meetings was that these people had a chance to discuss the issues with their colleagues—something many of them are often too busy to do. While too numerous to name individually, they shared their experiences, pointed us to valuable resources, and formed the basis of a fantastic network of people around the country upon whom the Foundation now relies for the latest information.

Each chapter of the resource book has been reviewed several times by people who are knowledgeable in the field. Their critiques helped sharpen our focus and strengthen the material. We appreciate your help.

This book comes alive because of the creative design work of Tom Ingalls, Caryl Gorska, and their wonderful group of illustrators. The words are reinforced by fantastic stills from the documentary film and special moments caught by terrific photographers from all across the country. Carolyn Knutson/The Regents deserves special thanks for great print management, as does Trisha Lamb Feuerstein for the comprehensive index. Frances Lennie generously contributed the software to deliver and maintain the index.

We worked hard to select schools for this book and documentary film that are representative of the many innovations in education today. We are excited that it captures the vision of The George Lucas Educational Foundation so well. The film is a production of State of the Art, Inc., Washington, D.C., and was produced and directed by Gerardine Wurzburg.

Space limitations don't allow us to name everyone who made important contributions to this effort, including attorneys, consultants, and others without whom this project wouldn't be the same.

The work that is being done at this Foundation is some of the most rewarding that I have ever been involved with. Having the opportunity to work with so many bright, creative, interesting people is everyone's dream. The fact that it is my job is unbelievable. Together, we have forged relationships, explored education and technology, and encouraged each other to think deeply about children and learning. I hope everyone who reads this book and watches the documentary film will share in the contagious enthusiasm we all feel about public education.

Patty Burness
Executive Editor

Introduction

Despite all of the talk of a crisis in America's public schools, our educational system is in the midst of one of the most **exciting** periods in its history. Rapid changes in society, technology, and the economy are creating an endless demand for well-educated people. Research is providing useful new insights into how children learn. New technologies are **transforming** communication and information, two of the main ingredients of education. And hundreds of schools across America are putting these developments to work, quietly demonstrating how we can give all children a fair chance to learn and live to their fullest **potential.**

Our public schools have historically pursued three **purposes:** to prepare young people to assume their responsibilities as **voters** and contribute to their communities, to give them the **skills** needed to be productive in the workplace, and to help them gain the knowledge and **wisdom** needed to fulfill their individual potential and lead satisfying lives.

> *"I can only say that I view education as the most important subject which we as a people can be engaged in."*
>
> **Abraham Lincoln, 1832**[1]

Almost everyone agrees that our public schools fall far short of serving these purposes today. We hear of employers who can't find qualified workers, universities that spend too much time teaching remedial math, and voters who can't muster enough interest to go to the polls. Hundreds of reports and articles have detailed the shortcomings of our **school system** as well. The gap between what people need to know to thrive in today's world and what they learn in school is very real.

Consider what it means for a student to be **prepared** for employment. Forty years ago, a high school dropout could work at a factory and earn enough to raise

1

a family. Today, even a high school diploma is no longer adequate to land a good job. Most people will have to change **careers** several times during their lifetimes and a high percentage of jobs require advanced knowledge and technological skills. Success in today's workplace, in short, requires an ability to continue learning and **adapting** to changing times.

> *"It is true that the aim of education is development of individuals to the utmost of their potentialities."*
>
> John Dewey, 1934[2]

Being an informed voter and contributing to **community life** are more difficult than ever before. We are flooded with advertisements and brief bits of news coverage about important local and global issues. What balance should we strike between preserving the environment and creating jobs? How can welfare be reformed to address problems without harming the truly needy? Do local schools need a bond measure for construction and renovation? In order to **participate** effectively in these debates, a person needs to know how to dig deeper—to find more information, evaluate it, and use it to craft an opinion or a solution.

Leading a **satisfying** personal life is also becoming more and more of a challenge. We're faced with choices every day that were unimaginable a generation ago. Instead of choosing a family doctor, many of us have to weigh the merits of differing health plans. Even a decision about childcare requires us to **evaluate** costs and risks.

Every young person, regardless of family background or circumstance, has the potential to make vital contributions to society. We waste that **potential** when we fail to prepare them for the **challenges** they will face in the modern world. Every student who fails means more than just an impoverished life for that individual.

Improving the System Our educational system was not designed to prepare youth for a rapidly changing, highly **technological** society; it was created for a simpler time. Over the past decade, attempts to fix the system one piece at a time haven't worked. That's why more and more people are now looking at a **systemic** approach to education reform. Every part of the system is being examined, with the understanding that a change in one part may require changing other parts.

Instead of mandating more specific requirements, like how many hours and years students should spend studying math, policy makers and other leaders are stepping back and looking at the **bigger picture.** The question most frequently heard is: "What do today's students need to know and be able to do?" As national organizations, state governments, school districts, and individual schools raise this question, they have discovered it is not easy to forge agreement on an answer. But almost everyone involved agrees that answering this question is the logical place to begin as we strive to create **effective schools** for the 21st century.

Many schools and districts on the leading edge of reform started their work by initiating a conversation about the mission and **goals** of their school. They often invited everyone with a stake in education to the table, including parents, students, teachers, administrators, policy makers, business people, children's advocates, community leaders, and concerned citizens. Each of these **stakeholders** has an important perspective, and their sustained support is critical to making fundamental, lasting improvements.

The mission and goals guide the development of a curriculum with specific standards for **content** and student performance, a process typically led by educators with input from the same broad range of stakeholders. In states that have adopted **standards** and curriculum frameworks, these serve as guidelines for **local curriculum** development. Schools also borrow from national-level standards developed by organizations of scholars and teachers in each academic discipline. Both national and state-level standards and **frameworks** are not intended as mandates, but as **guidelines** that give communities flexibility to design curriculum reflecting local needs, interests, and resources. To prevent the curriculum from becoming outdated, some **communities** are setting up processes for regular review and updating.

> *"If the children...are untaught, their ignorance and vices will in future life cost us much dearer in their consequences, than it would have done, in their correction, by a good education."*
>
> **Thomas Jefferson, 1818** [3]

Giving Teachers More Authority and Responsibility Defining goals and standards is only the first step in creating effective schools. The second step is deciding how best to help students—*all* students—reach the standards. Traditionally, those decisions have been made by people, like board members and administrators, who may not have been in a classroom for years. Many of the **reforms** implemented during recent decades have pushed decisions about teaching and learning even further from the classroom, to the state and national level. An ever-increasing web of rules and regulations has dictated what **teachers** should teach and when and how they should teach it. This top-down approach was based on a flawed assumption: that there is one best way to teach all children. The system was designed as though all children were similar enough that they could learn the same things in the same way at the same rate. But, as **research** and experience have shown, the ways children learn are as varied as their personalities.

One of the most promising developments in education today is the growing recognition that teachers—the people working daily with students—should be given more **flexibility** to make decisions about teaching and learning. As the Carnegie Corporation's Task Force on Teaching as a Profession said in its report, *A Nation Prepared*: "If schools are to compete successfully with medicine, architecture, and accounting for staff, then teachers will have to have comparable **authority** in making the key decisions about the services they render. Within the context of a limited set of clear goals for students set by state and local policy makers, teachers, working together, must be free to exercise their **professional** judgment as to the best way to achieve these goals. This means the ability to make—or at least strongly influence—**decisions** concerning such things as the materials and instructional methods to be used, the staffing structure to be employed, the organization of the school day, the assignment of students, the consultants to be used, and the allocation of **resources** available to the school."[4]

> *"The main part of intellectual education is not the acquisition of facts but learning how to make facts live."*
>
> Oliver Wendell Holmes, Jr., 1886[5]

Most teachers understand that there are better ways to teach than the methods they learned in college. But they don't have the time, support, or resources to learn different strategies. In too many schools, professional development is limited to occasional workshops, organized only by administrators and scattered throughout the year.

At schools where teachers have been given **control** over their own professional development, they are avid learners working to boost their effectiveness. With the growing number of computer **networks,** teachers are able to connect with others around the world and access information **globally.** Given enough time and resources, they also observe in each others' classrooms, work together to research and develop curriculum, talk over problems and strategies, and **consult** with experts of their own choosing. These teachers report

> *"Knowledge is of two kinds: we know a subject ourselves, or we know where we can find information upon it."*
>
> Samuel Johnson, 1775[6]

that they no longer feel isolated in their classrooms and **enjoy** their jobs more.

Teaching and Learning with Technology Teachers know that to help all students succeed, they have to treat each one as an **individual,** getting to know their needs and interests and finding the keys to unlock their motivation to learn. They also know that students learn better when they have **opportunities** to talk about what they are doing, when they have time to ask questions, test assumptions, and make sense of information at their **own pace.** Throughout history, humans have used a wide variety of methods to pass down knowledge and skills: storytelling, dialogue, apprenticeships, real-world experiences—the list goes on and on. But, in many schools, scheduling conflicts and other logistical problems prevent teachers from having students work in more engaging ways than reading textbooks, listening to lectures, or other whole-class activities.

Incorporating a full range of teaching and **learning** methods in today's schools is getting easier thanks to advances in technology. Teachers and students can structure **projects** that take advantage of the rich array of information and expertise available via the **Internet** and other telecommunications technologies. In project work that involves grappling with complex problems or creating a product, students can dig deeper into any dimension that interests them while also accomplishing the curricular goals of the project. They are no longer bound by the knowledge contained in textbooks or the teacher's head.

Interactive multimedia **technologies** that incorporate audio, video, and graphics **engage** students' interests and open additional avenues for them to express their ideas and demonstrate what they have learned. The schools that have the freedom to set and pursue their own **visions** are finding that technology offers powerful tools to help translate their ideas into reality.

> *"There are... two educations. One should teach us how to make a living and the other how to live."*
>
> **James Truslow Adams, 1929[7]**

Moving Ahead The challenge we face is to take a hard look at what we expect our **public schools** to do, discard the practices that are not working, and support **changes** that promise a better future for all of our nation's children. That's the principle behind setting high standards for learning and then giving schools the freedom, support, and **responsibility** to produce results.

The schools in this book, like many others of equal accomplishment, show how creativity and dedication can lead to more **effective** education. They also show that the process of transforming a school requires a lot of hard work and sustained **support** from everyone concerned about children's welfare. To provide similar opportunities for all students will require a major investment of time, energy, and resources. But it's worth it. After all, education is the most important investment we can make in our **future.** ●

[1] Reprinted, with changes, from **The Abraham Lincoln Encyclopedia,** by Mark E. Neely, Jr. *McGraw-Hill: New York, NY, 1982, 94.*

[2] **John Dewey on Education: Selected Writings,** Reginald D. Archambault, ed. *Modern Library: New York, NY, 1964, 12.*

[3] **Thomas Jefferson Memorial Foundation, Inc.,** http://www.monticello.org/. "Education: Jefferson Quotations," http://www.monticello.org/Matters/interests/education.html (23 August 1996).

[4] **A Nation Prepared: Teachers for the 21st Century,** by the Task Force on Teaching as a Profession, Carnegie Forum on Education and the Economy. *Carnegie Forum on Education and the Economy: Washington, DC, 1986, 58.*

[5] **The International Thesaurus of Quotations,** Rhoda Thomas Tripp, comp. *Harper & Row: New York, NY, 1970, 173.*

[6] Ibid., 338.

[7] **Webster's New World Dictionary of Quotable Definitions,** 2nd Edition, Eugene E. Brussell, ed. *Prentice Hall: New York, NY, 1988, 163.*

Students

Alice Carlson Applied Learning Center, Fort Worth, TX • Photo by Paul Moseley

Students

The most important question anyone can ask when discussing how to improve schools is: "What's best for our children?" At least part of the answer is clear: today's students need to learn much more than reading, writing, and arithmetic, because advances in human knowledge and technology are transforming the ways we work, play, and communicate. In order to succeed in a complex and changing world, students need to develop sophisticated thinking and problem-solving skills and, above all,

Shorecrest High School, Shoreline, WA

Alice Carlson Applied Learning Center, Fort Worth, TX

8

the ability to continue learning throughout their lives. To accomplish this, many educators are using hands-on projects and interactive technologies, which motivate students to learn. At the same time, they are seeking better ways to evaluate student achievement so that assessment furthers the learning process. In this section, we put children front and center as we explore efforts to change curriculum, instruction, and assessment designed to help all students reach their full potential. ●

Dzantik'i Heeni Middle School, Juneau, AK

The future belongs to young people who know where the knowledge is, how to get it, how to think about it, and how to turn it into better work, better products, better lives.

Rexford Brown,[1] Executive Director, P.S. 1 Charter School and Urban Learning Communities, Inc.

MAX SEABAUGH

Students

Chapter 1: Learning

14 Introduction

16 Imagine the Possibilities:
Building a Bridge to Knowledge for Every Child
by Judy Pace & Howard Gardner

22 From the Front Lines:
A Hundred Times More Rewarding
by Alexis Carrero

24 From the Front Lines:
The Power of Project-Based Learning
by Terry Thode

26 Snapshots
Innovative Schools & Programs

30 Access to Information
Organizations, Periodicals, Readings & Contact Information

Chapter 2: Assessment

40 Introduction

42 Imagine the Possibilities:
Show What You Know As You Go
by Grant Wiggins

46 From the Front Lines:
Creating a Culture of Student Reflection
by Clyde Yoshida

48 Snapshots
Innovative Schools & Programs

52 Access to Information
Organizations, Periodicals, Readings & Contact Information

Chapter 1
Learning

In this world of rapid change, where information is expanding exponentially and increasing in complexity, learning is a **survival** skill. Mastering the basics—reading, writing, and arithmetic—is as important as ever, but it is no longer enough. Today's students need to learn more than previous generations. They need to know how to find and use new **information,** to make informed decisions about complicated issues, and to **collaborate** as part of a team. Since the pace of change shows no signs of slowing in the future, students also need to learn how to learn.

A growing number of educators, business leaders, community representatives, and government officials are working to clarify the **goals** of education. They are identifying the skills and knowledge **essential** for literacy in each of the academic disciplines, and are beginning to create a set of benchmarks to measure student achievement. With clearly articulated **standards,** schools and educators can be held accountable for ensuring that all students are well prepared for life beyond school.

Asking students to learn more—and expecting everyone to meet higher standards—means that schools have to adopt better **strategies.** This chapter describes how educators and researchers, working with new insights into the nature of intelligence, thinking, and learning, are demonstrating that the goal of educating **all students** is within reach.

Cognitive scientists are finding that learning is an **active** process of sense making, not just fact gathering. It entails interpreting new information, connecting it in some way to our own prior **knowledge,** and applying it appropriately. Conventional curriculum and instruction, with its focus on discrete skills and isolated facts and little **connection** to anything beyond the classroom, does not advance real learning.

How many of us ever made **sense** of square roots or understood why we diagrammed sentences? In classrooms around the country, educators are replacing memorization and rote learning with **challenging** activities that demand thinking and understanding.

This chapter highlights efforts by innovative educators to design interdisciplinary curriculum that **motivates** students by engaging them in real-world **projects.** In these activities, students **investigate** radiation in their town or examine life in a changing sea. With teachers as their guides, students are getting opportunities to follow individual areas of interest or to pursue **intriguing** leads, rather than simply turn pages in a book. Using technology, they uncover **rich resources,** work with peers and experts many miles away, or use scientific software to help them visualize abstract concepts. As students decide how they are going to proceed, and what strategies to use, they develop the skills they need to take **responsibility** for their own learning.

Students are **sharing** their individual talents and expertise as they work on these projects together. **Cooperative learning** accommodates individual differences among students and allows them to learn by talking over ideas with others, explaining their thoughts, and listening to other perspectives—the same way **adults** do in their lives.

What students need to learn **today** doesn't fit neatly into separate subjects with predetermined solutions that can be completed in 50-minute time periods. The efforts presented in the following pages take different approaches to addressing this problem, but all share one basic goal: to **improve** student learning and achievement. ●

Imagine the Possibilities

BY JUDY PACE AND HOWARD GARDNER

BUILDING A BRIDGE TO

knowledge for

When visitors walk through King School, they are often surprised. It is very different from the schools they attended and from others they have seen. Instead of children sitting quietly in rows facing the teacher at the front of the room, they find youngsters returning from a field study with jars and basins full of pond specimens. They see students working in cooperative groups, creating visual aids for a day of student-led workshops on environmental issues for the entire school community. Another group is rehearsing a musical about South Africa, called *Sarafina,* on the stage in the performing arts center. Children of all ages are updating their digital portfolios at computer stations throughout the school to prepare for student-teacher-parent conferences.

Instead of a class working its way through a textbook, our visitors notice students conducting their own research using a wide variety of resources. Some are analyzing data on water pollution. Other students are discussing their interviews with community members about last week's local elections. Another group is in the media center locating books, articles, videos, and films related to the history of South Africa.

Rather than worksheets and short-answer tests, our visitors find students reading each other's stories and giving feedback on strong and weak points. One teacher and student review a portfolio, which contains all of the planning, interviewing, drafting, and editing that went into a news report on a local incident. In the art studio, a student is presenting a series of her paintings to an audience of classmates, discussing what she has learned from each one and how her work has evolved.

At first our visitors are somewhat perplexed because King clashes so much with their own experience of school. But they notice how inviting and alive the school feels, how engaged students and teachers seem to be, how interesting and sophisticated the children's work looks. They are curious to know more about what makes it different.

Unfortunately, King School exists only in our imagination. It represents a dramatically different approach to learning than American education has traditionally embraced. Most of the ideas that King illustrates can be found here and there in innovative schools, but this idealized institution is meant to show what a school could look like when all the best ideas are brought together in one place.

Toward a Deeper Understanding Through conversations with various people, our visitors learn that King School is an integral part of its community, a mid-size town whose population has become increasingly diverse. School-related decisions are made with input from a variety of groups, including school staff, family members, students, the

Judy Pace[2] is a graduate student in education at Harvard University. Howard Gardner[2] is a professor of education at the Harvard Graduate School of Education and co-director of Harvard Project Zero.

E V E R Y
child

At a nearby pond, young scientists collect samples of pond life and bring them back to the lab to study under microscopes. They keep written records and make drawings of their observations. They show our visitors how to test the pond water for pollutants, and log on to the computer network to compare their findings with those of students in other communities.

In the video studio, young newscasters prepare for an interactive news program in which they relay and comment on important local, national, and international events, respond to questions, and facilitate discussion. Students do the writing and the production work for the program.

King's community knows that in order to leave school with real understanding in various fields, students need to have time to investigate a limited number of topics in depth. In a conversation with teachers, visitors learn more about how children come to school with their own previous knowledge, experiences, and ideas about the world in which they live, some of which are attuned to school learning, and others of which may be at odds with the messages of school. Teachers explain how they tap into this prior knowledge and help students make connections between old and new information.

Students are involved in activities that have clear value in a particular field in order to develop deep and important understandings.

Teachers also help students relate what they are learning to other topics they've studied and to their personal lives and community. For example, before studying the issue of racial segregation, students give examples of segregation and discrimination from their own lives and write journal entries on their experiences. Then they are better able to relate to the issue of segregation from a personal perspective.

In-depth exploration also serves the purpose of confronting misconceptions, stereotypes, and other naive theories that children develop before they even come to school. In the pond study, young children discuss their initial thoughts about the differences between living and non-living, or between plants and animals. Only after many observations and discussions regarding biological

town council, and the business community. In this racially and economically diverse setting, decision makers strive to make a match between the school and the needs, values, and interests of the larger community.

Our visitors hear repeatedly that the school's intent is to foster understanding, which it defines as the ability to apply knowledge to new situations. Students are involved in activities that have clear value in a particular field in order to develop deep and important understandings. For example, a group of young historians discusses the connections and the differences between *Brown v. the Board of Education* and the overthrow of apartheid in South Africa. This discussion is based on their analysis of newspaper articles, films, and interviews.

characteristics, growth and change, production of energy, and reproduction of a species do students begin to understand these categories in a way consistent with systematic thinkers, such as biologists and ecologists.

Questions and Themes The King School community has confronted the challenge of deciding what students need to learn as a consequence of considerable research, dialogue, and planning in committees made up of teachers, administrators, parents, community members, and students. They agree that student learning should be driven by provocative, overarching questions that are revisited throughout the primary and secondary curriculum. These questions bring coherence and integration to learning within and across domains. Students' investigations increase in complexity and sophistication as they get older. Questions may include the following: Who am I and how do I fit into my community? How do I know what is true? How do people solve problems? What is the nature of the physical environment?

To investigate these universal questions, students study topics and themes that are relevant and rich in possibilities. Because committee members agree that they must choose a few strategic areas to probe in depth—rather than cover many topics superficially—the question of which topics and themes to pursue becomes a matter of critical importance. The committee decides to use topics and themes at the heart of real-world issues, such as power and conflict, preservation of the natural environment, and the struggle for equality. Some topics and themes are central to a discipline, such as life cycles in biology, civil rights in social studies, and statistics in mathematics. Others cut across disciplines, such as diversity and commonality, the nature of argument and evidence, or patterns.

Much of the curriculum at King is interdisciplinary. Students explore real-world issues through different lenses, while using disciplinary knowledge as needed. For example, to investigate apartheid in South Africa, students do research on the history, politics, and economics of the country. They read the literature and listen to the music of South Africans. They come to understand how one discipline informs another, and why many real-world problems require an interdisciplinary team to address them.

This kind of learning helps students make connections and generalizations across disciplines, while they identify differences among them as well. They learn that the way in which historical

King's teachers are aware that, in order for students to do interdisciplinary work of good quality, they must have solid grounding in the academic disciplines.

facts and explanations are arrived at differs from the determination of scientific facts and models. King's teachers are aware that, in order for students to do interdisciplinary work of good quality, they must have solid grounding in the academic disciplines. Interdisciplinary studies also provide students opportunities to pursue areas of individual interest and strength. They engage in work that combines ways of knowing and can be so seamless that it is tough to say where art begins, history ends, or science takes off.

Working on Projects A major part of the curriculum is project-based. Students get involved in work that revolves around a central topic or theme, is sustained over a long period of time, and culminates in a final product or performance. Through projects, students apply their knowledge and skills to create a whole and meaningful exhibit or performance that they share with an audience. Although there are certain requirements, there is room for choice; students have some control over the content of their work and the activities they will perform. Students become engaged in the creative process, which they document in portfolios that record all of the work and thinking that goes into these projects. And they participate in critiquing and evaluating their own and others' projects.

Students who are studying samples of pond life become so interested in what they are discovering that they decide to investigate the pond's entire ecosystem. One line of inquiry leads to another, and they learn about the life cycle of the pond as well as the impact of human beings on this ecosystem. Students chat on-line with a biologist from a nearby college and interview a parent who is a naturalist. They also poll members of the school community on their awareness and use of the pond. Students break into small groups to do research on an area of particular interest and share their findings with the rest of the large group.

In order to convince people about the importance of preserving and appreciating the value of

the pond, the students decide to make a presentation to the broader community. Students consult with a friend of the school who designs exhibits at a science museum. They display what they've learned about the pond's ecosystem by creating an interactive multimedia exhibit with their own drawings, dioramas, photos, videos, databases, maps, and reports on pond life. The students collect signatures on a petition to protect the pond from unrestricted fishing and pollution and send it to a local environmental policy group.

Learning Together Students at King frequently work in cooperative, multi-age groups of mixed abilities. These cooperative groups are based on the idea that learning takes place through social interaction and dialogue; indeed students teach each other by working together to solve problems or create products. Students make unique contributions to the group based on their strengths and support each others' weaknesses. Students with greater understanding in certain areas increase it by explaining ideas to others, whereas those with less developed understanding can reach for the level that is modeled by their peers. Through group work, students learn important skills like

collaboration and role-taking, thus developing their interpersonal intelligence. In such social contexts, students feel motivated to participate and show what they can do.

Along with cooperative groups, technology is a critical element in students' learning and is drawn upon in a natural and seamless way. Students are aided by the computer as they engage in all kinds of simulations and problem solving, from learning to fly airplanes to constructing an ideal town. They research projects on electronic databases that contain vast amounts of human knowledge. Students collaborate with peers and access experts worldwide through computer networks. They develop multimedia portfolios to document their work. During conferences, parents can click on a computer screen and hear their child describing the architectural design they are seeing or watch a video clip of a dance performance and read the child's reflection on how it conveys the theme of interdependence.

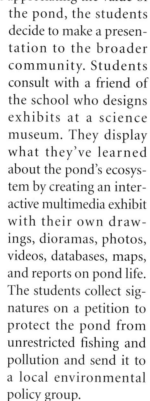

Students collaborate with peers and access experts worldwide through computer networks.

Measuring Progress How can we be sure that students at King are developing an understanding of the concepts and topics identified as important, as well as the skills to build and express these understandings? Assessment of student learning occurs continually in many different ways, and is inseparable from the process of teaching and learning. As has long been the case in the arts and athletics, assessment is centered on students' performances. A master pianist coaches a young musician on her execution of a piece according to certain criteria, such as accuracy of the notes and rhythm as well as appropriate interpretation and expression in phrasing and dynamics. So, too, a teacher coaches a student on her debate in terms of the accuracy of information, use of evidence to make an argument, and persuasive delivery. Much of the assessment takes place in the course of rehearsal. Students are totally involved in the assessment process as they reflect on their own work and use their reflections and feedback from teachers and peers to revise their performances. Parents and other community members also become involved in reviewing portfolios, questioning students about their learning, and helping to evaluate major projects and performances.

One of the striking features of King School is the number of opportunities to learn in different ways. The community has put a lot of thought into one of the toughest challenges for educators: how to reach all students. Community members believe that it is crucial to pay attention to individual differences. Teachers approach their work with students in ways that affirm and tap into the range of intelligences shared by all people: linguistic, logical-mathematical, spatial, musical, bodily-kinesthetic, interpersonal, and intrapersonal. (Linguistic and logical-mathematical intelligences are the areas that have always been emphasized in schools— they concern words and numbers. But the other intelligences can be equally important to learning. A student who has a high level of spatial intelligence, for example, will likely be more engaged when working with physical shapes and models; a student who excels in bodily-kinesthetic intelligence engages more when working in the context of physical activities, such as dance or sports.) Recognizing that children, as well as adults, have different areas of strengths and interests, King's teachers provide a variety of ways for students to engage with a new topic.

Recognizing that children, as well as adults, have different areas of strengths and interests, King's teachers provide a variety of ways for students to engage with a new topic.

Instead of students showing what they know by taking a written test or some other prescribed format that may target an area of weakness instead of a strength, to some extent they choose how they will demonstrate their understanding. In this way, assessment supports students' learning. Among the group of students studying the food web in the pond, for example, one is writing an explanation while another is drawing a diagram.

Translating Research into Practice King School is an example of a school that builds a bridge between educational research and teaching; theory and practice inform one another. The school's practices are coherent and sound because they are based on ideas that are mutually reinforcing and that revolve around education for deep understanding. These ideas are discussed by teachers and shared with the larger community so that important decisions about curriculum and instruction can be made by representatives of different groups and understood by all stakeholders. In this context, everyone in the school community becomes a learner.

In summary, at King School, learning is driven by students' questions about themselves, their communities, and the world. Teachers target central concepts and issues in their work with students. Students explore these questions, concepts, and issues through a variety of activities.

Learning is integrated across disciplines so that students are working on real-world problems, making connections across disciplines, and becoming complex thinkers. Students and teachers take time to investigate a few important areas in depth using a wide range of school and community-based resources. Students create projects in which they apply knowledge and demonstrate understanding in multiple ways. Learning is a collaborative and inclusive activity in which individuals—students, teachers, parents, and others—bring different strengths that contribute to the whole. The entire community supports and benefits from the educational process. ●

From the Front Lines

BY ALEXIS CARRERO

a hundred times more

When I was in the fifth grade, my family moved from New York to Florida for a year where I attended a traditional, neighborhood school. Before we moved, my mother researched the local schools, and my school was considered one of the best in the area. I don't remember much of what I learned that year, but a couple of things do stick in my mind. One day, our homework assignment was to answer the questions at the back of a chapter in one of our textbooks. The last question was a "What do you think?" type of question. When I got my homework back, my teacher told me that my answer was wrong. I never got over how she could say my opinion was wrong. The message was clearly that my opinion didn't matter.

I moved back to New York for the sixth grade and went back to Central Park East (CPE). It was like a breath of fresh air. I wasn't just a student, I was also a teacher and an equal. My opinions and ideas were respected. I had always been treated this way at CPE, but at my Florida school, I kind of forgot that this was the way I should be treated as a student.

My teachers in Florida only wanted kids to do what they were told: read the book, answer the questions, take a test. When we studied the Revolutionary War, we had to memorize the information in our textbook, including a poem about Paul Revere. It was very important to know the poem exactly, but it had no meaning to me. If you had asked me to recite the poem a week later, I wouldn't have been able to. What purpose did this poem have? Why was it so important for me to memorize? After learning this poem, our lesson on Paul Revere was over and we moved on to another topic.

At CPE, memorizing wasn't good enough. We were expected to study a topic until we really understood it, then come up with some kind of creative way of presenting what we learned. When we studied the Civil War at Central Park East Secondary School (CPESS), our group had to become experts and teach what we discovered to the rest of the class. We had to do a lot of research, reading letters from the time and books written by people with different points of view. Then we had to make a presentation and explain and defend our ideas. My friends and I created the Civil War News, a simulated broadcast on the important battles, turning points, and significance of the war. At the end we had a news flash announcing the end of the war. I remember a lot more of what I learned about the Civil War that year than what I learned in Florida about the Revolutionary War.

An important part of the approach at CPESS is that teachers allowed us to influence what we were learning and how we learned it. When we were studying the history of the 1920s and '30s, for example, we found that our textbooks lacked information from varied points of view and dealt with the history of people of color in a superficial manner. So this inspired us to create our own textbook about the '20s and '30s. We chose our topics, assigned our own homework, and scheduled our class time to discuss and organize the textbook. By the end of the class, our book had sections about topics ranging from the Apollo Theater to the women's suffrage movement. Everyone in the class worked harder because it became our work, and instead of our teacher feeling like he had lost control, he encouraged us 100 percent.

My friends thought that CPESS sounded cool, that we had a lot of freedom and could talk with our teachers. They thought our work sounded easier because everything didn't lead up to a test, and they thought taking a test was a lot harder than what we were doing. But I think memorizing a bunch of facts and answering multiple-choice questions on a test is easier, because it's

It feels good to get a high grade on a test, but when you do a portfolio—presenting your ideas and then defending them—it's a hundred times more rewarding. And it's interesting and even fun.

portfolio, I combined math with social issues and designed a women's health center for East Harlem. I had to justify why I chose this community, and show that it did not have enough services for women. I had to draw the center to scale, both floor plans and elevations, and solve problems like how to support the weight of water in a pool on the second floor. I had to apply the formulas I had learned in other math and geometry classes. In a traditional math class, I would have just memorized the formulas and repeated them on a test. It feels good to get a high grade on a test, but when you do a portfolio—presenting your ideas and then defending them—it's a hundred times more rewarding. And it's interesting and even fun.

It's easy for me to write about the experiences I had at CPE and CPESS because the teachers went out of their way to make sure I understood what I was doing and had a good time doing it. I

rewarding

not really learning. You don't have to think as much as we did at CPESS.

During my last two years at CPESS, which are called the "Senior Institute," I had to complete 14 portfolios to show what I had learned in 14 different areas, including literature, science and technology, history and social studies, and practical skills. Each one was a major project, and eight of them had to be presented and defended to a four-person committee made up of two teachers, a student, and a person of my choice. For my math

remember always being asked if I liked school and, to most people's surprise, I would tell them that I loved school and that it was like a second home to me. My days in CPE and CPESS will never be forgotten; they prepared me to keep learning for the rest of my life. ●

Alexis Carrero[3] is a graduate of Central Park East Secondary School in New York City, and is currently enrolled at Syracuse University.

From the Front Lines

BY TERRY THODE

the power of project-

I'm the luckiest teacher I know because my job at Hemingway Elementary School in Ketchum, Idaho, is to learn along with students. As a technology teacher in charge of a hands-on learning laboratory, I spend my days immersed in an educational environment that lets children explore their world through exciting and relevant project-based education.

Envision a room filled with all kinds of electronic equipment, from computers to wind tunnels to robots. There's a hum of voices as busy hands and minds explore, discuss, create, and invent. Students work cooperatively or independently to solve real-world problems. They absorb science, math, language arts, geography, art, reading, social studies, and music by using technological tools that, as they constantly tell me, make "learning seem like fun, not work."

Educators should never underestimate the abilities of students or the effectiveness of letting them follow their interests. Instead of trying to mold them to learn our curriculum, we should try to understand where they are and tap into the natural motivation within them.

On any given day, kindergarten through sixth-grade students at my school elect to be structural engineers and use computer-aided design software to plan and construct scale-model space structures, skyscrapers, or entire cities. Others work as genetic engineers to change variables that affect plant growth and share their research results with peers in the school and the district via modem. Some act as safety-design engineers and master computer 3-D modeling and physics software to study impact forces, then apply what they've learned to build model cars that protect egg drivers and passengers in high-speed collisions. Budding television producers use cameras connected to multimedia computers to edit video yearbooks for their classes and for the entire school.

The Hemingway hands-on learning laboratory was created more than a decade ago by educators, parents, and community members who wanted to harness the power of project-based learning. Since it's impractical to fund equipment for individual classrooms, the district allocates money for a teacher specialist and a dedicated room in the school for the program. Parents and community members provide supplies, equipment, and additional funding. Every class at Hemingway spends scheduled time in my lab, but many pupils also drop in during open hours before and after school and at lunch to do tasks like research assignments on the Internet.

These students' work is not aimed at merely making drawings or dioramas to take home to impress Mom and Dad. In a true project-based learning environment like the one at Hemingway, the "minds-on" process of thinking and creating is as important as the final product. Doing projects requires pupils to plan, evaluate, anticipate, critique, analyze, and develop other higher-order thinking skills. They know that if something doesn't come out the way they intended, they haven't failed. It just means they learned what doesn't work, and that is just as important. They understand that they can try again, changing their assumptions and approaches based upon what they learned the first time.

I stress to my students that I am only one resource in the room, and most often should be their last resource. In this day and age, it is an impossible task for me or any other educator to

based learning

subjects. The most important lesson I've learned as a project specialist is that educators should never underestimate the abilities of students or the effectiveness of letting them follow their interests. Instead of trying to mold them to learn our curriculum, we should try to understand where they are and tap into the natural motivation within them.

One of the key parts of our program is the time parents and community members give us. Many professionals come into the lab to help students work on projects related to the adult's expertise, which most find more interesting than volunteering as a teacher aide. I hold open houses for "parents only" where they explore new technologies, and I find they get much more excited about their children's schooling when their own imaginations are ignited.

Sometimes, in pondering the success our school has had with project-based education, I recall the first day of my student teaching assignment in a large urban school many years ago. My supervising teacher, an extremely creative and energetic person, was in the middle of a science lesson that wasn't going as planned. She stopped the class, questioned students to confirm her assessment, and then said immediately, "Forget it. This isn't working." I was amazed that she could do that and still feel confident that her credibility was intact. That was my first experience with a teacher and students being equal partners in establishing the learning environment.

There was a lesson in that for me, but I also think there's a lesson there for all educators. When things aren't working—as they aren't in so many schools—don't be afraid to try something new that makes children active partners in their education. That's exactly what I do every day—and I'm having a ball. ●

Terry Thode[4] is a technology teacher at Hemingway Elementary School.

know everything. I tell the children that there are many other resources—from community members to electronic databases around the world—they can turn to that have better, more accurate knowledge than I do about a particular subject. No one waits for me to tell them what to do next, and students are constantly sharing new information that they've uncovered with me. We explore, research, discuss, analyze, test, and evaluate together. I am a true partner in discovery.

In my room, you can't tell the students who are labeled gifted and talented from those who are called learning disabled. Project-based education is the great leveler for kids of different abilities and learning styles. It allows each individual to progress in the way that best suits him. I constantly see students who struggle in a traditional classroom find success and self-worth in this setting.

This kind of project-based learning is so effective because it's tied to real-world knowledge, not memorization and abstractions. Students are driven by their own excitement and curiosity when they can see how their learning is relevant to their lives. They are turned on by being allowed to explore different types of knowledge at the same time, rather than being limited to narrow academic

Snapshots

Adolescents in Charge

"Our students never ask 'Why are we learning this?'" says Donna Imatt, a teacher at Brown Barge Middle School in Pensacola, Fla. "We connect to our students because our curriculum reflects the special needs and interests of adolescents." Each year, parents are surveyed to determine their opinions about the skills and knowledge necessary for their children, and the school's 535 students are asked to identify their concerns about themselves and the world in which they live. The school's faculty considers the survey answers in creating thematic courses of study for the year, with the goal of making the middle school experience more meaningful. "When kids feel that their work is important and worth their time, they'll take responsibility for their learning," says Imatt. "The way our kids take charge, I think some of them could run a business!"

A flexible schedule allows teachers to work together to plan and implement 12-week units called "streams," of which students select three per year. Streams are designed to help the sixth- through eighth-grade students acquire subject knowledge and to challenge them to use what they've learned in creative ways. In a culminating activity for a stream on "Flight," for example, students build hot air balloons. "To do this," says principal Camille Barr, "they need to know physics concepts like lift, thrust, and drag. They're motivated to learn the necessary skills in math and physics because they actually build and fly the balloons." ●

Brown Barge Middle School Escambia County School District, 151 East Fairfield Drive, Pensacola, FL 32503 **Contact:** Camille C. Barr, Principal • Phone: (904) 444-2700 • Fax: (904) 444-2779 • E-mail: barr_c@popmail.firn.edu

Equal Opportunities

Paideia is an educational program that has its roots in a democratic ideal: that society has a responsibility to provide all students with the same education currently offered to the best students. First advanced by Mortimer Adler in his book, *Paideia Proposal,* the program outlines a demanding curriculum and three instructional strategies: lecturing, coaching, and group seminars based on the Socratic method.

The Paideia program is being used in a number of schools across the country, including the Chattanooga School for the Arts and Sciences (CSAS) in Tennessee. The school draws a diverse student body from all corners of the city, and all 1,150 students take the same course of study, including math, science, history, literature, drama, visual arts, and instrumental, string, and vocal music. In addition, starting in kindergarten, every student learns Spanish or French as a second language.

Teachers at CSAS place a high premium on developing students' abilities to think deeply and reason well. Each week students meet with peers for a seminar that challenges them to develop and defend opinions about such things as a sculpture or a passage from literature. Before the seminars, teachers help students develop the background they'll need to engage in a thoughtful exchange of ideas. To prepare for a discussion on Martin Luther King Jr.'s *Letter from a Birmingham Jail,* students would have to know about the historical context in which it was written. Such seminars help students improve their skills in thinking, speaking, and listening, while at the same time they learn to respect the different opinions of others. ●

Chattanooga School for the Arts and Sciences Chattanooga Public Schools, 865 East Third Street, Chattanooga, TN 37403 **Contact:** Judi R. Shirley, Principal K-5, or William D. Kennedy, Principal 6-12 • Phone: (423) 757-5495 • Fax: (423) 757-5331 • E-mail: KennedyW@utc.campus.mci.net

Grappling with Messy Problems

Students at Illinois Mathematics and Science Academy (IMSA) don't shy away from problems. In fact, problems are an important feature of the curriculum at this three-year residential public high school. A problem-based approach to teaching and learning, modeled on a strategy originally used in medical schools, presents students with a "messy" problem for which, as in life, there is no simple answer. At IMSA, students assume the roles of doctors, scientists, historians, or other stakeholders as they grapple with problems such as: "Should the Park Service reintroduce wolves into Yellowstone Park?" Students become "apprentice investigators," using knowledge and skills from a variety of disciplines and employing appropriate technologies to develop solutions. They also have many opportunities to work with professionals in their fields of interest, both within and outside the school.

Though IMSA is a competitive-admissions school that serves students who display a high aptitude for math, science, and technology, The Center for Problem-Based Learning, located at the school, provides materials and workshops for other educators nationwide interested in implementing this approach to learning for their students. ●

Illinois Mathematics and Science Academy 1500 West Sullivan Road, Aurora, IL 60506 **Contact:** Brenda Buschbacher, Coordinator of Public Information • Phone: (630) 907-5000 • Fax: (630) 907-5976 • E-mail: Brenda@imsa.edu • URL: http://www.imsa.edu/

Virtual Argonauts

Students around the world get the chance to learn science while participating in real scientific expeditions thanks to the capabilities of modern technologies and the resources of the JASON Project. Founded in 1989 by Dr. Robert Ballard, who discovered the wreck of the Titanic, the JASON Project is a multi-faceted program that sponsors yearly expeditions for kids, provides curriculum spanning grades K-12, professional development programs for teachers, and on-line networks connecting students, educators, and scientists. The project draws expertise and support from numerous public and private organizations. At specially equipped museums, universities, and research centers, for example, students view satellite broadcasts of the explorations, use advanced telecommunications technologies to interact with scientists, and even operate an underwater robot called a ROV (Remotely Operated Vehicle).

Each year, between 8 and 20 students and teachers, called "Argonauts," are selected to join expeditions in the field for a week or two. In January 1996, Argonauts explored how life adapts to a changing sea in the Florida Bay. One field team compiled information on crocodiles. "We trudged through the mangroves to get to a crocodile nest that hadn't hatched... When we uncovered the nest, the stench was overpowering... The crocodile eggs are about the size of goose eggs. When we finished burying them again, we checked our location using the GPS (Global Positioning System)." This is an excerpt from a journal written by 9th- and 10th-grade Argonauts. The journal is posted on-line where students and teachers around the world can get a first-hand account of the expedition and ask questions of the Argonauts about their work. Since its inception, the JASON Project has reached well over a million students. With advances in telecommunications technologies, the project hopes to be able to provide a window into science for millions more. ●

The JASON Foundation for Education

395 Totten Pond Road, Waltham, MA 02154 **Contact:** Timothy W. Armour, Executive Director • Phone: (617) 487-9995 • Fax: (617) 487-9999 • E-mail: info@jason.org • URL: http://seawifs.gsfc.nasa. gov/JASON/HTML/JASON.html

Nurturing Different Kinds of Intelligences

The Key Renaissance School in Indianapolis extends to middle school students the educational programs originally established at the Key School in 1987. Key School was one of the first schools to develop curriculum based on psychologist Howard Gardner's theory of multiple intelligences. Gardner is well known for advancing the notion that intelligence is not a single entity fixed at birth. Instead, he maintains that individuals use at least seven intelligences in varying combinations when they approach

problems or create products. These include linguistic and logical-mathematical intelligences—the focus of most traditional courses of study. But they also include musical intelligence and bodily-kinesthetic intelligence—aspects of student development that are often considered to be frills.

At both schools, music, dance, foreign language, and art have as much prominence in the program as math and history. Subjects are woven together in a theme-based curriculum that is designed to encourage students to develop and use their different intelligences.

In addition to themed courses, students at Key Renaissance select a year-long enrichment course designed to challenge and appeal to individuals with similar capacities

and interests. Some may study photography, holography, and computer graphics, while others learn how to lobby decision makers in city and state government. Throughout the school year, groups of students plan and participate in community service activities, such as working with homeless people, helping mount art exhibits, planting a peace garden, and developing a tour of the city by and for teens. The rich array of activities at Key Renaissance helps ensure that all students remain excited about—and successful at—learning. ●

The Key Renaissance School Indianapolis Public Schools, 222 East Ohio Street, Indianapolis, IN 46204 **Contact:** Patricia Bolaños, Principal • Phone: (317) 226-4996 • Fax: (317) 226-3049

Getting Into Things

Shutesbury Elementary School
Erving School Union #28, 23 West Pelham Road, Shutesbury, MA 01072
Contact: Laura Baker, Principal • Phone: (413) 259-1212 • Fax: (413) 259-1531 • E-mail: shuteses@crocker.com

Several years ago, officials in rural Shutesbury, Mass., received a report that gave a comprehensive picture of radon (a radioactive gas with potential cancer-causing properties) in their community. The report, complete with computer-generated charts and graphs, was also sent to government radon specialists and anyone requesting copies. The report seemed to have been written by professionals, but it wasn't: the data was collected, analyzed, written, and published by 11-year-old students from Shutesbury Elementary School.

At Shutesbury, a school serving 250 students from early childhood through sixth grade, projects are the norm. The school's offices and classrooms display a variety of books, models, and art that were produced by students during the course of work on topics ranging from ancient Egypt to current water quality. In-depth projects like this not only help students understand and use scientific inquiry methods, manage data, and summarize findings, but also require them to collaborate and be self-directed. Students learn to critique each other's work and become accustomed to making multiple revisions based on feedback from both peers and teachers. Their final drafts or products serve as models for other students. "This is not like a robot's school," says student Ken Comish. "You don't just look at textbooks and stare blankly at the board. You really get into things." ●

"This is not like a robot's school. You don't just look at textbooks and stare blankly at the board. You really get into things."

Creating and Testing New Ideas

"We view ourselves as a school where new ideas are invented and tested," says Grace Arnold, principal of Open Charter School in Los Angeles. Founded in 1977 by parents interested in non-traditional educational programs, the Open Charter School now serves almost 400 students in kindergarten through sixth grade selected by lottery from applicants all over Los Angeles. In 1987, the school added a strong dose of technology to its program when it was picked as a site for Apple Computer, Inc.'s Vivarium Project, which explored ways that computers can support learning. "We know how to create our own programs on the computer—animation, video games, pictures—not just use programs someone else made," boasts 11-year-old Danny Cronin. Though the Vivarium Project is now over, the school continues to work on other projects with Apple, and technology is well integrated into instructional programs.

The school's courses emphasize learning through exploration, creativity, and physical expression. Basic skills are taught in small groups and reinforced with hands-on activities in a variety of meaningful contexts. The school's 2,000 square foot garden, for example, serves as a classroom where students measure and sequence growing patterns, write poetry, make weavings, learn about nutrition, analyze soil, and track rates of decomposition. They use computers to chart and graph their garden data and to design animations to examine changes. Students also design and build a scale model of a city using found objects such as milk cartons and cereal boxes. The model becomes a vehicle to learn civic concepts such as urban planning and city administration. "The school philosophy," principal Arnold says, "centers around the child as he or she interacts with the environment in a meaningful way." ●

Open Charter School Los Angeles Unified School District, 6085 Airdrome Street, Los Angeles, CA 90035 **Contact:** Grace Arnold, Principal • Phone: (213) 937-6249 • Fax: (213) 937-2884 • E-mail: opencharter@applelink.apple.com • URL: http//www.ed.gov/pubs/ EdReformStudies/EdTech/opencharter.html

Connecting to Life Beyond the Classroom

At a MicroSociety school, it's not uncommon to find a room full of sixth-grade students debating the need for income taxes, jury duty, or enforcement agencies. After all, MicroSociety students learn by developing their own governments and free-market systems. The idea was conceived in the 1960s by George H. Richmond, who was looking for a way to help students connect their academic studies to their lives beyond school. He settled on an approach in which students create and operate simplified models of businesses and government institutions.

More than 175 schools in 29 states have since adopted the Micro-Society approach. Students in kindergarten through eighth grade spend part of each day learning academic skills and the other part participating in miniature versions of society. Some schools have teamed up with business partners and crafts people to create elaborate edifices of banks, shops, and post offices, while others simply set up shop at whatever tables and desks are at hand. The appearances vary, but when they are open for business, MicroSociety activities resemble a busy town filled with students who are creating and selling merchandise, presiding over trials, and solving all types of problems that come with the territory. ●

MicroSociety®, Inc. 53 North Mascher Street, Suite 3, Philadelphia, PA 19106 **Contact:** Leonette Boiarski, Director of Communications • Phone: (215) 922-4006 • Fax: (215) 922-3303 • E-mail: msocinc@aol.com

Organizations

American Association for the Advancement of Science (AAAS) **Description:** A nonprofit professional association with more than 143,000 members, including scientists, engineers, educators, policy makers, and interested citizens. **Purpose:** To advance scientific and technological excellence across all disciplines, to promote and improve education in science, and to increase public understanding of science and technology. **Activities:** Education-related programs include Project 2061, a long-term initiative to reform K-12 science, mathematics, and technology education. This project develops curriculum guidelines and learning goals, holds workshops for educators, collaborates with government and education organizations to set criteria for science literacy, and publishes resources such as *Science for all Americans* and *Benchmarks for Science Literacy,* available in both print and electronic formats. The Education and Human Resources Directorate operates numerous programs designed to improve science education at all levels and to increase participation of women, minorities, and people with disabilities in science, mathematics, and engineering. These programs include the AAAS Science Library Institute and professional development programs for teachers, The AAAS National Network of Minority Women in Science, and Kinetic City Super Crew, a children's science radio show with a World Wide Web site (http://www.aaas.org/ehr/kcsuper.html). **Contact:** Mary Koppal, Communications Manager, Project 2061 • American Association for the Advancement of Science, 1333 H Street NW, Washington, DC 20005 • Phone: (202) 326-6643 • Fax: (202) 842-5196 • E-mail: mkoppal@aaas.org • URL: http://www.aaas.org

Center for Civic Education Description: A nonprofit corporation established by the State Bar of California in 1981 that currently has programs in all 50 states. **Purpose:** To help students become informed, responsible citizens through programs of civic education in the schools. **Activities:** Develops K-12 curriculum materials on topics ranging from principles of democracy to the development of public policy. Publishes a curriculum framework, *The National Standards for Civics and Government,* and a variety of teaching materials. Disseminates information through in-service training, a newsletter, and on-line materials. Organizes leadership institutes for educators and administers the *We the People...* competition and awards program for students and teachers nationwide. **Contact:** Charles Quigley, Executive Director • Center for Civic Education, 5146 Douglas Fir Road, Calabasas, CA 91302 • Phone: (818) 591-9321 • Fax: (818) 591-9330 • E-mail: center4civ@aol.com • URL: http://www.primenet.com/~cce

> *"In order for successful restructuring to take place, the principal must be a visionary willing to share power with teachers."*
>
> Camille C. Barr,[5] Principal, Brown Barge Middle School

Clear View Charter School, Chula Vista, CA • Photo by Matthew Rivaldi

Cooperative Learning Center (CLC) Description: A university-based center established by cooperative learning pioneers David and Roger Johnson. **Purpose:** To promote the use of cooperative learning strategies and conflict-mediation programs in schools nationwide. **Activities:** Sponsors annual training workshops for teachers and administrators at sites across the country, provides technical assistance, and publishes a variety of resources. **Contact:** David Johnson or Roger Johnson, Co-Directors • Cooperative Learning Center, University of Minnesota, 60 Peik Hall, 159 Pillsbury Drive SE, Minneapolis, MN 55455 • Phone: (612) 624-7031 • Fax: (612) 626-1395 • URL: http://www.coled.umn.edu

American Educational Research Association (AERA) Description: An international membership organization of educators, policy makers, behavioral scientists and graduate students. **Purpose:** To improve education by encouraging scholarly inquiry into learning at all levels, from early childhood through higher education. **Activities:** Hosts an annual conference where thousands of research studies are presented. Distributes research news through books, papers, reports, and video and audio tapes. Publishes numerous journals, including *Educational Researcher* and *Education Evaluation and Policy Analysis.* **Contact:** Denise McKeon, Director of Outreach • American Educational Research Association, 1230 17th Street NW, Washington, DC 20036 • Phone: (202) 223-9485 • Fax: (202) 775-1824 • E-mail: dmckeon@gmu.edu • URL: http://tikkun.ed.asu.edu/aera/home.html

Developmental Studies Center (DSC) **Description:** A nonprofit educational organization founded in 1981. **Purpose:** To foster ethical, social, and intellectual development in children. **Activities:** Sponsors the Child Development Project, a program that helps elementary schools become supportive learning communities for all children and adults. Offers literature-based language arts and cooperative math curricula; guides for improving classroom management and family and community involvement; documentary videos; and professional development and consulting services. **Contact:** Eric Schaps, President • Developmental Studies Center, 2000 Embarcadero Drive, Suite 305, Oakland, CA 94606 • Phone: (510) 533-0213 • Fax: (510) 464-3670 • E-mail: Info@devstu.org • URL: http://www.devstu.org

EQUALS Description: A research and development organization. **Purpose:** To increase the participation of female and minority students in math education, create enthusiasm for the subject, and increase awareness of math-related occupations. **Activities:** Develops math curriculum, publications, and assessments for kindergarten through 12th-grade educators; models instructional techniques; and offers workshops for teachers, parents, and administrators. Programs include a six-day EQUALS workshop, which provides new teaching strategies and hands-on activities that help all students, particularly underrepresented groups, develop an understanding of mathematics; FAMILY MATH, which promotes family participation in math learning; and SEQUALS, an ongoing professional development program. Publishes resource books as well as classroom instructional materials and provides access to networks of people interested in gender and racial equity issues. **Contact:** José Franco, Director • EQUALS, Lawrence Hall of Science, University of California Berkeley, Berkeley, CA 94720 • Phone: (510) 642-1823 • Fax: (510) 643-5757 • E-mail: equals@uclink.berkeley.edu • URL: http://equals.lhs.berkeley.edu

O'Farrell Community School, San Diego, CA

Education Development Center, Inc. (EDC) Description: An international research and development organization. **Purpose:** To improve the effectiveness and quality of education in the U.S. and worldwide. **Activities:** Designs curriculum materials and offers professional development to promote hands-on, inquiry-based learning. Manages more than 150 programs. The Center for Learning, Teaching, and Technology creates materials and instructional methods to help learners deepen their understanding of mathematics and science. The Center for Children and Technology develops prototypes of, and conducts research on, technology-enhanced learning environments. EDC is a partner in ATLAS Communities, one of the design models for "break-the-mold" schools sponsored by New American Schools. **Contact:** Dan Tobin, Director of Communications • Education Development Center, Inc., 55 Chapel Street, Newton, MA 02158 • Phone: (617) 969-7100 ext. 2204 • Fax: (617) 969-5979 • E-mail: DanT@edc.org • URL: http://www.edc.org/

The Exploratorium Description: Interactive museum and education center founded in 1969. **Purpose:** To provide exciting activities to learn about science, nature, art, and technology. **Activities:** Museum features more than 650 interactive exhibits, sponsors formal and informal science lessons, hosts lecture series, and publishes newsletters and other materials. Operates the Center for Teaching and Learning, which offers professional development for preservice and in-service educators, sponsors a Teacher in Residence program to help prepare district science specialists, and publishes materials such as *Science Snackbook*, a book of hands-on science activities written by educators. **Contact:** Linda Dackman, Public Information Director • The Exploratorium, 3601 Lyon Street, San Francisco, CA 94123 • Phone: (415) 563-7337 • Fax: (415) 561-0307 • E-mail: pubinfo@exploratorium.edu • URL: http://www.exploratorium.edu/

"Teachers need to integrate technology seamlessly into the curriculum instead of viewing it as an add-on, an afterthought, or an event."

Heidi Hayes Jacobs,[6] Educational Consultant, Curriculum Designers, Inc.

Alice Carlson Applied Learning Center, Fort Worth, TX

Institute for Research on Learning (IRL) Description: A nonprofit research organization established in 1987. **Purpose:** To further the understanding of learning in real-world settings and to translate results of research into practice. **Activities:** Engages in research on the nature of learning in schools, workplaces, and the community. Uses findings to develop technology applications for learning and create math and science curriculum materials. Assesses and designs organizational structures within schools and workplaces. Publishes research reports. Works with school districts and collaboratives such as Multimedia Makers to develop technology-enriched educational programs. **Contact:** Peter Henschel, Executive Director • Institute for Research on Learning, 66 Willow Place, Menlo Park, CA 94025 • Phone: (415) 614-7900 • Fax: (415) 614-7957 • E-mail: peter_henschel@irl.org • URL: http://www.irl.org/

Learning Research and Development Center (LRDC) Description: A university-based research center founded in 1963. **Purpose:** To expand scientific knowledge of all aspects of learning, including thinking, knowing, and understanding; and to support the application of research in various instructional settings. **Activities:** Conducts research on learning in five main areas: processes of learning, learning in school, education policy and reform, learning and the world of work, and learning and technology. Through its New Standards Project, LRDC is developing standards and assessments and is helping teachers learn new instructional methods. Plays a key role as a partner in the National Alliance for Restructuring Education, one of the innovative school design models sponsored by New American Schools. Disseminates research findings in print, on-line, and at conferences, and publishes *Learning,* a semiannual newsletter for teachers. **Contact:** Shari Kubitz, Communications Specialist • Learning Research and Development Center, University of Pittsburgh, 805 LRDC, 3939 O'Hara Street, Pittsburgh, PA 15260 • Phone: (412) 624-2881 • Fax: (412) 624-3051 • E-mail: shari@lrdc3.lrdc.pitt.edu • URL: http://www.lrdc.pitt.edu

Center for Research on Education, Diversity and Excellence (CREDE)
Description: A national research center funded by the U.S. Department of Education. **Purpose:** To find ways to improve education by addressing primary risk factors of language, race, poverty, and geographic location facing students from kindergarten through twelfth grade. **Activities:** Conducts research and disseminates information and reports. **Contact:** Roland Tharp, Director • Center for Research on Education, Diversity and Excellence • University of California Santa Cruz, 252 Social Science II, Santa Cruz, CA 95064 • Phone: (408) 459-3500 • Fax: (408) 459-3502 • E-mail: crede@cats.ucsc.edu

National Paideia Center Description: A university-based resource center. **Purpose:** To promote the Paideia program, a curriculum and instruction framework originally developed by Mortimer Adler and the Paideia Group to provide quality education for all students. **Activities:** Facilitates networking and provides staff development and long-term technical assistance for schools adopting the Paideia approach to teaching and learning. Collects and disseminates information related to educational quality and equity. **Contact:** Terry Roberts, Executive Director • National Paideia Center, University of North Carolina at Chapel Hill, Campus Box 8045, Chapel Hill, NC 27599 • Phone: (919) 962-7380 • Fax: (919) 962-7381 • E-mail: npc@unc.edu • URL: http://www.unc.edu/depts/ed/cel-paideia.html

"When I was a beginning teacher, I tried to teach the way I had been taught, but I wasn't meeting the needs of my students. What I found is that students learn best when they are part of the decision-making process, determining the content and direction of projects."

Brad Thode,[7] Technology Education Teacher, Wood River Middle/High School

The National Association for Sport and Physical Education (NASPE)
Description: Membership association for physical education teachers and the largest group in the American Alliance for Health, Physical Education, Recreation and Dance. **Purpose:** To integrate knowledge about sports and physical activity into the school curriculum. **Activities:** Projects include research, development of standards and benchmarks in physical education, professional development programs, and publication of resource materials for teachers. **Contact:** Paula Kun, Director, Public Relations • The National Association for Sport and Physical Education, 1900 Association Drive, Reston, VA 22091 • Phone: (703) 476-3461• Fax: (703) 476-8316 • E-mail: naspe@ aahperd.org • URL: http://www.aahperd.org/naspe.html

National Science Resources Center (NSRC) Description: A resource center established jointly by the Smithsonian Institution and the National Academy of Sciences. **Purpose:** To improve the quality of science education for all children. **Activities:** Develops hands-on science curriculum for grades one through six and maintains a database of elementary and middle school science materials developed by others. Publishes a resource guide for teachers and a newsletter for NSRC members. Holds summer leadership institutes for school district teams and provides ongoing technical assistance. **Contact:** Leslie J. Benton, Program Officer • National Science Resources Center, Smithsonian Institution, Arts & Industries Building, Room 1201, Washington, DC 20560 • Phone: (202) 287-2063 • Fax: (202) 287-2070 • E-mail: outreach@nas.edu • URL: http://www.si.edu/nsrc

National Telemedia Council (NTC) Description: Founded in 1953, NTC is the oldest nonprofit professional media literacy organization in the U.S. **Purpose:** To support the development of media literacy programs in the schools and promote mindful viewing and reflective judgment of print and visual media materials. **Activities:** Sponsors the National Media Literacy Clearinghouse and Center, which maintains an electronic database of media-related resources. Offers research and consulting services, sponsors workshops and conferences, and publishes *Telemedium, the Journal of Media Literacy.* **Contact:** Marieli Rowe, Executive Director • National Telemedia Council, 120 East Wilson Street, Madison, WI 53703 • Phone: (608) 257-7712 • Fax: (608) 257-7714 • E-mail: NTelemedia@aol.com • URL: http://danenet.wicip.org/ntc

Harvard Project Zero Description: A university-based research organization founded in 1967. **Purpose:** To advance knowledge about intelligence, creativity, and learning; and to blend theory and practice in schools, classrooms, and communities. **Activities:** Conducts research on topics such as learning for understanding, the role of technology in education, and the nature of creativity. Conducts workshops for educators, helps develop assessment strategies, publishes classroom materials, and disseminates research findings. Project Zero is a partner in ATLAS Communities, one of the design models for "break-the-mold" schools sponsored by New American Schools. **Contact:** Harvard Project Zero • Graduate School of Education, Harvard University, 13 Appian Way, Cambridge, MA 02138 • Phone: (617) 495-4342 • Fax: (617) 495-9709

> *"When used effectively in the curriculum, technological tools enable children to work like experts—scientists, mathematicians, historians, writers, dramatists, musicians, artists—doing real work and using the resources productive adults use."*
>
> Vicki Hancock,[8] Regional Director, Northwest Region, Association for Supervision and Curriculum Development

Alice Carlson Applied Learning Center, Fort Worth, TX

TERC Description: A nonprofit education research and development organization. **Purpose:** To improve mathematics and science education by creating innovative curricula, fostering professional development, pioneering creative uses of technology, investigating learning, and developing equitable opportunities for underserved learners. **Activities:** Conducts a wide variety of research and development projects, including: Visualizing Earth, which explores geographic information systems and remote sensing as an avenue for students to investigate our planet; Global Laboratory, which uses telecommunications to unite students from more than 20 countries in research on environmental issues; Lab Net, an electronic network for kindergarten through 12th-grade science and math teachers; Investigations in Number, Data, and Space, a K–5 curriculum for students to develop fluency in solving mathematical problems; and research projects on science education in culturally diverse classrooms. TERC develops curriculum and staff materials and publishes numerous resources, including *Hands On!*, a semiannual newsletter. **Contact:** Peggy Kapisovsky, Communications Director • TERC, 2067 Massachusetts Avenue, Cambridge, MA 02140 • Phone: (617) 547-0430 • Fax: (617) 349-3535 • E-mail: Communications@terc.edu • URL: http://www.terc.edu

Shorecrest High School, Shoreline, WA

Periodicals

ASCD Curriculum/Technology Quarterly
Description: Journal for kindergarten through 12th-grade educators. **Focus:** Profiles exemplary uses of technology for learning, reviews print and electronic resources, and reports on trends and research findings. **Publisher:** Education and Technology Resources Center, Association for Supervision and Curriculum Development, Alexandria, VA • Phone: (800) 933-2723.

"Besides teaching our children the three R's, we might better prepare them for the 21st century by developing their capacity for the three C's – comprehension, creativity, and compassion."

Ken Sakatani,[9] Arts &Technology Coordinator and Teacher, Bayside Middle School for the Arts and Creative Technology

West Des Moines Community School District, West Des Moines, IA

Journal of Science Education and Technology
Description: Quarterly journal for science educators at all levels. **Focus:** Invited and contributed articles address various aspects of the discipline of science education, including research, practice, and policy. **Publisher:** Plenum Publishing, New York, NY • Phone: (212) 620-8470.

Technology & Learning
Description: Magazine for educators, parents, and technology resource people. **Focus:** Features articles on technology and education, descriptions and reviews of hardware and software, and other industry news. **Publisher:** Peter Li, Dayton, OH • Phone: (800) 543-4383 ext. 121.

Live Wire Description: A quarterly publication for parents and educators. **Focus:** The newsletter of MicroSociety, Inc. contains portraits of noteworthy student activities, grant developments, and program changes at affiliated schools across the country. Also provides information on training and conferences offered by the national consortium. A column by founder George Richmond elaborates on the MicroSociety philosophy of active, real-world learning. **Publisher:** MicroSociety®, Philadelphia, PA • Phone: (215) 922-4006.

The Quarterly Description: A journal for educators. **Focus:** Offers resources and ideas about the writing process and the teaching of writing. Topics range from research by teachers to learning to write as a means of communication in all subjects. **Publisher:** National Writing Project and the National Center for the Study of Writing and Literacy, Berkeley, CA • Phone: (510) 643-7022.

The Web Description: The monthly newsletter of an organization established to design innovative schools. **Focus:** Contains articles and reviews by educators implementing the Expeditionary Learning Outward Bound approach to schooling. Topics range from student assessment to professional development expeditions for educators. **Publisher:** Expeditionary Learning Outward Bound®, Cambridge, MA • Phone: (617) 576-1260.

Readings

Anderson, Ronald D., Beverly L. Anderson, Mary Ann Varanka-Martin, et al. **Issues of Curriculum Reform in Science, Mathematics and Higher Order Thinking Across the Disciplines.** *Government Printing Office: Washington, DC, 1994.* Phone: (202) 512-1800. ● For educators, policy makers, and curriculum developers, this report reviews literature on science and math education, discusses the need for changes, and describes current reform efforts.

Bruner, Jerome. **The Culture of Education.** *Harvard University Press: Cambridge, MA, 1996.* Phone: (800) 448-2242. ● The author argues that one role of education is to assimilate students to present-day cultural norms. At the same time, it must help equip students to think about and understand their changing world.

Beane, James A. **A Middle School Curriculum: From Rhetoric to Reality, 2nd Edition.** *National Middle School Association: Columbus, OH, 1993.* Phone: (800) 528-6672. ● Offers insights into the distinct learning needs of adolescents and suggests a thematic curriculum that integrates their concerns with broader social concerns.

Carnegie Corporation of New York. **Years of Promise: A Comprehensive Learning Strategy for America's Children.** *Carnegie Corporation of New York: New York, NY, 1996.* Phone: (301) 843-0159. ● Addresses the importance of child development as a precursor to educational achievement. Focuses on strategies that contribute to academic success in the elementary school years, including expanding childcare opportunities, strengthening families, and linking them with community-based institutions.

"*How students interact with each other in school has a substantial impact on their learning. A classroom that is trying to get the best out of each student should have them working cooperatively a majority of the time, just as was done in the best of the one-room schoolhouses.*"

Roger Johnson,[10] Co-Director, Cooperative Learning Center, University of Minnesota

Beane, James A., ed. **Toward a Coherent Curriculum: The 1995 ASCD Yearbook.** *Association for Supervision and Curriculum Development: Alexandria, VA, 1995.* Phone: (800) 933-2723. ● This collection of essays by scholars, curriculum developers, and researchers exposes the weaknesses of the traditional curriculum, which tends to be a collection of isolated processes, fragmented ideas, and disconnected facts, and presents ideas about creating coherent curriculum.

Alice Carlson Applied Learning Center, Fort Worth, TX • Photo by Paul Moseley

Cawelti, Gordon, ed. **Handbook of Research on Improving Student Achievement.** *Educational Research Service: Arlington, VA, 1995.* Phone: (703) 243-2100. ● Provides brief descriptions of effective classroom practices in K-12 education, summaries of supporting research, and references for more complete information about the studies.

Cobb, Nina, ed. **The Future of Education: Perspectives on National Standards in America.** *College Board Publications: New York, NY, 1994.* Phone: (212) 713-8165. ● Contributors to this book offer a diverse range of views about national standards and their implications for policy, curriculum, and school reform.

Brooks, Jacqueline Grennon, and Martin G. Brooks. **In Search of Understanding: The Case for Constructivist Classrooms.** *Association for Supervision and Curriculum Development: Alexandria, VA, 1993.* Phone: (800) 933-2723. ● Presents the theory and implementation of constructivism, an approach to teaching and learning in which students derive meaning and understanding by actively finding appropriate information, developing strategies to make sense of it, and applying what they learn to complex problems.

"Technology is about connections—connecting people to each other, to ideas, and to possibilities. Imagine being able to sample the atmosphere of a planet millions of miles away and go hands-on with the universe—this is the stuff that gets kids excited about science! What's there not to love?!"

Shirley Malcom,[11] Head, Directorate for Education and Human Resource Programs, American Association for the Advancement of Science ★ FILM

Research and Policy Committee. **Connecting Students to a Changing World: A Technology Strategy for Improving Mathematics and Science Education.** *Committee for Economic Development: New York, NY, 1995.* Phone: (212) 688-2063 ext. 212. ● Published by a group of national business and education leaders, this report explains how technologies that have changed the workplace can be used to improve math and science education. Addresses issues of school management, curriculum standards, and planning for technology integration.

Fosnot, Catherine T., ed. **Constructivism: Theory, Perspectives, and Practice.** *Teachers College Press: New York, NY, 1996.* Phone: (800) 575-6566. ● Educators and researchers present diverse perspectives on the constructivist theory of knowledge and learning and its implications for teaching.

Cousins, Emily, and Melissa Rodgers, eds. **Fieldwork: An Expeditionary Learning Outward Bound Reader, Vol. 1.** *Kendall/Hunt Publishing: Dubuque, IA, 1995.* Phone: (800) 228-0810. ● Presents information about a design model for innovative schools based on experiential learning. Includes the design proposal, information about implementation efforts, and excerpts from the organization's newsletter.

Davidson, Neil, and Toni Worsham, eds. **Enhancing Thinking Through Cooperative Learning.** *Teachers College Press: New York, NY, 1992.* Phone: (800) 575-6566. ● In this collection, scholars and practitioners explain how cooperative learning can improve student thinking, increase understanding of content, and develop important collaborative skills for the workplace. Presents theory as well as practical strategies for implementing cooperative learning in the classroom.

Alice Carlson Applied Learning Center, Fort Worth, TX

Bruer, John T. **Schools for Thought: A Science of Learning in the Classroom.** *Massachusetts Institute of Technology Press: Cambridge, MA, 1993.* Phone: (617) 253-5646. ● Describes research findings on how people learn. Concludes that schools should structure curriculum to move learners beyond the novice level to the expert level of competence and provides examples of instructional strategies in various academic disciplines.

Daggett, Willard R. **Defining Excellence for American Schools.** *International Center for Leadership in Education: Schenectady, NY, 1994.* Phone: (518) 372-7544. ● Presents an analysis of math, science, and language arts standards in America compared with several other industrialized nations. Concludes that, while America has similar content standards, our graduates are less prepared to use their knowledge outside of school than their peers in other nations.

Gardner, Howard. **Multiple Intelligences: The Theory in Practice.** *BasicBooks: New York, NY, 1993.* Phone: (800) 331-3761. ● Provides an overview of the author's influential theory of the nature of intelligence and its implications for curriculum, assessment, and educational reform. Describes efforts to apply the theory of multiple intelligences to classroom practice and offers insights from practical research.

Glatthorn, Alan A., ed. **Content of the Curriculum: 2nd Edition.** *Association for Supervision and Curriculum Development: Alexandria, VA, 1995.* Phone: (800) 933-2723. ● A comprehensive look at suggested content, standards, research, and resources in 10 subject areas. Written by experts and academics for state, district, and school curriculum leaders, this book warns that curriculum development and reform must be a continuous process to keep pace with a changing world.

Alice Carlson Applied Learning Center, Fort Worth, TX

Kendall, John S., and Robert J. Marzano. **Content Knowledge: A Compendium of Standards and Benchmarks for K–12 Education.** *Mid-continent Regional Educational Laboratory: Aurora, CO, 1996.* Phone: (303) 337-0990. ● Offers concise summaries of issues, activities, and developments related to standards and benchmarks for each major subject area at every grade level from K–12.

Kovalik, Susan, and Karen Olsen. **ITI: The Model: Integrated Thematic Instruction, 2nd Edition.** *Susan Kovalik & Associates: Kent, WA, 1993.* Phone: (206) 630-6908. ● Describes integrated thematic instruction, an approach to teaching and learning based on current knowledge of how the brain works. Presents eight elements for classroom application, explains how to develop year-long themes, and gives examples of curriculum.

"'Every child can learn to a high standard.' This must not be just a slogan but a practical organizing principle behind everything a school does. It must be the minimum goal of school reform."

Robert Slavin,[12] Co-Director, Center for Research on the Education of Students Placed At-Risk, The Johns Hopkins University

Ravitch, Diane. **National Standards in American Education: A Citizen's Guide.** *The Brookings Institution: Washington, DC, 1995.* Phone: (202) 797-6252. ● Written for the lay person, this book traces the history of the effort to define what students should know and be able to do in each academic discipline. Discusses problems of developing and implementing national content standards and assessments.

Goleman, Daniel. **Emotional Intelligence: Why It Can Matter More Than IQ.** *Anchor Books: New York, NY, 1995.* Phone: (800) 232-9872. ● The author contends that emotional intelligence—abilities such as self control, empathy, and persistence—is critical to an individual's potential to excel in life. Describes research on the brain's role in emotions, provides insight into social problems arising from lack of control, and argues that emotional development must be addressed in the school curriculum.

Johnson, David W., Roger T. Johnson, and Edythe Johnson Holubec. **The New Circles of Learning: Cooperation in the Classroom and School.** *Association for Supervision and Curriculum Development: Alexandria, VA, 1994.* Phone: (800) 933-2723. ● A classic work that defines cooperative learning, presents various cooperative learning strategies, and explains its benefits for students of all ages.

Jacobs, Heidi Hayes, ed. **Interdisciplinary Curriculum: Design and Implementation.** *Association for Supervision and Curriculum Development: Alexandria, VA, 1989.* Phone: (800) 933-2723. ● Explains why curriculum integration is necessary to improve student learning, describes various methods of integration, provides step-by-step procedures, and offers insight into classroom practice.

Murnane, Richard J., and Frank Levy. **Teaching the New Basic Skills: Principles for Educating Children to Thrive in a Changing Economy.** *Free Press: New York, NY, 1996.* Phone: (800) 323-7445. ● Economists argue that schools should expand basic skills instruction to include the ability to apply English and math to real-world problems. They call for schools to be evaluated by looking at how their students will fare in the workplace.

Miller, Bruce A. **Children at the Center: Implementing the Multiage Classroom.** *Northwest Regional Educational Laboratory and the ERIC Clearinghouse on Educational Management: Portland, OR, 1994.* Phone: (800) 438-8841. ● A primer on the idea and practice of grouping students of varying ages in classrooms. Places multiaged classrooms in the context of student learning and overall education reform, presents four case studies showing the promises and pitfalls of this organizational approach, and offers guidelines for implementation.

Contact Information

[1] **Rexford Brown** Executive Director •
P.S. 1 Charter School and Urban Learning Communities, Inc., 901 Bannock
Street, Denver, CO 80204 •
Phone: (303) 575-6690 •
Fax: (303) 575-6661 •
E-mail: rbrown@usa.net

[2] **Judy Pace** Graduate Student, and
Howard Gardner Professor of Education •
Graduate School of Education,
Harvard University, Larsen Hall,
2nd Floor, Cambridge, MA 02138 •
Phone: (617) 495-4342 •
Fax: (617) 496-4855 •
E-mail: paceju@hugse1.harvard.edu

[3] **Alexis Carrero** Student • c/o Center for
Collaborative Education, 1573 Madison
Avenue, Room 201, New York, NY 10029 •
Phone: (212) 348-7821 •
Fax: (212) 348-7850 •
E-mail: ancarrer@mailbox.syr.edu

[4] **Terry Thode** Technology Teacher •
Hemingway Elementary School,
Blaine County Schools #61,
Box 298, Ketchum, ID 83340 •
Phone: (208) 726-3348 •
Fax: (208) 726-7160 •
E-mail: tthode@wrmsmail.bcsd.k12.id.us

[5] **Camille C. Barr** Principal • Brown Barge
Middle School, Escambia County School
District, 151 East Fairfield Drive,
Pensacola, FL 32503 •
Phone: (904) 444-2700 •
Fax: (904) 444-2779 •
E-mail: barr_c@popmail.firn.edu

[6] **Heidi Hayes Jacobs** Educational
Consultant • Curriculum
Designers, Inc., 26 Allendale Drive,
Rye, NY 10580 •
Phone: (914) 921-2046 •
Fax: (914) 921-2046 •
E-mail: curricdes@aol.com

[7] **Brad Thode** Technology Education
Teacher • Wood River Middle/High
School, Blaine County School District
#61, PO Box 1088, Hailey, ID 83333 •
Phone: (208) 788-3523 •
Fax: (208) 788-4598 •
E-mail: bthode@wrms.bcsd.k12.Id.us

[8] **Vicki Hancock** Regional Director, Northwest
Region • Association for Supervision and
Curriculum Development, 1250 North
Pitt Street, Alexandria, VA 22314 •
Phone: (800) 933-2723 ext. 740 •
Fax: (703) 299-8638 •
E-mail: vhancock@ascd.org

[9] **Ken Sakatani** Arts & Technology
Coordinator and Teacher • Bayside
Middle School for the Arts and Creative
Technology, San Mateo-Foster City
Schools, 2025 Kehoe Avenue, San Mateo,
CA 94403 • Phone: (415) 312-7660 •
Fax: (415) 312-7634 •
E-mail: ksakata@aol.com

[10] **Roger Johnson** Co-Director • Cooperative
Learning Center, University of Minnesota,
60 Peik Hall, 159 Pillsbury Drive SE,
Minneapolis, MN 55455 •
Phone: (612) 624-7031 •
Fax: (612) 626-1395 •
E-mail: Johns009@maroon.tc.umn.edu

[11] **Shirley Malcom** Head • Directorate for
Education and Human Resource Programs,
American Association for the Advancement
of Science, 1200 New York Avenue NW,
6th Floor, Washington, DC 20005 •
Phone: (202) 326-6680 •
Fax: (202) 371-9849

[12] **Robert Slavin** Co-Director • Center for
Research on the Education of Students
Placed At-Risk, The Johns Hopkins
University, 3505 North Charles Street,
Baltimore, MD 21218 •
Phone: (410) 516-8809 •
Fax: (410) 516-8890 •
E-mail: rslavin@inet.ed.gov

Chapter 2
Assessment

When a professional skater takes to the ice, he faces a challenging **test** of his abilities. He's trained for years and knows that his score from the judges depends upon how well he **demonstrates** what he's capable of. Under the guidance of a coach, he's learned essential skills, set personal goals, built on his strengths, and worked to overcome his weaknesses. He understands how to incorporate feedback, constantly **monitor** his own performance, and strive for higher levels of excellence. As he begins his program, he has the advantage of knowing the standards against which he'll be judged.

Educators across the country are working to adapt a similar approach to measure learning. Called "**performance assessment**," this approach includes a wide variety of strategies and techniques that share a common characteristic: they require students to demonstrate their ability to **use** a range of knowledge and skills. Performance assessments can be as straightforward as writing a short story or as complicated as creating a multimedia project. Unlike selecting answers from a list, performance assessments more closely resemble challenges people face in the **real world.**

Traditionally, we have depended upon letter grades to report student progress and standardized tests to evaluate program effectiveness. While each provides some **useful** information, neither provides a complete picture of what students know and are able to do. Letter grades are not **reliable** because they vary so much from classroom to classroom. Standardized tests suffer from other limitations. Most consist of multiple-choice questions useful in measuring students' recall of factual information, but not in assessing their ability to use the information in any meaningful way.

In this chapter, we focus on performance assessments as part of a broader **system** of tests and evaluations being used in education today. Accurate, reliable, and useful assessments are essential in education for several reasons. They foster **learning** in the classroom, help teachers develop programs that meet the needs of students, and give parents a way to monitor their child's learning. Certain kinds of evaluations allow administrators and policy makers to monitor programs so they can ensure that the system is working **effectively** for all students and they help college admissions officers or employers **evaluate** a potential candidate.

Portfolios—carefully selected **collections** of student work—are another element of a comprehensive assessment system. Like those compiled by artists and writers, student **portfolios** provide tangible records of achievement over time. The act of selecting examples for a specific purpose reveals student **thinking** about their own learning and their understanding of the standards of quality against which their work is measured. As **technology** becomes more common in classrooms, portfolios are no longer limited to written products. An even more detailed picture of a learner's progress is being captured on audio or video and stored in **digital** form. Samples of a student's work from many years can be accessed from a single disk or over a network, making it readily available for review.

When students, like skaters, understand what constitutes **excellence** and have the opportunity to show what they know, they develop the capacity to monitor their own progress—a skill essential for **lifelong learning**. In combination with clearly defined standards and improved tests, performance assessments offer all stakeholders a better **understanding** of how well students and schools are achieving their goals. ●

Imagine the Possibilities

BY GRANT WIGGINS

show what you know as you go

My vision of meaningful assessment begins simply enough, not with images but with sounds—snippets of talk. Listen to students: They no longer ask teachers: "Is this what you want?" or "Is this going to be on the test?" Instead, students know right from the start what they are expected to learn. Like athletes and actors, they've studied models of high performance and monitor their own progress towards those yardsticks. You can hear them asking each other or their teachers: "How can I improve this?" or "How can I find more evidence to support my conclusion?"

Teachers talk about "more sophisticated performance," not "higher scores." One hears almost no talk about averages or normal curves, because the goal is for every student to achieve at the highest possible level. Teachers seek as much information as possible about how students are learning in order to provide them with better coaching and guidance. They draw on actual samples of student work, easily accessible in electronic databases, as they talk about how to improve achievement. Teachers spend part of their time developing and refining ways of assessing student learning and helping students learn the skill of self-assessment.

Outside of school, policy makers and the media are no longer heard judging programs, schools, districts, or states solely on the basis of test scores. They understand that no single standardized test is an adequate measure of learning. They've stopped trying to use tests to improve schools, realizing this strategy makes as much sense as trying to improve government by giving legislators a multiple-choice test. Rather, policy makers and the media use a broad range of indicators to monitor schools, looking for appropriate gains when current performance is compared with past performance. Accountability measures are based on the goal of having every student meet high standards.

The common thread in all these discussions is a different understanding of the purpose of assessment: it's not a way of designating winners and losers at the end of the game. Tests and other assessments are valuable only when they provide worthwhile information that can be used to improve student achievement. This information is needed long before the end of a lesson or a year so that adjustments can be made before it is too late.

Seeing is Believing What do we see as we wander around a school, then? The assessment process is so unobtrusive to students and teachers, so seamless with teaching and learning, that it is indistinguishable

Grant Wiggins[1] is the president and director of programs at The Center on Learning, Assessment, and School Structure. ★ FILM

from what takes place during good instruction. We see kids working together and critiquing each other, science experiments being brought to fruition, art exhibits being finished, and debate points being honed. In short, we see authentic assessments—learning activities that closely resemble the ways that students will be expected to use their knowledge and skills in the real world.

We still see students working and teachers observing carefully, taking notes—the oldest and most revealing mode of assessment. In some schools, we see teachers using computers and audio or video recorders to help them monitor student work, building databases that can help identify the ways a particular student learns best.

Some students are taking tests that are standardized to allow comparisons among schools, districts, states, and nations. But these tests no longer consist of multiple-choice questions so they can be easily scored by a machine. Instead, most tests are scored by hand, to ensure that student

In short, we see authentic assessments— learning activities that closely resemble the ways that students will be expected to use their knowledge and skills in the real world.

performance is judged against sophisticated criteria. Reliable scores are achieved through training teachers in the standards and criteria measured by each test (a scoring system used for decades for Advanced Placement examinations). Hundreds of standardized tests are available, and they are used primarily by teachers to assess both their own and their students' progress.

Older observers, used to silence and blue books, are surprised to learn that a lively discussion between a teacher and a small group of students is actually a formal and rigorous assessment. The teacher is asking probing questions of a group of students working on a project. She wants to know not only what assumptions the students started with and what decisions they have made, but also why they are using certain strategies and what they might do differently. The conversation is being recorded and will be transcribed for later, more careful analysis by the teacher and a colleague whose students are working on a similar project hundreds of miles away.

Some students are working on their digital portfolios, assembling the elements required for each of their learning plans. They select work that demonstrates what they are learning, including papers, test results, and video or audio recordings. They also complete a self-assessment that prompts them to think about what they are learning, to recognize quality work, and to plan how they can perform better in the future.

Others are building bridges, staging plays, and mounting museum exhibits, using computer simulations instead of physical materials. Such simulations require students to demonstrate their understanding of knowledge, skills, and ideas by using them in context. They also allow teachers to gauge the student's ability to self-adjust in response to the typical problems of each context. Feedback is immediate, just as it has always been on the job or the playing field, and part of what is being measured is the degree to which a student solicits, ponders, and effectively uses the feedback.

Better Information Pinpoints Learners' Needs For the most part, a whole class of students is almost never seen taking the same test at the same time. Advances in technology allow assessments to be personalized to reflect the goals and current areas of focus for each individual student. Computer simulations, for example, quickly adapt to a student's responses and apparent level of understanding. And the simulations have memory: the student's past achievements are used as a benchmark for assessing new gains.

Instead of comparing students to each other, based on arbitrary timetables, students can be compared against performance standards and benchmarks.

Teachers, students, and parents have instantaneous access to detailed achievement profiles, including where each student's current performance level can be placed on a career-long scale (as has long been done in chess or gymnastics).

Helping students understand standards and the criteria for meeting them is now seen as an important part of the teaching process. When they understand what they are expected to learn, students can play a major role in setting immediate and long-range goals and assessing their own progress, much as they track their scores on computer games and their performances in athletics. Self-assessment is finally recognized as a vital skill for success in the world outside of school.

Computerized portfolios of each student's performance over time give teachers and students access to information that is invaluable in helping design and adjust individualized learning plans. Both the assessments and subsequent reports allow monitoring of student learning at a level of detail never before practical, so teachers can focus activities much more directly to the specific needs of a single pupil or group of students. And they can draw on a wider array of information to track progress towards more elusive goals, such as perseverance, craftsmanship, and effective problem solving.

Fair and Useful Accountability The accumulated database of student work provides policy makers with better information to help determine whether or not particular schools and districts are measuring up to agreed-upon standards. Since school sites have diverse goals, they are not judged against each other, but against themselves. Schools are assessed based on achieving their own goals and on demonstrating improved student achievement over time. Thus, the process of holding schools and districts accountable for results is more equitable and useful.

States no longer give tests. They test tests: They certify that local assessment systems are up to standards, and that schools and districts regularly monitor their progress toward their goals. Random audits of district and school databases help officials monitor local assessment processes and make sure they meet established criteria. Officials call up sets of student papers to make sure that performance standards are high and that scoring is consistent. Based on these audits, state personnel

make recommendations and assist in improving local assessment systems.

At the local level, teams of teachers routinely collaborate on assessments to ensure consensus and consistency in the scoring of work. Any teacher or student can easily access an international database of tasks, criteria, benchmarks, and student work products which enable longitudinal assessment—a continuum from "rank novice" to "expert"—for almost any subject or course imaginable. And teachers from other schools come in periodically to judge performance and help conduct audits to ensure validity and reliability.

Significantly, teachers are not the only people setting standards or evaluating student work. College professors and business people help make sure that standards prepare students for the world beyond school and help judge major assessments of student portfolios and performance. In fact, since schooling has become a community-wide affair, teachers don't hesitate to ask for help from anyone whose expertise might be valuable during a particular learning activity. These "guests" don't simply impart their wisdom and leave, but stick around to help evaluate what was learned by students, teachers, and even themselves.

When they understand what they are expected to learn, students can play a major role in setting immediate and long-range goals and assessing their own progress, much as they track their scores on computer games and their performances in athletics.

Employers and college admissions officers each devise different ways of interpreting the database or portfolio of work presented by candidates. Some choose to combine quantifiable results into a single, ranked score, while others take the time to look more deeply at specific qualities needed for success. Either way, few ever pine for the days when all the information they had about a candidate's education was a grade-point average and a couple of numerical test scores.

Not Just a Vision, A Reality Is such a system of personalized, rigorous, ongoing assessment desirable? Many of us think so. Feasible? Yes. Most of the scenes described above can be witnessed somewhere in the world, right now, as you imagine the possibilities. ●

From the Front Lines

BY CLYDE YOSHIDA

Creating a Culture

The seventh and eighth graders in my math class at O'Farrell Community School in San Diego work in groups of five or six. One student in each group presents a stamp that they designed for the country of Guinea. They had started the assignment by creating small versions of their designs, then rendered them as large posters—learning math by calculating ratios as they increased their artwork in size. (Art was my college major, and I'm always looking for ways to link math and visuals.) The presenters in each group explain the decisions they made as they worked on the project, and ask their classmates for feedback on how they can revise and improve their work.

These sessions are called "critique circles." They are one of many innovative educational practices adopted at O'Farrell as part of a comprehensive restructuring effort. As a member of the school's curriculum and portfolio committees, I worked on devising ways to help students become more reflective and critical about their work. We want them to be able to judge for themselves whether a piece of work is excellent or falls short of the school's standards. It may seem like a lot to ask of adolescents but, once we started using strategies like critique circles and portfolios, students quickly showed they were willing and able to take more responsibility for the quality of their work. Teachers clearly define their expectations, then give students feedback indicating whether the work "does not meet," "meets," or "exceeds" expectations. We find that this kind of feedback

encourages students to reflect on their work and, when necessary, to revise it to meet the standards.

O'Farrell's students regularly work in cooperative learning groups, so they feel comfortable critiquing the work of their peers in constructive ways. Everyone understands that all work is subject to revision and that suggested changes don't mean a student failed the first time. Teachers monitor these discussions and push them to become more substantive. When I supervised circles in my math classes, I wasn't just looking at whether or not students calculated correctly. I also evaluated things like how well they were communicating— were they being clear, direct, and helpful?

A critical factor in getting students to assume responsibility for monitoring the quality of their work is to establish clear expectations ahead of time. When they begin to compile their portfolios, students first identify how their work addresses one or more of the school's six challenges, such as completing a research project or serving the community. Then they create a "personal reflection" describing what they learned in completing the assignment, identifying the work's strong points, and detailing what they would improve with more time. Finally, they craft three questions that serve as prompts for discussion with others. For a science and math assignment, for example, a student might ask: "Are my calculations correct?" "Are they pertinent to the lab?" and "How could I have explained the procedures I used better?"

After a critique circle, students can choose to revise work for another round of evaluation or include it "as-is" in their portfolios. (When students have the skills to observe and measure their own growth, they will often go the extra mile to

# of Student Reflection

improve their assignments.) At the end of each year, students use the contents of their portfolios for an exhibition that requires them to show how they have grown and that they are ready to move on. The presentations take place before a panel that may include parents, community members, teachers from other schools, district officials, and business people.

Students learn a lot from this portfolio process. By presenting their work to peers, they get a different perspective on it. They begin to understand how they learn (what educators call "metacognition"). They realize that revising a project—sometimes even starting over—and collaborating with others are natural parts of real-world work. They feel a greater ownership of what they create and try harder to make it as good as possible because it will be seen by a larger audience. They learn to take responsibility for evaluating their own efforts, rather than waiting for the teacher to pass judgment on them. And they know that their school work is valuable, because the teacher asks them to keep it rather than throw it away after it's graded. They can see their progress over time because they have a tangible record of their learning.

Letter grades, by contrast, stigmatize students by labeling work as "good" or "bad," often without giving them opportunities or support to improve it. Portfolios help students focus on bettering themselves rather than ranking their work in comparison with the achievement of others.

This system also benefits teachers. When one student says to another, "Oh, you solved the problem a different way. How'd you do it?" it shows educators that what we are actually doing is teaching children how to become better learners. The feedback students get on their work is also feedback on ours. And, as a teacher, I like to be able to show real examples of student work to my principal, parents, and colleagues as proof that these kids are learning.

It may seem like a lot to ask of adolescents but, once we started using strategies like critique circles and portfolios, students quickly showed they were willing and able to take more responsibility for the quality of their work.

As technology becomes pervasive, the power of portfolios to improve learning is bound to expand. Because almost any kind of work can be captured and stored digitally, schools will soon be able to keep an electronic archive showing a student's development over his entire K-12 career. Portfolios stored on digital media are portable and accessible. Employers and college admissions officers will be able to easily look at relevant examples of a candidate's school work.

I recently got a visit from a former student that reinforced my conviction that portfolios change how students view learning. "My high school doesn't use portfolios," the student confided to me, "but you know what? I keep one anyway." ●

Clyde Yoshida[2] is a former teacher at O'Farrell Community School, and a consultant on curriculum and assessment.

Snapshots

Statewide Influence

When teachers in the Carroll County Public Schools in Maryland initiated a hands-on science curriculum more than 10 years ago, it was the start of a revolution. The curriculum was designed to encourage students to develop useful scientific skills, such as the ability to observe, measure accurately, and use data to support conclusions. It attracted widespread attention and is now used to teach more than 700,000 students nationwide. It also sparked changes in the

way the state measures science achievement—the Maryland Science Performance Assessment Program (MSPAP), adopted in 1993, incorporates the kinds of hands-on tasks that Carroll County pioneered.

MSPAP is a model of how state assessments can better match classroom activities and the skills that students need to master. "Teaching to the test can be a good thing when the test is valid and reflects your goals in the classroom," says Suzanne Peters, a science teacher.

The district is also working to make sure that all of its 25,000 students, regardless of their abilities and backgrounds, can meet standards that require them to analyze and think independently. Carroll

Carroll County Public Schools
55 North Court Street, Westminster, MD 21157 **Contact:** Brad Yohe, Supervisor of Science • Phone: (410) 751-3000 • Fax: (410) 751-3003 • URL: http://www.carr.lib.md.us/ccps/welcome.htm

County teachers incorporated animation and sound into problems like those encountered on the MSPAP to produce a CD-ROM used for independent practice. Recent results show that Carroll County students consistently rank among the highest in the state on the MSPAP, despite attending one of Maryland's lower-income districts. ●

Alice Carlson Applied Learning Center, Fort Worth, TX • Photo by Paul Moseley

South Brunswick Public Schools
Four Executive Drive, PO Box 181, Monmouth Junction, NJ 08852
Contact: Willa Spicer, Director of Curriculum and Instruction • Phone: (908) 297-7800 • Fax: (908) 422-8054 • E-mail: l.ray@applelink.apple.com

Testing What is Taught

In 1989, teachers in South Brunswick, N.J., changed the way they taught reading and writing to focus more on comprehension. But the district's tests continued to focus on isolated skills. This split, between what was taught and what was tested, challenged teachers to find an approach that measured reading comprehension but still retained the reliability of traditional, standardized tests. With help from the Educational Testing Service (ETS), the nation's largest test publisher, teachers created the Early Literacy Portfolio (ELP) for kindergarten through second grades. The ELP helps document a child's development of reading comprehension through work samples and teacher observations and interviews.

ETS helped teachers develop a six-point scale to score a child's abilities in reading and writing. Beginning readers can identify letters of the alphabet and their corresponding sounds; the most advanced can read independently, understanding a variety of material. The scale helps teachers assess literacy among groups of students within a class as well as across the district. District teachers get together periodically to read, discuss, and score each others' ELPs. The meetings give teachers a common understanding of quality work and ensure a consistent interpretation of the scale. "ETS helped us clarify what we truly want to assess," says Willa Spicer, director of curriculum and instruction. ●

In Gauging Learning

"We ask 'what do students need to learn, what strengths do they bring to the task, and how can we best teach them?'" says Frederika French, principal of Morristown Elementary School in Vermont. For many years, the pre-K through sixth-grade school has been piloting a wide variety of assessments to supplement traditional tests.

To help gauge a student's readiness to learn, the school uses portfolios containing samples and revisions of a student's work that reflect progress toward criteria in each content area. The goals for student work are clear and the standards against which their progress is measured are modeled by benchmarks—examples of work ranging in quality from poor to excellent.

The school has also adopted the New Standards assessments in mathematics, a rigorous performance assessment based on real tasks and projects. Fourth-grade students, for example, are asked to show how they could set up an aquarium within a budget of $50, explaining their choices of equipment, fish, and food. In order to implement this or any other performance-based assessment successfully, Morristown has learned that it is critical to help students understand the standards they are expected to meet. Since audiences of classmates, parents, teachers, and other community members often help evaluate performances, they, too, have to understand the standards. One of the ways Morristown has communicated the importance and usefulness of standards is to enlist community members to share the criteria for excellence in their own fields.

The school's leadership role in the assessment field continues to evolve. "In order to help a child move from one point to another, the teacher needs to continually assess where the student is in relationship to the standard or desired result," French says. ●

"We ask 'what do students need to learn, what strengths do they bring to the task, and how can we best teach them?'"

Morristown Elementary School Lamoille South Supervisory Union School District, Route 15A, Morrisville, VT 05661 **Contact:** Barbara Percy, Administrative Assistant • Phone: (802) 888-3101 • Fax: (802) 888-6721 • E-mail: morristown55@morristown.k12.vt.us

The Power of Portfolios

The limitations of multiple-choice tests are apparent in subjects such as writing, music, and visual arts—a good test score indicates very little about a student's ability to analyze or create an essay, a musical composition, or a work of art. The best way to assess a person's abilities and understanding in these fields is to review samples of their work. That is why professionals in these fields compile portfolios, and it is also why portfolios are now used in all of Pittsburgh's secondary schools to assess student learning in writing, music, and visual arts.

Each of the district's 18,900 6th through 12th graders compile portfolios containing a history of their learning on selected projects. The portfolios contain a range of work, such as initial sketches, early and final drafts, and self- and peer-assessments. The work collected in the portfolios is used as a source of instruction.

Teachers used samples of student work to develop models of excellence along a six-point scale. At annual districtwide portfolio audits, portfolio samples are evaluated by teachers and administrators from different schools, as well as by community members. As a result, score reliability has been very high.

The emphasis on meaningful tasks, self-reflection, and self-assessment are natural outgrowths of portfolios. "Student reflection opened the door to what was missing in my experience and my knowledge as a writing teacher," says Kathy Howard, a Pittsburgh teacher. "There is a shift in the power base from teacher to students. Students start looking at models of good writing and setting their own criteria and standards for good work." ●

Pittsburgh Public Schools 1501 Bedford Avenue, Pittsburgh, PA 15219 **Contact:** Lynn A. Mariaskin, Coordinator: Teaching, Learning, and Assessment • Phone: (412) 338-8049 • Fax: (412) 338-8045

Digital Portfolios

Educators at North Star Elementary School in rural Alaska understand that effective assessment begins when students look at their own work and compare it to meaningful individual goals. To enhance this process, North Star has developed a unique type of parent conference that uses digital

North Star Elementary School Kenai Peninsula Borough School District, PO Box 8629, Nikiski, AK 99635 **Contact:** Donna Peterson, Principal • Phone: (907) 776-5575 • Fax: (907) 776-8423 • E-mail: dpeterson@kpbsd.k12.ak.us • URL: http://www.kpbsd.k12.ak.us

portfolios to help students reflect on their academic development and discuss it with their parents.

From kindergarten on, teachers help North Star's 340 students collect samples of their writing, math, and artwork. The selection of samples is a lesson itself, as students work with peers and teachers learning how to identify and evaluate quality work. These samples are then scanned into a computer and digitally stored, so they can be reviewed over the years.

In the fall of the fourth grade, students present their digitized portfolios to their parents, sharing what they have collected and answering questions their parents might have. Although the teacher participates, students are expected to take the lead in these conferences, showing how their skills

have developed over the years and identifying and discussing their goals for the coming semesters. "The conferences let me see my daughter taking responsibility for her progress," says Pam Lettington, a parent. "I was really happy to see her recognize that she has weaknesses while still feeling proud of her accomplishments."

The school has seen improvements in standardized test scores and other traditional indicators of student learning. As a result of the portfolio process, parents and students exhibit a stronger understanding of the skills and knowledge not yet mastered. "We believe this kind of assessment is the key to real learning," says Donna Peterson, North Star's principal. ●

Assessing Mastery

"Teachers and administrators are committed to meaningful assessment throughout this district," says Randall Pfeiffer, teacher leader for assessment in the Upper Arlington City Schools in Columbus, Ohio. "We don't just try to plug in assessment in place of standardized testing. We use it as a guide to improve student performance."

Upper Arlington's 12-year commitment to finding more effective ways to evaluate students is built on a foundation of solid research. After studies at nearby Ohio State University showed that numerical test results do not provide a complete picture of how students' skills develop, the district started looking for better assessment alternatives. Teachers now evaluate students by asking them to apply their skills in ways that reflect how

"We don't just try to plug in assessment in place of standardized testing. We use it as a guide to improve student performance."

they are used in the real world—a method known as performance-based assessment. Students might demonstrate their mastery of mathematics by figuring out how much it would cost to paint their own house, or show their ability to write by producing a brochure.

To ensure accurate and consistent assessment results from class to class, Upper Arlington regularly provides teachers with training, opportunities to observe colleagues, and chances to have their students' work evaluated by others. As this process has evolved,

the district has developed a set of performance standards—with detailed descriptions and examples of each standard—to guide the evaluation process at each level. Teachers also collect student work in portfolios to document progress. "Our assessment practices have not only given us a much better idea of how we need to help individual students, it's also caused the students and the community to start to reflect more on their learning," Pfeiffer concludes. ●

Upper Arlington Assessment Program Upper Arlington City Schools, 1650 Ridgeview Road, Columbus, OH 43221 **Contact:** Randy Pfeiffer, Teacher Leader for Assessment • Phone: (614) 487-5258 • Fax: (614) 487-5238

Right of Passage

In order to earn a diploma, students at Walden III Middle/High School in Racine, Wis., have to complete the Right of Passage Experience (ROPE). Developed by Walden's teachers in 1973, ROPE is a demanding set of projects and presentations designed to evaluate student achievement and preparation for post-secondary life. The program is based on the principle that students' knowledge is cumulative and that they should be able to demonstrate an ability to apply what they have learned. ROPE requires students to present evidence of their mastery in 16 areas—such as English, mathematics, science, government, ethics, and physical challenge—before a committee of teachers, peers, and community members. ROPE does not specify detailed criteria or standards for any of the areas assessed. Each student has to decide how best to present what she has learned and can do; and each committee has to decide whether the student's achievement sufficiently prepares her to carry out her post-secondary plans.

Walden III Middle/High School
Racine Unified School District, 1012 Center Street, Racine, WI 53403
Contact: Patricia Stephens Rodgers, Directing Principal • Phone: (414) 635-5860 • Fax: (414) 631-7121

Students prepare for their demonstrations in a semester-long course led by the ROPE instructors who will later evaluate their performance. During the course, students assemble a portfolio of classroom work they began as early as the sixth grade and complete a major research paper in U.S. history. In addition, they demonstrate their mastery of subjects such as mathematics, government, and world geography by making oral presentations and responding to questions. The ROPE committee evaluates all of these components and issues a final grade. Students who are unsuccessful in meeting the standards pursue further studies before the committee reconvenes. ROPE's instructors say the spirit of their program goes beyond measurement and scores to helping students assess their own skills and potential before leaving high school. ●

Graduation by Exhibition

University Heights High School
New York City Public Schools District 10, University Avenue and West 181st Street, New York, NY 10453 **Contact:** Deborah Harris, Assistant Principal • Phone: (718) 289-5300 • Fax: (718) 295-7572 • E-mail: paul_allison@cce.org

Although many students enroll at University Heights High School in the Bronx because it is an alternative school offering a second chance at a diploma, they soon discover that they've got their work cut out for them. Instead of having to pass a certain number of courses, they have to demonstrate that they meet a set of detailed standards of learning and achievement. "No student gets a diploma simply for being here a certain amount of time. Our students have to prove they measure up," explains faculty member Phil Farnham.

University Heights students demonstrate their accomplishments and prove their skills to a "roundtable" of peers, teachers, community members, and other critical friends—a system known as "graduation by exhibition."

The school requires students to present evidence of skills in each of seven areas, such as thinking critically; communicating clearly with numbers, words, and scientific data; and demonstrating responsible citizenship. The evidence that students can offer ranges from traditional standardized test scores and research papers to videotaped performances and digitized collections that show a student's work over time. The standards that each presentation is judged against, however, stay constant and explicit.

After three years, the round-table process seems to have had a positive effect for these students from mostly low-income, minority families. Three-quarters of all graduates go on to college. Students who pass with distinction have, as a rule, experienced comparable success at the university level. This has created an atmosphere in which it is assumed that all of the school's students will succeed at high levels and be prepared for college. "It's what happens when you build on the expectation that all students must prove their competence to their community and to themselves," says Paul Allison, a University Heights teacher. ●

Organizations

Assessment and Accountability Program (A&A)
Description: A research, development, and training program of the Northwest Regional Educational Laboratory (NWREL) that assists state education agencies, school districts, colleges, and businesses. **Purpose:** To promote effective, system-wide, K-12 student assessment programs. **Activities:** Conducts applied research and development activities and provides technical assistance and instruction in effective assessment practice and program evaluation. Also offers research assistance through the Test Center, a lending library of more than 2,000 assessment resources, and publishes bibliographies of its collected materials. **Contact:** Judith Arter, Assessment Unit Manager • Assessment and Accountability Program, Northwest Regional Educational Laboratory, 101 SW Main Street, Suite 500, Portland, OR 97204 • Phone: (800) 547-6339 or (503) 275-9500 • Fax: (503) 275-0450 • E-mail: arterj@nwrel.org • URL: http://www.nwrel.org

> *"Teachers have always known the power of assessment to drive classroom instruction. What is exciting now is how motivated they become when they feel in control of assessment practices."*
>
> Bena Kallick,[4] Vice President, Technology Pathways

ERIC Clearinghouse on Assessment and Evaluation
Description: One of 16 federally funded education clearinghouses of the Educational Resource Information Center (ERIC) system. **Purpose:** To provide educators, policy makers, and the general public with information about assessment and evaluation. **Activities:** Collects, abstracts, and indexes thousands of relevant journal articles, research reports, curriculum guides, books, and conference papers. **Contact:** Lawrence Rudner, Director • ERIC Clearinghouse on Assessment and Evaluation, Catholic University of America, 210 O'Boyle Hall, Washington, DC 20064 • Phone: (800) 464-3742 • Fax: (202) 319-6692 • E-mail: eric_ae@cua.edu • URL: http://www.cua.edu/www/eric_ae/

> *"We need separate, parallel assessment systems: the first to give teachers and students rich information about an individual's progress, and the second to give the public useful information about how the school and district are doing relative to curriculum standards. We are asking too much of any single system when we expect it to do both."*
>
> George Madaus,[3] Boisi Professor of Education and Public Policy, Center for the Study of Testing, Evaluation and Educational Policy, Boston College

Center on Learning, Assessment, and School Structure (CLASS) **Description:** An educational research and consulting organization working with schools, districts, and state education departments. **Purpose:** To improve teaching and learning by providing services, products, and ideas for the enhancement and redesign of assessment systems, curriculum, and teaching strategies. **Activities:** Sponsors workshops, seminars, and conferences. Publishes print material and video resources. **Contact:** Everett Kline, Senior Staff Associate • Center on Learning, Assessment, and School Structure, 648 The Great Road, Princeton, NJ 08540 • Phone: (609) 252-1211 • Fax: (609) 252-1268 • E-mail: info@classnj.org • URL: http://www.classnj.org

Center for Performance Assessment **Description:** Started in 1992 as a research and development center at the Educational Testing Service (ETS). **Purpose:** To contribute to the theoretical understanding, design, and use of performance assessments intended to promote effective learning and teaching. **Activities:** Conducts research on the design, implementation, consequences, and technical quality of assessments in a variety of educational contexts. **Contact:** Mimi Perez, Senior Administrative Assistant • Center for Performance Assessment, Educational Testing Service, Rosedale Road, Mail Stop 11-P, Princeton, NJ 08541 • Phone: (609) 734-5521 • Fax: (609) 734-5115 • E-mail: mperez@ets.org • URL: http://www.ets.org

Center for the Study of Testing, Evaluation, & Educational Policy (CSTEEP)
Description: An international research center serving school districts, education and government agencies, private foundations, and corporations. **Purpose:** To advance the study of educational testing, evaluation, and policy so as to improve the quality and fairness of education. **Activities:** Conducts research and evaluation, provides technical assistance, and distributes information on assessment practices and policies. Current projects include the Third International Mathematics and Science Study (TIMSS) and research into the use of multimedia technology in student performance assessment and national testing systems. **Contact:** Albert Beaton, Director • Center for the Study of Testing, Evaluation, & Educational Policy, Boston College, Campion Hall, Room 323, Chestnut Hill, MA 02167 • Phone: (617) 552-4521 • Fax: (617) 552-8419 • E-mail: beatonal@bc.edu • URL: http://www.csteep.bc.edu

Four Seasons Network

Description: Four Seasons began as a collaborative project to investigate assessment by classroom practitioners from Harvard Project Zero, the Coalition of Essential Schools (CES), Foxfire, and the National Center for Restructuring Education, Schools, and Teaching (NCREST). It has evolved into a network of educators engaged with broader issues of school restructuring. **Purpose:** To examine the links between assessment, curriculum, and instruction, and to share collective knowledge from the field. **Activities:** Members learn and share information through institutes, consultations, and projects. Ongoing communication and collaboration is facilitated by an electronic network. **Contact:** Ann Lieberman, Co-Director • Four Seasons Project, National Center for Restructuring Education, Schools, and Teaching, Teachers College, Columbia University, Box 110, New York, NY 10027 • Phone: (212) 678-3432 • Fax: (212) 678-4170 • E-mail: al136@ columbia.edu • URL: http://www.tmn.com/ ncrest/fourseasons.html

National Center for Fair & Open Testing (FairTest) **Description:** An advocacy organization that serves as a national clearinghouse for information on testing and other kinds of assessments. **Purpose:** Promotes reform of the current system of standardized testing for American students, with an emphasis on equity and appropriate uses of assessments. **Activities:** Provides technical assistance, monitors standardized testing, and organizes public education campaigns. Publishes a quarterly newsletter, *The Examiner;* annotated bibliographies; and other materials on testing from pre-kindergarten through higher education and employment. **Contact:** Bob Schaeffer, Public Education Director • National Center for Fair and Open Testing, 342 Broadway Avenue, Cambridge, MA 02139 • Phone: (617) 864-4810 • Fax: (617) 497-2224 • E-mail: fairtest@aol.com • URL: http://www.essential.org/fairtest

The National Center for Research on Evaluation, Standards, and Student Testing (CRESST) **Description:** A federally funded research center and clearinghouse for information on assessment systems. **Purpose:** To promote improved approaches to assessment and evaluation in public schools. **Activities:** Provides technical assistance to educators, designs prototype assessments, develops training and assessment resources, and conducts on-site studies. Maintains an on-line database containing descriptive listings of new assessments in practice. Publishes a monograph series, technical reports, resource papers, and a semi-annual research-based publication, all available on-line. **Contact:** Ron Dietel, Communications Director • National Center for Research on Evaluation, Standards, and Student Testing, University of California Los Angeles, 1320 Moore Hall, Mailbox 951522, Los Angeles, CA 90095 • Phone: (310) 206-1532 • Fax: (310) 825-3883 • E-mail: ron@cse.ucla.edu • URL: http://www.cresst96.cse.ucla.edu/cresst.htm

> *"Anything we can do to improve the quality and timeliness of feedback is very valuable. Technology does this by hooking kids into a community of people that will give them frequent, well-educated feedback on the work they're producing."*
>
> Phil Daro,[5] Executive Director of Assessment Development, New Standards

National Assessment of Educational Progress (NAEP) **Description:** An educational assessment program established by Congress in 1969. **Purpose:** Monitors levels of academic achievement to help policy makers improve the quality of public education. **Activities:** Develops and conducts national and state-level assessments of student performance in reading, math, science, writing, history, geography, and other curricular areas. Publishes reports outlining trends in what American students know and are able to do. **Contact:** Sheida White, Statistician • National Assessment of Educational Progress, National Center for Education Statistics, U.S. Department of Education, 555 New Jersey Avenue NW, Washington, DC 20208, Phone: (202) 219-1675 • Fax: (202) 219-1801 • E-mail: sheida_white@ ed.gov • URL: http:// www.ed.gov/NCES/naep/

New Standards **Description:** A voluntary partnership of states and school districts committed to school restructuring through establishing high standards for all students. A joint project of the National Center on Education and the Economy (NCEE) and the Learning Research and Development Center (LRDC). **Purpose:** To design and implement a national system of rigorous content and performance standards for student achievement in each academic discipline. **Activities:** Conducts research on education standards nationally and worldwide. Develops standards in various curricular areas and builds assessment systems, including portfolios and performances, to gauge progress toward the standards. Conducts pilot projects across the country. Publishes reports and materials, provides training, and hosts conferences. **Contact:** Eugene Paslov, Executive Director • New Standards, National Center on Education and the Economy, 700 Eleventh Street NW, Suite 750, Washington, DC 20001 • Phone: (202) 783-3668 • Fax: (202) 783-3672 • E-mail: epaslov@ncee.org • URL: http://www.ncee.org

Performance Assessment Collaboratives for Education (PACE) Description: A multi-year project supporting innovative approaches to assessment and learning at urban middle schools nationwide. **Purpose:** To help teachers use and improve portfolios and performance assessments. **Activities:** Conducts research and provides on-site support in developing new approaches to assessment. Hosts an annual national summer institute on assessment reforms for educators. **Contact:** Dennie Palmer Wolf, Director • Performance Assessment Collaboratives for Education, Graduate School of Education, Harvard University, 8 Story Street, Cambridge, MA 02138 • Phone: (617) 496-2770 • Fax: (617) 496-2777 • E-mail: wolfde@hugse1.harvard.edu • URL: http://hugse1.harvard.edu/~pace

State Collaborative on Assessment and Student Standards (SCASS) Description: A series of assessment-development projects in which 43 states participate under the direction of the Council of Chief State School Officers (CCSSO). **Purpose:** To help states develop high-quality, cost-effective assessments. **Activities:** Helps states develop alternative assessment standards, materials, and staff development resources. Conducts surveys of student assessment programs nationwide and maintains an electronic database of results available to policy makers, educators, and community members interested in state-level assessment. Publishes an annual report of assessment program information. **Contact:** Edward Roeber, Director, Student Assessment Programs • State Collaborative on Assessment and Student Standards, State Education Assessment Center, Council of Chief State School Officers, One Massachusetts Avenue NW, Suite 700, Washington, DC 20001 • Phone: (517) 347-1145 • Fax: (517) 347-1145 • E-mail: edroeber@aol.com • URL: http://www.ccsso.org

> *"Improving assessment involves not just creating more ways to measure learning, but also changing curriculum, instruction, and record keeping to build on the strengths of new assessments."*
>
> Robert Marzano,[6] Deputy Director of Training and Development, Mid-continent Regional Educational Laboratory

Periodicals

> *"New assessments must be reliable, practical, and credible. Technology can help by portraying student growth in ways that people can understand—not just with numbers in tables, but with authentic examples."*
>
> Eva L. Baker,[7] Co-Director, National Center for Research on Evaluation, Standards, and Student Testing, University of California Los Angeles

Educational Assessment Description: A quarterly scholarly journal. **Focus:** Offers articles, editorials, and empirical research exploring the theoretical frameworks and debates surrounding national assessment issues. **Publisher:** Lawrence Erlbaum Associates, Mahwah, NJ • Phone: (201) 236-9500 ext. 235.

Educational Measurement: Issues and Practice Description: Quarterly publication aimed at teachers and other users of educational assessments. **Focus:** Presents a variety of perspectives on current assessment-related issues, including the quality of new assessments, equity concerns, and the role of computers. **Publisher:** National Council on Measurement in Education, Washington, DC • Phone: (202) 223-9318.

The CRESST Line Description: A quarterly newsletter of the National Center for Research on Evaluation, Standards, and Student Testing (CRESST) for educators of all levels. **Focus:** Offers information about CRESST research, publications, conferences, and activities related to standards and assessment. **Publisher:** UCLA Center for the Study of Evaluation, Los Angeles, CA. • Phone: (310) 206-1532

Readings

Darling-Hammond, Linda, Lynne Einbender, Frederick Frelow, et al. **Authentic Assessment in Practice: A Collection of Portfolios, Performance Tasks, Exhibitions, and Documentation.** *National Center for Restructuring Education, Schools, and Teaching, Teachers College, Columbia University: New York, NY, 1993.* Phone: (212) 678-3432. ● An extensive collection of various approaches to assessment from schools and districts. Covers a wide range of academic disciplines and skills.

Educational Leadership. **"Using Performance Assessment."** *Vol. 49, No. 8, May 1992. Association for Supervision and Curriculum Development: Alexandria, VA.* Phone: (800) 933-2723. ● Nineteen articles by assessment pioneers provide a variety of perspectives and research on performance and portfolio assessments.

The ERIC Review. "**Performance-Based Assessment**." *Vol. 3, Winter 1994. ACCESS ERIC: Rockville, MD.* Phone: (800) 443-3742. ● Provides an overview on the subject, including descriptions of innovative projects and listings of resources for more exploration.

Mitchell, Ruth. **Testing for Learning: How New Approaches to Evaluation Can Improve American Schools.** *Free Press: New York, NY, 1992.* Phone: (800) 223-2336. ● Intended for policy makers and others interested in system-wide assessment reform, this book profiles performance-based systems implemented in Arizona, California, Maryland, and Vermont.

National Forum on Assessment. **Principles and Indicators for Student Assessment Systems.** *National Center for Fair and Open Testing: Cambridge, MA, 1995.* Phone: (617) 864-4810. ● Outlines seven principles for transforming assessment as part of comprehensive education reform, such as: the primary purpose of assessment is to improve learning; the broader community should be involved in assessment development; and the assessment system should be reviewed and improved regularly.

Rothman, Robert. **Measuring Up: Standards, Assessments, and School Reform.** *Jossey-Bass: San Francisco, CA, 1995.* Phone: (800) 956-7739. ● Using case studies, this book examines schools that have adopted performance assessments as a central strategy in school-wide restructuring.

Herman, Joan L., Pamela R. Aschbacher, and Lynn Winters. **A Practical Guide to Alternative Assessment.** *Association for Supervision and Curriculum Development: Alexandria, VA, 1992.* Phone: (800) 933-2723. ● The authors review the purposes of assessment and present numerous examples of how they can best be achieved through assessments that conform to current research on learning and cognition.

Northwest Regional Educational Laboratory. **Innovative Assessment: Bibliography of Assessment Alternatives: Portfolios: Fall 1995 Edition.** *NWREL: Portland, OR, 1995.* Phone: (800) 547-6339. ● An annotated bibliography of more than 180 portfolio-related articles reviewed by NWREL staff.

Phillips, S.E. **Legal Implications of High-Stakes Assessment: What States Should Know.** *North Central Regional Educational Laboratory: Oak Brook, IL, 1995.* Phone: (708) 571-4700. ● Explains the web of legal issues and case law surrounding the use of test scores as a principle factor in decisions such as student tracking and graduation.

Stiggins, Richard J. **Student-Centered Classroom Assessment.** *Macmillan College Publishing: New York, NY, 1994.* Phone: (800) 947-7700. ● Written for classroom teachers and other educators, this book describes the importance of involving students in self-assessment and integrating assessment with classroom instruction. Numerous practical ideas draw upon both traditional and innovative techniques.

Newmann, Fred M., Walter G. Secada, and Gary G. Wehlage. **A Guide to Authentic Instruction and Assessment: Vision, Standards, and Scoring.** *Wisconsin Center for Education Research: Madison, WI, 1995.* Phone: (608) 263-4214. ● The authors describe how learning and assessment can be integrated in activities that simulate real-world tasks and present examples of classroom instructional strategies, assessment tasks, and scoring procedures.

Perrone, Vito, ed. **Expanding Student Assessment.** *Association for Supervision and Curriculum Development: Alexandria, VA, 1991.* Phone: (800) 933-2723. ● Contributors examine problems with current standardized testing systems and explore ways to move assessment closer to the work of teachers and learners. Offers recommendations for engaging students as active participants in learning and self-assessment.

> "At the moment we have an educational system that falls far short of our goals for students. We need to find better ways of teaching and assessing that promote thoughtful, engaged, active learning about complicated subject matter to high levels of achievement."
>
> Karen Sheingold,[11] Director, Center for Performance Assessment, Educational Testing Service

Sheingold, Karen, and John Frederiksen. **Linking Assessment with Reform: Technologies that Support Conversations about Student Work.** *Center for Performance Assessment: Educational Testing Service, Princeton, NJ, 1995.* Phone: (609) 734-5521. ● This report examines how video, computer, and telecommunications technologies can be used in the design and delivery of assessments that measure student understanding and performance.

Wiggins, Grant. **Assessing Student Performance: Exploring the Purpose and Limits of Testing.** *Jossey-Bass: San Francisco, CA, 1993.* Phone: (800) 956-7739. ● The author explains the limitations of traditional standardized tests and describes new systems of assessment that promise more useful results.

Contact Information

[1]**Grant Wiggins** President and Director of Programs • The Center on Learning, Assessment, and School Structure, 648 The Great Road, Princeton, NJ 08540 • Phone: (609) 252-1211 • Fax: (609) 252-1268 • E-mail: info@classnj.org

[2]**Clyde Yoshida** Former Teacher • O'Farrell Community School, San Diego Unified School District, 6130 Skyline Drive, San Diego, CA 92114 • Phone: (619) 263-3009 • Fax: (619) 263-4339

[3]**George Madaus** Boisi Professor of Education and Public Policy • Center for the Study of Testing, Evaluation and Educational Policy, Boston College, 140 Commonwealth Avenue, Chestnut Hill, MA 02167 • Phone: (617) 552-4521 • Fax: (617) 552-8419 • E-mail: madaus@bc.edu

> "The goal of changing our assessment system should be to align assessments with good teaching. You know you have a good assessment when it can be used interchangeably as a good teaching activity."
>
> Richard J. Shavelson,[12] Dean, School of Education, Stanford University

[4]**Bena Kallick** Vice President • Technology Pathways, 12 Crooked Mile Road, Westport, CT 06880 • Phone: (203) 227-7261 • Fax: (203) 227-7261 • E-mail: bkallick@aol.com

[5]**Phil Daro** Executive Director of Assessment Development • New Standards, UCOP, 4th Floor, 300 Lakeside Drive, Oakland, CA 94612 • Phone: (510) 987-9465 • Fax: (510) 238-8475 • E-mail: pdaro@ncee.org

[6]**Robert Marzano** Deputy Director of Training and Development • Mid-continent Regional Educational Laboratory, 2550 South Parker Road, Suite 500, Aurora, CO 80014 • Phone: (303) 337-0990 • Fax: (303) 337-3005 • E-mail: bmarzano@mcrel.org

[7]**Eva L. Baker** Co-Director • National Center for Research on Evaluation, Standards, and Student Testing, University of California Los Angeles, 3rd Floor GSE&IS Building, 405 Hilgard Avenue, Los Angeles, CA 90095 • Phone: (310) 206-1532 • Fax: (310) 825-3883 • E-mail: eva@cse.ucla.edu

[8]**Dennie Palmer Wolf** Director • Performance Assessment Collaboratives for Education, Harvard University, 8 Story Street, Cambridge, MA 02138 • Phone: (617) 496-2770 • Fax: (617) 496-2777 • E-mail: wolfde@hugse1.harvard.edu

[9]**Jay McTighe** Director • Maryland Assessment Consortium, c/o Urbana High School, 3471 Campus Drive, Ijamsville, MD 21754 • Phone: (301) 874-6039 • Fax: (301) 874-6057 • E-mail: jmcTigh@aol.com

[10]**Richard J. Stiggins** Director • Assessment Training Institute, 50 SW Second Avenue, Suite 300, Portland, OR 97204 • Phone: (503) 228-3060 • Fax: (503) 228-3014 • E-mail: 73704.2432@compuserve.com

[11]**Karen Sheingold** Director • Center for Performance Assessment, Educational Testing Service, Mail Stop 11P, Princeton, NJ 08541 • Phone: (609) 734-5521 • Fax: (609) 734-5115

[12]**Richard J. Shavelson** Dean • School of Education, Stanford University, Stanford, CA 94305 • Phone: (415) 725-9090 • Fax: (415) 725-7412 • E-mail: rich.s@forsythe.stanford.edu

Alice Carlson Applied Learning Center, Fort Worth, TX • Photo by Paul Moseley

Teachers

In schools committed to change, teachers are breaking out of the isolated confines of their classrooms and developing new relationships with students, colleagues, and communities. With increased knowledge about teaching and learning, they are redefining their roles and becoming facilitators of learning as well as assessment specialists, mentors, managers, and lifelong learners. Many teachers who have access to advanced technologies are searching

Alice Carlson Applied Learning Center, Fort Worth, TX • Photo by Paul Moseley

out the most up-to-date information about education and creating ways to share ideas with others. In this section, we look at how teachers are preparing for this expanded role and at schools that are providing opportunities for ongoing professional development. The most promising reform efforts recognize the value of teachers' knowledge and experience and give them a voice in helping lead the way to better schools. ●

Working with a team of dedicated teachers, having a voice in curriculum and management decisions, and having access to new technologies has made my work more challenging and rewarding than I ever dreamed possible.

Shirley Cothran,[1] Teacher and Kentucky Alliance Consultant, Calloway County Schools

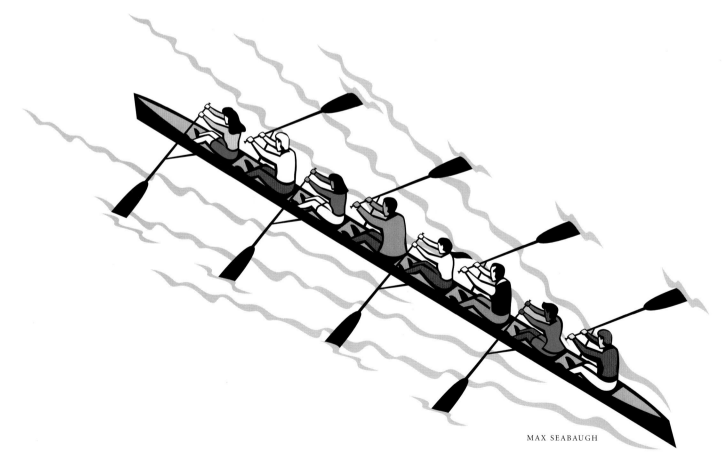

MAX SEABAUGH

Teachers

Chapter 3:
Role of the Teacher

64 Introduction

66 Imagine the Possibilities:
Redefining the Role of the Teacher
by Judith Taack Lanier

70 From the Front Lines:
The Teacher as Learning Guide
by Bonnie Bracey

72 Snapshots
Innovative Schools & Programs

76 Access to Information
Organizations, Periodicals, Readings & Contact Information

Chapter 4:
Learning to Teach

82 Introduction

84 Imagine the Possibilities:
Becoming a Teacher: A Never-Ending Journey
by Linda Darling-Hammond

88 From the Front Lines:
Good Teaching is a Voyage of Discovery
by Lynn Cherkasky-Davis

90 Snapshots
Innovative Schools & Programs

94 Access to Information
Organizations, Periodicals, Readings & Contact Information

Chapter 3
Role of the Teacher

n too many schools today, teachers are isolated and powerless. Decisions about what and how to teach are made far from the **classroom** by a central hierarchy of administrators. Teachers are expected to cover the curriculum at a pre-set pace, repetitively **teaching** the same thing in the same way and treating all students as if they were alike. Teachers, too, are considered interchangeable, with few opportunities to gain **recognition** for quality work or advance in the profession without leaving the classroom.

Many teachers, of course, bring enough **commitment** and enthusiasm to their jobs to overcome the "teacher-proof" materials they have to work with. They make a tremendous **difference** in the lives of students and are the teachers we remember fondly throughout our lives. Others, though, become demoralized by the constraints that prevent them from doing what they know is **best** for the children in their care. As many as half of all new teachers respond by leaving the profession.

In this chapter, we look at places where teachers are supported, their **experiences** valued, and where they have the lead in creating better schools. They are **redefining** what it means to be a teacher. Many are becoming managers, coaches, and facilitators of learning. By developing stronger **relationships** with their students and a deeper understanding of learning, they are better able to meet the needs of each individual.

The most important changes are taking place in the classroom. Thanks to new technologies like **multimedia** software and the Internet, teachers don't have to be the only source of knowledge and information. Students are now able to easily tap data and **expertise** from around the world, so teachers can focus on assisting them as they learn. Instead of telling children how to approach an assignment, teachers can help students identify strategies, **guide** them in appropriate directions, and make sure that they have access to ample resources.

In order to improve their professional practice, teachers are finding they have to **organize** their work lives in different ways. They are forming teams that remain with a group of students over several years, rather than working alone with a class for a single year. **Team teaching** allows educators to pool their expertise, share their strengths, and allocate their time more effectively.

Outside the classroom, teachers are broadening their role and responsibilities as well. As members of school **management** teams, they are making decisions about everything from schedules and budgets to curriculum and technology. As **advocates** for the students in their charge, teachers are working with parents and health and social service organizations to help foster childrens' overall development. They are serving as **ambassadors** to their communities, encouraging parents, business people, and others to participate in schools. And as **professionals** who enthusiastically pursue their own learning, teachers model an attitude essential for success in the modern world. ●

Imagine the Possibilities

BY JUDITH TAACK LANIER

Redefining the role of

Imagine a school where teaching is considered to be a profession, rather than a trade. The role of teachers in a child's education—and in American culture—has fundamentally changed. Teaching differs from the old "show-and-tell" practices as much as modern medical techniques differ from practices like applying leeches and bloodletting.

Instruction isn't primarily lecturing to students who sit in rows at desks dutifully listening and recording what they hear, but offers each and every child a rich, rewarding, and unique learning experience. The educational environment isn't confined to the classroom, but extends into the home, the community, and around the world. Information isn't bound primarily in books, but is available everywhere in bits and bytes. Students aren't consumers of facts, but active creators of knowledge. Schools aren't bricks and mortar, but centers of lifelong learning. And, most importantly, teaching is recognized as one of the most challenging and respected career choices, absolutely vital to the social, cultural, and economic health of our nation.

Today, as we count down the final years of the 20th century, the seeds of such a dramatic transformation in education are being planted. Prompted by massive revolutions in knowledge, information technology, and public demand for better learning, schools nationwide are slowly but surely restructuring themselves. Leading the way are thousands of teachers who are rethinking every part of their jobs—their relationship with students, colleagues, and the community; the tools and techniques they employ; their rights and responsibilities; the form and content of curriculum; what standards to set and how to assess whether they are being met; their preparation as teachers and their ongoing professional development; and the very structure of the schools in which they work. In short, teachers are reinventing themselves and their occupation to better serve schools and students.

New Relationships and Practices Traditionally, teaching was a combination of information dispensing, custodial childcare, and sorting out academically inclined students from others. The underlying model for schools was an education factory in which adults, paid hourly or daily wages, kept like-aged youngsters sitting still for standardized lessons and tests. Teachers were told what, when, and how to teach. They were required to educate every student in exactly the same way and were not held responsible when many failed to learn. They were expected to teach using the same methods as past generations, and any deviation from traditional practices was discouraged by supervisors or prohibited by a myriad of education laws and regulations. Thus, many teachers simply stood in front of the class and delivered the same lessons year after year, growing gray and weary of not being allowed to change what they were doing.

Judith Taack Lanier[2] is a Distinguished Professor of Education at Michigan State University.

the Teacher

Many teachers today, however, are encouraged to adapt and adopt new practices that acknowledge both the art and science of learning. They understand that the essence of education is a close relationship between a knowledgeable, caring adult and a secure, motivated child. They grasp that their most important role is to get to know each student as an individual in order to comprehend her unique needs, learning style, social and cultural background, interests, and abilities. This attention to personal qualities is all the more important as America continues to become the most pluralistic nation on earth. Teachers have to be committed to relating to youngsters of many cultures, including those young people who, with traditional teaching, might have dropped out—or have been forced out —of the education system.

The underlying model for schools was an education factory in which adults, paid hourly or daily wages, kept like-aged youngsters sitting still for standardized lessons and tests.

Their job is to counsel students as they grow and mature—helping them integrate their social, emotional, and intellectual growth—so the union of these sometimes separate dimensions yields the abilities to seek, understand, and use knowledge; to make better decisions in their personal lives; and to value contributing to society. They must be prepared and permitted to intervene at any time and in any way to make sure that learning occurs. Rather than seeing themselves solely as masters of subject matter such as history, math, or science, teachers increasingly understand that they must also inspire a love of learning.

In practice, this new relationship between teachers and students takes the form of a different concept of instruction. Tuning into how students really learn prompts many teachers to reject teaching that is primarily lecture-based in favor of instruction that challenges students to take an active role in learning. They no longer see their primary role as being the king or queen of the classroom, a benevolent dictator deciding what's best for the powerless underlings in their care.

They've found they accomplish more if they adopt the role of educational guides, facilitators, and co-learners.

The most respected teachers have discovered how to make students passionate participants in the instructional process by providing project-based, participatory, educational adventures. They know in order to get a student to truly take responsibility for her own education, that the curriculum must relate to her life, learning activities must engage her natural curiosity, and assessments must measure real accomplishments and be an integral part of learning. Students work harder when teachers give them a role in determining the form and content of their schooling—helping them create their own learning plans and deciding the ways in which they will demonstrate that they have, in fact, learned what they agreed to learn.

Rather than broadcasting content, the day-to-day job of a teacher is becoming one of designing and guiding students through engaging learning opportunities. An educator's most important responsibility is to search out and construct meaningful educational experiences that allow students to solve real-world problems and show that they have learned the big ideas, powerful skills, and habits of mind and heart that meet agreed-upon educational standards. The result is that the abstract, inert knowledge that students used to memorize from dusty textbooks, comes alive as they participate in the creation and extension of new knowledge.

New Tools and Environments One of the most powerful forces changing teachers' and students' roles in education is new technology. The old model of instruction was predicated on information scarcity. Teachers and their books were information oracles, spreading knowledge to a population with few other ways to get it. But today's world is awash in information from a multitude of print and electronic sources. The fundamental job of teaching is no longer to distribute facts, but to help children learn how to use them by developing their abilities to think critically, solve problems, make informed judgments, and create knowledge that benefits both the students and society. Freed from the responsibility of being primary information providers, teachers have more time to spend working one-on-one or with small groups of students.

Recasting the relationship between students and teachers demands that the structure of school changes as well. While still the norm in many places, the practice of isolating teachers in cinder-block rooms with age-graded pupils rotating through classes every hour across a semester—or every year in the case of elementary traditions—is being abandoned in more and more schools that want to give teachers the time, space, and support to do their jobs. Extended instructional periods and school days, as well as reorganized yearly schedules, are all being tried as ways to avoid chopping learning into often arbitrary chunks based on limited time. Rather than inflexibly grouping students in grades by age, many schools feature mixed-aged classes in which students spend years with the same teachers. And ability groups, from which those judged less talented can rarely break free, are being challenged by a recognition that current standardized tests do not measure many abilities or take into account the different ways people learn best.

One of the most important innovations in instructional organization is team teaching, in which two or more educators share responsibility for a group of students. This means that an individual teacher no longer has to be all things to all students. It allows her to apply her strengths, interests, skills, and abilities to the greatest effect, knowing that children won't suffer from her weaknesses because there's someone with a different set of abilities to back her up. To truly professionalize teaching, in fact, we need to further differentiate the roles a teacher might fill. Just as a good law firm has a mix of associates, junior partners, and senior partners, schools should have a greater mix of teachers who have appropriate levels of responsibility based on their abilities and experience levels.

Just as much of a lawyer's work occurs outside the courtroom, so too, should we recognize that much of a teacher's work is done outside the classroom.

New Professional Responsibilities Aside from rethinking their primary responsibility as directors of student learning, teachers are also taking on other roles in schools and in their profession. They are working with colleagues, family members, politicians, academics, community members, employers, and others to set clear and obtainable standards for the knowledge, skills, and values that we should expect America's children to acquire. They are participating in day-to-day decision making in schools, working side-by-side to set priorities and dealing with organizational problems that affect their students' learning. Many teachers also spend time researching various questions of educational effectiveness, expanding the understanding of the dynamics of learning. And more teachers are spending time mentoring new members of their profession, making sure that college of education graduates are truly ready for the complex challenges of today's classrooms.

Teachers have discovered how to make students passionate participants in the instructional process by providing project-based, participatory, educational adventures.

Reinventing the role of teachers inside and outside the classroom can result in significantly better schools and better educated students. But while the roots of such improvement are taking hold in today's schools, they need continued nurturing to grow and truly transform America's learning landscape. The rest of us—politicians and parents, superintendents and school board members, employers and education school faculty —must also be willing to rethink our roles in education to give teachers the support, freedom, and trust they need to do the essential job of educating our children. ●

From the Front Lines

BY BONNIE BRACEY

The Teacher as Learning

Alex, a fourth grader in my class at Ashlawn Elementary School in Arlington, Va., broke into tears. He'd been working on the design for Marsville, a colony on the fourth planet from the Sun. Through the project, sponsored by the Challenger Center for Space Science Education, kids not only learn facts about Mars, but they also grapple with the problems humans would encounter living and working in an alien environment. Alex was trying to figure out a way to cook his favorite food—hamburgers —in space. He'd been consulting with a British scientist via the Internet about the question. The tears started when the man told Alex that he'd soon be visiting Washington, D.C., for a National Science Foundation meeting. Could he and Alex get together and "do lunch?" "I didn't tell him that I'm only in the fourth grade," sobbed Alex, thinking he'd done something wrong. "I don't know how to 'do lunch.'"

Such are the wonderful—yet sometimes bumpy —educational adventures that arise when students take responsibility for their own learning. Traditionally, the teacher is an all-knowing fountain of wisdom spouting facts that students are expected to soak up. During more than three decades in education, however, I've come to believe that the proper role of the teacher is to be a learning guide, an educational facilitator, and a broker of learning opportunities.

In my early days of teaching—during the 1960s and '70s—the classroom sometimes felt like a cell, with both the students and myself prisoners of time and the educational climate. As I explained lessons to the students, their little faces would glance longingly at the real world outside the classroom window. One day, a little boy stood up and said, "I'm tired of all of this talking. You just talk, talk, talk all the time."

He was bored to death, and, frankly, so was I. I wanted to be a creative teacher inspiring students to learn. I wanted my students to care about being in school. So I decided to reinvent my teaching. Rather than trying to dominate my class, I learned to make it a shared experience. In the spirit of such self-directed learners as Thomas Jefferson and George Washington Carver, I taught kids that they didn't have to depend on someone else for their education—they could learn on their own. My job was to observe, to assist, to suggest, and, when

Photo by Richard Nowitz ©National Geographic Society

things were going well, to fade into the corners of the classroom.

The most important change I made was to see my job through the eyes of children and to really get to know the students in my care. I began to devote the first month of school to learning about my kids—a mixed group of fourth and fifth graders. We made visual maps of their family trees, interests, and ideas. We created timelines and wrote autobiographies. I arranged camping trips and museum visits that bonded the class into a group. Each child got a new start with me; I trusted and believed in them no matter what their official records said.

My goal was to tap into the spirit of curiosity and exploration that all children share. When kids are allowed free time on playgrounds, they form little groups to investigate a mud puddle or trace the paths of ants. They are forever solving problems

Guide

and making things—tree houses, drawings, model airplanes. So I filled our classroom with a treasure chest of goodies, making it a hands-on learning laboratory for kids to explore. There were rocks and rockets, petrified wood and fossils, pots and pans, maps and atlases, paintings and posters, calculators and incubators, greenhouses and butterfly boxes, masks and artifacts from around the world, even a tile from a space shuttle.

Occasionally, students sat at desks as I talked to them, but most of their time was spent doing projects that combined knowledge with creative problem solving. As part of a National Geographic Kids Network project called "What is Water?" we measured and monitored the water quality in a stream outside our school. We took field trips to the Chesapeake Bay and stomped through mud in search of plankton and tiny crabs. We observed the effects of acid rain on historic buildings in Alexandria, Va. We created stories, poems, magazines, and murals based on water themes. Using computers, we mapped and graphed and shared

and compared data about water resources with other children around the world.

Over the years I took advantage of every opportunity to learn about—and obtain grants for—high-tech tools for my classroom. Finally, we had computers, CD-ROM players, and modems that allowed learning to reach beyond the confines of the school into the real world. Through the Internet, a virtual faculty of teachers, students, and experts was available to me and my kids. This global networking allowed the tiniest fingers to explore the biggest ideas.

I saw myself as a co-learner with my kids, and I gave myself permission to learn as much as I needed to be a good teacher. I studied marine biology and met huge mosquitoes as I tromped in wading boots through creeks and marshes. As a Challenger Center fellow, I set off a rocket, stood in a wind tunnel, flew kites, and piloted a glider.

Occasionally, students sat at desks as I talked to them, but most of their time was spent doing projects that combined knowledge with creative problem solving.

A couple of years ago, I left the classroom to expand my role as a change agent in education. I worked with the National Infrastructure Information Advisory Council to bring electronic networking to schools, libraries, and homes, so that every student can have the kind of access to learning that my kids did. I've also helped to launch the Online Internet Institute (URL: http://oii.org), an electronic network dedicated to teachers teaching teachers, a place in cyberspace where educators can learn and grow together.

The underlying goal of this work, however, is the same one I've always had: to offer kids the rich education I never got as a child. The most important role for a teacher, I believe, is to introduce children at early ages to a wealth of wonderful learning opportunities so that they are inspired to think about who they can be and what they can do for the rest of their lives. ●

Bonnie Bracey[3] is a technology teacher in residence at the Arlington Career Center and the director of education networks at The McGuffey Project.

Snapshots

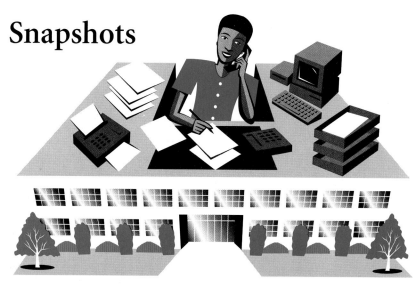

Teachers in Charge

"I've taught at other schools before, but I've never been this happy and satisfied with my work," says Jean Hurst, a second-grade teacher at The Children's School of Rochester (CSR). "The excitement that comes from helping govern the school really keeps me focused. I'm designing curriculum. I'm determining what the report card will look like. I'm making decisions about the school's budget. Talk about teacher autonomy!"

CSR's staff of 15 teachers, together with the principal, support staff, and family members, are jointly responsible for the academic and administrative operation of the K-3 school. This shared responsibility takes time—faculty work long hours and spend a lot of time in meetings and on the phone—but the teachers say it's worth it, because they feel free to create the best possible school.

To manage these non-traditional duties, the staff has organized itself into permanent work groups that address issues from staff development to technology integration. Each teacher is also a member of a grade-level team that identifies goals, objectives, and the subject matter knowledge they want students to acquire. They then collect electronic and print resources—such as software programs and children's literature—and create interdisciplinary projects based around a broad theme. The second-grade team, for instance, used the theme "winter weather in the tropical and temperate zones," to create a project in which students turned the team's two adjoining classrooms into representations of winter in two different climates.

CSR's faculty uses their autonomy to constantly improve the school's teaching and learning environment. "We are truly treated as professionals here," says second-grade teacher Deanne Delehanty, "so we really try to live up to those expectations for ourselves." ●

The Children's School of Rochester Rochester City School District, 494 Averill Street, Rochester, NY 14607 **Contact:** Edward J. Witaszek, Principal • Phone: (716) 262-8830 • Fax: (716) 262-8834 • E-mail: Edward_Witaszek@mistand.com

High-Tech Teaching

Teachers at ACT Academy in McKinney, Tex., are using technology to transform the way they teach, develop curriculum and assessment, and communicate with students and other educators. Founded in 1993 as a "school of the future," the suburban K-12 school of 250 students is run entirely by its teachers, staff, and family members. "One of the hardest things to do was to let go of some of the old paradigms and change our role as teachers," says Nana Hill, a teacher at ACT. "We literally had mock funerals for things like ditto sheets and 45-minute schedules."

ACT Academy serves as a laboratory for the district, hosting visitors interested in learning more about educational technology and teacher-designed curriculum. Its teachers make extensive use of electronic networks, including the Texas Education Network (TENET) and the Internet, to locate resources for student projects, download lesson plans, and communicate with other educators around the country. Each teacher has a portable networked computer and there are phones in every classroom—a practice still unheard of in most schools. ●

ACT Academy McKinney Independent School District, 510 Heard Street, McKinney, TX 75069 **Contact:** Judy Bratcher, Director • Phone: (214) 569-6455 • Fax: (214) 542-2924 • E-Mail: JBratcher@tenet.edu

Teaching Externships

Each year, 48 middle and high school teachers in the Miami area are released from regular classroom responsibilities for nine weeks to research, develop, practice, and evaluate curriculum and teaching methods. Under a program run by the Dade Academy for the Teaching Arts (DATA), based at Miami Beach Senior High School, these teachers, known as "externs," use their sabbaticals to work on projects related to their interests and disciplines. Their teaching duties are assumed by a cadre of highly trained replacement teachers.

Externs receive support from DATA resident teachers—classroom teachers who spend part of their time helping externs refine their research, identify resources and experts, and arrange visits to innovative programs and classrooms. The DATA teachers, who were selected for their high levels of expertise, also conduct seminars for the externs on issues such as child development and technology integration. "At DATA, the word 'professional' is really upheld," says Ricki Wehye, a DATA resident teacher. "We give our teachers recognition for a job well done, treat them as friends, and make them proud again of being a teacher."

Since DATA's creation in 1987, externs have completed more than 600 projects ranging from the development of a curriculum unit on the Holocaust to the creation of a mentoring program that pairs high-achieving students with less advantaged peers. The externs share their projects with interested colleagues and the entire collection of projects has been indexed and made available to every school in the district. ●

"At DATA, the word 'professional' is really upheld. We give our teachers recognition for a job well done, treat them as friends, and make them proud again of being a teacher."

Dade Academy for the Teaching Arts Miami Beach Senior High School, Dade County Public Schools, 2231 Prairie Avenue, Miami Beach, FL 33139 **Contact:** Evelyn C. Campbell, Teacher-Director • Phone: (305) 532-0846 • Fax: (305) 672-8231

Ready, Aim, Foxfire

Isaac Dickson Elementary School in Asheville, N.C., is the only elementary school in the nation with an entire teaching staff trained in the Foxfire approach to instruction. Under the Foxfire approach, which evolved from student-produced magazines and books about Southern Appalachian folklife, teachers develop curriculum that draws on the unique resources of their communities.

Teachers and students agree on projects that give students a hands-on way to learn the curriculum and lead to a product that shows they have learned the material. To study weather, for example, students constructed rain gauges and weathervanes, which they used to keep detailed records of local weather patterns. While students work on projects, teachers spend much of their time carefully observing, assessing each child's progress, and devising ways to make sure each student's instructional needs are met.

This approach to instruction requires teachers to be creative, eager to learn new things, and willing to constantly hone their teaching skills. Dickson's teachers use a regional network of Foxfire educators for much of their professional development. Members of this professional network exchange ideas, information, and resources, and visit each other's schools and classrooms. Weekly faculty meetings serve the same purposes within the school. Dickson teachers say that the entire staff's participation in Foxfire has helped them develop into a cohesive unit with a common focus and direction. ●

Isaac Dickson Elementary School Asheville City Schools, 125 Hill Street, Asheville, NC 28801 **Contact:** Robert J. McGrattan, Principal • Phone: (704) 255-5376 • Fax: (704) 255-5589 • URL: http://www. ashvillecityschools.edu/issacdickson

On-the-Job Research

Every teacher doubles as an educational researcher at Coal Creek Elementary in Louisville, Colo. Each year, the staff at this suburban elementary school identifies questions about teaching and learning that they want to explore either individually or as a school-wide team. One project, for example, looked at how the questions children ask can be used to identify differences in their learning styles and social development. Teachers gather data by observing classrooms and interviewing children, colleagues, and family members. Paraprofessionals and family members help with interviewing and documenting findings. Teachers turn to the Internet and a large professional library to help inform their research.

Coal Creek Elementary School
Boulder Valley Public Schools, 801 West Tamarisk, Louisville, CO 80027
Contact: Ellen Goering, Principal • Phone: (303) 666-4843 • Fax: (303) 661-9892 • E-mail: loverhls@bvsd.k12.co.us • URL: http://bvsd.k12.co.us/schools/coalc/Pages/Home.html

"Our research gives us a constructive way of dealing with challenges and problems," says Ellen Goering, Coal Creek's principal. "We collect and research information and we hash it out together." Substitute teachers staff the school one day each month so teachers can meet to share research topics and strategies and evaluate work on curriculum and assessment. Through partnerships with local universities, research projects often evolve into professional development courses that provide teachers with graduate credits and help hone their research skills and methods. ●

Teachers as Leaders

"We are fortunate to have a district that says, 'We want things to be better for kids, so we are going back to teachers to make that happen.'"

Gorham School Department
270 Main Street, Gorham, ME 04038
Contact: Tim W. McCormack, Superintendent • Phone: (207) 839-5000 • Fax: (207) 839-5003 • E-mail: TIMM@gorham.k12.me.us • URL: http://MaineEd.cybertours.com/MaineEd/Gorham

As the designated Teacher Scholar at Narragansett School in Gorham, Maine, Debbie Loveitt recently enjoyed an experience more familiar to university professors than to kindergarten through 12th-grade teachers. She was freed from her classroom responsibilities for a full year to pursue professional interests that she would not otherwise have time for. Debbie used the year to learn more about student assessment and educational technology and to share her knowledge with other teachers through workshops, presentations, and one-on-one sessions. "I'd always seen myself as a leader in my own classroom," she says, "but this experience gave me the opportunity to use those leadership skills to help others."

For more than a decade, the Gorham School Department, a suburban school district of 2,400 students in southern Maine, has encouraged teachers to become leaders with the idea that they'll then pioneer new practices for their peers. Each year, teachers and staff at each of the district's six schools create special leadership positions for experienced educators and allocate funds to support them. Up to a third of the district's 170 classroom teachers assume these roles in any given year, usually in addition to their regular teaching duties. The teacher-leader positions allow educators to take on new challenges and advance in their profession without leaving the classroom to become administrators. They learn new teaching skills and are better able to manage student learning.

Gorham's schools use block scheduling and common planning times to give all teachers opportunities to work together, and provide phones and networked computers in classrooms to encourage communication. "We are fortunate to have a district that says, 'We want things to be better for kids, so we are going back to teachers to make that happen,'" says Michael Carter, a teacher-leader in social studies. ●

Teachers Supporting Teachers

Cincinnati's Peer Assistance and Evaluation Program (PAEP) addresses problems that vex many school districts: how to find sufficient time to evaluate teachers, help those who are inexperienced or aren't performing up to par, and avoid a protracted dismissal process for those who fail to improve. PAEP, like similar programs in a handful of other districts across the nation, solves these problems by empowering teachers to evaluate and monitor their own ranks.

Under PAEP, experienced teachers are released from classroom duties for two years to supervise and assist new teachers, as well as evaluate and support veteran teachers who are experiencing difficulties in their classrooms. These teachers, known as "consulting teachers" or "CTs," are trained in clinical supervision and curriculum development and observe models of effective teaching at the district's professional development academy. They are then assigned a maximum of 14 new and veteran teachers and spend between 40 to 100 hours with each one, observing and commenting on their practice, assisting in the design of curricula and assessments, modeling lesson plans, and helping establish discipline procedures.

Both teachers and administrators say the program is achieving its goal of improving the competency of the district's teachers. At the same time, it has improved relations between the district and its teachers' union and made it easier to dismiss teachers who fail to make agreed-upon improvements. ●

Peer Assistance and Evaluation Program Cincinnati Public Schools, Aiken High School Annex, 5641 Belmont Avenue, Cincinnati, OH 45224 **Contact:** Franki Bryant, Facilitator • Phone: (513) 853-8468 • Fax: (513) 853-8466

Dzantik'i Heeni Middle School, Juneau, AK • Photo by Brian Wallace

Magnets for Innovation

Gardendale Elementary Magnet School in Merritt Island, Fla., is actually four theme-based schools in one. Its School of Performing Arts emphasizes projects in the areas of music, dance, and drama. The School of Math and Science features hands-on activities such as growing tobacco worms and observing metamorphosis. The School of Arts and Culture concentrates on world cultures and languages. In the School of Microsociety, students engage in real-world activities like operating an in-school postal system, managing a bank with its own currency, and publishing newspapers.

In order to guide all this activity, teachers take leadership roles in all of the schools' operations. Each school is managed by a lead teacher who works with the faculty and principal on academic and administrative issues. Another teacher serves as a specialist in the school's theme, helping fellow educators gather resources, plan units, and develop projects.

Other innovations at Gardendale enable teachers to expand their roles beyond traditional teaching. Adjoining classrooms make it easier for teachers to collaborate or serve as mentors to each other. The school's year-round schedule of nine weeks in, three weeks out, reduces teacher burnout and gives them time to further their professional development and create thematic units reflecting each school's focus. ●

Gardendale Elementary Magnet School Brevard County, Florida Public Schools, 301 Grove Boulevard, Merritt Island, FL 32953 **Contact:** Albert Narvaez, Jr., Principal • Phone: (407) 452-1411 • Fax: (407) 454-1094

Organizations

Center for Research on the Context of Teaching (CRC) **Description:** Research center affiliated with the Stanford University School of Education. **Purpose:** To identify and investigate factors such as school environment, organization, and policy that affect teaching and learning. **Activities:** CRC researchers analyze how teaching and learning are shaped by the policies, cultures, and organizational structures of schools. Findings are available in books, papers, and reports. **Contact:** Julie Cummer, Project Administrator • Center for Research on the Context of Teaching, School of Education, Stanford University, CERAS Building, Stanford, CA 94305 • Phone: (415) 723-4972 • Fax: (415) 723-7578 • E-mail: cummer@Forsythe.Stanford.edu

American Federation of Teachers (AFT) Educational Issues Department
Description: Division of the American Federation of Teachers that focuses on professional issues. **Purpose:** To help teachers strengthen their own teaching and assume leadership in school reform efforts. **Activities:** Offers workshops, professional development programs, and individualized assistance on reform-related issues. Helps teachers disseminate their work throughout AFT's affiliate network. Annual conferences bring together teachers, community leaders, and organizations to develop and advocate policy changes. Also publishes regular reports on a variety of policy and practice issues and a newsletter, *QuESTLINE,* which provides a forum for AFT views on current educational reform initiatives. **Contact:** Eugenia Kemble, Assistant to the President • Educational Issues Department, American Federation of Teachers, 555 New Jersey Avenue NW, Washington, DC 20001 • Phone: (202) 879-4463 • Fax: (202) 393-7483

Foxfire Fund, Inc. Description: Foxfire is an educational organization that works with teachers, primarily through training and other support programs, to encourage changes in schools. Foxfire got its start as a classroom project in which high school students produced a magazine and several best-selling books on Appalachian folklore. **Purpose:** To assist teachers in developing more effective relationships and creating a hands-on, learner-centered curriculum. **Activities:** Offers professional development and networking opportunities. Publishes *Hands-On: A Journal for Teachers.* **Contact:** Kim Cannon, Executive Assistant • Foxfire Fund, Inc., PO Box 541, Mountain City, GA 30562 • Phone: (706) 746-5318 • Fax: (706) 746-5829 • E-mail: foxfirefnd@aol.com • URL: http://www.foxfirefnd.com

> *"I spend a lot of time on-line, downloading lesson plans, keeping in touch with other educators, and sharing information. Then I take the knowledge I gain and share it with the rest of the school."*
>
> Nana Hill,[4] Learning Facilitator, ACT Academy, McKinney Independent School District

Center for Teaching and Learning (CTL)
Description: A division of the National Education Association that houses the National Center for Innovation, the National Foundation for Improvement of Education, and the Center for Education Technology. **Purpose:** To improve public schools and colleges of education, foster effective professional development and teacher leadership, integrate technologies with reform efforts, and support school improvement legislation. **Activities:** Offers publications, workshops, grants for teachers, and on-site assistance at selected locations. **Contact:** Laurie Wheeler, Program Assistant • Center for Teaching and Learning, National Education Association, 1201 16th Street NW, Washington, DC 20036 • Phone: (202) 822-7013 • Fax: (202) 822-7974 • URL: http://www.nea.org

Computer–Using Educators, Inc. (CUE)
Description: A California-based nonprofit educational organization with more than 10,000 members worldwide. **Purpose:** To help kindergarten through 12th-grade and university educators integrate technology with teaching and learning. **Activities:** Holds two annual conferences, the oldest and largest educational technology gatherings in the nation. Maintains a network of 23 regional organizations in California, which gives members grants to integrate technology with instruction and sponsor regular meetings to facilitate information sharing. Publishes a bimonthly newsletter, *CUE,* offering information and ideas for using technology in the classroom. **Contact:** Gloria Gibson, Assistant Director • Computer-Using Educators, Inc., 1210 Marina Village Parkway, Suite 100, Alameda, CA 94501 • Phone: (510) 814-6630 • Fax: (510) 814-0195 • E-mail: Cueinc@aol.com • URL: http://www/cue.org

Clear View Charter School, Chula Vista, CA • Photo by Matthew Rivaldi

National Board for Professional Teaching Standards (NBPTS) **Description:** An independent board with 63 members, a majority of whom are classroom teachers. Proposed in *The Nation Prepared,* a 1986 report of the Carnegie Task Force on Teaching as a Profession. **Purpose:** Dedicated to improving student learning by helping to professionalize teaching and bring it the respect and recognition the work deserves. **Activities:** Under the auspices of the National Board, some of the nation's preeminent education researchers, together with practicing teachers, have developed a process for certifying kindergarten through 12th-grade teachers who demonstrate "professional teaching excellence." They are defining standards of accomplishment in teaching and are testing new ways of assessing teaching quality, such as reviewing portfolios and videotapes of teachers' work. **Contact:** James A. Kelly, President • National Board for Professional Teaching Standards, 26555 Evergreen Road, Suite 400, Southfield, MI 48076 • Phone: (810) 375-4444 • Fax: (810) 351-4170 • E-mail: NBPTS@aol.com

National Center for Restructuring Education, Schools and Teaching (NCREST) **Description:** A university-based research and networking organization with more than 50 affiliates. **Purpose:** To identify and promote changes needed to transform schools so they better meet children's needs. **Activities:** Quarterly newsletter, *Resources for Restructuring,* provides information about school change efforts around the nation. Maintains an electronic network focusing on comprehensive assessment. Offers a collection of videos that feature learner-centered schools and classrooms. Numerous publications include the *NCREST Affiliates Directory,* a guide to leading reform organizations, as well as research on student-centered practice throughout the country. **Contact:** Diane Harrington, Director of Communications • National Center for Restructuring Education, Schools and Teaching, Teachers College, Columbia University, Box 110, 525 West 120th Street, Room 411 Main Hall, New York, NY 10027 • Phone: (212) 678-3015 • Fax: (212) 678-4170 • URL: http://www.tc.columbia.edu/~ncrest

Impact II—The Teachers Network **Description:** Started in the New York City public schools more than 15 years ago, IMPACT II has grown into a nationwide, educational, nonprofit networking organization composed of more than 30,000 teachers at 27 sites. **Purpose:** To connect innovative teachers, disseminate good ideas, and improve classroom instruction. **Activities:** Awards grants to teachers to package and adapt successful classroom projects, and helps them disseminate their work through workshops, conferences, and annual publications. Impact II's Web site, TeachNet, provides descriptions of model projects and provides a forum for discussions on issues such as school restructuring and teacher leadership. **Contact:** Ellen Meyers, Vice President, Programs and Communications • Impact II—The Teachers Network, 285 West Broadway, New York, NY 10013 • Phone: (212) 966-5582 • Fax: (212) 941-1787 • E-mail: teachnet@teachnet.org • URL: http://www.teachnet.org

Quest Center **Description:** An arm of the Chicago Teacher's Union created to support school reform efforts. **Purpose:** To help teachers achieve effective and sustainable change in Chicago's schools. **Activities:** Staff members provide assistance to individuals and teams of teachers working to restructure their practice and their schools. Offers print and video resources, on-site workshops, and regular conferences. Also helps teams of teachers develop school-based research studies. **Contact:** Allen Bearden, Director • Quest Center, Chicago Teachers Union, 222 Merchandise Mart Plaza, Suite 400, Chicago, IL 60654 • Phone: (312) 329-9100 • Fax: (312) 329-6203

South Carolina Center for the Advancement of Teaching and School Leadership **Description:** Created with state school-restructuring funds, the Center is a network of 26 public and private teacher preparation colleges and more than 120 schools. **Purpose:** To help prepare teams of teachers and administrators to lead change in schools and teacher preparation programs. **Activities:** Provides management training to help school-based teams develop a common vision, learn how to work together effectively, and identify areas for focused reform efforts. Helps develop school-university partnerships. Supports an electronic network to enable teams to remain in touch with the Center and with teams at other schools. **Contact:** Larry Winecoff, Executive Director • South Carolina Center for the Advancement of Teaching and School Leadership, College of Education, University of South Carolina, Columbia, SC 29208 • Phone: (803) 777-3084 • Fax: (803) 777-1585 • E-mail: Larry.Winecoff@scarolina.edu

> *"In order for students to be active, engaged, and willing to learn from their experiences, teachers have to be active, engaged, and willing to learn from their experiences."*
>
> Nancie Atwell,[5] Director, Center for Teaching and Learning

Periodicals

American Educator **Description:** Quarterly magazine for American Federation of Teachers members. **Focus:** Features in-depth essays by kindergarten through 12th-grade teachers, administrators, scholars, and other education professionals on topics such as curriculum and assessment, instructional strategies, and school culture. **Publisher:** American Federation of Teachers, Washington, DC • Phone: (202) 879-4420.

> *"Technology holds great promise as a tool to help teachers help students. Suppose, for example, that instead of constantly struggling to come up with original lesson plans and activities, every teacher had access to a comprehensive computer database of the very best instructional ideas from across the nation."*
>
> Al Shanker,[6] President, American Federation of Teachers

Classroom Connect **Description:** Newsletter published nine times a year for teachers and students; available both in print and electronic formats. **Focus:** Covers educational electronic networking, including resources available to teachers on the Internet. **Publisher:** Wentworth Worldwide Media, Lancaster, PA • Phone: (800) 638-1639.

On the Road Ahead! **Description:** A quarterly newsletter of the National Foundation for the Improvement of Education (NFIE). **Focus:** Reports on the progress of sites involved in *The Road Ahead* program, established to connect schools and community-based organizations and to help integrate technology in the curriculum. **Publisher:** NFIE, Washington, DC • Phone: (202) 822-7840.

Raising Standards **Description:** Annual journal containing articles written by classroom teachers, paraprofessionals, and leading education reformers. **Focus:** Emphasizes effective teaching in a multicultural environment. **Publisher:** Rochester Teachers Association, Rochester, NY • Phone: (716) 546-2681.

Teacher Magazine **Description:** Newsmagazine for teachers published nine times a year. **Focus:** Informs educators about current issues affecting K-12 teaching. Profiles exemplary teachers and programs and features regular columns on topics such as research and curriculum. **Publisher:** Editorial Projects in Education, Washington, DC. Phone: (800) 347-6969.

Teacher-To-Teacher **Description:** The Galef Institute's semiannual newsletter. **Focus:** Features teacher-authored accounts of classroom practice; in-depth essays focusing on such areas as curriculum, assessment, and instructional strategies; and editorials written by students and teachers. Also provides updates on the Institute's activities. **Publisher:** Galef Institute, Los Angeles, CA • Phone: (800) 473-8883.

Teaching and Change **Description:** Quarterly journal for kindergarten through 12th-grade teachers. **Focus:** A scholarly forum for teachers to describe and reflect upon their classroom projects and instructional strategies. **Publisher:** National Education Association Professional Library and Corwin Press, Thousand Oaks, CA • Phone: (805) 499-9774.

Totally for Teachers **Description:** Newsletter published six times a year. **Focus:** Provides a vehicle for classroom teachers to exchange practical instructional strategies, activities and lesson plans, classroom management tips, and print and electronic resources. **Publisher:** Totally for Teachers, Pittsford, NY • Phone: (716) 385-2849.

Readings

Dzantik'i Heeni Middle School, Juneau, AK • Photo by Brian Wallace

Maeroff, Gene I. **Team Building for School Change: Equipping Teachers for New Roles.** *Teachers College Press: New York, NY, 1993.* Phone: (800) 575-6566. ● Documents common hurdles that teachers and administrators face when working in teams within their schools and offers innovative approaches to issues such as managing schedules, making decisions, and fostering an atmosphere of collaboration.

McLaughlin, Milbrey W., and Joan E. Talbert. **Contexts That Matter For Teaching and Learning: Strategic Opportunities for Meeting the Nation's Educational Goals.** *Center for Research on the Context of Secondary School Teaching: Stanford University, Stanford, CA, 1993.* Phone: (415) 723-4972. ● A summary of five years of research examining curriculum and the dynamics of classroom interactions among teachers and students. Provides strategies for incorporating these research results into national restructuring efforts.

Serim, Ferdi, and Melissa Koch. **NetLearning: Why Teachers Use the Internet.** *Songline Studios and O'Reilly & Associates: Sebastopol, CA, 1996.* Phone: (707) 829-6500. ● Offers practical advice and examples of classroom use of the Internet. Includes a list of e-mail addresses of experienced users and a selection of Web site addresses. Comes with a CD-ROM that provides Internet service and a Web-authoring tool.

Johnson, Susan Moore. **Teachers at Work: Achieving Success in Our Schools.** *BasicBooks: New York, NY, 1990.* Phone: (800) 331-3761. ● Focusing on the school as a workplace, the author explores how such features as physical settings and organizational structures affect the quality of instruction and recommends changes in these areas to improve teaching and learning.

Impact II—The Teachers Network. **Teachers Guide to Cyberspace.** *Impact II: New York, NY, 1996.* Phone: (212) 966-5582. ● Written by teachers, this how-to book offers information about using computers in the classroom. Comes with disks containing examples of projects developed by teachers around the country.

Marzano, Robert J. **A Different kind of Classroom: Teaching with Dimensions of Learning** *Association for Supervision and Curriculum Development: Alexandria, VA, 1992.* Phone: (800) 933-2723. ● Provides a framework for K–12 instruction that reflects what is known about how children learn. Includes suggestions for curriculum design and student assessment.

Hollingsworth, Sandra, and Hugh Sockett, eds. **Teacher Research and Educational Reform: Ninety-third Yearbook of the National Society for the Study of Education Part 1.** *University of Chicago Press: Chicago, IL, 1994.* Phone: (800) 621-2736. ● A collection of scholarly essays that traces the development of teachers as researchers within their own schools and classrooms, provides examples of current research approaches, and examines the potential for teacher research to affect education reform initiatives.

Lieberman, Ann, ed. **The Changing Contexts of Teaching: Ninety-first Yearbook of the National Society for the Study of Education, Part 1.** *University of Chicago Press: Chicago, IL, 1992.* Phone: (800) 621-2736. ● In scholarly essays, leading researchers in the field of teaching explore how school restructuring is influencing the professionalization of teachers.

"With the aid of technology, teachers are becoming guides and one-on-one mentors for their students, rather than drill sergeants and lecturers. They are sharing in the decision making regarding curriculum, scheduling, and other key educational issues. The long isolation of the American teacher behind a closed door in the school is finally ending."

Keith Geiger,[7] Past President, National Education Association

"For schools to be vibrant places in which kids' intellectual interests come to life, teachers need to be involved in deciding what is taught, how it is taught, and how it is measured—all at the same time."

Patricia A. Wasley,[8] Dean of Graduate School, Bank Street College of Education

U.S. Congress, Office of Technology Assessment. **Teachers & Technology: Making the Connection.** OTA-EHR-616. *GPO: Washington, DC,* April 1995. Phone: (703) 487-4679. Presents results of a two-year study by the Office of Technology Assessment evaluating the integration and use of technology by kindergarten through 12th-grade teachers in American schools. Noting that few teachers know about, are comfortable with, or use technology, the report offers a plan for training educators to use high-tech tools to support instruction.

Wasley, Patricia A. **Stirring the Chalkdust: Tales of Teachers Changing Classroom Practice.** *Teachers College Press: New York, NY, 1994.* Phone: (800) 575-6566. ● Case studies of five teachers involved in comprehensive school restructuring reveal the challenges and benefits of implementing changes in curriculum, assessment, and instruction.

Seashore-Louis, Karen, and Sharon D. Kruse. **Professionalism and Community: Perspectives on Reforming Urban Schools.** *Corwin Press: Thousand Oaks, CA, 1995.* Phone: (805) 499-9774. ● Argues that supportive and engaging school environments are the key to helping teachers become effective instructors and offers a framework for evaluating whether a school is a high-quality professional community.

Shulman, Judith H., and Amalia Mesa-Bains, eds. **Diversity in the Classroom: A Casebook for Teachers and Teacher Educators.** *Research for Better Schools and Lawrence Erlbaum Associates: Hillsdale, NJ, 1993.* Phone: (215) 574-9300. ● Case studies by teachers explore the challenges of teaching heterogeneous groups of students and offer approaches to improve teachers' understanding of ethnic, racial, and cultural diversity.

Contact Information

"Teachers working alone cannot transform schools into successful places. They need opportunities to come together to solve problems, develop curriculum, and enhance their own learning."

Milbrey McLaughlin,[9] Director, Center for Research on the Context of Teaching, Stanford University

[1]**Shirley Cothran** Teacher and Kentucky Alliance Consultant • Calloway County Middle School, Calloway County Schools, 2108-A College Farm Road, Murray, KY 42071 • Phone: (502) 759-3568 • Fax: (502) 762-3216 • E-mail: ACOTTOCKYS@aol.com

[2]**Judith Taack Lanier** Distinguished Professor • College of Education, Michigan State University, 201 Erickson Hall, East Lansing, MI 48824 • Phone: (517) 353-3874 • Fax: (517) 353-6393 • E-mail: jlanier@msu.edu

[3]**Bonnie Bracey** Director of Education Networks • The McGuffey Project, 888 17th Street NW, 12th Floor, Washington, DC 20006 • Phone: (202) 429-8744 • Fax: (202) 296-2962 • E-mail: BBracey@aol.com

[4]**Nana Hill** Learning Facilitator • ACT Academy, McKinney Independent School District, 510 Heard Street, McKinney, TX 75069 • Phone: (214) 569-6455 • Fax: (214) 542-2924 • E-mail: Nanahill@aol.com

[5]**Nancie Atwell** Director • Center for Teaching and Learning, 3605 Cross Point Road, Edgecomb, ME 04556 • Phone: (207) 882-9706 • Fax: (207) 882-9706

[6]**Al Shanker** President • American Federation of Teachers, 555 New Jersey Avenue NW, Washington, DC 20001 • Phone: (202) 879-4440 • Fax: (202) 879-4545 • E-mail: afteditor@aol.com

[7]**Keith Geiger** Past President • National Education Association, 1201 16th Street NW, Washington, DC 20036 • Phone: (202) 822-7200 • Fax: (202) 822-7292

[8]**Patricia A. Wasley** Dean of Graduate School • Bank Street College of Education, 610 West 112th Street, New York, NY 10025 • Phone: (212) 875-4400 • Fax: (212) 875-4753 • E-mail: paw@bnk1.bnkst.edu

[9]**Milbrey McLaughlin** Director • Center for Research on the Context of Teaching, Stanford University, CERAS Building, Room 402, Stanford, CA 94305 • Phone: (415) 723-4972 • Fax: (415) 723-7578 • E-mail: milbrey@Forsythe.Stanford.edu

Chapter 4
Learning to Teach

Over the past few decades, we've made great strides in unlocking the **mysteries** of how people learn. Cognitive scientists are mapping how the brain works, showing how people process new information and acquire new skills. Educators have applied this **research** to develop approaches to curriculum, instruction, and assessment that are more effective with a diverse range of students. And technological breakthroughs have created a whole array of powerful new **electronic tools** for teachers and students.

Unfortunately, teacher preparation and continuing education have lagged behind educational **innovation.** Many teachers have been left ill-equipped for the challenges of applying an ever-expanding body of professional **knowledge,** adopting the latest technologies, and changing how they do their jobs.

This chapter explores some of the ways that educators and others are working to **reinvent** teacher education from the start of college throughout a teacher's career. In schools, colleges, and universities, they are designing a new model of professional development with more **rigorous** academic standards and plenty of opportunities for hands-on experience under the guidance of skilled educators. **Ongoing** learning—keeping up with the latest practices, research, and technological advances—is becoming recognized as an important part of every educator's job description.

To prepare a new generation of teachers, institutions of **higher education** are collaborating with K–12 schools to create laboratories for the study of teaching.

On-the-job teachers and college faculty members are taking a fresh look at what **education students** should know and be able to do. Undergraduate education programs are incorporating the latest **technologies** so that new teachers can learn to use these tools effectively. New programs are being created to attract the best and brightest to the profession, particularly from underrepresented minority groups.

But better preparation for future teachers is not enough—teachers face new **challenges** throughout their careers. Recognizing that beginning teachers, in particular, need more support, many states and districts are creating programs to pair them with veteran teachers who act as **mentors.** Schools that are on the leading edge understand that this support has to extend beyond the first years. Instead of offering a few programs on specific days, these schools provide more time, money, and other resources, so learning becomes an **integral** part of professional practice. This gives teachers the opportunity and responsibility to guide the content and form of their own educational development.

Teachers are finding new ways to **network** with colleagues and other experts through telecommunications links and at conferences and workshops. In their daily life at school, they are **supporting** and learning from each other as they strive to improve their teaching. Indeed, most of the programs profiled throughout this book owe their success to teachers who are **committed** to keeping their knowledge and skills up to date. ●

Imagine the Possibilities

BY LINDA DARLING-HAMMOND

BECOMING A TEACHER: a

For as long as she could remember, Maria loved teaching. As a little girl, she would read to toddlers, play school with her friends, and explain the mysteries of the universe to anyone who would listen. As a peer tutor in middle school, she discovered there was no better feeling than when someone she was working with finally grasped challenging concepts like photosynthesis or the

never-

Pythagorean theorem. In high school, her favorite times were spent sharing with friends what she'd learned researching reports and projects on the Internet. As she faced choosing a college and career, she knew exactly what she wanted to do.

The children of today who, like Maria, dream of becoming teachers have a lot to look forward to. The mysteries of how people learn are gradually being revealed through the careful scrutiny of scientists, researchers, and practicing teachers. A growing stock of new tools and strategies is enabling educators to be more effective than ever in meeting student needs. Slowly but surely, we're heading toward a time when teachers have the knowledge and freedom to help all children achieve at high levels.

For the next generation of teachers, getting there will be exciting, but it won't be easy. Education students will find that it's harder to become proficient; there's more to study, more to learn, more to practice. To get a glimpse of how best to prepare fledgling educators for this challenge, let's imagine what lies in store for Maria on her quest to become a teacher.

Learning the Basics After lots of research, Maria settled on a five-year college program leading to a master of arts in teaching. She chose math as her major because she had always loved grappling with complex mathematical ideas and problems.

During her first years in college, Maria immersed herself in educational philosophy and research, studying the works of trailblazers like John Dewey, Jean Piaget, and Maria Montessori. In courses on teaching practices and curriculum development, she learned ways to engage students in experiences that allow them to integrate skills into hands-on activities and to conduct their own inquiries and experiments. She explored how technologies like the Internet and sophisticated computer simulations can open a whole new world of possibilities for classroom learning and make the curriculum more meaningful for

ending

students. Her professors didn't lecture from textbooks or measure learning with multiple-choice tests. Instead, they modeled the strategies Maria herself would use as a teacher; they created learning opportunities that enabled their students to apply knowledge in real teaching situations.

Linda Darling-Hammond[1] is the executive director of the National Commision on Teaching and America's Future and the co-director of the National Center for Restructuring Education, Schools and Teaching, Teachers College, Columbia University. ★ FILM

journey

Maria spent a lot of time in schools observing experienced teachers and working with students. These chances to apply her classwork meant that she never found studying theory to be dull or abstract. To the contrary, she found it gave her a powerful set of lenses through which to view the classroom. During one semester, she conducted a case study of John, a seven-year-old boy she tutored at a local school. As she observed him in class and at play, either in person or on videotape, she could see what she'd learned in her classes coming to life before her eyes. She engaged in long discussions with her professors and fellow students about how John's physical and social development affected his academic performance, and talked about how these areas could be supported and stretched. She noticed that the boy was proficient in some skills, like building models, but struggled with others, like reading. These observations helped her understand the usefulness of studying theories on different types of intelligences, like those of educational researcher Howard Gardner. She concluded that one of her biggest challenges as a teacher would be to discover each student's unique strengths and to find ways to use them to overcome the student's weaknesses.

Her professors didn't lecture from textbooks or measure learning with multiple-choice tests. Instead, they modeled the strategies Maria herself would use as a teacher; they created learning opportunities that enabled their students to apply knowledge in real teaching situations.

The Fifth Year Maria's fifth and final year of college was an internship at a professional development school—a middle school committed to providing state-of-the-art teacher preparation as well as state-of-the-art education for children. There, she joined a small team of student teachers under the guidance of both university faculty and expert teachers. In seminars and in classrooms, the team examined ways to identify and accommodate different learning styles and needs, strategies for addressing misconceptions students hold about certain subjects, and approaches to common learning problems like dyslexia.

Her classroom work, guided by a mentor team, included observing specific children and documenting their learning, evaluating lessons, tutoring and working with small groups, and sitting in on family conferences. She also took part in school and team planning meetings, visited homes and community agencies, planned field trips and curriculum segments, and taught lessons and short units. Finally, at the end of the year, she assumed responsibility for a class for a month.

This work was supplemented by reading and discussions of case studies of teaching. Some were drawn from an electronic database compiled by teachers all over the country; others were videotaped by teachers at her professional development school. These case studies enabled student teachers like Maria to look at practice from many angles, examine how situations in the classroom arose from incidents in the past, see how strategies actually turned out, and understand the thinking teachers used to make decisions about students, subjects, and curriculum goals.

The combination of classroom work, research, and seminars during her year-long internship helped Maria learn to observe and listen to students to understand their experiences, prior knowledge, and learning strengths. She discovered how to provide emotional support and develop teaching strategies responsive to their particular needs. She found out how to create engaging tasks that would stretch and motivate students, and how to manage the learning process so they could succeed at this challenging work. She began to better juggle and balance the competing demands between individuals and groups, between curriculum goals and student interests, and between helping students versus challenging them. She developed the skills to reach out to students who might otherwise slip past or fall through the cracks. She learned always to question what she was doing and constantly to reexamine her own teaching and that of her colleagues.

A Beginning Teacher When Maria finished her rich, exhausting internship year, she was ready to try her hand at what she knew would be an equally demanding first year of teaching. She submitted a portfolio of her college work for review by the state professional standards board, passed the rigorous performance examination required for an initial teaching license, and was offered a teaching position at an innovative middle school.

In her first months on the job, Maria found herself delighted and intrigued by her students. Although she found teaching challenging, she did not feel overwhelmed by classroom management issues the way beginning teachers once had. Her extensive internship had really prepared her to establish a well-functioning classroom from the start.

She still had a lot to learn, though. She was grateful for the support from her district that

included assigning her a mentor teacher and providing time off to continue her professional studies. The mentor teacher spent several hours each week observing and assisting Maria in her classroom, helping her examine and adjust teaching strategies. In addition, all the district's mentor teachers and beginning teachers met periodically to discuss specific problems of practice. They interacted frequently via an on-line network, through which they could chat, post questions, and share ideas and materials.

Thanks to team teaching and flexible scheduling that provided her with periods when she was not responsible for students, Maria was able to regularly observe in other classrooms and meet with groups of teachers at her new school. She and other math and science teachers got together weekly to discuss curriculum plans and share

demonstration lessons. Maria also consulted often with her five-member teaching team, which consisted of teachers from different subject areas. This team used its time together to discuss interdisciplinary connections and the progress of the students for whom they shared responsibility. When a concern arose about a particular student's progress, teachers in the team held a review session to examine the student's work and behavior using their pooled experiences and insights. Maria found that these sessions helped her learn about particular students and ways to address their needs, and also helped her better understand learning in general and specific strategies that strengthened her teaching.

Maria appreciated having access to her colleagues' knowledge and thinking about both subject-matter issues and student concerns. She never felt as though she was alone in her efforts to tackle the many challenges of beginning teaching. She always had peers to turn to for advice, counsel, and support.

A Lifetime of Learning Maria soon became aware of the rich array of ongoing professional development courses and experiences offered teachers by local universities, school districts, and even area businesses. In her spare moments at her computer, she sometimes cruised the rich offerings of teacher-oriented Web sites or visited forums where teachers and other experts were holding lively discussions about different aspects of learning. As she understood more about such resources, she realized that her development as a teacher would never be over. Her experiences in college and during her first year on the job were the beginning, not the end, of her quest to be a better teacher. She was just starting a lifelong learning adventure. ●

In her spare moments at her computer, she sometimes cruised the rich offerings of teacher-oriented Web sites or visited forums where teachers and other experts were holding lively discussions about different aspects of learning.

From the Front Lines

BY LYNN CHERKASKY-DAVIS

My 25 kindergartners sit in the literature circle deep in conversation about Ezra Jack Keats' illustrations. Nearby at the art center, Barb Turk, an education student from National Louis University, prepares paste, glue, water, brushes, fabric, scissors, paper, and paints. She works quickly to get back to the children in time to watch how I direct the transition from group discussion to related hands-on activities at the various discovery centers in the classroom. Barb is doing the classroom observation required by the state of Illinois to qualify her to teach. To say she's just observing, though, misstates her active participation in classes, staff meetings, and parent conferences during her visits to The Foundations School. She and others come to this Chicago public school to learn from us. We learn from them, too.

I hope Barb's professional development path will be less difficult than mine. My teacher education, at a highly regarded university more than a quarter century ago, included teaching-methods courses, a research-based curriculum, hands-on course work, and a wonderful, yet quite myopic, nine-week student teaching experience. Then I graduated, a licensed teacher with the minimum competencies required by the state, and was placed in a classroom of my own.

Among educators at the time, further professional development, other than pursuing a master's degree, was seen as a weakness. Asking for advice would signal incompetence. The only mentoring I got was casual discussion in the teachers' lounge. That was enough for a while, because I didn't know any better. The district provided me with "teacher-proof" guides and curriculum from which to work. My job was to pour what was in those books into pupils' heads. I didn't need an educational philosophy—I had ditto sheets.

After teaching elementary grades for several years and then moving to a kindergarten, I began to have nagging doubts about what I was doing. My kids were scoring well on tests, so the district concluded I was a good teacher. Yet I saw students who were frustrated or bored, which in turn led to behavior problems. One student jarred me by bringing me different kinds of pins each time I asked him to retrieve a pen. I realized that, even though he could complete the phonics tests, he couldn't hear the difference between "pen" and "pin." It wasn't his fault. The teaching methods I had grown up with weren't providing the kind of education he needed because they didn't connect with his world or his culture.

Good Teaching is a Voyage

Then, at the beginning of the 1983–84 school year, I opened my classroom door to find something missing. The textbooks and workbooks had disappeared; the central office hadn't come through with money to buy them. I panicked. After six years of teacher education and several years in the classroom, I was not prepared. It was time for me to learn new ways of teaching content, and at the same time address the longing I'd felt for a better way of teaching the whole child.

And so my professional development journey began. I started furiously reading and experimenting with what I was learning in my own classroom. I knew I had to take risks in order to grow, just as I was asking my kids to do.

The following summer I discovered the Illinois Writing Project, which helped me understand the developmentally appropriate, hands-on, language-rich methods through which five-year-olds really learn. It introduced me to other teachers whose dissatisfaction with traditional teaching methods had launched them on their own journeys of learning and exploration. Finally, in groups like Teachers Applying Whole Language, I found colleagues who were as eager as I was to network, to share, and to learn.

Over the next several years, I immersed myself in all of the professional development opportunities I could find. Through workshops offered by local universities and private educational consultants, I studied topics such as hands-on math, parent involvement, and new forms of assessment. I took personal days to visit teachers in other schools. Every time I learned something new, I alerted my colleagues and principal, constantly trying to spark a professional dialogue.

My teaching changed radically and my students achieved more than I had ever imagined

others' classrooms, talk over our concerns, offer suggestions, and support each other. Our group, "Teacher Talk," evolved into a serious forum for professional development in which we investigated topics ranging from multi-age classrooms to performance assessment to peer tutoring.

When our principal was replaced by one less willing to give teachers authority and autonomy, Teacher Talk set out to create our own school. The result was The Foundations School, the first teacher-designed and teacher-led school in Illinois.

Through partnerships with a consortium of universities and the Chicago Teachers Union's Quest Center, we strive to be a place where a new generation

I opened my classroom door to find something missing. The textbooks and workbooks had disappeared; the central office hadn't come through with money to buy them.

# of Discovery

possible. Both they and I were having a good time learning. I won several teaching awards and was asked to serve on professional boards. Still, since the district didn't provide sufficient resources for professional development, I had to pay my own way and take uncompensated time to continue my education.

One year, I discovered how technology could help me. I videotaped myself teaching, then watched the tapes and saw things I never realized I was—or wasn't—doing. I'd rethink my teaching, talk to other professionals, and try again. I found graduate students at local teacher-training institutions who were available to tape me if I would allow them to use the tapes as case studies in their classes.

In 1989, I transferred to a school where the principal shared my philosophy of education. A group of 12 of us began meeting every Wednesday over a two-year period to tour each

of educators can learn. One day a week, our school becomes a professional development clinic. A steady parade of visitors comes to learn such innovative practices as peer evaluation, interdisciplinary curriculum, and teacher leadership.

We work closely with education students like Barb Turk to help them become satisfied and effective educators. Her journey to exemplary teaching may be just as long as mine, but it has started earlier and won't be as treacherous. Our education leaders are realizing that if students are to learn more, work harder, and be more accountable for what they do, we must take a hard look at how we prepare new teachers and support continuing development throughout their careers. ●

Lynn Cherkasky-Davis[2] teaches at The Foundations School. She is also a director of the National Board for Professional Teaching Standards.

Snapshots

Learning with Technology

They say you teach the way you have been taught, and for Sophia Sullivan, a recent graduate of the University of Virginia's Curry School of Education, that is a good thing. Because her training required her to study advanced

"We are trying to get them to break away from the methods they saw when they were in school."

technology and up-to-date research on teaching and learning, Sophia says she was well prepared for her work as a special education teacher. "The things we were learning at the University were readily tied to classroom experiences," she says. "I was prepared for the types of challenges I would face and the children I would see."

Connecting studies to professional work is a major emphasis at Curry, which offers a five-year program leading to a master's degree in teaching and a bachelor's degree in a liberal arts discipline. Students are placed in nearby public schools in their sophomore year, and over the next four years they undertake an increasingly sophisticated succession of field experiences culminating in a semester-long school internship. The program aims to prepare educators to integrate technology with their teaching and be adept at making decisions that affect everything from classroom learning to schoolwide governance.

Technology is an integral part of methods courses and field experiences. Using case studies

drawn from World Wide Web sites, for example, small teams of teacher education students from four universities analyze "real-life situations not unlike the ones they will encounter in the teaching world," says Joanne Herbert, an assistant professor at Curry. "We are trying to get them to break away from the methods they saw when they were in school." ●

Curry School of Education University of Virginia, Ruffner Hall, Room 220, Charlottesville, VA 22903 **Contact:** Greta Morine-Dershimer, Director • Phone: (804) 924-0748 • Fax: (804) 924-0747 • E-mail: gm4p@ virginia.edu • URL: http://curry.edschool.Virginia. edu/curry/TeacherEd/

Teachers Teaching Teachers

The idea behind the Learning/ Teaching Collaborative (LTC) in the Boston area is simple: When it comes to preparing education students for the classroom, practicing teachers have abundant knowledge and experience to offer. Unlike most student teaching programs,

The Learning/Teaching Collaborative
Brookline Public Schools, 345 Harvard Street, Brookline, MA 02146 **Contact:** Vivian Troen, Coordinator of the Learning/Teaching Collaborative • Phone: (617) 730-2520 • Fax: (617) 730-2474 • E-Mail: vivian_troen@brookline.mec.edu

LTC was conceived and is run mostly by on-the-job teachers.

The centerpiece of LTC is a year-long internship for students who are pursuing graduate degrees and teaching certification at Wheelock College or Simmons College, two small, urban colleges renowned for their teacher preparation programs. Throughout the year, the graduate students work closely with teams of classroom teachers at one of eight elementary schools affiliated with LTC. The teams include a college faculty member who supervises interns,

attends team meetings, and co-teaches school-based seminars with LTC teachers. The teams meet regularly to share instructional strategies and discuss interns' progress. As a result of having interns in the classroom, teachers have one day a week to conduct research, develop curriculum, lead workshops for colleagues, or teach courses at the colleges. LTC teachers say the program has improved their confidence in themselves as professionals, improved their practice, and reduced their isolation. ●

Connect, Inform, and Empower

For many teachers, the four walls of a classroom can feel like an "isolation barrier" that prevents them from continuing their own learning. Genentech, Inc., a leader in the biotechnology field, is helping break down that barrier with Access Excellence, an on-line network that puts biology teachers in touch with colleagues, scientists, and new information. Biology teachers can access the network to share lesson plans, read scientific literature, participate in "live" conferences and forums, and communicate with other teachers and with Genentech scientists. The company's goal is to inform and empower teachers and, indirectly, inspire students to enjoy and excel in science.

In addition to the network, Access Excellence also hosts an annual fellowship program. Each participant is given a laptop computer, training on Genentech's network and the Internet, and the opportunity to attend a biology education summit. One Access Fellow, Steve Case, a biology teacher at Olathe East High School in Olathe, Kan., spent a recent summer working in a protein chemistry lab at Genentech. He's excited about the program that "helps me let my students do real science." ●

Access Excellence Genentech, Inc., 460 Point San Bruno Boulevard, South San Francisco, CA 94080 **Contact:** Geoffrey Teeter, Senior Program Manager • Phone: (415) 225-8171 • Fax: (415) 225-1657 • E-mail: teeter.geoffrey@gene.com • URL: http://www.gene.com

ProTech, Boston, MA

Essentials for Educators

More than 20 years ago, Alverno College in Milwaukee, Wis., realized that a well-prepared teacher is someone who can do more than just get good grades and pass traditional tests in undergraduate education courses. The urban liberal arts college for women in Milwaukee remade its entire approach to teacher education to focus on 13 essential abilities that teachers need to succeed in the classroom (8 are required of all Alverno undergraduates, such as the ability to communicate effectively; 5 are specific to education students, such as the ability to diagnose learning difficulties and the ability to coordinate resources to support learning goals).

There are no grades or final exams in the undergraduate teacher preparation program; instead, students demonstrate what they know in other ways. To show that they can coordinate resources, for example, Alverno students might download fine arts resources from an electronic community network and integrate them in an elementary curriculum for arts, physical education, and social studies. In a math methods course, students demonstrate conceptualization skills by approaching a problem from three different perspectives—arithmetically, geometrically, and algebraically. Student presentations are videotaped and reviewed by the student and his professors to identify areas needing further study.

The future teachers also spend a great deal of time practicing the 13 essential skills in local classrooms, often in Milwaukee's inner city neighborhoods. Alverno alumni are prepared to continue learning throughout their careers and many choose to work in the city's most challenging schools. ●

College of Education Alverno College, 3401 South 39th Street, PO Box 343922, Milwaukee, WI 53234 **Contact:** Mary Diez, Dean • Phone: (414) 382-6213 • Fax: (414) 382-6354 • E-mail: alverdie@class.org • URL: http://www.alverno.edu

Mentoring for Success

Liberal arts graduates interested in becoming teachers get an intensive dose of both theory and practice in the University of Southern Maine's Extended Teacher Education Program (ETEP). University faculty and teachers at five area schools collaborated in designing the program and work as full partners in operating it. The core of ETEP is a yearlong internship that pairs interns with experienced teachers who are trained for their role as mentors. Interns participate in the daily activities and routines of a teacher, observe instruction, co-plan and teach lessons, and eventually assume full-time teaching responsibilities. At the same time, they take graduate courses taught by both teachers and university faculty. The program encourages interns to reflect on their teaching practices and on the relationship between theory and practice.

Many ETEP interns are experienced professionals seeking a career change who bring valuable knowledge to their schools. At Yarmouth High School, for example, an intern with substantial experience in interactive multimedia design helped teachers integrate multimedia in the curriculum. ●

Extended Teacher Education Program
Admissions and Advising Office, College of Education and Human Development, University of Southern Maine, 118 Bailey Hall, Gorham, ME 04038 • **Contact:** Carol Lynn Davis, USM Coordinator for ETEP's Yarmouth Site • Phone: (207) 780-5068 • Fax: (207) 780-5043 • E-mail: CLDavis@usm.maine.edu • URL: http://www.usm.maine.edu

Grow Your Own Teachers

South Carolina Center for Teacher Recruitment Canterbury House, Rock Hill, SC 29733 **Contact:** Janice Poda, Executive Director • Phone: (803) 323-4032 • Fax: (803) 323-4044 • E-mail: janice.poda@ bbs.serve.org • URL: http://www1.winthrop.edu/scctr/

Many youngsters begin making decisions about their future careers as early as the seventh grade. So that's when South Carolina begins recruiting its best and brightest students to consider a career in teaching. Under a statewide program begun in 1989, middle school students are given opportunities to learn about the work of teaching and the requirements to become a teacher. Those who show an interest enter a pipeline of programs that provide support and encouragement through high school, college, and their first years of teaching.

A key part of South Carolina's effort is the Teacher Cadet program, a yearlong elective course for outstanding students offered at 77 percent of the state's high schools. Practicing teachers wrote—and regularly revise—the Teacher Cadet curriculum, which covers such topics as child development, effective teaching, and the organizational aspects of schools. In one language arts project, for example, students write an original script and create hand puppets for use in an elementary classroom. Cadets also attend regional conferences at local universities. Some 7,500 former Teacher Cadets have enrolled in teacher education programs, forming the core of a next generation of teachers that will increase the racial and ethnic diversity of the state's teaching force and alleviate teacher shortages in areas such as science, math, and special education. ●

Learning to Write, Writing to Learn

Each summer, a select group of 20 teachers gets a taste of what their students go through when they sit down to write. In daily writing sessions, participants in the Bay Area Writing Project's Summer Invitational Institute learn firsthand about the anguish of writer's block and the joy of a well-turned phrase. The goal of these sessions is to help teachers gain a greater understanding of the writing process so they can become better teachers of writing.

During the five-week Institute, participants—who are chosen for the innovative ways they use writing in their classrooms—also work with staff to create workshops on their writing practices and philosophy. Topics ranged from alternative approaches to teaching grammar to incorporating science facts into fiction. After the Institute, they join a network of about 500 project alumni who teach other teachers at workshops in area schools, conduct classroom research, and continue to hone their leadership abilities.

While the explicit goal of the project is to improve the teaching and learning of writing, alumni say the biggest benefits are an increased feeling of professionalism and the chance to be a part of a peer network. The success of the Bay Area Writing Project paved the way for the National Writing Project, which has spawned more than 150 similar endeavors throughout the United States. ●

Bay Area Writing Project
School of Education, University of California Berkeley, 5511 Tolman Hall, Berkeley, CA 94720 **Contact:** Carol Tateishi, Director • Phone: (510) 642-0971 • Fax: (510) 642-4545 • E-mail: tateish@uclink4.berkeley.edu • URL: http://www-gse.berkeley.edu/research/nwp/nwp.html

Partners in Professional Preparation

Every Wednesday morning at Holt Senior High School, the school's 60 staff members can be found discussing issues like adolescent development, reviewing the research they've done, or planning how to improve the school. Thanks to a modified schedule and extended calendar, teachers have these three hours each week away from their classroom duties to concentrate on professional development. "The kinds of discussions we have are different than those at most schools," explains Dean Manikas, assistant principal at Holt. "Most

"Most teachers talk about questions such as, 'What lesson plans are we going to choose?' We focus on questioning why we do what we do."

teachers talk about questions such as, 'What lesson plans are we going to choose?' We focus on questioning *why* we do what we do."

Holt's commitment to ongoing self-improvement is a key reason they were selected to be a Professional Development School (PDS) for Michigan State University's College of Education (MSU). PDSs are partnerships between teacher education programs and schools that serve as laboratories where educators from the two arenas work together to improve both institutions.

Each year, a group of MSU students is placed at Holt for their teaching internships. The interns are supervised by both school and university faculty and participate in Holt's professional development efforts. Faculty from both schools also collaborate to conduct research and teach classes.

Charles Thompson, MSU's co-director of PDSs, sums up the appeal of the partnership: "The kind of concerns about serving the needs of students that Holt has makes it a good place for our education students to learn to teach," he says. "Ideally, we not only want them in classrooms with different approaches to curriculum and instruction, but in a whole different kind of school environment. Holt has created that." ●

Holt Senior High School Holt Public Schools, 1784 Aurelius Road, Holt, MI 48842 **Contact:** Dean Manikas, Assistant Principal • Phone: (517) 694-2162 • Fax: (517) 699-3451

Organizations

> *"Professional sports teams are built progressively, starting with developmental leagues for little kids and ending with world-class competition. We need a comparable approach for supporting educators across their career continuum."*
>
> David Haselkorn,[3] President, Recruiting New Teachers, Inc.

American Association of Colleges for Teacher Education (AACTE)

Description: A national membership organization for colleges and universities with teacher education programs and individuals with ties to public schools and government. **Purpose:** To provide support for members in areas such as data gathering, equity concerns, leadership development, networking, policy analysis, scholarly research, and other professional issues. **Activities:** Keeps members informed and involved through study groups, forums, a journal, and an annual conference. Maintains comprehensive databases of teacher education programs and state teacher policies. **Contact:** Research and Information Services • American Association of Colleges for Teacher Education, One Dupont Circle NW, Suite 610, Washington, DC 20036 • Phone: (202) 293-2450 • Fax: (202) 457-8095 • URL: http://www.aacte.org

Center for Educational Renewal

Description: A partnership of 25 colleges and universities working with more than 100 public school districts. **Purpose:** To improve K-12 education and university-level teacher preparation. Based on the ideas set forth by John Goodlad, co-founder and director, in his books, *A Place Called School* and *Teachers for Our Nation's Schools.* **Activities:** Publishes conceptual papers and progress reports. **Contact:** Roger Soder, Associate Director • Center for Educational Renewal, College of Education, University of Washington, 313 Miller Hall, Box 353600, Seattle, WA 98195 • Phone: (206) 543-6230 • Fax: (206) 543-8439

ERIC Clearinghouse on Teaching and Teacher Education

Description: One of 16 federally funded education clearinghouses of the Educational Resource Information Center (ERIC) system. **Purpose:** To provide the public and educators at all levels with information about teaching and teacher education. **Activities:** Collects, abstracts, and indexes thousands of relevant journal articles, research reports, curriculum guides, books, and conference papers. This information is compiled in a database available in print, on-line, or on CD-ROM. Clearinghouse staff will conduct searches on specific topics for a fee. Also provides free or low-cost resources on a variety of topics. **Contact:** Dorothy Stewart, User Services Coordinator • ERIC Clearinghouse on Teaching and Teacher Education, American Association of Colleges for Teacher Education, One Dupont Circle NW, Suite 610, Washington, DC 20036 • Phone: (800) 822-9229 • Fax: (202) 457-8095 • E-mail: ericsp@inet.ed.gov • URL: http://www.ericsp.org

The Galef Institute

Description: A nonprofit education organization founded in 1989 that developed *Different Ways of Knowing,* a school-change initiative. **Purpose:** To improve student achievement and accelerate school reform by helping teachers adopt an arts-infused interdisciplinary curriculum. **Activities:** Works year-round over a period of three to five years with teachers, administrators, and school communities to help improve curriculum and classroom practices. Through *Different Ways of Knowing,* the Institute provides classroom tools for teachers and students, professional development institutes, workshops, and ongoing technical assistance and study group meetings. Publishes a newsletter, *Teacher-To-Teacher,* in which teachers offer advice and recommend resources. **Contact:** Sue Beauregard, Vice President Programs and Communications • The Galef Institute, 11050 Santa Monica Boulevard, Third Floor, Los Angeles, CA 90025 • Phone: (310) 479-8883 • Fax: (310) 473-9720 • E-mail: sue@galef.com

Interstate New Teacher Assessment and Support Consortium (INTASC)

Description: A consortium of state education agencies, higher education institutions, and national education organizations established in 1987. Members represent more than 36 states. **Purpose:** To help restructure teacher preparation, licensing, and professional development. Developing model licensing standards and performance assessments in six subject areas based on emerging national standards for students. **Activities:** Maintains a clearinghouse of resources and holds annual seminars to help members plan and carry out teacher education reforms in their own states. **Contact:** Jean Miller, Director • Interstate New Teacher Assessment and Support Consortium, Council of Chief State School Officers, One Massachusetts Avenue NW, Washington, DC 20001 • Phone: (202) 336-7048 • Fax: (202) 789-1792 • URL: http://www.ccsso.org

> *"Good teaching is not just writing engaging lesson plans; it's thinking deeply about what we are doing and looking for ways to do it better."*
>
> Joan Cone,[4] English Teacher, El Cerrito High School, West Contra Costa Unified School District

Massachusetts Field Center for Teaching and Learning

Description: Statewide professional development organization led by teachers. **Purpose:** To help ensure that teachers' voices and experiences influence school change and educational policy. **Activities:** Holds annual conferences for educators and policy makers. Provides grants to individuals and teams of kindergarten through 12th-grade teachers for research and ongoing, school-based study groups. Conducts a professional development academy for educators. Publishes *Teaching Voices*, a bimonthly newsletter. **Contact:** Karen O'Connor, Executive Director • Massachusetts Field Center for Teaching and Learning, University of Massachusetts at Boston, 100 Morrissey Boulevard, Boston, MA 02125 • Phone: (617) 287-7660 • Fax: (617) 287-7664 • E-mail: oconnor@umbsky.cc.umb.edu

National Center for Research on Teacher Learning (NCRTL)

Description: A university-based education research center. **Purpose:** To explore how teachers learn and how to improve teacher education. The Center's research is based on its earlier finding that teachers are inadequately prepared to teach challenging academic content to diverse learners. **Activities:** More than 100 publications present current research on how teachers learn and explore how these insights can improve teacher preparation. **Contact:** Robert Floden, Co-Director • National Center for Research on Teacher Learning, College of Education, Michigan State University, 116 Erickson Hall, East Lansing, MI 48824 • Phone: (517) 355-9302 • Fax: (517) 432-2795 • E-mail: floden@msu.edu • URL: http://ncrtl.msu.edu

National Staff Development Council (NSDC) **Description:** A nonprofit organization with more than 8,000 individual and organizational members worldwide. **Purpose:** To ensure success for all students by serving as an international network for educators and by supporting individual and organizational development. **Activities:** Helps members share information through annual conferences, periodic workshops, and numerous publications. Offers a customized, two-year professional development program for schools and districts. **Contact:** Shirley Havens, Business Manager • National Staff Development Council, PO Box 240, Oxford, OH 45056 • Phone: (513) 523-6029 • Fax: (513) 523-0638 • E-mail: nsdchavens@aol.com • URL: http://www.nsdc.org

> *"All teachers, both preservice and in-service, must be given ample opportunities to experience the power and excitement of teaching and learning with technology."*
>
> Neal Strudler,[5] Associate Professor and Coordinator of Educational Computing, College of Education, University of Nevada, Las Vegas

National Urban Alliance for Effective Education (NUA) **Description:** Partnership of school systems, universities, publishers, telecommunications agencies, and educational organizations launched in 1989. **Purpose:** To improve instruction in urban schools through staff development. **Activities:** Works with schools and communities to design comprehensive professional development programs, focusing on areas ranging from leadership development to strategies that encourage collaboration among educators and community members. Trained participants serve as program coordinators in their districts. Services include distance learning, production of instructional video tapes and guides, symposia, and conferences. **Contact:** Eric Cooper, Executive Director • National Urban Alliance for Effective Education, Teachers College, Columbia University, 525 West 120th Street, Box 149, New York, NY 10027 • Phone: (800) 682-4556 • Fax: (908) 604-0711

National Council for Accreditation of Teacher Education (NCATE) **Description:** A professional accrediting agency founded by 29 national organizations of educators and policy makers. **Purpose:** To encourage teacher education programs to meet national standards. The New Professional Teacher (NPT) project is an effort to draft performance-based standards for teacher preparation compatible with standards for kindergarten through 12th-grade students in various subjects. **Activities:** NCATE provides a free list of accredited schools of education nationwide. NPT offers state forums to help educators, policy makers, and parents explore changes needed in teacher preparation to ensure good teaching. **Contact:** Jane Leibbrand, Director of Communications • National Council for Accreditation of Teacher Education, 2010 Massachusetts Avenue NW, Suite 500, Washington, DC 20036 • Phone: (202) 466-7496 • Fax: (202) 296-6620 • E-mail: ncate@ncate.org

Recruiting New Teachers, Inc. (RNT) **Description:** Nonprofit educational organization founded in 1986. **Purpose:** To help improve teacher recruitment, development, and diversity for the nation's schools. **Activities:** Sponsors, with the Advertising Council, a national public service advertising campaign to raise appreciation for teaching and attract new candidates to the profession, especially persons of color and potential teachers for urban schools. Provides information and counseling services to prospective teachers and links candidates with schools and colleges of teacher education. Assists educational policy makers, promotes pre-collegiate teacher recruitment programs, and offers publications, conferences, networking, and technical assistance. A recent report, *Breaking the Class Ceiling,* identifies 149 programs that prepare workers such as paraprofessionals or volunteers to be teachers. **Contact:** David Haselkorn, President • Recruiting New Teachers, Inc., 385 Concord Avenue, Suite 103, Belmont, MA 02178 • Phone: (617) 489-6000 • Fax: (617) 489-6005 • E-mail: rnt@tiac.net • URL: http://www.rnt.org

> *"My teacher education program helped me learn how to continually monitor my weaknesses and strengths. Now I'm confident in my teaching, but I'll never stop learning and improving."*
>
> Karen Ambrosh,[6] Milwaukee Public School Teacher and Alverno College Alumna

Shorecrest High School, Shoreline, WA

Periodicals

Journal of Teacher Education: The Journal of Policy, Practice, and Research in Teacher Education **Description:** A scholarly journal published five times per year. **Focus:** Each issue centers around specific themes, such as urban education or gender issues, exploring how policies, research, and practice in those areas impact the field. **Publisher:** American Association of Colleges for Teacher Education and Corwin Press, Thousand Oaks, CA • Phone: (805) 499-0721.

Journal of Technology and Teacher Education **Description:** Quarterly academic journal. **Focus:** Presents the latest research and practices for integrating technology into both preservice and in-service teacher education. Issues range from the role of electronic networking in professional development to profiles of technology-infused teacher preparation programs. **Publisher:** Association for the Advancement of Computing in Education, Charlottesville, VA • Phone: (804) 973-3987.

Journal of Computing in Teacher Education

Description: Quarterly academic journal featuring research articles and book reviews. **Focus:** Examines efforts, both successful and unsuccessful, to infuse technology into preservice teacher education. **Publisher:** International Society for Technology in Education, Eugene, OR • Phone: (800) 336-5191.

Journal of Staff Development

Description: Quarterly journal with scholarly and thematic articles. **Focus:** Explores theory, research, and best practices of staff development as it relates to improving schools. **Publisher:** National Staff Development Council, Oxford, OH • Phone: (513) 523-6029.

Pathways **Description:** Biannual newsletter of the DeWitt Wallace-Reader's Digest Pathways to Teaching Careers Program, Northeast & Midwest Expansion Project. **Focus:** Each issue provides updates on the 11 colleges and universities that are part of a multi-year effort to improve teacher recruitment and preparation. The project targets paraprofessionals and other uncertified teachers, particularly minorities, who are currently working in the public schools. **Publisher:** Bank Street College of Education, New York, NY • Phone: (212) 875-4528.

Readings

Corcoran, Thomas C. **Transforming Professional Development for Teachers: A Guide for State Policymakers.** *National Governors' Association: Washington, DC, 1995.* Phone: (301) 498-3738. ● A useful guide intended for state policymakers interested in improving the effectiveness of their K-12 professional development programs. Describes the vital role of professional development in school reform and offers tips for allocating financial and human resources.

The National Commission on Teaching & America's Future. **What Matters Most: Teaching for America's Future.** *The National Commission on Teaching & America's Future: New York, NY, 1996.* Phone: (212) 678-3015. ● Argues that a well-prepared teaching force is essential to educational reform. Recommends setting higher standards for teachers, improving preparation programs, organizing schools to support collaboration and professional growth, and establishing a strict accountability system that also rewards excellence.

Goodlad, John. **Educational Renewal: Better Teachers, Better Schools.** *Jossey-Bass: San Francisco, CA, 1994.* Phone: (800) 956-7739. ● A leading expert in the field offers a detailed look at his evolving vision of how reforms in teacher education and public schooling can proceed hand-in-hand. Goodlad argues that education professors need to band together with colleagues from the math and sciences and public school faculty to form "centers of pedagogy" that integrate scholarly inquiry with extended experiences in public schools.

Committee on Biology Teacher Inservice Programs, Board on Biology, Commission on Life Sciences, et al. **The Role of Scientists in the Professional Development of Science Teachers.** *National Academy Press: Washington, DC, 1996.* Phone: (800) 624-6242. ● A how-to guide for scientists interested in helping to improve science education by assisting in the professional development of practicing teachers.

Lieberman, Ann, and Lynne Miller. **Staff Development for Education in the 90's: New Demands, New Realities, New Perspectives. 2nd Edition** *Teachers College Press: New York, NY, 1991.* Phone: (800) 575-6566 ● Leading educators argue that effective staff development cannot be dictated from above, but must be based on needs identified by teachers. Their essays offer tips to help teachers take control of continued learning and urge communities to make a sustained commitment to ongoing professional development.

ProTech, Boston, MA • Photo by Christopher Fitzgerald

Professional Development. The ERIC Review. *Vol. 3, ACCESS ERIC: Rockville, MD. Winter 1995.* Phone: (800) 538-3742. ● Leaders in preservice and in-service education describe different approaches to professional development for kindergarten through 12th-grade teachers through profiles of innovative programs and short articles. Includes a list of print and organization resources.

Darling-Hammond, Linda, Arthur E. Wise, and Stephen P. Klein. **A License to Teach: Building a Profession for 21st Century Schools.** *Westview Press: Boulder, CO, 1995.* Phone: (800) 242-7737. ● Describes efforts to develop performance-based standards and assessments for teacher licensing. The authors profile pioneering efforts in California and Minnesota and discuss the challenges of implementing this work on a national scale.

The Holmes Group **Tomorrow's Schools of Education: A Report of the Holmes Group.** *Holmes Group: East Lansing, MI, 1995.* Phone: (517) 353-3874. ● Classroom teachers and university faculty from many of the nation's most prestigious schools of education propose a blueprint for reforming teacher preparation. They recommend creating professional development schools to forge stronger connections between university-based studies and classroom realities.

Rényi, Judith. **Teachers Take Charge of Their Learning: Transforming Professional Development for Student Success.** *The National Foundation for the Improvement of Education: Washington, DC, 1996.* Phone: (202) 822-7840. ● Addresses the importance of making professional development a part of the daily work of teachers. Offers suggestions for improving professional practice to meet the needs of students in the 21st century.

Dzantik'i Heeni Middle School, Juneau, AK • Photo by Brian Wallace

Tyson, Harriet. **Who Will Teach the Children? Progress and Resistance in Teacher Education.** *Jossey-Bass: San Francisco, CA, 1994.* Phone: (800) 956-7739. ● Through portraits of teacher education in Oregon and at five schools of education in the South and Midwest, the author conducts an in-depth examination of teacher preparation, including structures and policies that can hamper or support real reform.

Villegas, Ana Maria, Beatriz Chu Clewell, Bernice Taylor Anderson, et al. **Teaching for Diversity: Models for Expanding the Supply of Minority Teachers.** *Policy Information Center, Educational Testing Service: Princeton, NJ, 1995.* Phone: (609) 734-5694. ● Examines successful strategies for recruiting, preparing, and graduating minority teacher education students. Several different approaches are explored, including helping paraprofessionals become certified teachers.

"Too many staff development programs are adult pull-out programs, where teachers are taken out of the classroom to be taught, but the job setting remains unaffected. Individual learning has to occur within the redesign of the workplace of teachers."

Dennis Sparks,[7] Executive Director, National Staff Development Council

Contact Information

[1] **Linda Darling-Hammond** Co-Director • National Center for Restructuring Education, Schools and Teaching, Teachers College, Columbia University, Box 86, 525 West 120th Street, New York, NY 10027 • Phone: (212) 678-4142 • Fax: (212) 678-4039

[2] **Lynn Cherkasky-Davis** Teacher • The Foundations School, 2040 West Adams Street, Chicago, IL 60612 • Phone: (312) 534-7605 • Fax: (312) 534-7604 • E-mail: LynnieCD@aol.com

[3] **David Haselkorn** President • Recruiting New Teachers, Inc., 385 Concord Avenue, Suite 103, Belmont, MA 02178 • Phone: (617) 489-6000 • Fax: (617) 489-6005 • E-mail: rnt@tiac.net

[4] **Joan Cone** English Teacher • El Cerrito High School, West Contra Costa Unified School District, 540 Ashbury Street, El Cerrito, CA 94530 • Phone: (510) 525 0344 • Fax: (510) 525-1810 • E-mail: joancone@uclink4.berkeley.edu

[5] **Neal Strudler** Associate Professor and Coordinator of Educational Computing • College of Education, University of Nevada, Las Vegas, 4505 Maryland Parkway, Las Vegas, NV 89154 • Phone: (702) 895-1306 • Fax: (702) 895-4898 • E-mail: strudler@nevada.edu

[6] **Karen Ambrosh** Milwaukee Public School Teacher and Alverno College Alumna • 1022 West Eden Place, Milwaukee, WI 53221 • Phone and Fax: (414) 483-6097 • E-mail: KDBrosh@aol.com

[7] **Dennis Sparks** Executive Director • National Staff Development Council, 1124 West Liberty Street, Ann Arbor, MI 48103 • Phone: (313) 998-0574 • Fax: (313) 998-0628 • E-mail: sparksnsdc@aol.com

Communities

Alice Carlson Applied Learning Center, Fort Worth, TX • Photo by Paul Moseley

Communities

When schools and communities work together, everyone prospers. Students get access to rich and rewarding learning experiences; communities gain healthy, responsible citizens; and businesses are assured of a well-prepared workforce. In this section, we look at how educators are creating new ways to work with family members, whose involvement is key to school success. We examine promising efforts in which community

Yarmouth High School, Yarmouth, ME

resources and social services are linked with schools, and schools, in turn, become centers for recreation and education for people of all ages. We explore school-business partnerships aimed at producing graduates who meet high standards and are prepared to learn throughout their lifetimes. And we see how technology can improve communication among all stakeholders who share responsibility for young people. ●

Partnerships between schools, families, communities, and businesses are necessary to transform the educational system from top to bottom. When these stakeholders join forces to provide support and resources, all children have a chance to succeed.

*Don Davies,[1] Founder,
Institute for Responsive Education,
Northeastern University*

MAX SEABAUGH

Communities

Chapter 5:
Involving Families

106   Introduction

108   Imagine the Possibilities:
The Home-School Team
by Norris M. Haynes and James P. Comer

112   From the Front Lines:
Parent With a Purpose
by Mary D. Colón

114   Snapshots
Innovative Schools & Programs

118   Access to Information
Organizations, Periodicals, Readings & Contact Information

Chapter 6:
Connecting Communities

124   Introduction

126   Imagine the Possibilities:
A Common Ground for Learning
by Michele Cahill

130   From the Front Lines:
Coming Together as a Community
by Stephany Hoover

132   Snapshots
Innovative Schools & Programs

136   Access to Information
Organizations, Periodicals, Readings & Contact Information

Chapter 7
Business Partnerships

142   Introduction

144   Imagine the Possibilities:
Working to Learn, Learning to Work
by Roberts T. Jones

148   From the Front Lines:
Building Bright Futures
by Juliette Johnson

150   Snapshots
Innovative Schools & Programs

154   Access to Information
Organizations, Periodicals, Readings & Contact Information

Chapter 5
Involving Families

We've known since the early days of public education that children learn more when their families and schools work closely **together.** Mothers, fathers, and other relatives are a young person's first teachers, and they know their child's needs and interests best. The values they instill and the **support** they offer throughout the K–12 years are essential to success in school. Because parents and teachers have different perspectives on a child, their collaboration offers a greater possibility of releasing a student's true **potential.**

Yet, due in part to the traditional structure of schooling and in part to the hectic demands of modern life, family **involvement** in education is all too rare. It's not unusual for communication to be limited to report cards and complaints about a child's behavior. Neither teachers nor parents have adequate **channels** to share information that could make the difference in a child's learning. Most teachers, for example, still do not have telephones in their classrooms.

This chapter delves into efforts by parents and educators to build powerful **partnerships** on behalf of children. Schools and teachers are learning how to reach out to families and **welcome** their active participation in the classroom. They provide volunteer opportunities to make use of parents' skills and talents, and find ways to involve families more **directly** in their children's education.

Educators are working with mothers, fathers, and guardians to design learning plans that respond to the needs and interests of individual students. More broadly, site-based **management** creates a new avenue for parents to be actively involved in making decisions about everything from the school's mission to how technology should be integrated. Parents, in turn, are acting as a **force** for change, venturing into the community to explain educational concerns and building public support for schools.

Technology is proving very useful in supporting closer **collaboration** between homes and schools. Electronic bulletin boards and e-mail help increase **communication** between teachers and parents. As technology assumes a greater role in the learning process, it is becoming increasingly important for every child to have **access** to a computer at home. Not only do they extend the time for learning, but computers allow parents to conveniently review student work. A growing number of schools, some profiled in this chapter, are arranging for children and families to **borrow** equipment at little or no cost.

When children see their parents and teachers working together, it sends a clear and consistent **message** about the value of learning. Research and common sense tell us that a true partnership between schools and families results in a greater likelihood of **success** for students, both in school and beyond. ●

Imagine the Possibilities

BY NORRIS M. HAYNES AND JAMES P. COMER

the home-school team

Children learn best when the significant adults in their lives—parents, teachers, and other family and community members—work together to encourage and support them. This basic fact should be a guiding principle as we think about how schools should be organized and how children should be taught. Schools alone cannot address all of a child's developmental needs: The meaningful involvement of parents and support from the community are essential.

The need for a strong partnership between schools and families to educate children may seem like common sense. In simpler times, this relationship was natural and easy to maintain. Teachers and parents were often neighbors and found many occasions to discuss a child's progress. Children heard the same messages from teachers and parents and understood that they were expected to uphold the same standards at home and at school.

As society has become more complex and demanding, though, these relationships have all too often fallen by the wayside. Neither educators nor parents have enough time to get to know one another and establish working relationships on behalf of children. In many communities, parents are discouraged from spending time in classrooms and educators are expected to consult with family members only when a child is in trouble. The result, in too many cases, is misunderstanding, mistrust, and a lack of respect, so that when a child falls behind, teachers blame the parents and parents blame the teachers.

At the same time, our society has created artificial distinctions about the roles that parents and teachers should play in a young person's development. We tend to think that schools should stick to teaching academics and that home is the place where children's moral and emotional development should take place.

Yet children don't stop learning about values and relationships when they enter a classroom, nor do they cease learning academics—and attitudes about learning—when they are at home or elsewhere in their community. They constantly observe how the significant adults in their lives treat one another, how decisions are made and executed, and how problems are solved. All of the experiences children have, both in and out of school, help shape their sense that someone cares about them, their feelings of self-worth and competency, their understanding of the world around them, and their beliefs about where they fit into the scheme of things.

These days, it can take extraordinary efforts to build strong relationships between families and

Norris M. Haynes[2] is associate professor at the Yale Child Study Center and the Department of Psychology and director of research for the School Development Program; James P. Comer[2] ★ FILM is Maurice Falk Professor at the Yale Child Study Center, associate dean of the Yale Medical School, and director of the School Development Program.

educators. Schools have to reach out to families, making them feel welcome as full partners in the educational process. Families, in turn, have to make a commitment of time and energy to support their children both at home and at school. The effort involved in reestablishing these connections is well worth it, as many communities across the country—including those we work with—are discovering. Our experience is that significant and meaningful parent involvement is possible, desirable, and valuable in improving student growth and performance.

A Starting Point The communities in which we are involved—mostly inner city neighborhoods—tend to start with relatively poor relationships between schools and families. Many of the parents experienced failure in their own school days and are reluctant to set foot inside their children's schools. Teachers commute to work and often know very little about the neighborhood outside the school. Before they can develop effective partnerships, educators and families in these communities first have to learn to trust and respect one another.

Before they can develop effective partnerships, educators and families in these communities first have to learn to trust and respect one another.

Although it is less obvious, the same is true in more affluent communities. The lack of trust and respect can be seen in the growing numbers of parents choosing to enroll their children in private schools or educate them at home, and in the growing reluctance of voters to approve school-bond issues. At the same time, relatively few schools have open-door policies allowing parents to visit at any time, and parents who insist on playing an active role in their children's education are often branded as "troublemakers."

The starting point in any community is to create opportunities where parents and teachers can learn that they both have children's best interests at heart. We applaud the growing trend to decentralize decision making from central offices to individual schools because it creates opportunities for parents and educators to work together, making decisions about school policies and procedures. Some may see this arrangement as shifting power from school staff to parents—but it's not power shifting, it's power sharing. It is empowering all of the adults who have a stake in children's development.

Participation on school-based planning and management teams gives parents a chance to learn about the professional side of schooling—to understand the inner workings of curriculum and instruction. It also allows them to educate school staff about the community and demonstrate that parents have much to offer if provided the opportunities to do so. Working together as full partners, parents, teachers, administrators, business people, and other community members can create an educational program that meets unique local needs and reflects the diversity within a school without compromising high performance expectations and standards. They can foster a caring and sensitive school climate that respects and responds to students' differences as well as their similarities.

A Wide Variety of Roles Besides participating in governance, parents can be involved in schools in many different roles. There are the traditional ways: encouraging children to complete homework, attending parent-teacher conferences, and being active members of their school's parent-teacher organization. There are also roles that require more commitment: serving as mentors, teacher aides, or lunchroom monitors, or providing assistance to schools and students in a myriad of other ways. At a time when schools are adopting curricula based on real-world problems and information, families can make a valuable contribution by sharing first-hand information about work, hobbies, history, and other personal experiences, either in-person or via a computer network. Perhaps most important, parents can simply take the time to go to their schools and observe, learning about what their children and their children's teachers are doing.

The hectic pace of modern life can make this kind of involvement seem out of reach for many parents. But there are positive signs that it is becoming more feasible. Employers, concerned about the quality of the future workforce, are starting to adopt policies that allow parents time off to participate on a school's planning and management team or volunteer time at regular intervals. And more schools are offering either daycare or preschool, which makes it easier for parents with young children to spend time at an older child's school.

This level of parent involvement in schools allows parents and staff to work together in respectful and mutually supportive ways, creating an environment where understanding, trust, and respect can flourish. At the same time, students get consistent messages from the important adults in their lives. When children observe that home and school are engaged in a respectful partnership for their benefit, they are likely to develop more positive attitudes about school and achieve more, compared to situations in which school and home are seen as being worlds apart.

Better Lines of Communication Regardless of a parent's direct involvement in school activities, it is vital for parents and teachers to communicate effectively with one another. Each has a piece of the picture of a child's development, and each can be more effective when information is shared. Constant

communication helps to ensure that both schools and homes are responsive to a child's unique needs and therefore support his overall development.

Some of this interaction should be face-to-face, either at the school, at home, at the parent's worksite, or at another convenient location. It must be considered an integral part of schooling, and adequate time must be provided during regular working hours for school staff to carry it out. At the same time, this communication must be recognized as a critical part of parenting, and parents must make the commitment to meet periodically with their children's teachers.

Technology can allow educators and parents to be linked into a sturdier web of mutual support than ever before. Schools and homes can be connected through computer networks that allow them to freely share information, via electronic

mail and bulletin boards, 24 hours a day, year-round. It's not hard to imagine a time in the near future when all parents at home will be able to quickly call up information such as a student's schedule for the week, current assignments, and suggestions from teachers about what they can do to support learning goals at home. They'll be able to review what the child has been doing by looking at actual samples of school work that have been collected in an electronic portfolio.

To ensure that everyone, regardless of income or other circumstances, has equal access to such electronic tools, some schools work with businesses and other partners to create computer lending programs for families. All schools should consider creating similar programs. The needed computers should also be available to parents at a variety of public settings like schools, libraries, and government buildings, and there should be free or low-cost classes to teach educators and parents how to use them to foster learning.

The establishment of computer networks linking schools and homes fits neatly with another positive trend we've noticed: more and more schools are broadening their mission to provide educational services for their entire community. Lifelong learning is rapidly becoming a requirement for success in the modern world. Parents and other community members can either attend classes at a school or study at home using distance learning technologies, with content supplied by their local school or by one miles away. Through these networks, parents can not only advance their own education, but also demonstrate for their children that adults need to keep working at learning, too.

But the biggest winners are the children. When we walk into a school and see parents and teachers working together, in all sorts of roles, it's a sure sign that the school challenges the very best in students and helps all, regardless of race, class, or culture, to realize their fullest potential. ●

When children observe that home and school are engaged in a respectful partnership for their benefit, they are likely to develop more positive attitudes about school and achieve more, compared to situations in which school and home are seen as being worlds apart.

From the Front Lines

BY MARY D. COLÓN

parent with a purpose

When people ask me what made me become so involved in my kids' schools, or why I started fighting for something so "hopeless" as education reform, I joke about growing up Irish Catholic and being driven by guilt to make the world a better place. But, the truth is, it was concern for my daughters, their friends, my nephew—people I knew personally. I'm not sure what makes me stay involved in something that, at times, can drive me crazy with frustration. I think it's hope—genuine hope that things have changed for the better and will continue to do so.

I've been involved in the schools here in Minneapolis since the oldest of my two daughters started preschool. She's now a sophomore in high school and my youngest is an eighth grader. When I first started as a parent volunteer, I was asked to do all the things that schools have traditionally asked of parents: PTA, fundraising, tutoring, and chaperoning field trips.

My girls flourished in school, but my nephew, who is the same age as my oldest daughter, was failing. His mother was terrified of teachers and principals and didn't trust the system because she had failed out of it at 14. She asked me to help.

I didn't realize it at the time, but her fear and distrust woke me up—it made me realize that there were many others like her and pushed me across some invisible boundary of parent involvement. I began asking about the types of services schools had available to help kids like my nephew. I found that individual teachers cared and tried to do what they could, but they didn't know how to make the system work for him any more than we did. They were tired and frazzled, dealing every day with hundreds of kids whose problems they couldn't solve. They suggested I go to the county social service system for help. I found that the county system and the school system worked in separate, fragmented, and openly territorial ways, often battling each other for dollars and turf. I didn't think there was any way to change that, so I just kept attending conferences with my nephew's teachers and helping however I could.

By the time my oldest daughter and my nephew reached middle school, she was an "A" student and he was in a "Level IV Behavior Program"—code for the kids the system can't handle. Eventually, a school social worker wrote a letter to the county, and he was referred to a mental health program. The program proceeded to cancel appointments for the next six weeks until I went in and refused to leave until someone saw him. My nephew finally got help, and I decided then and there that I would fight to make mental health a priority area in the schools.

My opening came through a new policy called "site-based management," under which many decisions were decentralized from the district offices of the Minneapolis Public Schools to local school buildings. A few years earlier, each school had been required to create a leadership team that included parents, as well as administrators, teachers, and other community members. The change to self-governance was frightening for those who were used to doing what they were told, and some teachers, principals, and even parents resisted the new policy.

So I was surprised when my husband and I went to an Open House for parents at my daughter's new school, Northeast Middle School. We were greeted warmly by the principal and staff at the door. They invited everyone who attended to join a new partnership called the Building Leadership Team.

Our team, comprised of 26 parents, teachers, administrators, business people, and students, put our heads, skills, and backgrounds together to address issues critical to the school. Finally, we were being asked to do more than sell chocolate for fundraising.

Our team, comprised of 26 parents, teachers, administrators, business people, and students, put our heads, skills, and backgrounds together to address issues critical to the school. Finally, we were being asked to do more than sell chocolate for fundraising. That first year was tough, as parents and educators tried to find equal footing on new ground. We received leadership and problem solving training from our school district and our business partner, AT&T. We had to learn to trust and respect each other. Ultimately, we found common ground because every member of the team was committed to viewing all students as *our kids.* Every decision we made was measured against the yardstick of: "Is this the best thing for our kids?"

Our team has accomplished a lot over the past several years. The project I'm proudest of is the Resource Center, which offers our students and their families on-site medical and mental health services, job-training and placement resources, parenting skills classes, adult education, after school activities, academic tutoring, family outreach programs, and emergency assistance (money, shelter, food, legal aid, and childcare). It wasn't created in time to help my nephew, but it has helped hundreds of other kids and their families.

Another important team initiative is bringing new technologies into the school. A homework hotline and voice mail system now allows parents to monitor assignments and leave extended messages for school staff. AT&T is wiring the building for classroom telephones and connections to the Internet. The company has also donated computers that help Resource Center staff document the use of Northeast's health and social services.

My nephew and my daughters have moved on from middle school to high school, where I've become vice chairperson of the Parent Leadership Team. The high school has also hired me as a part-time family outreach person. I help kids with reading, and I also keep in constant touch with parents by phone and through home visits. Sometimes they get angry when I raise concerns with them about their children, but mostly they are tickled to death to hear from me. Their lives and those of their kids are often out of control and they're grateful to have another parent there to help.

There is a line in Alice Walker's novel, *The Color Purple,* that captures what it is about kids that makes me want to work hard for them. In the book, the main character, Ceely, has led a hard life full of abuse, neglect, violence, poverty, and racism. While talking to the first real friend she's ever had, she muses: "I think God gets pissed at us when we walk by the color purple and don't even see it."

Kids are like the color purple. Teachers, administrators, and parents are often too busy or too tired to see the potential and beauty in them. We forget that, ultimately, it's about all of our kids—about trying to make sure that they succeed academically and socially, about seeing the color purple before it fades. ●

Mary D. Colón[3] is the co-chair of Redesign, an initiative to expand the Resource Center model throughout Hennepin County, Minn.

Snapshots

A Democratic Alternative

Graham & Parks Alternative Public School in Cambridge, Mass., was established in 1972 in response to lobbying by parents who were dissatisfied with traditional educational practices. "We were committed to creating a democratic learning community right from the start," principal Len Solo says.

For about 25 years, parents and teachers have worked collaboratively to operate the school, which has an enrollment of 380 students in kindergarten through eighth grade. The result is an educational program that meets the academic, social, and emotional needs of individual students. Instead of traditional classes grouped strictly by age, for instance, students are grouped in multi-age classes where they stay for two years with the same teacher. This permits parents, teachers, and students to develop stronger relationships.

Parents also contribute time and expertise to the school's daily life. They serve as room parents, help produce the school's literary magazine, help set up community service activities, and contribute in a myriad of other ways. "I really enjoy being able to come into school every morning to work with computers and with my sons and other students," says parent Bob Filmore. "They get the idea that parents support them and the school, so they work harder and do better." A full-time parent coordinator reaches out to parents who may be reluctant to become involved. She also conducts orientations and supports volunteers. ●

Graham & Parks Alternative Public School
Cambridge School Department, 15 Upton Street, Cambridge, MA 02139 **Contact:** Len Solo, Principal • Phone: (617) 349-6612 • Fax: (617) 349-6615 • E-mail: solo@puck.rosa.parks.cambridge.k12.ma.us. • URL: http://puck.rosaparks.cambridge.k12.ma.us/

Parents as Students

When parents told Charles Mingo, principal at DuSable High School in Chicago, that they were afraid to volunteer at school because they hadn't graduated themselves, he turned what could have been an impediment into an opportunity.

"Seeing parents at the school regularly and having them in class inspires our students, parents, and staff."

Since 1993, the school has allowed parents to earn their diplomas and volunteer in their children's school at the same time. Under the Parent Academic Success Service (PASS) program, parents who left school in the 11th or 12th grade can simply re-enroll at DuSable as regular students subject to the same behavioral and performance expectations as their teenagers. "The parents, just by being there, help to keep classes calm and provide our teenaged students with strong adult role models," says parent coordinator Mary Jones.

DuSable recognizes that its older students have special needs. A full-time parent program coordinator meets with them regularly and helps resolve problems that arise from their dual roles as parents and students.

DuSable was able to establish PASS because, like other Chicago schools, it is run by a local school council composed of the principal, six parents, two teachers, and two community members.

Approximately 20 parents participate in PASS each year, but its impact goes far beyond numbers. Other parents respond to PASS as a symbol of the school's commitment to taking their needs and ideas seriously. The school gets good attendance at workshops and meetings designed to connect families to services, help parents support learning, and keep them informed. "Seeing parents at the school regularly and having them in class inspires our students, parents, and staff," the principal says. ●

DuSable High School Chicago Public Schools, 4934 South Wabash, Chicago, IL 60615 **Contact:** Mary Jones, Parent Coordinator • Phone: (312) 535-1100 • Fax: (312) 535-1004 • E-mail: maryj@dusable.cps.k12.il.us • URL: http://www.dusable.cps.k12.il.us

Making Points for Parent Involvement

In searching for a way to make parent involvement more effective, educators at Turnbull Learning Academy decided to develop a list of the most critical activities that parents should do. Then they assigned points to each activity, which range from helping children track assignments to volunteering at school. Finally, they asked families who choose to enroll their children in the school to commit to earning 18 points worth of school-involvement credits each month to support their children's learning. "Parents won't participate in schools just to participate. They'll do it to help their children perform better academically," says co-principal Barbara Adams.

Turnbull, a magnet school in San Mateo, Calif., adopted its emphasis on family involvement in 1993 in conjunction with a redesign of its buildings and educational programs. Teachers have noticed that reading skills improve more quickly when students can count on active family involvement. The regular presence of parents at this 300-student school has also created a stronger sense of community. "Naturally, when parents gather the talk turns to how their kids are doing in school and how they can help one another," says J.B. Tengco, the liaison for Partners in Innovation, an organization that helps Turnbull with its community programs. Parents formed a group to trade services like babysitting, mechanical work, and translation help, so they can spend more time helping their children learn. ●

Turnbull Learning Academy San Mateo-Foster City School District, 715 Indian Avenue, San Mateo, CA 94401 **Contact:** Evelyn Taylor or Barbara Adams, Co-Principals • Phone: (415) 312-7766 • Fax: (415) 312-7729

A Vision Realized

Maplewood K-8 School Edmonds School District, 8500 200th Street SW, Edmonds, WA 98026 **Contact:** Laurie Gerlach, Public Relations Coordinator • Phone: (206) 670-7515 • Fax: (206) 670-7519 • URL: http:// mwel.edmonds.wednet.edu

Parents who choose to enroll their children at Maplewood K–8 School in Edmonds, Wash., agree to give 90 hours each year, mostly in teaching roles under the guidance of a classroom teacher. Under the Parent Cooperative Education Program (PCEP), each school year begins with a meeting between the teacher and a parent room-coordinator to determine how parents will be a part of curriculum planning and implementation. Working with the classroom teacher, parents select lessons that best suit their skills.

These lessons, called "rotations," take place in the core academic areas as well as elective areas, such as foreign language, art, and advanced science. Groups of six to eight students spend part of their day moving from one rotation to another. "With these rotations, students get the individual attention they need," says Laurie Gerlach, a parent who serves as public relations coordinator at this 470-student school.

Many area employers have agreed to flexible schedules to allow parents to participate in the school. When parents have a scheduling conflict, they can arrange for a substitute parent, sometimes even a grandparent. Those families who are unable to participate in teaching rotations help with activities outside of the classroom, such as organizing assemblies and chaperoning field trips. ●

Computers in Every Home

West Des Moines Community School District, West Des Moines, IA

While many dream of the day when all students will have computers in their homes, it's a reality today in many of Indiana's fourth- and fifth-grade classrooms. Thanks to The Buddy System Project, a state-sponsored program, selected schools across the state are able to provide families of fourth and fifth graders with a computer, modem, printer, and training in how to use them. The technology allows students to reinforce and extend skills learned at school and creates a new kind of connection between school and family.

"With e-mail, teachers let parents know instantly if a child had a good day or needs help. Even posting assignments electronically allows parents much greater involvement than sending work home with the child," says Candace Swanson, principal of Solon Robinson Elementary School in Crown Point, Ind., a participant in The Buddy Project.

Solon Robinson teachers post discussion questions for parents to explore with their children and suggest ways that parents can reinforce learning at home. Students and parents can work together on activities like developing a spreadsheet for a monthly food budget. "The parents of my students now have much more say in how their children learn in my class and a better understanding of how I teach," says Carolyn Vertesch, a teacher and Buddy site coordinator.

Although the project is primarily intended to benefit children, its effects can be far-reaching. "One of the most exciting things is seeing parents enhance their own careers as they learn these new skills along with their children. I've seen it transform lives," says Nancy Miller, implementation manager for The Buddy System Project. ●

"With e-mail, teachers let parents know instantly if a child had a good day or needs help..."

The Buddy System Project Corporation for Educational Technology, 17 West Market Street, Suite 960, Indianapolis, IN 46204 **Contact:** Alan Hill, President • Phone: (317) 464-2074 • Fax: (317) 464-2080 • E-mail: ahill@vonnegut.buddy.k12.in.us • URL: http://www.buddy.k12.in.us/

A Community-Wide Committee

"Our town is small, so the families here just seem to feel like everyone is needed to make the school work," says Chris Farley, mother of three students in the Flambeau School District, which serves 700 students in a rural community in Wisconsin. More than three-fifths of all households have participated in focus groups

Flambeau School District PO Box 86, Tony, WI 54563 **Contact:** Chuck Ericksen, Community Education Director • Phone: (715) 532-7760 • Fax: (715) 532-5405 • E-mail: erickson@centuryinter.net

that set educational priorities in the district. Begun in 1994, the project, known as the Flambeau Action Committee on Education for Tomorrow, brings together family members, educators, and local officials to redesign the community's education system.

"The families in this community learned about education reform through the focus groups, but they have also taken to these groups as a way to make certain that their interests are identified and prioritized in the school," says Chuck Ericksen, Flambeau's full-time community education director. The result has been an

emphasis on skills identified by the community as essential to their children's success. While these include the usual competency in math, reading, and writing, parents also identified problem solving, critical thinking, and creativity as equally important. "The parents here saw the need to transform their kids into self-reliant learners," says Ericksen.

Parents and other adult family members routinely offer their time and knowledge to support school activities. For instance, family members helped set up 360 classroom computers and wire dedicated ISDN lines to provide fast connections to the Internet. ●

Parents Helping Parents

"We teach our parents to help each other, because they understand this community and its needs better than any outsider," says Teresa Martiato, coordinator of the Referral and Information Network (RAIN) at Fienberg-Fisher Elementary School in Miami Beach, Fla. RAIN was created in 1991 after a survey of families identified access to information as the most pressing need in this mostly Spanish-speaking, low-income community. "Many families here come from countries where they have to accept what's given to them. Our program helps them understand what their rights are in this country," explains Martiato, who started as a parent volunteer herself.

RAIN provides parents with 40 hours of training that is part class instruction and part community outreach. Families learn how to locate community resources, how to better support their children's learning, and, eventually, how to train other parents. Parents staff a RAIN room at the school that serves as a center for the program's activities. "The program has given our families active voices in our community. The kids have performed better because they see that their parents care," says Annette Weissman, assistant principal. ●

Fienberg–Fisher Elementary School
Dade County Public Schools, 1420 Washington Avenue, Miami Beach, FL 33139 **Contact:** Grace Nebb, Principal • Phone: (305) 531-0419 • Fax: (305) 534-3925

Alice Carlson Applied Learning Center, Fort Worth, TX

The Sum of Parental Involvement

On any given day, dozens of parents and other family members can be found at Emma E. Booker Elementary School in Sarasota, Fla., assisting in classrooms, meeting with service providers, or helping with special events. The school's unusually high level of family involvement is credited to the School Development Program (SDP).

SDP, developed by Dr. James Comer and the Yale Child Study Center, is designed to overcome the mistrust and misunderstanding often found between families and educators in inner city schools. The effort to build these relation-

Emma E. Booker Elementary School Sarasota School District, 2350 Martin Luther King Jr. Way, Sarasota, FL 34234 **Contact:** Gwendolyn Rigell, Principal • Phone: (941) 361-6480 • Fax: (941) 361-6484

ships starts right at the top: Parents help set the school's direction as members of a Planning and Management team whose composition reflects the school's multiracial community.

Booker Elementary, which serves 820 students, has been using the SDP approach since it opened in 1990. To encourage readiness for school and early parental involvement, Booker identifies children as young as two who need extra help and could benefit from its pre-K programs. After kindergarten, students stay with the same set of teachers for three years in multi-age groups that allow greater familiarity between parents, teachers, and children. Families are continually invited to the school to see their children take part in monthly school-wide presentations, to recognize student achievement, and for school and social functions.

This welcoming atmosphere makes it easier for Booker to stress another Comer concept: serving the needs of the child by serving the family. To support families and help them better provide for their children, 27 agencies provide services on-site, including a computer training program, a variety of health care programs, and a literacy program to develop parents' reading and writing skills. The sum of all this family involvement is clear to parent Connie Ruby: "My kids feel special here because everyone knows who I am." ●

Organizations

Center for the Study of Parent Involvement

Description: A national information clearinghouse created in 1973. **Purpose:** To strengthen home-school partnerships. **Activities:** Provides training and technical assistance to families, educators, and community leaders. Conducts research on parent involvement programs. Sponsors conferences and workshops; publishes a newsletter, *Apple Pie;* and develops curricula on family involvement for teacher-credentialing programs. **Contact:** Dan Safran, Director • Center for the Study of Parent Involvement, John F. Kennedy University, 12 Altarinda Road, Orinda, CA 94563 • Phone: (510) 254-0110 • Fax: (510) 254-4870 • E-mail: dsafran@jfku.edu

"It's very simple. When teachers see that you are actively involved in your child's education, they are more motivated because they know their efforts are supported at home. When that happens, it all seems to come together."

Kenyetta Redwood,[4] School Assistant, White Career Academy, Chicago Public Schools

Clear View Charter School, Chula Vista, CA • Photo by Matthew Rivaldi

Hispanic Policy Development Project

Description: An advocacy resource group for Hispanic parents and families. **Purpose:** To increase the involvement of Hispanic families in the educational system. **Activities:** Advises schools on ways to improve family-school partnerships. Publishes informational pamphlets and bilingual books for families to read to kids. Produces reports, including, *Together is Better,* which analyzes why some parent involvement programs work and others don't. **Contact:** Siobhan Nicolau, President • Hispanic Policy Development Project, 36 East 22nd Street, 9th Floor, New York, NY 10010 • Phone: (212) 529-9323 • Fax: (212) 477-5395 • E-mail: Siobhan96@ aol.com

Hand in Hand

Description: A national public education campaign sponsored by the Mattel Foundation. **Purpose:** To encourage family participation in schools. **Activities:** Sponsors a national "Take Our Parents to School Week;" coordinates media events that promote time off work for parents to participate in schools; and develops coalitions of parents, educators, and public officials in eight cities, including San Antonio, Philadelphia, Portland, and Birmingham. Publishes guides and other materials that help parents and teachers work together. **Contact:** Wendy Russell, Field Director • Hand in Hand, 1001 Connecticut Avenue NW, Suite 310, Washington, DC 20036 • Phone: (800) 953-HAND • Fax: (202) 872-4050 • E-mail: hand@iel.org

Home Instruction Program for Preschool Youngsters USA (HIPPY)

Description: An international network of families and educators. **Purpose:** To help families create home environments that help preschool children learn and get prepared for school. Focuses on involving hard-to-reach families that have low incomes and low levels of education. **Activities:** The HIPPY national office publishes and distributes activity packets. Local programs conduct home visits and group meetings for families. **Contact:** Miriam Westheimer, Executive Director • Home Instruction Program for Preschool Youngsters USA, Teachers College, Columbia University, 525 West 120th Street, Box 113, New York, NY 10027 • Phone: (212) 678-3500 • Fax: (212) 678-4136

Institute for Responsive Education (IRE)

Description: A nonprofit, public-interest research and advocacy organization founded in 1973. **Purpose:** To promote citizen participation in educational decision making as the foundation of school improvement. **Activities:** IRE provides research, policy development, and on-site technical assistance to support family-school-community partnerships and school improvement. Sponsors the League of Schools Reaching Out, an international network of 90 schools working to improve learning through partnerships between families and communities. Publishes a journal, *New Schools, New Communities.* **Contact:** Tony Wagner, President • Institute for Responsive Education, Northeastern University, 50 Nightingale Hall, Boston, MA 02115 • Phone: (617) 373-2595 • Fax: (617) 373-8924 • E-mail: t.wagner@nunet.neu.edu

National Asian Family-School Partnership Project Description: A network of family-advocacy programs sponsored by the National Coalition of Advocates for Students. **Purpose:** To support the involvement of immigrant Asian families in public schools. **Activities:** Supports pilot projects in six cities that connect families to social service agencies, provide translators, and organize retreats. Each project focuses on different Asian immigrant groups. The national organization brings educators together with Asian families, offers workshops to help bridge the cultural gap between immigrant families and public schools, and establishes parent groups to represent Asian concerns in the schools. It also hosts conferences and publishes books and a newsletter, *Network News,* to help promote these initiatives. **Contact:** Bouy Te, Project Director • National Asian Family-School Partnership Project, National Coalition of Advocates for Students, 100 Boylston Street, Suite 737, Boston, MA 02116 • Phone: (617) 357-8507 • Fax: (617) 357-9549

National Coalition for Parent Involvement in Education (NCPIE) Description: A coalition of major educational associations and child-advocacy groups. **Purpose:** To encourage the involvement of families in education and to foster relationships between homes, schools, and communities. **Activities:** Provides resources and legislative information to membership organizations to help promote parent involvement. **Contact:** Sue Ferguson, Chairperson • National Coalition for Parent Involvement in Education, 1201 16th Street NW, PO Box 39, Washington, DC 20036 • Phone: (202) 822-8405 • Fax: (202) 872-4050 • E-mail: ferguson@iel.org

"When well implemented, these six types of family involvement help schools reach important goals: parenting, communicating, volunteering, helping children learn at home, participating in school decision making, and collaborating with the community."

Joyce Epstein,[5] Director, Center on School, Family, and Community Partnerships, The Johns Hopkins University

The National PTA Description: National child-advocacy organization. **Purpose:** To promote the welfare of children in the home, school, and community, bringing parents and teachers together to cooperate in the education of children. **Activities:** Publishes materials for families and PTA leaders and supports affiliated local and state chapters in schools throughout the country. Offers training and leadership programs at national and state levels, and sponsors conferences on increasing the role of parents in education. **Contact:** Patty Yoxall, Director of Public Relations • The National PTA, 330 North Wabash Avenue, Suite 2100, Chicago, IL 60611 • Phone: (312) 670-6782 • Fax: (312) 670-6783 • URL: http://www.pta.org

National Urban League (NUL) Description: A nonprofit, community-based, social service and civil rights organization founded in 1910 with 114 affiliates in 34 states and the District of Columbia. **Purpose:** To assist African-Americans achieve economic and social equality. **Activities:** Provides information and training to families, educational administrators, and policy makers about issues that affect African-Americans. Sponsors employment and career-development programs. Supports research and outreach to increase public awareness of the conditions of African-Americans and to build bridges between different races in a pluralistic society. With a grant from the Pew Charitable Trusts, NUL is developing academic benchmarks to help parents measure their children's progress. **Contact:** Hugh Price, President and Chief Executive Officer • National Urban League, 500 East 62nd Street, New York, NY 10021 • Phone: (212) 310-9011 • Fax: (212) 755-2140 • URL: http://www.nul.org

Parent Institute for Quality Education (PIQUE)
Description: Advocacy institute for parents and families. **Purpose:** To help families become effective partners in their children's education. **Activities:** Offers training courses to parents covering topics requested by families, including ways to help their children learn both at school and home, how to get the most out of parent-teacher conferences, and how school systems function. PIQUE reaches out to all communities, with an emphasis on immigrants who may have different cultural expectations of schools or whose own education was curtailed at an early age. **Contact:** Patricia O. Mayer, Executive Director • Parent Institute for Quality Education, 6306 Riverdale Street, San Diego, CA 92120 • Phone: (619) 285-9905 • Fax: (619) 285-0865

Clear View Charter School, Chula Vista, CA

Parents' Educational Resource Center (PERC) Description: Membership organization of more than 2,000 families and professionals established in 1989 by the Charles & Helen Schwab Foundation. **Purpose:** To provide families with information and guidance relating to learning disabilities. **Activities:** Provides information and referral services by telephone or at the Center. Offers outreach seminars to San Francisco Bay Area communities. Maintains a resource library and publishes the *Parent Journal.* **Contact:** Amy J. Hughes, Program Director • Parents' Educational Resource Center, 1660 South Amphlett Boulevard, Suite 200, San Mateo, CA 94402 • Phone: (415) 655-2410 • Fax: (415) 655-2411 • E-mail: perc@netcom.com

Center on School, Family, and Community Partnerships Description: Research and development organization. **Purpose:** To study how families, schools, and communities can work together to strengthen their relationships and improve student performance. **Activities:** Conducts research, analyzes policies, and publishes information. Their National Network of Partnership-2000 Schools helps schools and states improve school-family-community connections. **Contact:** Joyce L. Epstein, Director • Center on School, Family, and Community Partnerships, Johns Hopkins University, 3505 North Charles Street, Baltimore, MD 21218 • Phone: (410) 516-8800 • (410) 516-8890 • E-mail: sfc@scov.csos.jhu.edu • URL: http://scov.csos.jhu.edu/p2000/p2000.html

School Development Program (SDP) Description: Established in 1968 as a collaboration between Yale University and the New Haven Public Schools, this school-improvement program is now used in more than 300 schools nationwide. **Purpose:** To build support systems between families and school staff, creating a better learning environment for students both at school and home. **Activities:** Helps school districts create and implement a healthy learning environment for the entire community based on three key strategies: a comprehensive school plan to address academic achievement, social environment, and public relations; staff development; and evaluation and modification of the plan to incorporate changes. Also publishes a newsletter, *Newsline.* **Contact:** Norris M. Haynes, Associate Professor and Director of Research • School Development Program, Child Study Center, Yale University, 230 South Frontage Road, New Haven, CT 06520 • Phone: (203) 785-2548 • Fax: (203) 785-3359 • E-mail: haynesnm@maspo1.mas.yale.edu

Parents for Public Schools, Inc. Description: A national organization with community-based chapters in 20 states. **Purpose:** To support enrollment in public schools and to provide families with a voice in developing education policy. **Activities:** Supports the formation of chapters in individual communities to work closely with superintendents, real estate agents, civic leaders, and the media. Chapters inform the community about public school programs and issues that affect the schools. Some chapters hold community forums on topics such as school finance and school safety; publish guides and newsletters; offer tours of local schools to parents; or set up committees that give families a voice in setting local educational priorities. **Contact:** Kelly Butler, Executive Director • Parents for Public Schools, Inc., PO Box 12807, Jackson, MS 39236 • Phone: (800) 880-1222 • Fax: (601) 982-0002 • E-mail: PPSchapter@aol.com

Periodicals

Children's Software Revue Description: A bimonthly newsletter for teachers and parents. **Focus:** Provides evaluations of children's software products to promote better use of technology at school and in the home. Software is field-tested by families, teachers, and students. **Publisher:** Active Learning Associates, Flemington, NJ • Phone: (800) 993-9499.

Education Today Description: Complimentary newsletter published eight times a year. **Focus:** Keeps parents informed about school reform. Each issue focuses on a popular area of concern, such as communicating with schools or supporting learning at home. Includes reviews of relevant publications and resources. **Publisher:** Educational Publishing Group, Boston, MA • Phone: (800) 927-6006.

> *"Much of the time, the problem between schools and families is simple fear. The families we work with are often afraid to approach teachers or administrators. They don't realize that educators, too, are often afraid to reach out to families from unfamiliar cultures."*
>
> Bouy Te,[6] Project Director, National Asian Family-School Partnership, National Coalition of Advocates for Students

Exceptional Parent Description: A monthly magazine for parents and educators. **Focus:** Explores issues of concern to families raising children and young adults with disabilities, as well as the professionals who work with them. Topics range from assistive technologies and classroom environments to health issues and family life. **Publisher:** Psy-Ed, Brookline, MA • Phone: (800) 247-8080.

KidsVoice Alert Description: Quarterly newsletter. **Focus:** Provides updates on developments in California public schools for members of KidsVoice, a grassroots parent organization. Tracks legislation, changes in school district policy, and new publications of interest to families and children. **Publisher:** KidsVoice, San Rafael, CA • Phone: (415) 721-4204.

Family PC Description: A magazine for computer-using families. **Focus:** Provides reviews of hardware and software, including educational products. Articles and columns offer resource information and ideas for family use of multimedia technologies. **Publisher:** Family PC, Des Moines, IA • Phone: (800) 413-9749.

Readings

Chavkin, Nancy F., ed. **Families and Schools in a Pluralistic Society.** *State University of New York Press: Albany, NY, 1993.* Phone: (800) 666-2211. ● Written by educational researchers, this compilation of articles examines the role of the family in schools. It presents research and current practices and offers strategies to increase minority parent involvement.

Harvard Family Research Project. **Raising Our Future: Families, Schools, and Communities Joining Together.** *Harvard Family Research Project, Graduate School of Education, Harvard University: Cambridge, MA, 1995.* Phone: (617) 496-4304. ● Provides parents, educators, and community leaders with profiles of more than 80 family involvement programs around the country. Also includes a comprehensive listing of resources, organizations, and publications.

> "When parents are involved in their children's education at home, their children do better in school. When parents are involved at school, their children not only go further, the schools become better for all children."
>
> Anne T. Henderson,[7] Education Policy Consultant, Center for Law and Education

Rutherford, Barry, ed. **Creating Family/School Partnerships.** *National Middle School Association: Columbus, OH, 1995.* Phone: (800) 528-6672. ● Provides a review of research and literature on family and community involvement with schools at the middle-grades level. Gives educators, parents, and community members summaries of programs and strategies that increase parent and community participation in education, including home activities and involvement in partnership and school restructuring efforts.

Kellaghan, Thomas, Kathryn Sloane, Benjamin Alvarez, et al. **The Home Environment and School Learning: Promoting Parental Involvement in the Education of Children.** *Jossey-Bass: San Francisco, CA, 1993.* Phone: (800) 956-7739. ● Directed toward educators and policy makers, this book presents research showing that the home environment has more of an impact on student learning than socioeconomic status or cultural heritage. It provides examples of ways parents can be helped to support their children and promote learning.

Levine, James A. and Edward W. Pitt. **New Expectations: Community Strategies for Responsible Fatherhood.** *The Families and Work Institute: New York, NY, 1995.* Phone: (212) 465-2044 ext. 237. ● A resource book that outlines strategies, identifies programs, and recommends readings that encourage greater paternal involvement in children's education.

Comer, James P., Norris M. Haynes, Edward T. Joyner, et al., eds. **Rallying the Whole Village: The Comer Process for Reforming Education.** *Teachers College Press: New York, NY, 1996.* Phone: (800) 575-6566. ● Explores the theory and practice of the renowned School Development Program that links parents and educators in support of children.

Henderson, Anne T., and Nancy Berla, eds. **A New Generation of Evidence: The Family is Critical to Student Achievement.** *National Committee for Citizens in Education: Washington, DC, 1994.* Phone: (202) 462-7688. ● This report describes and analyzes the research on collaborations among families, communities, and schools. Concludes that schools must plan and sustain efforts to involve families.

Rioux, J. William, and Nancy Berla. **Innovations In Parent & Family Involvement.** *Eye on Education: Princeton Junction, NJ, 1993.* Phone: (609) 395-0005. ● Describes parent involvement programs across the country for preschool through grade 12 in rural, suburban, and urban areas. Includes descriptions of program goals and the schools and communities involved, evaluations, and contact information.

> *"Many minority parents are unfamiliar with the expectations of schools, and many teachers and administrators are unfamiliar with the parenting practices and cultural strengths of minority families. If children are to achieve their potential, parents and schools must understand each other's cultures, goals, hopes, and needs."*
>
> Siobhan Nicolau,[8] President, Hispanic Policy Development Project

Shore, Kenneth. **The Parents' Public School Handbook: How to Make the Most of Your Child's Education, from Kindergarten through Middle School.** *Simon & Schuster: New York, NY, 1994.* Phone: (800) 223-2336. ● This resource for parents provides information about public schools and outlines ways parents can be involved in their children's education. Encourages parents to insist on having a voice in schools.

Shartrand, Angela, Holly Kreider, and Marji Erickson-Warfield. **Preparing Teachers to Involve Parents: A National Survey of Teacher Education Programs.** *Harvard Family Research Project, Graduate School of Education, Harvard University: Cambridge, MA, 1994.* Phone: (617) 496-4304. ● A survey of teacher education programs that include parent involvement as an integral component in preparing new teachers.

Papert, Seymour. **The Connected Family: Bridging the Digital Generation Gap.** *Longstreet Press: Marietta, GA, 1996.* Phone: (770) 980-1488. ● This book offers parents and educators ways to explore issues related to learning with computers. It comes with a CD-ROM and has a Web site at http://www.ConnectedFamily.com.

U.S. Department of Education. **Strong Families, Strong Schools: Building Community Partnerships for Learning.** *USDOE: Washington, DC, 1994.* Phone: (800) 872-5327. ● This report gives specific suggestions for parents, teachers, and business people to help families become more involved in schools. Describes the U.S. Department of Education's "Strong Families, Strong Schools" initiative.

Contact Information

[1]**Don Davies** Founder • Institute for Responsive Education, Northeastern University, 50 Nightingale Hall, Boston, MA 02215 • Phone: (617) 373-8275 • Fax: (617) 373-8924

[2]**Norris M. Haynes** Director of Research, and **James P. Comer** Director • School Development Program, Yale Child Study Center, 230 South Frontage Road, New Haven, CT 06520 • Phone: (203) 785-2548 • Fax: (203) 785-3359 • E-mail: haynesm@maspo1.mas.yale.edu

[3]**Mary D. Colón** Co-Chair of Redesign • 3200 Cleveland Street NE, Minneapolis, MN 55418 • Phone: (612) 789-6354 • Fax: (612) 627-3100

[4]**Kenyetta Redwood** School Assistant • White Career Academy, Chicago Public Schools, 1136 West 122nd Street, Chicago, IL 60643 • Phone: (773) 535-5671 • Fax: (773) 535-5644

[5]**Joyce Epstein** Director • Center on School, Family and Community Partnerships, The Johns Hopkins University, 3505 North Charles Street, Baltimore, MD 21218 • Phone: (410) 516-8807 • Fax: (410) 516-8890 • E-mail: jepstein@scov.csos.jhu.edu

[6]**Bouy Te** Project Director • National Asian Family-School Partnership, National Coalition of Advocates for Students, 100 Boylston Street, Suite 737, Boston, MA 02116 • Phone: (617) 357-8507 • Fax: (617) 357-9549 • E-mail: BouyTe@aol.com

[7]**Anne T. Henderson** Education Policy Consultant • Center for Law and Education, 1875 Connecticut Avenue NW, Suite 510, Washington, DC 20009 • Phone: (202) 986-3000 • Fax: (202) 462-7687 • E-mail: HN1669@handsnet.org

[8]**Siobhan Nicolau** President • Hispanic Policy Development Project, 36 East 22nd Street, 9th floor, New York, NY 10010 • Phone: (212) 529-9323 • Fax: (212) 477-5395 • E-mail: siobhan96@aol.com

Chapter 6
Connecting Communities

I n an era when institutions that support families are under increasing pressure, more **responsibility** for children is falling to the schools. They are bombarded with demands to provide a **safe** environment in an unsafe world, opportunities to learn new skills, and a broader range of **services** to meet the social, emotional, and physical needs of children and their families.

Many schools have struggled under this burden. Others, like those featured in this chapter, are meeting the **challenge** by bringing together families, businesses, and the community at large. They are transforming themselves into a new kind of school—a **community learning center** that meets the broad needs of citizens, young and old.

Some communities are using the school site as the place to **coordinate** local services for children and their families. In certain cases, this means providing space within a school for medical and dental clinics, social service agencies, and other community groups. In others, it means offering **resource and referral** information and advising parents as they navigate through the frustrating bureaucracies that often prevent the most needy from getting help. The goal is to have healthy and happy students who are better able to focus on **learning.**

A t the same time, more schools are inviting those outside education to become **partners** in children's learning. Educators are asking community members to assist in setting standards for what young people should know and be able to do. They are working together to develop curriculum and learning experiences that link academics with **real-world** challenges. The communities are **extensions** of the classroom where teachers and students are spending time learning at offices, hospitals, factories, libraries, museums, parks, and theaters. Community service programs give students opportunities to apply what they've learned in class, while letting them give something back to their hometowns. And members of the community share their knowledge and act as mentors to kids who may have few positive role models in their lives.

Technology can enhance the **connections** between schools and communities. E-mail, computer networks, and other communication technologies allow community members to take advantage of local **resources** from home and school, 24 hours a day. Schools are becoming technological **hubs,** opening their doors for adult computer classes, Internet access, video conferencing, and other services not available elsewhere in the community.

In a growing number of communities, schools are **multipurpose** facilities used for adult education, childcare, teen programs, and recreational and cultural activities. Schools have always helped shape the social, civic, and economic **life** of our towns and cities. By extending their hours of operation and offering a wider range of programs and activities, many are now making even greater **contributions** to the local quality of life. ●

Imagine the Possibilities

BY MICHELE CAHILL

a

It's a Thursday evening in July and Joanne Diaz is pulling her car into the parking lot of the Daly Community Learning Center a few miles from her home. She's exhausted from a long day as an administrative assistant at a local hospital and grateful that she doesn't have to face the second shift of family life alone.

While Daly includes the school where her 14-year-old son, Jason, will enter the ninth grade in the fall, it is much more than a school. It's

traditionally served as stabilizing forces in young people's lives. Instead of following the trend of expecting educators to serve not only as teachers, but also as parents, social workers, counselors, doctors, protectors, mentors, role models, and friends to increasing numbers of children, these centers bring in other professionals to take on the responsibilities for which they have been trained. The centers also mobilize the talents of parents, young people, and other residents to contribute

common ground

the center of community life for thousands of children and adults, open all year from early in the morning until late at night. It's nothing less than a new kind of societal institution—one designed to meet the full range of children's developmental needs, to strengthen and support families, to advance the knowledge and skills of adults, to serve as a connection to health and social services, and to be a focal point of civic life.

Daly (named in tribute to New York City principal Patrick Daly, who was shot to death by stray bullets from gang members while trying to contact a troubled student after school) is a fictitious composite of the many school-community centers springing up around the country. I call them "community learning centers or CLCs."

CLCs are being created in response to the weakening of other institutions—such as families, churches, and communities—that have

to youth and community development. The mix of services offered in today's centers varies widely based on local needs and priorities, but my imaginary Daly represents many of the programs and philosophies these evolving institutions have in common.

Support for Children and Families Like so many parents, Joanne worries about Jason getting involved with drugs or other negative temptations of adolescence. She's grateful that he's spending the summer participating in Daly's many programs: teen sports, cultural arts, community service,

Michele Cahill[1] is the vice president and director of the Youth Development Institute, Fund for the City of New York.

for learning

youth entrepreneurship, career exploration, and education programs. Jason is a member of the Center's drama group and loves to explore the World Wide Web at the computer center, but his favorite activity is one that exposes him to career options by matching him with community mentors. Through these encounters, Jason has set his sights on becoming either an engineer or an architect.

CLCs like Daly help to ensure that vulnerable children grow up in a positive, supportive atmosphere. The aim of these institutions is to mobilize community members to form close and nurturing relationships with kids in an era when family members and friends are often absent or negative influences.

Through a variety of broad-based programs, CLCs like Daly help to ensure that vulnerable children grow up in a positive, supportive atmosphere. The aim of these institutions is to mobilize community members to form close and nurturing relationships with kids in an era when family members and friends are often absent or negative influences. In simple terms, they give kids a safe place to go, challenging things to do, friends with whom they can bond, caring adults to guide them, and opportunities to make informed decisions about their lives.

Joanne's first stop at Daly is to pick up her nine-year-old daughter, Rebecca, from the summer camp for elementary school children. Under the guidance of several educators, Rebecca and the other students in the program use Daly's art rooms, science labs, auditorium, library, swimming pool, computer center, gardens, playing fields, and gymnasium for recreational and educational activities. Rebecca is particularly excited about working on an oral history of her hometown, for which she's taking photographs and recording interviews with local senior citizens. She'll assemble the material into a multimedia presentation to show at the end-of-summer Daly Family Festival.

When she sees her mother at her classroom door, Rebecca excitedly tells her about everything she's done that day. Then the two head to the dining room to meet Jason for the weekly Family Dinner and Game Night. They share a spaghetti supper with other families they've met at the Center, swapping community news and gossip. Afterwards, while Rebecca plays Mousetrap and Jason shoots baskets with friends, Joanne browses the Center's parenting library for advice on how to answer her daughter's recent questions about babies and sex.

Daly's support programs for youth and families, as well as its other services, are made possible by partnerships between schools and public and private service organizations. The community has changed its definition of a "school" from an age-segregated and limited-use building that's the exclusive turf of school district employees, to a social institution that's a setting for activities run cooperatively by many different individuals and groups. In some ways this arrangement is similar to the Latin American plaza, where community members can find diverse services offered by interdependent entities, which collectively form the social infrastructure of the community.

Obviously, the practical issues of operating a community learning center can be formidable. They range from big questions such as where to get the money to fund such an ambitious institution to small, but important ones, like how to assure educators that classrooms won't be trashed if they're also used by community organizations while school is out. There's ample experience from existing school and community partnerships, however, to show that these hurdles can be overcome if both educators and others are truly committed to meeting young people's needs.

Centers of Lifelong Learning Joanne loves working at the hospital, but feels ready for something more challenging and rewarding than a clerical job. She's decided to expand her skills to become a physician's assistant so, two nights each week, she takes an anatomy course at Daly, where several adult classes are offered in conjunction with a local community college. The Center provides evening childcare for Rebecca and teen programs for Jason, so Joanne can try to improve her life without worrying about who will watch her kids.

The Center's extensive technology infrastructure is one of the most important resources available for Joanne and the other adults who come to Daly for additional job training or to pursue their interests. In making her decision about what new career to pursue, Joanne used Daly's computer network to find information about occupations and employment trends. Using e-mail, she contacted professional associations and asked questions of experts in the field about what their jobs are really like. Because she can't afford to have a computer at home, she's glad that such technology is available in a public place.

Just as health clubs offer communities specialized equipment, programs, and support to keep the body fit, CLCs offer resources to keep the mind active. They represent a civic commitment to an educated populace, which benefits local schools, employers, and society. They serve as models, showing young people that learning will continue to be important throughout their lives. And experience shows they increase family involvement in efforts to restructure and improve schools.

Connection to Services and Civic Life Joanne feels lucky to have a steady job with good benefits, but she knows that many of her neighbors aren't so fortunate. They depend on Daly as a link to health and social services. These range from the

Center's on-site pediatric clinic to its affiliated network of government and community agencies that help children and adults cope with crises such as unemployment, alcohol or drug dependency, child or spousal abuse, and homelessness. Such services are coordinated through the school under the simple assumption that children can't learn if their basic health and welfare needs aren't met.

Daly is also a center of civic life for the community. During the recent mayoral election, Joanne attended a forum at which she was able to question candidates about their positions on proposed programs. Several organizations meet regularly at the Center, drawing people together for events like anti-violence discussions and neighborhood cleanup days. The community views Daly as a place where people can come together to discuss issues and solve problems, meet with public officials, and volunteer their time and talents.

The Center's extensive technology infrastructure is one of the most important resources available for Joanne and the other adults who come to Daly for additional job training or to pursue their interests.

Educators at Daly have students whose needs are fulfilled and, therefore, who can focus more on learning. They have also been freed of the burden of being all things to all students; the enormous workload of ensuring that kids are cared for—and cared about—is spread among many partners. And educators are more satisfied with their jobs because they are now truly in tune with their fundamental missions of developing healthy, happy young people and being a beacon of lifelong learning for community members.

Thanks to the Center's activities, Daly's community is a safer, more secure place to live for both young and old. Residents have numerous ways to expand their knowledge and skills, creating an environment of constant improvement that boosts the local quality of life. The community boasts an active, energetic civic culture that brings neighbors together to help one another. Most of all, the community cares for its young people, and they know it. ●

From the Front Lines

BY STEPHANY HOOVER

coming together as a community

It was my third day as coordinator of the Byck Family Resource Center at Dann C. Byck Elementary School in Louisville, Ky. The "Center" was just me and a chair in the school's office. So far I'd done little but answer the phone.

A pregnant woman walked in with one small child in her arms and another clinging to her leg. The mother held a brown bill—a notice from the utility company that her power was going to be cut off. She said she'd just come from the hospital. The child clutching her leg had recently had a tumor removed from his eardrum and the doctor had given her a $75 bottle of medicine for him, but it required refrigeration. The mother was in tears over how to chill the medication without electricity.

She was just the first of many parents and students who have come to the Center for help over the past few years. The idea behind centers like ours is that school is the logical place for communities to connect low-income school children and their parents with the health and social services they need to deal with the many ills affecting them—homelessness, hunger, alcohol and drug abuse, mental illness, and violence. After teaching first and second grades at Byck for seven years, I knew that such problems prevented many kids from learning. No matter how creative my fellow teachers and I were, we found that by the time our students entered kindergarten, we were literally five years too late to help them.

Our Center was made possible by the Kentucky Education Reform Act of 1990, which provided for full-service family resource centers to be established in or near elementary schools where at least 20 percent of the student population is eligible for free school meals. Byck qualified handily, because 92 percent of our students receive free or reduced-price lunches. Our community is typical of many inner city neighborhoods: 79 percent of families in our census tract make do with incomes below the federally defined poverty level, 71 percent are headed by women, and 60 percent of adults lack a high school diploma.

Our school staff was eager to establish a family resource center and applied for state funding as soon as it was available. Our proposal was accepted in July of 1991, and the principal hired me to lead the program.

The Byck Family Resource Center helps people with basic needs. We maintain a food pantry for hungry families and a clothes closet filled with underwear, socks, shoes, and other apparel for kids who do not have enough clothes to keep clean for a week or who have "accidents" while at school. We have a licensed after school and summer childcare program, and we train local childcare providers to meet state-licensing requirements.

Among the many other services we offer is The Cradle School, which prepares children from birth to age four for kindergarten. The children

Later the same day, the woman called after arranging to keep her utility service. She was sobbing with joy. She told her story to everyone she knew and people started showing up for help, first in a trickle, then a flood. That's okay, though. I know how to swim.

participate in early childhood education classes and their parents learn about subjects such as health, nutrition, and child development. Another program, Families in Training, gives new and expectant parents information about prenatal and postnatal care through classes and home visits. The Center also coordinates health services for children and adults—immunizations, physicals, hearing and vision screening, and mental health counseling can be obtained on-site or by referral to a neighborhood clinic.

Since social and recreational opportunities for children and parents are almost nonexistent in our community, that's another area we address. One night a week we baby-sit the kids so a group of moms (The Tuesday Night Tootsies) and dads (The Tootsie Pops) can do whatever they want at the school—play volleyball, hold baby showers, sing, make crafts. We arrange special events such

as an evening in the computer lab, during which parents can learn about keyboarding, word processing, and working with graphics. At another time, parents and students might get together to use the Center's laptops to compose stories and create Christmas cards. This access to technology, as limited as it is, gives even the poorest parents the chance to develop computer literacy skills.

The secret to making the Center work is our close partnerships with other community organizations. I'm in constant contact with government agencies, service organizations, churches, social service providers, charities, businesses, and others—all of whom come together to help individuals when they need it, rather than bog them down in the bureaucracy.

The woman who came to me for help with her utility bill was the first to benefit from this partnership. I immediately called the local gas and electric company and determined how much money they'd accept to leave her power on. Then I gave her the phone numbers of community agencies that would help her pay the bill. I was tempted to make the calls myself, but decided that the Center would serve parents better by empowering them to solve their own problems.

Later the same day, the woman called after arranging to keep her utility service. She was sobbing with joy. She told her story to everyone she knew and people started showing up for help, first in a trickle, then a flood. That's okay, though. I know how to swim.

This work is often heartbreaking. I sometimes find myself crying along with the families I try to help. But mostly I get great satisfaction from it. The reward isn't a plaque on the wall, but something more personal. My parents died about eight months apart a couple of years ago. During both of their funerals at my church, I looked behind me and saw pews filled with parents, children, and babies from the Center. They had come all the way across town to be with me, to support me and cry with me. They helped me in all the ways my job description says I should help them. They are some of the most beautiful people I've ever known in my life. ●

Stephany Hoover[2] is the coordinator of the Byck Family Resource Center.

Snapshots

Where the Neighborhood Hangs Out

"If our kids are not home in the evening," parent Lidia Aguasanta says, "they're usually at school in some supervised activity." But it's not just the children in New York City's Washington Heights neighborhood who find a reason to be at Intermediate School (IS) 218 after hours. One parent says that, whether for recreation, career training, community-development activities, or health and social services, "It's where the neighborhood hangs out."

Indeed, IS 218 has become a hub of life for the neighborhood. "People say it's hard to get parents involved in their children's schooling because they have so many pressing problems," says Rosa Agosto, community schools director for the Children's Aid Society, who is based at the school. "We make that involvement possible by providing the support parents need at school."

The health clinic on-site, for example, means families don't have to contend with unfamiliarity, long waits, and anonymity at city hospitals. From 7 AM to 10 PM every weekday, the clinic offers medical exams, immunizations, and dental services for a nominal fee. A full-time social worker makes sure community members get other services they need. If a student gets sick or has personal problems, professional help is just down the hall, not across town. "We can help children here at the school as soon as they need it," Agosto says.

The school has a "Family Room," furnished with sofas, a television, and a constant flow of coffee, where parents can deepen their understanding and involvement not only in their children's education, but also in community issues. A sense of ownership prevails, according to Ariel Briones, a recent graduate who comes back to volunteer in the school library: "The adults and older kids here taught us to contribute back to our community—not just live in it." ●

Intermediate School 218 New York Community School District 6, 4600 Broadway, New York, NY 10040 **Contact:** Betty Rosa, Principal • Phone: (212) 567-2322 • Fax: (212) 567-2974

Community Improvements

How can schools engage young people in work that not only advances their education, but also the quality of life in their communities? The answer in West Philadelphia is the "university-assisted community school," an effort to link area public schools with the University of Pennsylvania's (Penn) resources and technical expertise. The linkage is provided by the West Philadelphia Improvement Corps (WEPIC), which helps schools provide year-round daycare, health care, social services, and educational and recreational activities for neighborhood residents of all ages.

At Turner Middle School, where WEPIC has been active the longest, the University provides a much-needed commodity: the energy and expertise of trained adults. University students and teachers from more than 40 WEPIC community-action classes at Penn work with Turner's teachers. Their focus is on health, a priority identified in a neighborhood survey. In one project, seventh graders are trained to teach elementary school students how to improve their diets. Work like this "is fun," says seventh grader Mikail Aswald, "but I also learned that it feels good to help my neighborhood." ●

Center for Community Partnerships University of Pennsylvania, 3440 Market Street, Suite 440, Philadelphia, PA 19104 **Contact:** Joann Weeks, Director, WEPIC Replication Project • Phone: (215) 898-0240 • Fax: (215) 573-2096 • E-mail: weeks@ pobox.upenn.edu • URL: http://www. upenn.edu/ccp/

Strengthening Families and Communities

A child's success in school depends partly on the overall health of the child's family and community. That's why the Denver Public Schools joined in partnership with the city of Denver, businesses, community organizations, parents, and foundations to create Family Resource Schools (FRS). FRSs increase the range of programs and activities offered by public schools in inner city neighborhoods. They strengthen the capacity of both families and communities to support children's learning.

Cheltenham Elementary School is one of 11 FRS sites. Before launching its effort, parents and residents at Cheltenham held focus group meetings to determine the needs of their neighborhood. As a result, the school offers programs and activities that can extend into evenings and on weekends. Cheltenham's programs include adult and parenting education; workshops on leadership, employment, and gang prevention; tutoring programs with parent participation; computer training; family math and reading programs; and childcare. City officials and the Department of Housing and Urban Development also help provide life-skills workshops, assistance in securing affordable housing, and an electronic database linking the school to the Department of Social Services.

Family Resource Schools Denver Public Schools, 975 Grant Street, Denver, CO 80203 **Contact:** Bruce Atchison, Director • Phone: (303) 764-3587 • Fax: (303) 839-8001

Here's what one parent has to say about the FRS program at Cheltenham: "The coordinator, Patsy Roybal, has worked wonders for the Spanish-speaking parents here. Before she came, we felt left out of things. Now we really feel that the FRS room is our home away from home. She's gotten us all involved in our kids' education and organizes workshops to teach us how to do that effectively. Because of FRS, putting my three kids through school here has been a wonderful experience." ●

A Center for Family Support

"Most of our students are poor and we try to provide them with the services they need to survive and succeed," says Mary Skrabucha, coordinator for the Family Support Services Center at O'Farrell Community School in San Diego, Calif. "But, to serve the individual student effectively, you often have to serve the entire family," she adds.

The Family Support Services Center occupies an entire wing of the school's main building and is a measure of O'Farrell's commitment to serving the physical, emotional, and social needs of its 1,400 middle-school students. At the Center, an assortment of full-time social workers, psychologists, and volunteers from various agencies provide a mix of preventative health care, gang-prevention workshops, and one-on-one counseling for parents, students, and staff.

Creating closer connections between the school and its community is a central goal of all significant activities at O'Farrell. The Center's staff meets regularly with teachers to discuss individual students and to plan ways to keep a sense of safety and inclusiveness throughout the school. Students are expected to play an active role in maintaining ties to the community—they are required to perform 12 hours of community service and give a tour of the school to an adult visitor.

Eighth grader John Roman knows O'Farrell is unusual. "I have adults I can trust here. I have counselors who work with me one-on-one and people who make it their business to look after me and my family. I know other schools don't have that." ● ★ FILM

Family Support Services Center O'Farrell Community School: Center for Advanced Academic Studies, San Diego City Schools, 6130 Skyline Drive, San Diego, CA 92114 **Contact:** Bob Stein, Chief Educational Officer • Phone: (619) 263-3009 • Fax: (619) 263-4339 • E-mail: bob_stein@qm.sdcs.k12.ca.us • URL: http://www165.24.15.174

"I have adults I can trust here. I have counselors who work with me one-on-one and people who make it their business to look after me and my family. I know other schools don't have that."

Listening to the Community

Before it opened in 1992, the Vaughn Family Center asked residents of its San Fernando, Calif., neighborhood how it could help improve the community. The

"Parents feel that they are being heard, that their experiences are important to someone else, and that everyone can make a difference."

Center's governing board, composed of half parents, and half social service providers, listened to the community and heard its pleas for economic renewal. So, in addition to programs to help keep children healthy and thriving, the Center adopted economic development as one of its goals.

One result of this focus is a program known as the Urban Village, which offers job training, computer classes, and employment counseling. In an effort to provide productive alternatives for youth gang members, the Urban Village helps them acquire the academic and job skills they need to become employable and then helps them find jobs.

The Family Center is located at the Vaughn Next Century Learning Center, a charter elementary school. Its presence has helped improve relations in the community. Most of the Center's activities, including childcare, medical and dental screenings, parenting classes, and a variety of soccer leagues and other recreational

activities for children, operate in a bilingual format. The Center has become a safe place in a troubled neighborhood, according to its director, Yoland Trevino. "Parents feel that they are being heard, that their experiences are important to someone else, and that everyone can make a difference." ●

Vaughn Family Center
Vaughn Next Century Learning Center, 13330 Vaughn Street, San Fernando, CA 91340 **Contact:** Lily Gonzalez, Administrative Coordinator • Phone: (818) 834-1485 • Fax: (818) 834-1492

Help Yourself by Helping Your Community

At Countee Cullen Community Center, a teen council promotes activities that encourage youngsters to take a proprietary interest in their neighborhood. The Center's teens produce public service videos, organize street cleanups, publish a newspaper, and operate a nighttime teen lounge. "Here, kids learn to help themselves by helping their community," says

Countee Cullen Community Center
P.S. 194, District 5, 242 West 144th Street, New York, NY 10030 **Contact:** Joseph Stewart, Co-Director • Phone: (212) 234-4500 • Fax: (212) 234-4694 • E-mail: BCountee@thorn.net • URL: http://www.thorn.net/~bcountee

Joe Stewart, co-director of the Center. They even successfully petitioned a billboard company to remove a Virginia Slims billboard from the neighborhood and replace it with an ad for the United Negro College Fund.

The Center is operated by the Rheedlen Center for Children and Families, a nonprofit organization, and is part of a citywide "Beacons" program that connects community services to neighborhoods. Located at Public School 194, the Center is open from 9 AM to sometimes well past midnight serving residents of all ages. Center staff provide case management for social services, job-readiness training, adult

education, and computer classes. The Center helps parents stay connected with their children through support groups, parenting workshops, and family recreational activities. For teens, the Center offers a homework help program as well as a version of Upward Bound, drug awareness programs, late-night basketball, and a movie series. Community identification with the Center is encouraged through high-visibility activities that include voter registration booths, Center t-shirts, and a neighborhood tree-planting project. ●

Many Things to Learn

"I didn't have the opportunity to go to college when I got out of high school. I'm getting that education now through our community education program," says Betty Winston, 72, who was born in West Des Moines, Iowa, and put three children through its schools. Winston is one of many residents benefiting from services offered by the West Des Moines Community School District, a district that for more than 20 years has followed a mission to serve all community residents, not just school-aged children.

The District's commitment to its community is reflected in every aspect of its operations. Parents and community members serve with teachers, business people, and representatives from city government on site improvement teams that set the direction for each of the District's 15 schools. In addition, a community education advisory council conducts a community-needs assessment every few years to determine what kinds of programs should be offered.

Even the District's school buildings have been designed with both student and community use in mind. Computer labs and media centers are open to the public after school hours and during the summer, and some businesses rent them for training sessions. In addition, school buildings are used for community organization meetings, inexpensive summer camps, and for community events, such as the annual Parent University and the Elder Fair. The connection between schools and community will be reinforced even further when the city completes construction of a new library and city offices on a school campus.

Parents and community members like Winston ensure that the schools have a steady supply of volunteers. School events attract as many as 95 percent of the parents, and community volunteers flow in and out of schools daily. "People wonder why we don't leave during the winter snow," Winston says. "I tell them, there are too many things going on in this community that we can take advantage of, too many friends, too many things to learn." ● ★ FILM

West Des Moines Community School District 3550 George M. Mills Civic Parkway • West Des Moines, IA 50265 **Contact:** Linda Sanda, Director of Community Education • Phone: (515) 226-2750 • Fax: (515) 226-2869 • E-mail: sandal@grpw.wdm.k12.ia.us

Networked Services

Technology can help coordinate educational and social services by reducing duplicate paperwork and ensuring that children don't fall through the cracks. That's the goal in Santa Rosa County, Fla., as school officials implement a 1990 state law permitting them to create "Full Service Schools." Using computer networks, the District's 15 schools and local social service providers are building a common database. This allows agencies to share pertinent information about children they serve, from changes of address to awards and achievements. As a bonus, the networks link schools to the Internet and to each other. Ongoing technology training for teachers and paraprofessionals helps to ensure that full advantage is made of the technology.

Technology hasn't replaced the human touch in this county. Multidisciplinary teams meet regularly at schools to provide comprehensive case management to children and families. Integrated educational, health, and social services are offered at or near the school site. In collaboration with the state, the county also offers a low-cost, sliding-scale health plan for children. Adults can go to schools for basic education, college courses, career assistance, and parenting and employment classes. ●

Florida Full Service Schools Santa Rosa County School Board, 603 Canal Street, Milton, FL 32570 **Contact:** Carol Calfee, Project Manager • Phone: (904) 983-5054 • Fax: (904) 983-5011 • E-mail: carolc5990@aol.com

ACCESS TO INFORMATION

Organizations

O'Farrell Community School, San Diego, CA

"As soon as families feel that their opinions are valued, they begin to articulate the kinds of services they need to improve themselves and their community. Working with these families has been the highlight of my career."

Yoland Trevino,[3] Director,
Vaughn Family Center,
Vaughn Next Century Learning Center

Child and Family Policy Center **Description:** A policy-oriented research organization established in 1989. **Purpose:** To create a stronger link between research and policy on issues vital to children and families. **Activities:** Consults with national organizations and foundations on the development of social service reform initiatives. Provides technical assistance to states and communities developing community education programs. Publishes reports on the integration of comprehensive, community-based services. Administers the Iowa Kids Count Initiative, a statewide campaign to invest in families with young children, and operates the National Center for Service Integration Clearinghouse. **Contact:** Charles Bruner, Executive Director • Child and Family Policy Center, Fleming Building, Suite 1021, 218 Sixth Avenue, Des Moines, IA 50309 • Phone: (515) 280-9027 • Fax: (515) 244-8997 • E-mail: HN2228@connectinc.com

Annie E. Casey Foundation
Description: A nonprofit, grant making foundation. **Purpose:** To advance the reform of policies, systems, organizations, and communities to improve the lives of disadvantaged children and their families. **Activities:** Provides funds and technical assistance to initiate, support, and promote reform demonstrations. Disseminates information through videos, reports, and conferences. Publishes *Kids Count Data Book,* an annual report that tracks the educational, social, economic, and physical well-being of American children. **Contact:** Tony Cipollone, Associate Director • Annie E. Casey Foundation, 701 St. Paul Street, Baltimore, MD 21202 • Phone: (410) 223-2926 • Fax: (410) 223-2927 • E-mail: Tony@AECF.org • URL: http://www.aecf.org

Center for Collaboration for Children Description: Research and information initiative operating at all campuses in the California State University system. **Purpose:** To promote working relationships among schools and social service providers to improve school and community-based services for children and families. **Activities:** Provides advice and technical assistance to public agencies, schools, and higher education institutions working together to provide a full range of services. Conducts research and disseminates findings. Publishes *Community Scorecard,* which assesses community health, social, and educational services and guides planning for improvements. **Contact:** Sidney Gardner, Director • Center for Collaboration for Children, California State University, Fullerton, EC 424, Fullerton, CA 92634 • Phone: (714) 773-3313 • Fax: (714) 449-5235 • E-mail: 103250.2112@ compuserve.com

Communities in Schools, Inc. (CIS) **Description:** A nonprofit network of more than 100 local CIS programs across the country. **Purpose:** To champion the connection of community resources with schools to help young people successfully learn, stay in school, and prepare for life. **Activities:** Develops partnerships among schools, social service agencies, businesses, and community groups to create effective stay-in-school programs. Operates CISNet, a computer network that links CIS programs nationwide. **Contact:** Bonnie Nance Frazier, Director of Communications • Communities in Schools, Inc., 1199 North Fairfax Street, Suite 300, Alexandria, VA 22314 • Phone: (703) 519-8999 • Fax: (703) 519-7123 • E-mail: cis@cisnet.org

Designs for Learning Description: Advocacy organization formed to promote an innovative educational program called "Community Learning Centers." Funded by the C.S. Mott Foundation. **Purpose:** To create powerful learning experiences for all ages by developing new schools and to transform existing programs by increasing their connections to the communities around them. **Activities:** Provides information and technical assistance to schools and school districts nationwide. **Contact:** Wayne Jennings, President • Designs for Learning, 1355 Pierce Butler Route, St. Paul, MN 55104 • Phone: (612) 645-0200 • Fax: (612) 645-0240 • E-mail: wayne@designlearn.com

Family Resource Coalition Description: Membership, consulting, and advocacy organization. **Purpose:** To provide resources and support to programs that serve families. **Activities:** Offers technical assistance, training, and consulting services to schools, community-based programs, and states. Publishes newsletters and manuals, sponsors conferences, and maintains a database of family support policies and programs. **Contact:** Gail Koser, Project Director, STATES Initiative • Family Resource Coalition, 200 South Michigan Avenue, 16th Floor, Chicago, IL 60604 • Phone: (312) 341-0900 • Fax: (312) 341-9361

Kentucky Family Resource/Youth Services Centers Description: School-linked, state-supported centers serving 559 Kentucky communities. **Purpose:** To coordinate and provide services as identified in the Kentucky Education Reform Act and deemed essential for each community to remove barriers to learning. **Activities:** Family Resource Centers, located in or near public elementary schools, provide coordination of and access to preschool childcare; after school childcare; parenting and adult education; and referrals for health and social services. Youth Services Centers, in or near public middle schools and high schools, offer access to employment counseling, training, and placement; summer and part-time job development; mental health counseling; and referrals for health and social services. An advisory council at each center includes parents, community members, and school staff in decision making. **Contact:** Marcia Morganti, Policy Analyst • Kentucky Family Resource/Youth Services Centers, 275 East Main Street, Frankfort, KY 40621 • Phone: (502) 564-4986 • Fax: (502) 564-6108

National Center for Community Education (NCCE) Description: A nonprofit training organization funded by the C.S. Mott Foundation. **Purpose:** To promote community and educational change with an emphasis on community schools. **Activities:** Brings key members of communities together for five days at the organization's headquarters in Flint, Mich., to attend leadership workshops, seminars, and area school visits. Participants focus on topics such as community education development, group facilitation, communications, collaboration, and needs assessment. Publishes a guide for improving community education. **Contact:** Dan Cady, Executive Director • National Center for Community Education, 1017 Avon Street, Flint, MI 48503 • Phone: (810) 238-0463 • Fax: (810) 238-9211 • E-mail: ncce@tir.com

National Community Education Association (NCEA) Description: Membership association for community education directors or coordinators, superintendents, state administrators, education professors, and state legislators. **Purpose:** To promote family and community involvement in public education, interagency partnerships, and lifelong learning opportunities for community residents. **Activities:** Disseminates information and hosts conferences and workshops. Publishes a monthly newsletter, *Community Education,* and the quarterly *Community Education Journal.* **Contact:** Starla Jewell-Kelly, Executive Director • National Community Education Association, 3929 Old Lee Highway, Suite 91-A, Fairfax, VA 22030 • Phone: (703) 359-8973 • Fax: (703) 359-0972 • E-mail: ncea@ids2.idson line. com • URL: http://www.idsonline.com/ncea/index.htm

"Community education brings citizens together to identify needs and link resources in a manner that helps people improve the quality of their lives."

Pat Edwards,[4] Associate Executive Director, National Center for Community Education and Executive on loan from the C.S. Mott Foundation

Human Services Policy Center Description: University-based information organization. **Purpose:** To encourage collaboration among social service providers in fields, such as education and nursing. **Activities:** Offers advice on advocacy and communications strategies. A database and network connects educators, health care professionals, social service providers, and policy makers. The Training for Interprofessional Collaboration program helps agencies become more effective by sharing information and coordinating efforts. **Contact:** Laurie Deppmann, Project Coordinator • Human Services Policy Center, University of Washington, Box 353060, Seattle, WA 98195 • Phone: (206) 685-3135 • Fax: (206) 616-5769 • E-mail: hspcnet@ u.washington.edu • URL: http://weber.u. washington.edu/ ~hspcnews

"Collaboration alone is not the answer if services are of mediocre quality and rendered grudgingly. Professionals must persevere and work respectfully with the people and communities they serve as well as with their colleagues."

Lisbeth Schorr,[5] Director, Project on Effective Interventions, School of Medicine, Harvard University

New York City Beacons Initiative Description: A network of 37 community centers in public schools throughout New York City. The centers are funded by the New York City Department of Youth Services and managed by community-based organizations working collaboratively with school boards, principals, service providers, and advisory boards composed of parents, educators, youth, and church leaders. **Purpose:** To provide services to youth and families before and after school and on weekends. **Activities:** Centers offer a mixture of recreation, social services, and educational and career-training programs. Participants often engage in activities to improve their neighborhoods, such as voter registration drives, street cleanups, and fundraisers. **Contact:** William Barrett, Program Manager • New York City Beacons Initiative, New York City Department of Youth Services, 44 Court Street, Brooklyn, NY 11201 • Phone: (718) 403-5364 • Fax: (718) 330-0964

Schools of the 21st Century Description: A child-care and family-support model developed by the Yale Bush Center in Child Development and Social Policy, adopted by more than 400 schools in 13 states. **Purpose:** To promote programs that help meet the social, nutritional, and educational needs of children and their families. **Activities:** Provides technical assistance and training to affiliated schools that offer before and after school care, childcare for preschoolers, medical screenings and referrals, nutrition help, and adult education classes. **Contact:** Matia Finn-Stevenson, Director • Schools of the 21st Century, Bush Center in Child Development and Social Policy, Yale University, 310 Prospect Street, New Haven, CT 06511 • Phone: (203) 432-9944 • Fax: (203) 432-9945

Smart Valley, Inc. Description: A partnership of 92 high-tech businesses that grew out of a grassroots effort to transform the Silicon Valley into a fully wired community. **Purpose:** To promote development of an electronic infrastructure that links schools, city governments, universities, businesses, and social service agencies. **Activities:** Recommends and publicizes standards for computer hardware and cabling acquired by schools and other public institutions. The Smart Schools' project uses corporate volunteers to train students and teachers on the Internet and develops a bank of donated equipment so that schools do not have to pay all the costs of acquiring the necessary hardware. Special events, such as Smart Schools NetDay, encourage corporate employees to help schools in the area get fully wired. A World Wide Web page serves as a central link for educational and career resources in the South Bay. **Contact:** Karen Greenwood, Project Director • Smart Valley, Inc., 2520 Mission College Boulevard, Suite 202, Santa Clara, CA 95054 • Phone: (408) 562-7707 • Fax: (408) 562-7677 • E-mail: KarenG@svi.org • URL: http://www.svi.org

Periodicals

Community Technology Center Review

Description: Semiannual publication. **Focus:** Covers developments that affect community-wide access to technology, particularly in socially and economically disadvantaged locales. Articles discuss legislation, policy issues, and community technology projects. **Publisher:** Community Technology Centers' Network, Education Development Center, Newton, MA • Phone: (617) 969-7101 ext. 2727.

The Future of Children

Description: A themed journal targeting policy makers, practitioners, professionals, and executives. **Focus:** Issues addressed include the long-term impacts of early childhood programs and the mounting problems faced by today's youth. Includes articles on research, programs, and policy. **Publisher:** Center for the Future of Children, The David and Lucile Packard Foundation, Los Altos, CA • Phone: (415) 948-7658.

The Prevention Report Description: Semiannual newsletter. **Focus:** Each issue looks at efforts to develop family-centered community services, including "one-stop" centers that offer childcare, parenting workshops, and health services. Profiles programs, reviews current research, lists resources, and reports on legislative changes. **Publisher:** National Resource Center for Family Centered Practice, Iowa City, IA • Phone: (319) 335-2200.

West Des Moines Community School District, West Des Moines, IA

Readings

Adler, Louise, and Sid Gardner, eds. **The Politics of Linking Schools and Social Services.** *Falmer Press: Bristol, PA, 1994.* Phone: (215) 785-5800.
● In this collection, leading scholars and practitioners from around the world make the case for linking education and other social services. Outlines roles of various institutions and describes existing programs.

Bruner, Charles, Karen Bell, Claire Brindis, et al. **Charting a Course: Assessing a Community's Strengths and Needs.** *Child and Family Policy Center, National Center for Service Integration: Des Moines, IA, 1993.* Phone: (515) 280-9027.
● This brief discusses strategies, such as the use of focus groups, for assessing community needs and resources as a step toward effective coordination and delivery of services to children and their families. Includes examples from communities that have successfully used these techniques.

"I felt good working on the needs assessment committee planning for lifelong learning for people in our community. When I take night classes at one of our schools, I always notice that just being in a public school classroom gets people more interested and involved in their children's education."

Betty Winston,[8] senior citizen and former member of the Advisory Council for the West Des Moines Community School District ★ **FILM**

Carnegie Council on Adolescent Development. **Great Transitions: Preparing Adolescents for a New Century.** *Carnegie Corporation of New York: New York, NY, 1995.* Phone: (202) 429-7979. ● Looks at ways to provide better community support during the critical stage of early adolescence (ages 11 to 14). Reviews the challenges and problems facing today's youth. Recommends integrating health services, strengthening ties within families, and developing community service programs for youth and adults.

West Des Moines Community School District, West Des Moines, IA

Komoski, P. Kenneth, W. Curtiss Priest. **Creating Learning Communities: Practical, Universal Networking for Learning in Schools and Homes.** *The Educational Products Information Exchange Institute: Hampton Bays, NY, 1996.* Phone: (516) 728-9100. ● This report outlines ideas for developing computer networks to link homes, schools, and communities. Hundreds of lessons drawn from existing network efforts help readers understand both the complexities and possibilities of connecting communities.

Kagan, Sharon L., and Bernice Weissbourd, eds. **Putting Families First: America's Family Support Movement and the Challenge of Change.** *Jossey-Bass: San Francisco, CA, 1994.* Phone: (800) 956-7739. ● This book explores the history, theory, policies, and practices behind efforts to support families. Since families are critical to the successful development of children, the book identifies programs that strengthen them, including those that offer health care, childcare, and links to other social institutions.

Dryfoos, Joy G. **Full-Service Schools: A Revolution in Health and Social Services for Children, Youth, and Families.** *Jossey-Bass: San Francisco, CA, 1994.* Phone: (800) 956-7739.
● The author proposes a comprehensive system of education that brings together health and social services for children and their families at school sites. She describes various types of partnerships between public schools and public agencies, profiles several exemplary programs, and addresses issues of implementation.

Kilbourne, Larry, Larry E. Decker, and Valerie A. Romney. **Rebuilding the Partnership for Public Education.** *Mid-Atlantic Center for Community Education, Curry School of Education, University of Virginia: Charlottesville, VA, 1994.* Phone: (703) 359-8973.
● Traces changes in the traditional roles and relationships among families, communities, and schools and explores the consequences of the breakdown of this partnership. Describes policies, programs, and practices that support education reform and promote successful collaboration among these institutions.

> *"Schools have been at the center of American communities for most of our history. But we are now rediscovering how important it is for schools and communities to work together—it's a prerequisite for serious education reform."*
>
> Sidney Gardner,[9] Director,
> Center for Collaboration for Children,
> California State University, Fullerton

Melaville, Atelia I., Martin J. Blank, and Gelareh Asayesh. **Together We Can: A Guide for Crafting a Profamily System of Education and Human Services.** *U. S. Government Printing Office: Washington, DC, 1993.* Phone: (202) 512-1800.
● This practical guide outlines a five-step process communities can follow to improve the coordination of social services. Includes tips on assessing needs, building community support, preparing staff, and designing and implementing programs. Also contains contact information for relevant programs, organizations, and other resources.

Schorr, Lisbeth B., and Daniel Schorr. **Within Our Reach: Breaking the Cycle of Disadvantage.** *Anchor Books: New York, NY, 1988.* Phone: (800) 232-9872.
● The authors argue that an investment in first-class services for disadvantaged children and their families will result in social and economic benefits to the entire society. They describe various programs that help to reduce poverty and ignorance among children.

Contact Information

[1]**Michele Cahill** Vice President •
Fund for the City of New York,
121 Avenue of the Americas,
New York, NY 10013 •
Phone: (212) 925-6675 •
Fax: (212) 925-5675 •
E-mail: mcahill@fcny.org

[2]**Stephany Hoover** Coordinator •
Byck Family Resource Center,
Dann C. Byck Elementary School,
Jefferson County Public Schools,
2328 Cedar Street, Louisville, KY 40212 •
Phone: (502) 485-8061 •
Fax: (502) 485-8805

[3]**Yoland Trevino** Director • Vaughn
Family Center, Vaughn Next Century
Learning Center, 13330 Vaughn Street,
San Fernando, CA 91340 •
Phone: (818) 834-1485 •
Fax: (818) 834-1492

[4]**Pat Edwards** Executive on loan from the
C.S. Mott Foundation and Associate
Executive Director • National Center
for Community Education,
1017 Avon Street, Flint, MI 48503 •
Phone: (810) 238-0463 •
Fax: (810) 238-9211 •
E-mail: ncce@tir.com

[5]**Lisbeth Schorr** Director •
Project on Effective Interventions,
School of Medicine, Harvard University,
3113 Woodley Road NW,
Washington, DC 20008 •
Phone: (202) 462-3071 •
Fax: (202) 319-7085 •
E-mail: 73134.3670@compuserve.com

[6]**Martin Blank** Senior Associate •
Institute for Educational Leadership, Inc.,
1001 Connecticut Avenue NW, Suite 310,
Washington, DC 20036 •
Phone: (202) 822-8405 ext. 17 •
Fax: (202) 872-4050 •
E-mail: blankm@iel.org

[7]**Wayne Jennings** President • Designs
for Learning, 1355 Pierce Butler Route,
St. Paul, MN 55104 •
Phone: (612) 645-0200 •
Fax: (612) 645-0240 •
E-mail: wayne@designlearn.com

[8]**Betty Winston** Senior Citizen •
Community Education, The Learning
Resource Center, 3550 George M. Mills
Civic Parkway, West Des Moines, IA
50265 • Phone: (515) 226-2750 •
Fax: (515) 226-2869

> *"Effective schools today must connect families with all types of human and community services. As learning centers, schools can become a major force for human growth and community development."*
>
> Larry E. Decker,[10] C.S. Mott Professor,
> College of Education, Florida Atlantic University

[9]**Sidney Gardner** Director • Center for
Collaboration for Children, California
State University, Fullerton, EC 424,
Fullerton, CA 92634 •
Phone: (714) 773-2166 •
Fax: (714) 449-5235 •
E-mail: 73160,1571@compuserve.com

[10]**Larry E. Decker** C.S. Mott Professor •
College of Education, Florida Atlantic
University, Building 47, Room 260,
777 Glades Road, Boca Raton, FL 33431 •
Phone: (561) 367-3599 •
Fax: (561) 367-3613 •
E-mail: ldecker@acc.fau.edu •
URL: http://www.fau.edu.80:divdept/
coe/ledhome.htm

Chapter 7
Business Partnerships

Businesses and education have flirted for decades. At countless meetings and conferences, educators and employers have confided their desire to work **together** to serve the interests of America's young people. They've shared their **perspectives** by visiting each others' classrooms and boardrooms and sitting down for frank discussions of their problems. They've formed **partnerships** to share funding, talent, technology, and other resources. They've sat on panels and stood at podiums to call for increased **cooperation** between the institutions that are shaping the next generation of American adults and the companies who will employ them.

Despite these repeated rendezvous, though, the **relationship** between business and education has remained somewhat distant, like that of a couple who spend a little time together and then retreat to their own separate lives. This chapter talks about efforts to take this relationship to the next step: a truly **committed** partnership that erodes the boundaries between school and the workplace.

More educators and employers are realizing how intimately their **interests** are intertwined. Educators understand that helping our youngest citizens develop the knowledge, skills, and attitudes they'll need in their jobs is a fundamental part of their work, though certainly not their entire mission. Employers recognize that changes in the **workplace** demand employees with the skills to solve problems, work with others, and learn on the job. In response, a growing number of schools and businesses are working together to rethink curriculum, instruction, and assessment to make it more **relevant.** They are creating ways to expose children to occupations at early ages, helping them to identify their interests and set career goals.

Offices, farms, factories, hotels, hospitals, and other work sites are becoming extensions of the learning environment, serving as locations where older students participate in internships, **apprenticeships,** and school-to-career programs. By moving learning out of the confines of the classroom and into the **community,** students see the links between their academic work and its relevance to the rest of their lives. These experiences allow teens to sample what different careers are really like, to receive on-the-job training, and to get a head start on **higher education.** Most importantly, these students are gaining the skills they need to be lifelong learners prepared to handle many transitions to different jobs.

Driven by the need for a **well-educated** pool of employees, more businesses are dedicating expertise, resources, funding, and personnel to support schools. Business organizations have been instrumental in providing computers and other **technology** to schools that would otherwise be unable to afford the latest high-tech learning tools. Companies are also supporting education by implementing school-friendly **employee** policies, which allow workers time to participate in schools, whether or not they have children.

Information and communication technologies are helping educators and business people form closer ties by providing new channels through which they can share **expertise** and other resources. They offer students and teachers real-time or recorded access to a wealth of business information and advice. And, using **simulation** software that replicates real-world situations like flying a plane or performing surgery, young people can get **realistic** work experience without ever leaving the classroom.

Closer **collaboration** among children's teachers and their future employers is an essential aspect of improving America's education system. As in any committed relationship, both parties will have to compromise, make adjustments, assume their share of **responsibility,** and remain open to change. ●

Imagine the Possibilities

BY ROBERTS T. JONES

working
to learn,
learning
to work

American business is caught in a painful paradox. When job openings are announced, applicants line up by the hundreds. Yet managers say they can't find people to fill jobs.

What these employers mean is they can't find people with the right skills—people who can read technical manuals, solve customer problems, handle a spreadsheet, work in teams, and think on their feet. Rapid changes in technology, the globalization of the marketplace, and the spread of new kinds of workplace organizations require more knowledge and skills from all employees. Even when the line of applicants stretches around the block, only a few may be able to handle such assignments.

Yet, often enough, that same line may contain scores of young people who did pretty well in school, and in their pain and disappointment lies a powerful lesson: the traditional school curriculum expects too little of students and fails to help them acquire the personal qualities and habits of mind demanded in today's workplace.

The Need for High Academic Standards By most indicators, school performance has improved in the last two decades. The problem is that schools have not kept pace with the demands of a rapidly changing world. For the most part, our education system is designed to prepare students for the world of work that existed a generation ago. Schools are compelled to help students score well on standardized tests, which is not the same thing as teaching the skills needed to be successful in life.

The single most important thing our nation can do to improve education is to develop high academic standards for all students, together with assessments to make sure the standards are being met. Our tradition of expecting only college-bound students to meet high standards is no longer sufficient. More than ever before, students preparing to enter the workforce need the same advanced academic skills. Stronger academic standards are the first step to ensuring that every student gains the knowledge and skills needed for responsible citizenship and productive work.

Business must help set those standards by communicating what skills are needed in the workplace. As a recent Brookings Institution study pointed out: "Although businesses have

Roberts T. Jones[1] is the president and chief executive officer of the National Alliance of Business.

145

frequently lamented the quality of workers they receive from schools, few have ever worked closely with schools to define the skills and abilities that they are seeking in prospective workers." A growing number of companies are participating in industry-skill standards projects to do just that. Others are actively involved in state-level efforts to develop academic standards and assessments.

Some states and districts have adopted sweeping education reforms and are now developing more detailed curriculum and assessment regimes. The standards-setting movement needs to be encouraged so that it extends to all states, districts, and individual schools. This stage will determine what kids are actually taught, and what will constitute acceptable levels of performance. Business input is critical—and will continue to be so as skill demands change.

As standards are being set, it's important to remember that the purpose of schooling is not simply to make students economically competitive, but to produce competent citizens, caring adults, and productive members of communities. At the same time, learning job skills does more than just prepare students to earn a living—it also helps students understand the world around them and how they fit into it.

Rather than asking students, "Are you going to work or to college?" we should ask students, "What career are you interested in pursuing?"

The Value of Work-Based Learning

In the classroom, motivating students to learn is one of the most important keys to success. Too often, though, students fail to understand how academic learning is applied in the real world. We should not ask them to prepare for their futures with blindfolds on—we should make sure they have as much information as possible about how to prepare themselves to be successful in a changing world. Business can play a critical role by helping to create links between academic subjects and the world of work.

With a closer partnership between education and business, project-oriented learning can be based, at least some of the time, on genuine business problems that allow students to develop, apply, and create knowledge. Students can be challenged, for example, to find the best way to transport a commodity from a supplier on the

other side of the world to a factory in their community. Through computer simulations, students can electronically tour the place where the commodity is produced—such as a kiwi grove in New Zealand or a silkworm farm in China—and learn about local customs and ways of doing business. They can access electronic databases to research different methods and routes of transportation, comparing time versus cost. They can consult with business people, either in-person or via the Internet, as they work to solve logistical problems. Finally, they can summarize their findings in a multimedia presentation that integrates text, audio, graphs, maps, animation, and video, and share it with teachers and students across the hall or around the globe. These kinds of practical experiences can link what students are expected to learn with what they'll be expected to accomplish as adults—and make learning exciting!

Learning in a real-world context is useful for all students, including those preparing for college. Separating students preparing for work and college implies that college-bound students never need to prepare for work. Rather than asking students, "Are you going to work or to college?" we should ask students, "What career are you interested in pursuing?" Only then can we provide students with an education that will keep all of life's doors open.

The Role of Business

There are many ways business can and should become involved in helping all children meet high standards. Over the past decade, thousands of businesses have entered partnerships with schools or districts in which they provide in-kind services or equipment. More recently, in order to help schools take full advantage of advanced technologies, companies have begun donating free cable connections or Internet access. Some companies are lending their technical professionals to assist schools with installing technology, such as determining the best way to wire networks within a school or among schools across town.

Aside from technology, businesses have a wealth of expertise that can help improve education. Businesses that have successfully re-engineered can help guide public school bureaucracies through the challenges of restructuring. Business leaders can contribute strategic planning help, budget guidance, and ideas about better forms of management systems. They can also help administrators adopt competitive contracting for services.

Employment policies can be recast to better support education. Some businesses are adopting new work schedules and structures that promote not only the continuing education of employees, but also participation in the schooling of young people, especially their own children. Parents get time off for conferences with teachers or school-governance meetings. Employees are encouraged to become mentors for students or make themselves available to help with classroom projects, sometimes via electronic networks.

Knowledge transfer is another key component of any successful business-education partnership. High school and community college faculties often are urged to teach about fast-breaking technologies and new workplace skills, but never see the inside of a real business where those innovations are being developed. Companies should bring teachers, administrators, professors, and students on-site, whether through visits, seminars, or internships. In some cases, similar experiences can be offered through electronic field trips, using video conferencing or virtual reality technology. Business can't complain about the lack of connection between school and work if they bar the door.

Many companies are becoming involved in promising new efforts to create better transitions between school and careers. These school-to-career programs, which typically involve both classroom instruction and on-the-job learning in the form of apprenticeships or structured internships, help students acquire skills like problem solving and the ability to collaborate that are vital in today's working environment. Unlike traditional vocational education, these programs are open to both college-bound and non-college-bound students and hold all participants to the same high academic standards. By working together, schools and employers are able to provide experiences that motivate youth to acquire high-level academic and workplace skills, which, in turn, can lead to rewarding employment and future learning opportunities.

Businesses have a lot of practice dealing with the acceleration of change driven by technology and global economics, and these forces are now poised at the schoolhouse door.

We Can Do Better! What will happen if all American students are truly expected to achieve at high levels? What can we anticipate if we commit ourselves to producing graduates with solid basic skills and mastery of a strong, well-rounded curriculum?

Of course, the most immediate beneficiaries would be our young people themselves. Not only would better schooling strengthen their minds and broaden their perspectives, it would also vastly enhance their economic prospects, enabling more of them to succeed in college; compete for rewarding careers; and earn the kind of wages and benefits needed to raise a family.

But companies would also benefit, since a more highly skilled workforce would enable them to adopt more efficient work strategies and increase productivity. In the long run, stronger educational standards would generate a larger domestic market as higher skills increase workers' wages and buying power.

It's time to stop pretending that education and commerce exist on different planets. Businesses have a lot of practice dealing with the acceleration of change driven by technology and global economics, and these forces are now poised at the schoolhouse door. The students inside need business and education to unite on their behalf. Our willingness to meet this challenge is the key to their future—and to the future economic security of our country. ●

From the Front Lines

BY JULIETTE JOHNSON

building bright

When I entered Brighton High School in Boston, Mass., as a student in 1957, preparing for the world of work was relatively simple. All I had to do was enroll in a college, business, or general course of study; take the required classes; and decide whether to go on to college or accept one of the many jobs available to high school graduates. As a female, my career choices were pretty much limited to secretarial work, cosmetology, nursing, sales, or education. I chose the college track, applied to teacher education programs, and, after getting my undergraduate degree, returned to the classroom to offer my students the same workplace preparation I had experienced.

Since then, the relationship between school and work has grown more complicated. Economic, social, and technological changes have created limitless career possibilities for both men and women, while at the same time increasing competition for employment. Basic reading, writing, and calculating skills are no longer enough to land a good job. Today's employers demand more specialized skills and knowledge as well as greater adaptability from workers.

Creating a smoother transition from school to work for Brighton's graduates has been an important part of my job since I became headmaster in 1982. The school I inherited was different in some ways than the one I attended: desegregation and demographic shifts had combined to produce an enrollment made up largely of minority students, many of whom had limited English-speaking proficiency. Despite all the changes in the outside world, however, the school's curriculum offerings and instructional practices were essentially the same as when I was a student. Our students and teachers ached for programs that would provide meaning and relevance.

Thanks to a collaboration with the Private Industry Council (PIC)—a coalition of business, government, education, and community leaders committed to helping prepare Boston's youth for work—we were able to begin addressing this problem during the 1980s. Funding and expertise from PIC helped many of Brighton's students develop job skills and find employment.

Then, in 1990, we were able to launch a more extensive school-to-career program. That year, Brighton established the School of Health Professions in response to a mandate that all Boston high schools develop a magnet theme. About 250 of our 1,100 students are in the program. Their core academic classes are supplemented by such courses as Introduction to Health Careers, Anatomy and Physiology, and Medical Techniques. During their junior year, these students spend 15 hours a week exploring and learning about more than 20 health occupations. They also have one afternoon a week when they rotate through different departments like pediatrics and physical therapy at six local hospitals. Seniors are placed in paid internships at health care facilities, getting hands-on work experience in specific medical specialties.

Some Health Professions students are part of a 2+2 course of study coordinated through Pro-Tech, a districtwide school-to-career program sponsored by PIC. They get two years of training in high school plus two years of higher education at local colleges and universities, graduating with an associate degree in a health care field.

As part of their studies, Health Professions students are exposed to many new technologies. They use the Internet to conduct research for class projects, exploring huge databases of health and medical information from government agencies, universities, professional associations, and other institutions. Their hospital rotations and internships give them a solid introduction to the many high-tech tools used in caring for patients. And every student at Brighton is required to take at least one computer science course to graduate, because we know technological literacy is a prerequisite for success in today's digital workplace.

futures

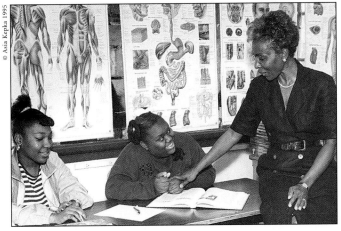

© Asia Kepka 1995

The curriculum for the Health Professions program reflects extensive research into the needs of employers. Our first year was spent forming relationships with local health care institutions, community colleges, and businesses. We also visited several high schools around the country with similar programs and got assistance from Pro-Tech. Periodic visits to health care employers help us keep our curriculum and instructional strategies relevant.

Health Professions faculty members model the "hard work" pathway to success by putting in long hours preparing instruction and continuing their professional development. Each has been extensively trained to integrate various computer technologies into subjects like biology,

biotechnology, and genetics. A full-time coordinator acts as a liaison between school and placement sites and is responsible for the program's overall management, which includes supervision and evaluation of teachers, parental outreach, development of internships, and student placement and monitoring.

For students in this program, school has more relevance to work, and work experience has reinforced the need for schooling. It helps them focus on real-world goals and develop their work ethic. They have a deeper understanding than the average high school graduate of the proficiencies, attitudes, and sophisticated skills it takes to survive in today's job market. They are more confident about their own abilities and sure of the direction in which their lives are headed. Their on-the-job experiences give them additional support in reaching their goals; hospital

For students in this program, school has more relevance to work, and work experience has reinforced the need for schooling. It helps them focus on real-world goals and develop their work ethic.

staff are role models and mentors who become involved with students' lives and have a stake in their success.

Of the 32 students in a recent graduating class from the School of Health Professions, 28 were accepted at two- and four-year colleges that offer degrees in health-related fields and the other four are working full-time in local hospitals. The program is still too new to have produced its first doctor, but I'm sure it will soon. We're considering expanding the school-to-career concept to additional occupations, because we see that students who attend school with a sense of purpose achieve greater success, have greater self-esteem and confidence, and get a clear head start on a bright future. ● ★ FILM

Juliette Johnson[2] is the headmaster at Brighton High School.

Snapshots

A Career Head Start

Considering they live in a community that boasts such renowned institutions as the Jet Propulsion Laboratory (JPL) and the California Institute of Technology (Caltech), it's not surprising that many students in Pasadena, Calif., aspire to careers in science, engineering, and space exploration. Some get a head start on their dreams at Pasadena's GeoSpace Academy, where they gain hands-on experience in fields such as aerospace research, laser technology, and computer-aided drafting. A few even get the opportunity to work side-by-side with some of the world's leading scientists.

The GeoSpace Academy, a partnership between the Pasadena Unified School District, JPL, Caltech, and others, is one of seven Pasadena Partnership Academies that together enroll more than 700 students. The other academies focus on health, technology, visual arts, computers, graphic communications, or business and finance. Located at various high schools, each offers a rigorous blend of academic and work-based learning to a broad spectrum of students, including those at highest risk for school failure. Thanks to dozens of partnerships with area businesses and institutions, academy students make full use of the technologies available in their chosen career field.

Academy graduates are well prepared for entry-level jobs in their particular field. "By the time they graduate, our students have resumes and a portfolio of their accomplishments; they've presented a senior project, visited colleges, put on health fairs, and worked extensively with adults," says Marla Keeth, coordinating teacher for the Health Academy. But, since they have also received a solid grounding in academics, the vast majority of graduates opt to continue their education at two- or four-year colleges. ●

Pasadena Partnership Academies Pasadena Unified School District, 351 South Hudson Avenue, Pasadena, CA 91109 **Contact:** Alma Dillard, Coordinator • Phone: (818) 568-4549 • Fax: (818) 795-1191 • E-mail: adillard@pasadena.k12.ca.us • URL: http://www.pasadena.K12.ca.us

A Working School

Hodgson Vo-Tech High School in Newark, Del., helps students acquire career-oriented skills and habits by applying the principles of the Coalition of Essential Schools, a national organization that encourages students to demonstrate what they've learned. Hodgson's 900 students build houses, assist in the dental clinic located at the school, or work with local employers. Their performance is evaluated in a work-readiness assessment that notes individual attendance, cooperation, and the ability to complete tasks. In order to graduate, all seniors must present a work-based project to a panel of experts who hold it to the standards of their field.

Hodgson guarantees its graduates will measure up on the job. Employers who are dissatisfied can send a graduate back to the school for retraining.

The emphasis on vocational skills does not come at the expense of academics. During the 9th through 11th grades, students take classes from a team of teachers who stress thinking and writing skills in every subject. In 1995, 84 percent of Hodgson students were rated competent or better on Delaware's writing assessment. "Traditional academic skills are an essential part of preparing students for the workplace," says principal Steven Godowsky. ●

Hodgson Vo-Tech High School New Castle County Vo-Tech School District, 2575 Summit Bridge Road, Newark, DE 19702 **Contact:** Steven Godowsky, Principal • Phone: (302) 834-0990 • Fax: (302) 834-0598

A Statewide Approach

Troubled by the recent death of his father and bored with high school, Mark Nordby seriously considered dropping out at the end of his sophomore year. Instead, he took a chance and enrolled in the Wisconsin Youth Apprenticeship Program. "I always learned better by doing and (with this program) I got to put into practice what I studied in school that same day," he says.

Three years later, Mark not only had his high school diploma, he also had earned a Certificate of Occupational Proficiency from the State Labor Department and was in his second year of technical college. As a lead worker at Serigraph Printing in West Bend, Wis., where he has been a paid employee since his junior year in high school, Mark routinely trains other workers. The former self-described "marginal student" now refers to himself as a "fast learner" and has become "a model representative for the company and the Youth Apprenticeship," according to Joe Klahn, an executive at Serigraph.

Under Wisconsin's School-to-Work Initiative, all of the state's school districts will be able to offer students opportunities similar to Mark's by the year 2000. Some 750 students have enrolled in state-sponsored youth-apprenticeship programs since 1992. While the specifics of local programs vary, certain basic elements do not. Applicants are required to be on track to graduate and willing to commit to a two-year program. During their apprenticeship, students must take a class relevant to their work experience. And by the end, they are expected to master essential entry-level workplace competencies identified by industry leaders. ●

Wisconsin Youth Apprenticeship Program, Office for Workforce Excellence, Wisconsin Department of Workforce Development, 201 East Washington Avenue, PO Box 7946, Madison, WI 53707 **Contact:** Joyce Christee, Youth Apprenticeship Coordinator • Phone: (608) 267-7210 • Fax: (608) 261-6698 • Email:chrisjo@DILHR.state.wi.us

Extending Learning through Technology

Apple Classrooms of Tomorrow (ACOT) is a research and development collaboration among public schools, universities, research agencies, and Apple Computer, Inc. Since 1985, this partnership has assisted numerous schools across the country in the creation of technology-rich learning environments and in the study of innovative instructional techniques. In ACOT classrooms, "students can collect information in multiple formats and then organize, visualize, link, and discover relationships among facts and events," says David Dwyer, former Apple Distinguished Scientist.

The underlying goal of the ACOT program is to empower students through technology integration. ACOT students can see how the work they're doing in the classroom is linked to the real world. "I'm doing complex spreadsheets like they do in businesses while I'm still a junior in high school," says one. Another student believes that ACOT classrooms are better "because of the family atmosphere. We develop relationships with students and teachers as we work together on projects."

ACOT also supports several Teacher Development Centers, created to study the impact of hands-on staff development on teaching. Through the centers, ACOT teachers and students work with teachers from their own districts and from schools across the country. Teachers collaborate to identify barriers to integrating technology throughout the curriculum and determine ways to overcome them. They also provide feedback to Apple regarding software applications or specific instructional strategies. "It's very important for teachers who have become comfortable with this new paradigm and the technological applications to share this knowledge with others," says Keith Yocam, manager for the ACOT program. ●

Apple Classrooms of Tomorrow Apple Computer, Inc., One Infinite Loop, MS: 301-3E, Cupertino, CA 95014 **Contact:** Apple Classrooms of Tomorrow • Phone: (408) 974-5992 • Fax: (408) 862-6430 • URL: http://www.research.apple.com/research/proj/acot

A Career Advantage

The hundreds of students who participate in Maine Career Advantage have an extra adult in their lives—an intern supervisor, whose role is modeled closely after that of German career mentors, called "meisters." According to director Susan Brown, "the intern supervisor experience is the key to the success of our program." Intern supervisors are not teachers, but instead are senior workers at local businesses across the state who help train and supervise students who have chosen to take on the challenge of combining school and work. The supervisors help high school and college students, usually on a one-to-one basis, as they learn to manage a weekly schedule which alternates school with full days at a work site.

The goal for students is to earn a Certificate of Skill Mastery guaranteeing employers that the holder has mastered a complex series of work-related skills identified by a state-assembled panel of industry leaders. The Center for Career Development backs up the guarantee by retraining any certificate holder deemed by an employer to lack core skills. Students who enroll in a full two-year internship also qualify for admission into one of Maine's seven technical colleges, where their supervised work experience and tuition-free courses give them up to a year's worth of credits. As the coordinating agency for the program, the Center for Career Development does not limit its role to training interns; it also helps train supervisors, develop curriculum, and facilitate communication among the hundreds of participating high schools and employers. ●

Maine Career Advantage Center for Career Development, Southern Maine Technical College, Fort Road, South Portland, ME 04106 **Contact:** Susan Brown, Director • Phone: (207) 767-5210 • Fax: (207) 767-2542 • E-mail: asbrown@ccd.mtcs.tech.me.us • URL: http://www.mtcs.tec.me.us

"Something magical happens to your understanding of your job when you have to explain it to a 10-year-old."

Ft. Worth Project C³ Ft. Worth Independent School District, 100 North University Avenue, Fort Worth, TX 76107 **Contact:** Debby Russell, School/Community Programs Coordinator • Phone: (817) 871-2313 • Fax: (817) 871-2548

Never Too Young

While most school-to-career programs focus on the high school years, the Fort Worth Project C³ (for "Community, Corporations, and Classrooms") serves students from kindergarten through 12th grade. After surveying 3,500 local workers about the levels and types of skills needed in their jobs, the Fort Worth City Schools used the results to link school work to careers and to encourage students to stay in school. Throughout their elementary and middle school years, students work on projects that put their learning in the context of real-world activities. A middle school English class, for example, redesigned the brochures for a county health agency. Another program helps fifth graders visit work sites like banks, the mint, and the airport. An air traffic controller had this to say about the visits: "Something magical happens to your understanding of your job when you have to explain it to a 10-year-old."

Starting in seventh grade, all students take part in Vital Link, a two-week program that provides students with a job-shadowing experience (in which a student follows a worker to see how a job is done). Tenth graders can participate in Next Link, a program which builds on Vital Link by offering longer paid internships. These experiences are closely tied to a redesigned applied-technology curriculum that actively engages students in subjects such as robotics manufacturing and computer-based publishing. More than 330 local businesses have already contributed to the success of Project C³. ●

Making a Connection

In 1990, a team of parents, educators, and business people helped Roosevelt High School in Portland, Ore., conduct a study and discovered what many students had long suspected: the school's academic program suffered from a lack of connection to students' lives and the demands of work. In response, the school launched Roosevelt Renaissance 2000. This school-improvement effort centers on occupational-cluster programs that help all 1,250

Roosevelt Renaissance 2000
Roosevelt High School, Portland Public School District, 6941 North Central Street, Portland, OR 97203 **Contact:** Janet Warrington, Project Coordinator • Phone: (503) 280-5138 • Fax: (503) 280-5663

Roosevelt students, including those bound for college, understand the connection between school and their future careers.

Roosevelt has been reorganized into six career paths: arts and communications, business and management, manufacturing and engineering technology, health services, human services, and natural resource systems. Ninth graders explore each path through a required course, Freshman Survey, which includes job shadowing (students follow a worker to see how she does her job) and class projects based on career skills. In the spring of ninth grade, students choose a career path for deeper exploration. In 11th and 12th grades, students take part in supervised work experiences with local employers.

An advisory group of local businesses helps with job placements, provides business-related materials, and helps match the curriculum to the demands of work. Janet Warrington, coordinator of the program, reports that "the experience opens students' minds to thinking about the world of work—both the

> *"The experience opens students' minds to thinking about the world of work—both the possibilities and the requirements."*

possibilities and the requirements." As a result, students are seeing the need for science and math, and enrollments in physics and chemistry have gone up. The school is exploring the possibility of offering a certificate of mastery to students who demonstrate acceptable levels of proficiency in reading, writing, and math. From all accounts, it seems that Renaissance 2000 may be living up to its name: student morale has improved and more students are staying in school. ●

The Missing Link

Each year, ProTech prepares hundreds of Boston inner city students for both high-skilled jobs and education beyond high school by reinforcing the ties between school and career. Beginning in the summer after 10th grade, workshops help students adjust their dress and behavior for the workplace, while classes at local colleges help them prepare for ProTech's academic requirements. Once they start 11th grade, ProTech students alternate classes at their high schools with paid 16-hour-per-week internships in health,

finance, environmental services, business, or public utilities. Specialized English and science classes help students link their studies to their jobs. Teachers get help incorporating workplace skills into these academic classes through work site visits, monthly meetings with ProTech counselors and workplace mentors, and summer curriculum workshops. At school and work, a personal counselor provides ProTech students with whatever it takes for them to stay on track, from tutoring or help with financial aid forms to more personal matters.

ProTech Boston Private Industry Council, 2 Oliver Street, Boston, MA 02109 **Contact:** Keith Westrich, Director • Phone: (617) 423-3755 • Fax: (617) 423-1041

So far, ProTech students are making the intended connections. More than two-thirds still work at companies where they apprenticed and more than 95 percent of the class of 1995 went on to two- or four-year colleges, where they can continue to consult with a ProTech counselor until they graduate. ●★ FILM

ACCESS TO INFORMATION

Organizations

American Youth Policy Forum (AYPF) Description: Informational organization linking federal policy makers with school-to-career program directors, staff, and researchers. **Purpose:** To help law makers make informed decisions about school-to-career programs. **Activities:** Conducts forums on topics such as national-skill standards and career preparation. Sponsors field trips for policy makers to observe model programs. Publishes reports and briefings by practitioners and researchers. **Contact:** Glenda Partee, Co-Director • American Youth Policy Forum, 1001 Connecticut Avenue NW, Suite 719, Washington, DC 20036 • Phone: (202) 775-9731 • Fax: (202) 775-9733

"We need young people who can demonstrate mastery of both rigorous academic and behavioral skills. Too often, we judge them on how many years they sit in classroom seats or how many written tests they pass by rote memorization."

Samuel Halperin,[4] Co-Director, American Youth Policy Forum

Business Coalition for Education Reform (BCER) Description: A coalition of 11 national business organizations: the American Business Conference, the Black Business Council, the Business Higher Education Forum, The Business Roundtable, the Committee for Economic Development, The Conference Board, the Chamber of Commerce of the United States, the National Alliance of Business, the National Association of Manufacturers, the National Association of Women Business Owners, and the U.S. Hispanic Chamber of Commerce. **Purpose:** To strengthen America's schools by supporting and expanding business involvement in education at the national, state, and local levels. **Activities:** Works with a network of local and state business-led coalitions to ensure standards reflect the academic and workplace skills needed for sustaining a growing economy, to help the public understand the need for academic standards and fundamental school reforms, and to provide expertise to states and communities who want to learn from others' experiences in advancing education reform. **Contact:** Aimee Rogstad Guidera, Project Director • Business Coalition for Education Reform, National Alliance of Business, 1201 New York Avenue NW, Washington, DC 20005 • Phone: (202) 289-2901 • Fax: (202) 289-1303 • E-mail: guideraa@nab.com • URL: http://www.bcer.org

The Business Roundtable (BRT) Description: An advocacy and information organization comprised of about 200 of the largest corporations. **Purpose:** Supports business leaders around the nation as they work to change education, primarily at the state level. **Activities:** Holds conferences, serves as an information clearinghouse, publishes reports, and supports education policy initiatives. **Contact:** Susan Traiman, Director, Education Initiative • The Business Roundtable, 1615 L Street NW, Suite 1100, Washington, DC 20036 • Phone: (202) 872-1260 • Fax: (202) 466-3509

High Schools that Work Description: A school-improvement program of the Southern Regional Education Board (SREB) that works with more than 550 schools in 21 states. **Purpose:** To replace traditional general and vocational tracks with a curriculum emphasizing academic skills, career concentrations, and integrated academic and technical studies for all students. **Activities:** Hosts conferences and workshops. Publishes books and reports on how to change practices and develop exemplary programs. Conducts assessments of students and teachers. **Contact:** Gene Bottoms, Director • High Schools that Work, Southern Regional Education Board, 592 10th Street NW, Atlanta, GA 30318 • Phone: (404) 875-9211 • Fax: (404) 872-1477 • E-mail: gbottoms@sreb.org • URL: http://www.peach.net/sreb/programs/high

Jobs for the Future (JFF) Description: A national, nonprofit policy and research organization that has worked with more than 20 states and 120 local partnerships to develop, improve, and evaluate school-to-career systems. **Purpose:** To enhance economic security and access to opportunities for all citizens by strengthening the transitions between learning and work. **Activities:** Conducts research, designs systems, provides technical assistance, and proposes policy innovation on the interrelated issues of work and learning. Helped develop the federal School to Work Opportunities Act of 1994. Publishes program briefings, manuals, and fact sheets. **Contact:** Mary Ellen Bavaro, Director of Communications • Jobs for the Future, One Bowdoin Square, Boston, MA 02114 • Phone: (617) 742-5995 • Fax: (617) 742-5767 • E-mail: mebavaro@jff.org

"A long-term investment in comprehensive school-to-work transition strategies will, for the first time in our history, create a level playing field for all youth."

William Bloomfield,[3] Executive Director, School & Main

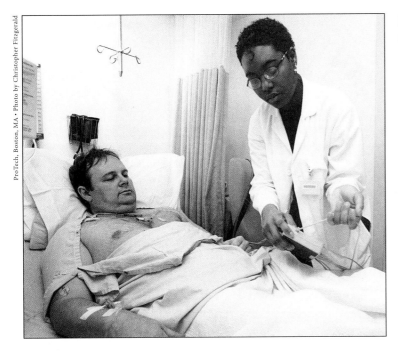

National Academy Foundation (NAF)

Description: A nonprofit organization established in 1989. **Purpose:** To promote "academies"—schools-within-schools that combine paid internships with concentrated studies in a particular industry, such as financial services, travel and tourism, or public service—in order to prepare graduates for careers or college. **Activities:** Provides assistance to more than 170 programs in 30 states and the District of Columbia. Helps forge local partnerships composed of school, business, and community leaders. Supplies instructional materials, funding advice, and staff development for local program directors and instructors. **Contact:** E. Bonnie Silvers, Director of New Initiatives • National Academy Foundation, 235 Park Avenue South, 7th Floor, New York, NY 10003 • Phone: (212) 420-8400 • Fax: (212) 475-7375 • URL: http://www.naf1.org

National Association of Partners in Education, Inc. (NAPE) Description: A national membership organization of schools, community groups, businesses, universities, and government agencies. **Purpose:** To promote partnerships among its members. **Activities:** Advises corporations on how to collaborate in support of community-wide education initiatives. Conducts research, provides technical assistance and training, holds conferences, and maintains a database of partnerships for members' use. **Contact:** Linda Beck, Director of Field Services • National Association of Partners in Education, Inc., 901 North Pitt Street, Suite 320, Alexandria, VA 22314 • Phone: (703) 836-4880 • Fax: (703) 836-6941 • E-mail: napehq@napehq.org • URL: http://www.napehq.org

National Center for Research in Vocational Education (NCRVE)

Description: The nation's largest center for work-related education research. Headquartered at the University of California Berkeley with eight consortium sites at other major research centers. **Purpose:** To strengthen education to prepare all individuals for lifelong employment and learning. **Activities:** Conducts research on work-related education, such as identifying exemplary practices. Uses findings to assist in the improvement of programs, including the development of training materials for integrating vocational and academic curricula. Disseminates research findings and conducts outreach through school networks, seminars, and conferences. **Contact:** Peter Seidman, Dissemination Program Director • National Center for Research in Vocational Education, University of California Berkeley, 2030 Addison Street, Suite 500, Berkeley, CA 94720 • Phone: (800) 762-4093 • Fax: (510) 642-2124 • E-mail: askncrve@vocserve.berkeley.edu • URL: http://vocserve.berkeley.edu

National School-to-Work Learning and Information Center Description: Federally funded information clearinghouse of the National School-to-Work Office. **Purpose:** To provide a central resource for the development of school-to-career efforts nationwide. **Activities:** Tracks and disseminates information on funding and legislative developments, conference announcements, and exemplary programs. Maintains a comprehensive database of programs, publications, and organizations. Information available through bulletins, workshops, and the Internet. **Contact:** Bryna Shore Fraser, Project Director • National School-to-Work Learning and Information Center, 400 Virginia Avenue SW, Room 210, Washington, DC 20024 • Phone: (800) 251-7236 • Fax: (202) 401-6211 • E-mail: stw_lc@ed.gov • URL: http://www.stw.ed.gov/

The Partnership for Kentucky School Reform Description: An advocacy organization made up of Kentucky business people, educators, and government officials. **Purpose:** To raise public awareness about, and support for, the educational reform provisions of the Kentucky Education Reform Act of 1990 (KERA). **Activities:** Identifies issues and strategies central to the implementation of KERA. Encourages businesses to inform employees about educational issues and helps them get involved in public schools. Provides advice to business and community members. Manages a resource center on educational reform, a speakers bureau, and a toll-free information line. **Contact:** Carolyn Witt Jones, Director • The Partnership for Kentucky School Reform, PO Box 1658, Lexington, KY 40592 • Phone: (800) 928-2111 • Fax: (606) 233-0760 • E-mail: partnerky@aol.com

Pioneering Partners Foundation Description: A national, nonprofit foundation that began as a partnership between the GTE Corporation, the Council of Great Lakes Governors, and selected school districts in eight states. **Purpose:** To improve the ways teachers teach and children learn through technology; to recognize outstanding teachers who have pioneered innovative technology applications; and to bring together leaders in education, business, and government in partnerships that expand technology opportunities. **Activities:** Selects teams of teachers and administrators each spring after a competitive application process. Grants funding, technical assistance, and ongoing support to help teams implement their technology-dissemination plans throughout the following school year. The Pioneering Partners Leadership Summit, held each summer, is an intensive, week-long, professional development program designed to promote education, business, and government collaboration. **Contact:** Ellen Jones, Program Manager • Pioneering Partners Foundation, 16 Bayberry Square, 1645 Falmouth Road, Centerville, MA 02632 • Phone: (508) 778-7200 • Fax: (508) 778-2553 • E-mail: PPFcapecod@aol.com • URL: http://www.macomb.k12.mi.us/pphome.htm

Workforce Skills Program Description: A program of policy analysis and technical assistance created in 1990 under the umbrella of the National Center on Education and the Economy (NCEE). **Purpose:** To advance the recommendations of the Commission on the Skills of the American Workforce as outlined in NCEE's 1990 report, *America's Choice: High Skills or Low Wages.* Among other recommendations, the report calls for strengthening preparation in academics and occupational skills and advocates the establishment of a system to certify that students have met specific performance standards. **Activities:** Works with regional, state, and local governments. Organized a consortium of states committed to restructuring their education, employment, and training systems. Holds workshops on academic and skill standards, school-to-career issues, and employment and training services issues. Arranges meetings between educators, business people, and community members. Publishes a variety of policy documents, guides, and videos. **Contact:** Betsy Brown Ruzzi, Associate Director • Workforce Skills Program, National Center on Education and the Economy, 700 Eleventh Street NW, Suite 750, Washington, DC 20001 • Phone: (202) 783-3668 • Fax: (202) 783-3672 • E-mail: BBrownruzzi@ncee.com

Tech Corps Description: A national, nonprofit organization of corporate volunteers. Currently active in 40 states. **Purpose:** To bring new technology into K-12 classrooms nationwide. **Activities:** Recruits volunteers from businesses to help schools integrate new technologies into the curriculum. Establishes guidelines for effective school-business partnerships, tracks individual state efforts, acts as an information clearinghouse for program developers, and maintains a Web page to help link businesses interested in education. **Contact:** Karen Smith, Executive Director • Tech Corps, PO Box 832, Sudbury, MA 01776 • Phone: (508) 620-7749 • Fax: (508) 875-4394 • E-mail: ksmith@ustc.org • URL: http://ustc.org

Periodicals

"When a majority of companies become involved in creating and supporting innovative programs in the schools and those efforts are backed by changes within schools, districts, communities, and education policy, then we will begin to transform the system so that each child has the opportunity to achieve an excellent education."

Diana W. Rigden,[5] Director of Teacher Education Programs, Council for Basic Education

Center Work Description: Quarterly journal. **Focus:** Presents key findings from important vocational education research, discusses successful practices around the country, and includes annotations of National Center for Research on Vocational Education publications. **Publisher:** NCRVE, Berkeley, CA • Phone: (800) 762-4093.

Visions Description: Annual newsletter of the Pacific Bell Foundation. **Focus:** Informs corporate employees and the general public about educational issues such as technology use, curriculum integration, and school-business partnerships. Newsletters include program descriptions and guides to resources for further information. **Publisher:** Education for the Future Initiative, Chico, CA • Phone: (916) 898-4482.

Crossroads Description: Semiannual newsletter. **Focus:** Tracks the activities of Jobs for America's Graduates programs throughout the country. Reports on pending legislation, funding developments, and school-to-career activities in various states. Includes information on national school-to-career events. **Publisher:** Jobs for America's Graduates, Alexandria, VA • Phone: (703) 684-9479.

IEE Brief Description: Quarterly research digest. **Focus:** Summarizes reports of the Institute's current research on critical school-to-career issues such as standards and the effectiveness of various programs for different types of students. Also includes bibliographic references for more in-depth study. **Publisher:** Institute on Education and the Economy, Teachers College, Columbia University, New York, NY • Phone: (212) 678-3091.

Readings

ProTech, Boston, MA • Photo by Christopher Fitzgerald

Bailey, Thomas, and Donna Merritt. **The School-to-Work Transition and Youth Apprenticeship: Lessons from the U.S. Experience.** *Manpower Demonstration Research Corporation: New York, NY, 1993.* Phone: (212) 532-3200. ● Since there is no comprehensive apprenticeship model in the U.S., this study examines four components of existing programs: student participation, educational content, location of instruction, and credentialing. Offers recommendations for program improvement and further study.

The Commission on the Skills of the American Workforce. **America's Choice: High Skills or Low Wages!** *National Center on Education and the Economy: Rochester, NY, 1990.* Phone: (716) 546-7620. ● An oft-cited report that warns that American students will be doomed to low-wage jobs or unemployment unless they meet high academic standards closely tied to skills required in advanced manufacturing and service occupations. Calls for states to certify high school graduates who meet national performance-based skills standards.

Council for Aid to Education. **Business and the Schools: A Guide to Effective Programs, 2nd Edition.** *CFAE: New York, NY, 1992.* Phone: (212) 661-5800. ● With descriptions of more than 125 programs, this volume provides an overview of school-business partnerships, offers strategies for business involvement, and focuses on key areas of educational reform. Includes a list of resource organizations and an annotated bibliography.

The Business Roundtable. **A Business Leader's Guide to Setting Academic Standards.** *BRT: Washington, DC, 1996.* Phone: (202) 872-1260. ● A guide for business leaders that explains the debate about academic and workplace standards, identifies ways businesses can be involved in setting standards, provides examples of approaches in various states, and offers resources for further exploration.

Goldberger, Susan, Richard Kazis, and Mary K. O'Flanagan. **Learning Through Work: Designing and Implementing Quality Worksite Learning for High School Students.** *Manpower Demonstration Research Corporation: New York, NY, 1994.* Phone: (212) 532-3200. ● This "how-to" guide prepared by Jobs for the Future offers 10 basic elements for successful worksite learning, such as coordinating school and work experiences and having students stay in programs for at least two years. Includes sample contracts, evaluation sheets, and observation forms.

National Alliance of Business. **The Challenge of Change: Standards to Make Education Work for All Our Children.** *NAB: Washington, DC, 1995.* Phone: (800) 787-7788. ● One of three booklets in a series on business support of academic standards. Outlines the underlying principles of educational standards and discusses the roles and responsibilities of business in their development.

National Alliance of Business and The Business Roundtable. **The Business Roundtable Participation Guide: A Primer for Business on Education.** *NAB and BRT: Washington, DC, 1991.* Phone: (202) 289-2888. ● This guide for business leaders discusses issues associated with restructuring education, including curriculum, site-based management, technology use, and accountability. Includes recommendations for effective business involvement in education.

> *"Once teenagers use their academic studies at work, they return to the classroom with renewed energy and purpose. They discover that learning can be relevant and engaging."*
>
> Stephen F. Hamilton,[6] Director, Cornell Youth and Work Program, Cornell University

Smith, Hedrick. **Rethinking America: A New Game Plan From the American Innovators: Schools, Business, People, Work.** *Random House: New York, NY, 1995.* Phone: (800) 793-2665. ● A journalist presents evidence of the need for innovation and a strong school-to-work system to keep America competitive in a global economy. Offers a range of views from international corporate executives to students enrolled in school-to-career programs.

Stern, David, Neal Finkelstein, James R. Stone III, et al. **School to Work: Research on Programs in the United States.** *Falmer Press: Bristol, PA, 1995.* Phone: (215) 785-5800. ● One of the most comprehensive studies to-date on school-to-work programs. Includes research on programs such as career academies, apprenticeships, and cooperatives. Concludes that these programs graduate students who enjoy somewhat higher wages and hold post-high school jobs longer than other students.

Secretary's Commission on Achieving Necessary Skills, U.S. Department of Labor. **What Work Requires of Schools: A SCANS Report for America 2000.** *U.S. Dept. of Labor, SCANS: Washington, DC, 1991.* Phone: (202) 512-1800. ● This report projects what jobs will be like in the year 2000 and details competencies that workers will need, including the ability to work as part of a team, understand complex systems, acquire and use information, manage time and resources, and work with various technologies.

Wentworth, Eric. **Agents of Change: Exemplary Corporate Policies and Practices to Improve Education.** *The Business Roundtable: Washington, DC, 1991.* Phone: (202) 872-1260. ● Identifies factors that are essential for successful school-business partnerships. Recommendations such as making time for employees to help in schools are supported with examples from programs around the country.

> *"Counselors and teachers must become familiar with the modern workplace through site visits, internships, and industry workshops so they can integrate career skills and high academic standards for all students."*
>
> Marilyn Raby,[7] Consultant, National Center for Research in Vocational Education, University of California Berkeley

Gold, Lawrence N. **States and Communities on the Move: Policy Initiatives to Create a World-Class Workforce.** *William T. Grant Foundation Commission on Work, Family and Citizenship: New York, NY, 1991.* Phone: (212) 752-0071. ● Profiles the efforts of more than a dozen states to help young people make the transition from school to career. Reviews legislation and funding; gives contacts for state programs.

Contact Information

> *"Working as partners with educators and the community, business can share expertise, personnel, and resources, as well as serve as a catalyst to increase public awareness of educational reform issues such as standards, assessment, accountability, and technology."*
>
> Ronn Robinson,[8] Corporate Director, Education Policy, The Boeing Company

[1] **Roberts T. Jones** President and CEO • National Alliance of Business, 1201 New York Avenue NW, Washington, DC 20005 • Phone: (800) 787-2848 • Fax: (202) 289-1303 • E-mail: info@nab.com

[2] **Juliette Johnson** Headmaster • Brighton High School, Boston Public Schools, 25 Warren Street, Brighton, MA 02135 • Phone: (617) 635-9873 • Fax: (617) 635-9892

[3] **William Bloomfield** Executive Director • School & Main, 750 Washington Street, NEMCH #328, Boston, MA 02111 • Phone: (617) 636-9151 • Fax: (617) 636-9158 • E-mail: bill.bloomfield@es.nemc.org

[4] **Samuel Halperin** Co-Director • American Youth Policy Forum, 1001 Connecticut Avenue NW, Suite 719, Washington, DC 20036 • Phone: (202) 775-9731 • Fax: (202) 775-9733

[5] **Diana W. Rigden** Director of Teacher Education Programs • Council for Basic Education, 1319 F Street NW, Suite 900, Washington, DC 20004 • Phone: (202) 347-4171 • Fax: (202) 347-5047 • E-mail: diana@c-b-e.org

[6] **Stephen F. Hamilton** Director • Cornell Youth and Work Program, Cornell University, G-57 Martha Van Rensselaer, Ithaca, NY 14853 • Phone: (607) 255-8394 • Fax: (607) 255-3769 • E-mail: sfh3@cornell.edu

[7] **Marilyn Raby** Consultant • National Center for Research in Vocational Education, University of California Berkeley, 30 Saddleback, Portola Valley, CA 94028 • Phone: (415) 851-2359 • Fax: (415) 529-0522 • E-mail: 76363.1733@compuserve.com

[8] **Ronn Robinson** Corporate Director, Education Policy • The Boeing Company, PO Box 3707, MS 14-50, Seattle, WA 98124 • Phone: (206) 544-1380 • Fax: (206) 655-2133 • E-mail: Robrex00@ccmail.ca.boeing.com

Schools

Perry High School photo courtesy of Ed Goodwin/Burgess & Niple Architects

Schools

Schools are shaped not only by people, but also by bricks and mortar, rules and regulations and, increasingly, by computers and telecommunications networks. Together, these elements create an environment that affects how well students learn and teachers teach. Educators and others are taking a fresh look at how schools are organized and governed to make them more autonomous

O'Farrell Community School, San Diego, CA

and responsive to local needs. Architects are working with local communities to create facilities that accommodate different groupings and a wide range of learning activities and, at the same time, inspire curiosity and imagination. Using the latest technologies, students and teachers are building connections to the world beyond the school and breaking through traditional limits on learning. ●

ProTech, Boston, MA

ProTech, Boston, MA

There are many compelling examples of the power of information-age technologies to improve teaching and learning. The challenge we face today is to move beyond examples and commit to creating a system that gives every student and teacher access to a vast array of resources and to the best environments for learning.

Linda Roberts,[1] Director, Office of Educational Technology, U.S. Department of Education

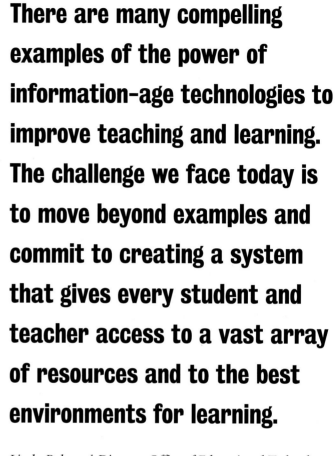

MAX SEABAUGH

Schools

Chapter 8: Reinventing Schools

166   Introduction

168   Imagine the Possibilities:
The Little School That…Could
by Robert S. Peterkin

172   From the Front Lines:
The Spirit of Group Governance
by Jayne John

174   Snapshots
Innovative Schools & Programs

180   Access to Information
Organizations, Periodicals, Readings & Contact Information

Chapter 9: Places For Learning

192   Introduction

194   Imagine the Possibilities:
Buildings That Teach
by Anne P. Taylor

198   From the Front Lines:
Designing a Dream
by K. John Jones

200   Snapshots
Innovative Schools & Programs

204   Access to Information
Organizations, Periodicals, Readings & Contact Information

Chapter 10: Technology

210   Introduction

212   Imagine the Possibilities:
The World at Your Fingertips
by Jan Hawkins

216   From the Front Lines:
Technology in Action
by John McSweeney

218   Snapshots
Innovative Schools & Programs

224   Access to Information
Organizations, Periodicals, Readings & Contact Information

Chapter 8

Reinventing Schools

For the last half of this century, our nation has engaged in an extended debate about how to improve **public schools.** Many different kinds of **reforms** have been tried, but none has achieved the dramatic gains in student learning needed for today's world.

About a decade ago, **leaders** in education, business, and government acknowledged the futility of piecemeal reform and began searching for better ways to improve schools. They examined previous efforts, realized that a change in one area, such as curriculum or assessment, was simply not enough, and concluded that the entire **system** needed to be "restructured." In the best schools, teachers and administrators were quietly ignoring counterproductive rules so they could implement **promising** strategies. They found many examples of successful pilot projects, but no concerted effort to make them available for all students.

Today, policy makers and others are trying to figure out how to provide schools with the **sustained** support needed for lasting improvement. National and state-level efforts focus on setting **standards** for student achievement and establishing policies to hold schools accountable for results. At the same time, they are giving local schools and communities more **freedom** to decide how best to help all students attain higher standards.

In a growing number of schools, educators, parents, business people, and community members are developing a common **vision** and establishing a clear set of **goals.** These schools and communities are grappling with questions like: "What do our students need to know and be able to do?" "What educational environment is most conducive to learning?" and "What organizational structures are most supportive?" These are **complex** questions, with no easy answers. But, as the programs in this chapter show, schools around the country are finding innovative **solutions** to these challenges.

With their new **authority,** local educators are making decisions about everything from personnel to technology integration, always keeping their eye on what is best for children. They are replacing outdated routines like lecture-only instruction and 45-minute class periods with more appropriate practices such as **project-based** learning and flexible scheduling. Some large schools are **reorganizing** their faculty and student body into smaller units where teams of teachers and students remain together for several years. This organizational structure enables teachers and students to get to know each other well and to develop the kinds of **relationships** that are critical for learning.

Teachers and principals are designing **challenging** curriculum and instruction for all students, not only the gifted and talented. They are working to ensure everyone has access to the best materials, including **global resources** and the latest technologies. With electronic links to experts and the world of ideas, **learning** is no longer limited to textbooks and bound by the four walls of the classroom.

Although there is little consensus, so far, on the details and methodology for improving the educational system, there is a growing **agreement** that the changes must be **fundamental** and supported over time, rather than one at a time and subject to shifting trends and fads. The schools and organizations listed in this chapter are applying hard work and common sense to the challenge of **reinventing** schools. ●

Imagine the Possibilities

BY ROBERT S. PETERKIN

the little school that...

Among the items on display in the foyer of Millennium School is a red metal school bell. Similar bells ring throughout the day in most American schools, signaling the beginning and end of each class period, much as factory whistles used to mark the start and finish of each work shift. The bell at Millennium, though, has been unhooked and put in a glass case, never again to interrupt the work of teachers and students.

The Millennium bell serves as a constant reminder of how far the school's staff has come in its effort to transform outmoded educational practices that, while well intentioned, actually impeded both teaching and learning. These teachers recognize that children are far too different —and learning much too complex—to fit into a rigid, uniform schedule. The thought that a bell could interrupt their work seems absurd to Millennium's staff, which has eliminated most of the ideas earlier schools borrowed from manufacturing, including the implausible notion that every student should learn the same things at the same rate like a slab of steel moving down an assembly line.

Although Millennium is fictional, its story is representative of the hundreds of schools across the country seeking a better way to educate our nation's children. These schools are discarding traditions that do not help students learn, turning instead to practices as ancient as Socrates and as modern as the World Wide Web. In the process, they are inventing new models of schools —models that can successfully prepare all children to meet life's challenges.

Starting at the School Level To govern innovative schools like Millennium, local school councils have been created. These groups are composed of administrators, teachers, parents, students, and other community members. They play a significant role in establishing community-wide standards and goals for education, in developing plans to meet those goals, and in monitoring progress toward achieving them. At Millennium, the council is responsible for overseeing most aspects of the school's operation including budget allocations, personnel matters, issues relating to the integration of technology, and to accountability. Council members also have responsibility for building community support for Millennium's programs and keeping them informed and involved.

The Millennium council started its work by asking its community members to help develop a vision for the school. Modeled along the lines of traditional New England "town meetings," groups of educators, families, students, business people, community leaders, and the principal spent many hours discussing children, education, and the requirements not only to succeed in today's world, but also to participate fully in our democracy. They looked at proven instances of effective educational practices in other schools, poured over the latest research, and investigated intelligent uses of the new technologies.

Local Control and Accountability Schools like Millennium may be on the leading edge of education reform, but they got there because of an idea borrowed from the earliest public schools: local

Robert S. Peterkin[2] is the director of the Urban Superintendents' Program at Harvard University.

COULD

control. Under a variety of policies adopted by states and school districts, including school-based management and charter schools, more and more schools are gaining the freedom needed to make lasting improvements. After decades in which decision making was increasingly centralized in state and district offices, authority is now being given back to those who are closest to students, including teachers, parents, principals, and other community members.

As integral members of the school council, teachers at Millennium were able to change outmoded school practices and bring them in line with their instructional innovations. The traditional 45-minute class period (and the need for bells) gave way to a flexible schedule with longer blocks of time that allows students to work without interruption. No more would individual teachers be assigned to a different group of students each year. Instead, they work in teams, over a longer time frame, reaping the benefits of professional collaboration while also developing close relationships with the students in their charge. And with new technologies, students and teachers not only learn from each other, but they are networked to, and interconnected with, a vast array of experts and resources around the globe.

When Millennium's teachers were freed from bureaucratic control and granted the autonomy others found in their professions, they assumed more responsibility for ensuring that their school measured up to high standards. The new schedules allowed them time to work together, enabling

These principles reflect the growing understanding that education is an interconnected system. In order for reform to work, roles, relationships, and responsibilities at all levels must be re-examined. Changes to one part of the system will not work unless other parts also change.

them to reflect on their efforts and to constantly help each other improve performance. Teachers with the most knowledge and experience took the role of mentors, sharing responsibility with the principal for reviewing and improving the performance of their junior colleagues—identifying weaknesses, providing support, and, when necessary, initiating dismissal proceedings.

Periodically, the Millennium staff supplements their internal accountability process by asking for independent reviews by teams of educators from other schools. Additionally, the neighborhood-wide "town meetings" give the community opportunities to discuss and update its vision for the school and review progress and accomplishments.

Principles for School Governance In a system that educates all students well, a few core principles are:
● Every child has a right to a high-quality education.
● Federal, state, and local governments are responsible for ensuring that every school has enough resources to educate children well.
● State and local policy makers work with educators, parents, and business and community leaders to define educational standards.
● Decisions about how to help students achieve those standards are left up to communities and educators at each school, who use the most effective strategies available to help each child succeed.
● Federal, state, and local governments are responsible for establishing a system of accountability that does not infringe upon school-level authority, but does ensure that all students and schools are performing at the highest possible level.

These principles reflect the growing understanding that education is an interconnected system. In order for reform to work, roles, relationships, and responsibilities at all levels must be re-examined. Changes to one part of the system will not work unless other parts also change.

A Supportive System Allowing schools the flexibility they need to increase student achievement requires a system willing to support change. Consider the following:

● At the community level, elected officials on local school boards help to ensure adequate funding and resources so each school can carry out its educational program. Giving schools the authority to solicit competitive bids for services creates incentives for districts to maximize efficiencies and eliminate services that are not responsive to the needs of their constituency. School boards monitor compliance with state and federal laws governing health, safety, and equal access to educational opportunities.

● Districts also support school efforts by helping provide needed professional development opportunities, establishing professional networks, and providing access to other resources. With the aid of advanced technologies, administration is streamlined and district personnel can coordinate services and provide referral information at the school site. Many districts also retain responsibility in areas such as collective bargaining and transportation.

● When states get out of the business of regulating individual schools, they can focus their efforts on a few key areas: helping to set standards that reflect society's interests in the goals of education, evaluating the adequacy of assessments designed to measure how well students are meeting those standards, working to improve teacher education, and ensuring that all students have equal access to the best educational opportunities. States can also support and disseminate educational research and provide ways for schools to network and collaborate. Some state educational agencies may provide direct services to schools that are geographically isolated or are not meeting agreed-upon levels of performance.

● The federal government, in turn, provides leadership to help ensure that everyone understands the importance of investing in education. It retains its traditional role of directing resources to the neediest communities and student populations, while allowing local school professionals to determine exactly how those students are to be educated. The idea should be to provide resources without burdening local communities with excess (and often times needless) bureaucracy. The federal government ensures equitable access to high-quality education for all students.

There is a lot of work ahead before this vision can become a reality—before school bells are only rung for emergencies and policy makers avoid quick fixes that ignore the complexity of learning. Consider another item in Millennium's display case, a yellowing copy of a quote from prominent 20th-century reformer Ron Edmonds: "We can whenever, and wherever we choose, successfully teach all children whose schooling is of interest to us. We already know more than we need to accomplish that task. Whether or not we do it must finally depend on how we feel about the fact that we haven't so far."[1] ●

Additionally, the neighborhood-wide "town meetings" give the community opportunities to discuss and update its vision for the school and review progress and accomplishments.

[1]As cited in **Shades of Brown: New Perspectives on School Desegregation**, Derrick Bell, ed. *Teachers College Press: New York, NY, 1980,* 121.

From the Front Lines

BY JAYNE JOHN

the spirit of group governance

A few years ago, after a month in which more than 300 visitors came to tour and observe at our school, I asked for student volunteers from each class to attend a problem solving meeting. As one of two teacher-directors at our 380-student, K–5 school, I explained to the children that something needed to be done to address the problems developing from the increasing numbers of visitors.

The kids decided that the first thing to do was to survey classrooms to find out what kinds of problems students and teachers were experiencing. After designing a survey instrument, the team met with each class to give an overview of the situation and gather data. Over the next several weeks, the team reviewed their data and discussed solutions. Among the changes they came up with were designating monthly visitor dates, hosting information sessions for visitors, providing guided tours of the building and classrooms, and implementing a plan to ensure more even distribution of visitors in classrooms. Over time, the students visited area museums and historic sites to learn from docents and tour guides and arranged for those professionals to provide training and consulting for the team. An unanticipated result has been

numerous invitations for the students to make presentations about our school to audiences such as the chamber of commerce, the school board, and groups from local universities and businesses.

While we continue to host many groups of visitors, the problems associated with accommodating them have diminished. At the same time, these youngsters learned some important lessons about taking responsibility for solving problems. Although the composition of the team changes each year as classrooms recruit new volunteers, it continues to provide a much-needed service to our community. In addition, we now have 12 other student teams that serve as conflict resolution mediators, school news broadcasters, safety inspectors, and software experts.

Getting children directly involved with school operations is very much in the spirit of group

governance that we've followed since opening the Alice Carlson Applied Learning Center in Ft. Worth, Tex. in 1992. We've established a management culture based on collaboration, communication, and consensus among all the school's stakeholders—educators, parents, students, and the community.

Our school was created during a restructuring of our district's education system. In the early 1990s, the superintendent, the school board, the chamber of commerce, and corporate leaders formed an alliance to implement several reform initiatives, including an active, project-based curriculum designed to connect school directly with real-life experiences. From that came a proposal for a public school of choice—open to all students in the district—focused on this kind of applied learning. The only requirement for a child to attend our school is an annual commitment of 20 hours of service per adult family member.

Like other schools in Texas, we follow a philosophy of site-based management, under which many choices about a school's operation are made locally. We're different, however, in the number of people we involve in decision making. As required by the state, we have a school management team made up of administrators and elected parents and staff members. But Alice Carlson is really run by six design teams comprised of volunteer parents and staff members. These teams are responsible for areas such as governance, the instructional program, operations, community involvement and services, special events, and communications. Every parent and faculty member is asked to join at least one design team, and though participation varies from person to person, we average about 60 adults actively involved in the school's governance.

All design teams meet on the same night every nine weeks and their meetings are open to the public. At the end of each meeting night, all the teams come together to update the entire group. During their work, team members can exchange e-mail and use the Internet to strengthen ties between our school and the greater community. Sometimes, two or more teams focus on different aspects of the same project. When the instructional design team, for example, identified a need for a database of parent and community resources that could be used by students and teachers, they asked the community team to assist with the effort.

As "teacher-directors"—a title that captures our role as instructional leaders better than "principal"—my co-director and I work hard to practice participatory management. I believe this model fosters the idea that learners must take informed risks, have a voice in governance issues, and develop autonomy. When the design teams were discussing issues such as how to develop and

evaluate projects and how to make assessment more meaningful, mine was but one voice among many. I do have to attend to some of the traditional duties of a principal, but I'm constantly in classrooms and working with children in different ways, taking a much stronger instructional role than most traditional administrators.

Our governance system reflects the philosophy that all members of our school community must learn to apply their skills and knowledge to concrete problems. We believe that better decisions get made when more voices are heard and everyone becomes part of a consensus. Parents aren't just made to feel welcome at our school; they are expected to participate as actual partners in teaching and learning. Faculty members are the managers of the curriculum—using state and district frameworks as guides, they decide what, when, and how to teach. Students have an unusual amount of freedom and responsibility for their own learning. They move about the building as needed to the library, science lab, art studio, offices, or anyplace they can find a free telephone, computer, printer, or scanner. We're not only teaching them to be proactive learners and to participate in decisions about their education, but we are also modeling that in the way we run the school.

We believe that better decisions get made when more voices are heard and everyone becomes part of a consensus.

Just before we opened, staff and parents met for a three-day working retreat to articulate a common mission for Alice Carlson and invent its system of shared governance. Several parents who worked with us throughout that time still talk about how being included made them feel. One told me: "It's amazing to think that a school faculty would take the chance on having parents sit in with them and plan how the school operates. You allowed us to give our ideas and have those ideas actually used. I knew that if the school respected and valued parents like that, my children were in good hands." ●

Jayne John[3] recently retired as one of two teacher-directors of the Alice Carlson Applied Learning Center.

Snapshots

Where Old Meets New

The first school in the tiny town of Cabot, Vt., was built in 1792 and served about 50 students of all ages. Cabot School currently enrolls approximately 250 students from pre-kindergarten

"Enormous changes have occurred since the first schoolhouse was built... We now write our papers on portable computers rather than slate tablets, and ride a bus to school rather than walk. Despite these differences, we know one thing has not changed, and that is the support of our town for our education."

through high school. Though the school's facade may have changed little over the years, inside the students are getting an education that prepares them not for the past, but for the future.

In 1990, as recipients of a Challenge Grant from the State of Vermont, Cabot community members joined parents and educators to begin hammering out a

mission statement for the school and a plan to revise the curriculum, improve professional practice, and increase parent and community involvement.

In 1992, as a pilot site for a "break-the-mold" school design of the National Alliance for Restructuring Education, Cabot received technology, training, and support from partners like the National Center on Education and the Economy, New Standards, and Apple Computer. This collaboration helped Cabot refine its plan and implement new techniques for teaching and learning. "I walked into a school that had a working document that acted like a road map for where the school had come from and where it was headed," says principal Halley.

One of the innovations adopted by Cabot is a synthesis course open to 11th and 12th graders who have mastered the basic curriculum by the end of 10th grade. In these courses, students pursue special areas of interest in depth as they apply their skills and

knowledge to challenging, real-world projects. Students in the first synthesis course studied the town's long history and produced a book, "Our Town Cabot," that was sent to every home. "As students studying the history of education in Cabot," they wrote, "we recognize the enormous changes that have occurred in our school system since the first schoolhouse was built... We now write our papers on portable computers rather than slate tablets, and ride a bus to school rather than walk. Despite these differences, we know that one thing has not changed, and that is the support of our town for our education." ●

Cabot School Cabot School District, PO Box 98, Cabot, VT 05647
Contact: Hasse Halley, Principal •
Phone: (802) 563-2289 •
Fax: (802) 563-2022 •
E-mail: Hassecabot@aol.com • URL: http://plainfield.bypass.com/~cabot

Speaking Up for Students

Making decisions by consensus can be difficult, yet the staff at Peakview Elementary School in Aurora, Colo., has found that this strategy is an essential ingredient for successful innovation. Everyone at Peakview has an opportunity to have their ideas heard—and a responsibility to express them.

Among the many innovative practices adopted by consensus at Peakview are a year-round schedule and cross-grade teams. The school's teachers and 700 students are divided into four K-5 teams. This structure gives teachers the flexibility to group students by abilities and interests rather than age, and encourages activities like "reading buddies," which pairs older and younger students. "We've had teams for five years now, and we are seeing extraordinary results," says Karen Peterson, Peakview's technology coordinator. "Everyone knows what's expected—older students have become models for younger ones and there is a real sense of continuity, commitment, and community."

Technology is used at Peakview to support various learning styles and extend learning experiences for students at all levels. Each classroom has four to six computers networked throughout the school, allowing students to access their work from any machine in the building. In addition, each team has access to laser-disc and CD-ROM players, scanners, still and video cameras, and a host of software. "We view technology as a tool and a resource, not an end in itself," Peterson says. "For instance, a teacher might come to me and ask about electronic resources for a unit on space or a project on the environment. Our technology provides opportunities to enhance the daily curriculum." ●

"Older students have become models for younger ones and there is a real sense of continuity, commitment, and community."

Peakview Elementary School

Cherry Creek School District, 19451 East Progress Circle, Aurora, CO 80015 **Contact:** David Livingston, Principal • Phone: (303) 766-1996 • Fax: (303) 766-0651 • E-mail: KarenP3@aol.com

Applying Learning to the Real World

Alice Carlson Applied Learning Center in Ft. Worth, Tex., was the first school in the district to open its doors to students from anywhere in the city. The school distinguishes itself by an emphasis on applied learning—an approach to education that connects classwork to the world beyond school and allows children to make choices and assume responsibilities. "We teach through projects," explains first-grade teacher Elizabeth Donaldson. "We don't just have children working from a book." Students learn data collection and graphing skills, for instance, while working on a local weather project. And, with the support of telecommunications technologies, they work with peers to integrate their findings into larger projects.

Teams of educators, parents, community members, and students share decision making responsibilities for all aspects of the school's operation, from instructional programs to purchases. Alice Carlson operates on a year-round calendar with three-week breaks between nine-week regular sessions. During the spring and fall breaks, students can register for workshops taught by teachers or members of the community on topics ranging from enriched academics to arts and crafts. ●

Alice Carlson Applied Learning Center

Ft. Worth Independent School District, 3320 West Cantey Street, Ft. Worth, TX 76109 **Contact:** Maria Lamb, Teacher-Director • Phone: (817) 922-6525 • Fax: (817) 922-6528 • E-mail: c.wms@tenet.edu

Alice Carlson Applied Learning Center, Fort Worth, TX • Photo by Paul Moseley

Turning On Lights and Opening Doors

"We are working toward developing a school in which students and teachers seek the highest levels through advanced technology, collaboration, problem-based learning, and meaningful assessment. We provide unlimited access to new learning tools and the support and safety necessary to see that all succeed."

Calloway County Middle School

Calloway County Schools, 2108-A College Farm Road, Murray, KY 42071 **Contact:** Cloyd J. Bumgardner, Principal • Phone: (502) 753-4182 • Fax: (502) 753-7648 • E-mail: KYcalloway@aol.com

"Look, the lights went on!" "We got our door to open automatically!" Excited voices of seventh graders in Kevin Brown's classroom spill out into the halls of Calloway County Middle School in rural Kentucky. The students are installing electrical circuits in shoebox structures they have designed and built. The project requires the students to work together to create a plan, conduct research, build a structure, and wire it so that lights and doors can be controlled by a switch. It's called, "Energy: The Ability to Do Work or Cause Change."

Change has become a way of life for Calloway's teachers, students, and parents, who have been working together for more than seven years to improve their school and to implement reforms required by the Kentucky Education Reform Act of 1990 (KERA). KERA redesigned the entire public school system in the commonwealth, establishing new guidelines for curriculum and assessment, expanding family-support services, planning for effective technology integration, and increasing decision making authority at school sites.

At Calloway, management councils were established to look at all aspects of restructuring at once. Making a shift from a departmentalized junior high structure to interdisciplinary teaching teams with flexible scheduling was one decision that had a major impact on the school. "I was ready to quit," says Nancy Schempp, a teacher who works on a team with Kevin Brown. "Now I'm excited again, and so are my students."

Calloway's involvement with the National Alliance for Restructuring Education (NARE) helped further the school's efforts. As a pilot site for this "break-the-mold" school design, Calloway received support from NARE's business and educational partners that included technology donations, professional development opportunities, and access to a network of experts and other teachers. "We are working toward developing a school in which students and teachers seek the highest levels through advanced technology, collaboration, problem-based learning, and meaningful assessment," says teacher Shirley Cothran. "We provide unlimited access to new learning tools and the support and safety necessary to see that all succeed." ●

A New Channel of Communication

Located in a rapidly growing suburb of Burlington, Vt., Williston Central School serves about a thousand kindergarten through eighth-grade students. From its technological infrastructure to the structure of its classes, Williston is in the process of implementing comprehensive reforms based upon the latest research about effective learning and successful organizations. Instead of grouping students by age, for example, they are organized into multi-age groups spanning two to four grade levels. In order to assure continuity in the learning program and flexibility in using time, students and teachers normally remain together for the full four-year duration. Each student has a personal learning plan that reflects district standards that all students are expected to achieve.

Williston's network of more than 400 computers supports its educational goals. Students can use tools like the Internet, two-way video conferences, or multimedia production as they work on projects that engage them in challenging and meaningful work. "The kids love it," says principal Lynn Murray. "Unlike traditional lessons when students tend to drift and daydream, you find that most are totally engaged in learning."

Electronic mail has opened up new channels of communication in the school. "When kids get to school in the morning they make a beeline to the computers to check their mail," says Murray. "They use it to communicate with their friends, teachers, and parents. Any kid can e-mail me and I'll answer. Kids who may not even like to write enough to

"The kids love it. Unlike traditional lessons when students tend to drift and daydream, you find that most are totally engaged in learning."

pass notes in class have had to improve their language skills because e-mail is so much a part of their social interaction. If someone abuses the system with foul language or nuisance mail and we revoke their access, it's like cutting off his or her tongue." ●

Williston Central School Chittenden South School District, 750 Williston Road, Williston, VT 05495 **Contact:** Lynn Murray, Principal • Phone: (802) 878-2762 • Fax: (802) 879-5830 • E-mail: murrayl@wcs3mail.wcs.cssd. k12.vt.us • URL: http://www.cvu.cssd. k12.vt.us/wcswww/wcs.htm

Clear View Charter School, Chula Vista, CA • Photo by Matthew Rivaldi

Everyone Can Learn

At Clear View Charter School, located close to California's southern border, approximately 60 percent of the 550 students in grades K-6, are new English learners and most come from low-income families. These are not the kind of demographics one would normally expect to find at a model school, yet Clear View and its principal have been recognized with numerous

"We just have to maintain high expectations and provide an environment that supports learning."

awards, and it is a model for its business partners IBM and Cox Communications.

Cox provided fiber optic links that connect students to the rest of the world, enabling them to engage in rich learning experiences designed by their teachers. Computers are integrated in the curriculum at every grade level from kindergarten, where students generate computer art to illustrate their stories, to sixth grade, where students access the information superhighway and create multimedia projects in multiple languages. In one project, fifth and sixth graders were linked through live video to scientists and medical students at San Diego State University, who helped with an investigation of insects by transmitting images from an electron microscope.

At Clear View, educators do everything they can to support continued learning, including working with parents and keeping the building open in the evenings so families and students can use its resources.

"For many years," says principal Ginger Hovenic, "I heard, 'You can't teach those kids. They can't learn.' But we can teach them and they can learn. We just have to maintain high expectations and provide an environment that supports learning." ● ★ FILM

Clear View Charter School Chula Vista Elementary School District, 455 Windrose Way, Chula Vista, CA 91910 **Contact:** Ginger Hovenic, Principal • Phone: (619) 498-3000 • Fax: (619) 498-3007 • E-mail: ghovenic@ cvesd.k12.ca.us • URL: http://www.cvesd.k12.ca.us

Collaboration for Achievement

Collaboration is the name of the game at Ysleta Elementary School in El Paso, Tex. For five years, teachers, administrators, parents, and representatives from community organizations have been involved in restructuring the school to improve students' academic achievement. They are working to integrate technology, align the curriculum across grades, increase professional accountability and interaction, and offer students the support

they need to succeed. In 1995, the school was organized into vertical teams composed of teachers and students from kindergarten through sixth grade. The teachers from each team meet regularly to discuss problems, develop strategies, and plan coherent curriculum for the students who remain in their charge throughout their years at Ysleta. Within these teams, called "families," students progress from grade to grade learning from each other and from teachers who know them well.

Ysleta receives support from the El Paso Collaborative, an organization dedicated to system-wide academic reform from kindergarten to college. The El Paso

Collaborative, in turn, is part of a national collaborative, the Education Trust, dedicated to the same goals. The Collaborative is working with Ysleta educators to establish standards and develop scoring guides to assess academic achievement across the grades. Ysleta's teachers, administrators, and parents participate in meetings sponsored by the Collaborative where educators focus on topics such as: "Math: From Kindergarten to College." Susana Navarro, director of the Collaborative, says: "I've seen secondary teachers learn strategies from elementary educators, and elementary teachers reexamine their practice when middle school teachers found they were having to re-teach too much." ●

Ysleta Elementary School Ysleta Independent School District, 9009 Alameda Avenue, El Paso, TX 79907 **Contact:** Dolores De Avila, Principal • Phone: (915) 859-8121 • Fax: (915) 859-9311

The Renaissance of Small Schools

"It takes about an hour for me to get here," says Charisse James, a 10th grader at Central Park East Secondary School (CPESS), "but it's safe and people learn." For Charisse and other students who travel to CPESS from all over New York City, the benefits of the school far outweigh the trouble it takes to get there. Founded in 1985, CPESS is a partnership between Community School District 4 and the Coalition of Essential Schools. It attracts a broad cross section of the city's 7th through 12th graders with a safe environment, personalized curriculum and instruction, and its small size—no more than 450 students and no more than 20 students per class. The school achieves this ratio under the same budget constraints as every other public school in New York City by making do without guidance counselors, music teachers, deans, or assistant principals, and with very little administrative and paraprofessional assistance.

An atmosphere of commitment and caring permeates the school. Students and teachers remain together for years and get to know each other both inside and outside of class. Teachers work together to plan and coordinate curriculum and devise meaningful assessments, rather than relying on textbooks to determine what kids study. And, as student advisors, they work with individual students guiding them to make appropriate life choices. "Teachers here are really doing three things at once: acting like counselors, developing curriculum, and teaching," says teacher Ed Canova.

As a member of the Coalition of Essential Schools, a nationwide reform partnership based at Brown University, CPESS has adopted an approach to curriculum that focuses on in-depth understanding of a limited number of concepts rather than cursory exposure to a prescribed list of information. There is a constant struggle to balance the depth and breadth in curriculum. "We know that to make good connections and to be able to evaluate things, students need lots of experiences," says Canova. "It's one of the things we talk about all the time."

In order to graduate, students must demonstrate mastery of skills and knowledge central to each academic discipline as well as proficiency in other CPESS requirements. Beginning in 11th grade, students develop in-depth projects and prepare portfolios of their work that reflect their understanding of the curriculum. Seven of these portfolios are then presented orally to a graduation committee composed of teachers, peers, and family or community members. ●

Clear View Charter School, Chula Vista, CA • Photo by Matthew Rivaldi

"Teachers here are really doing three things at once: acting like counselors, developing curriculum, and teaching."

Central Park East Secondary School New York City Community School District 4, 1573 Madison Avenue, New York, NY 10029
Contact: Paul Schwarz, Co-Director • Phone: (212) 427-6230 • Fax: (212) 876-3494

Organizations

Association for Supervision and Curriculum Development (ASCD) Description: An international, nonprofit education association of almost 200,000 administrators, teachers, students, parents, and others. Founded in 1943. **Purpose:** To improve teaching and learning for all learners, to promote educational equity, and to act as an information service. **Activities:** Hosts conferences and meetings, including interactive satellite teleconferences that focus on emerging issues and exemplary programs. Offers professional development institutes and technical assistance. Sponsors almost 50 networks of educators interested in specific issues. Publishes books and periodicals as well as audio, video, and electronic materials covering theoretical and practical aspects of education and reform. **Contact:** Susan Hlesciak Hall, Public Information Director • Association for Supervision and Curriculum Development, 1250 North Pitt Street, Alexandria VA 22314 • Phone: (800) 933-2723 • Fax: (703) 549-3891 • E-mail: shall@ascd.org • URL: http://www.ascd.org

> *"Technology and restructuring education go hand in hand. Computers, telecommunications, and multimedia tools make possible powerful new kinds of learning for both students and teachers."*
>
> Jane L. David,[4] Director, Bay Area Research Group

Consortium for Policy Research in Education (CPRE) Description: A consortium of education research institutions funded by the U.S. Department of Education. **Purpose:** To promote the use of research to inform policy and improve the quality of education for all students. **Activities:** Examines education reforms and their effects on teaching and learning; conducts research on policy and finance issues related to school improvement; and publishes results in reports and a newsletter entitled *Policy Briefs.* Serves as a federal resource center providing information and advice to policy makers, including governors and members of Congress. **Contact:** Tom Corcoran, Co-Director • Consortium for Policy Research in Education, University of Pennsylvania, 3440 Market Street, Suite 560, Philadelphia, PA 19104 • Phone: (215) 573-0700 • Fax: (215) 573-7194 • E-mail: CPRE@nwfs.gse.upenn.edu

Center for Leadership in School Reform, "The Schlechty Group" (CLSR)
Description: A nonprofit educational organization founded in 1988 by Phillip Schlechty, a leader in the field of school organization. **Purpose:** To advance fundamental reform in the public schools by improving leadership and management, developing a vision of schools and their relationship to the community, establishing a focus on the student as customer, and ensuring sustained support for school restructuring efforts. **Activities:** Promotes the notion that restructuring requires an examination of the roles and relationships within school districts as well as in communities, families, and public agencies. Provides consulting services for districts on issues such as program evaluation. Helps secure financial, political, and technical support for districts in the process of fundamental restructuring. Prepares and distributes reports and conducts seminars, workshops, and institutes. Collaborates with the Leadership Development Center, housed at JCPS/Gheens Professional Development Academy, to provide training and development for educators from Jefferson County, Ky. **Contact:** Ron Barber, Senior Associate • Center for Leadership in School Reform, "The Schlechty Group", 950 Breckenridge Lane, Suite 200, Louisville, KY 40207 • Phone: (502) 895-1942 • Fax: (502) 895-7901 • E-mail: info@clsr.win.net • URL: http://www.win.net/~clsr

Dzantik'i Heeni Middle School, Juneau, AK • Photo by Brian Wallace

Council of Chief State School Officers (CCSSO) Description: A nationwide, nonprofit organization composed of officials who head departments of education in the states, the District of Columbia, the Department of Defense Dependent Schools, and five extra-state jurisdictions. **Purpose:** To express members' views to Congress, federal agencies, professional and civic associations, and the public, and provide leadership on major educational issues. **Activities:** Through a structure of special and standing committees, works to develop consensus on key educational issues and express those views in appropriate forums. CCSSO forms coalitions with many other educational organizations to provide leadership for a variety of policy concerns affecting elementary and secondary education. With the support of foundations and federal agencies, undertakes projects that assist states with new policy and administrative initiatives and assist federal agencies and foundations in implementing their programs. Research studies and reports are developed and widely disseminated. **Contact:** Paula L. Delo, Director of Communications • Council of Chief State School Officers, One Massachusetts Avenue NW, Suite 700, Washington, DC 20001 • Phone: (202) 408-5505 • Fax: (202) 408-8072 • E-mail: info@ccsso.org • URL: http://www.ccsso.org

Designs for Change Description: A grassroots research and reform organization founded in 1977. **Purpose:** To serve as a catalyst for major improvements in urban public schools, with an emphasis on the Chicago Public Schools. **Activities:** Conducts applied research about urban schools and communities and advocates for public policies that serve the needs of these communities. Provides advice and support to educators, parents, and community leaders working to improve urban schools. Distributes resource materials, including a newsletter, *Closer Look.* **Contact:** Donald R. Moore, Executive Director • Designs for Change, Six North Michigan Avenue, Suite 1600, Chicago, IL 60602 • Phone: (312) 857-9292 • Fax: (312) 857-9299 • E-mail: dfc1@aol.com

"In order to increase student achievement, reforms at the school level need to be supported by all parts of the education system. State requirements, teacher training, curriculum materials, and tests all need to be designed around clear, focused goals for student learning."

Susan H. Fuhrman,[5] Chair, Management Committee, Consortium for Policy Research in Education, Graduate School of Education, University of Pennsylvania

Coalition of Essential Schools (CES)

Description: A membership network of schools established in 1984 at Brown University by Ted Sizer. Members are guided by nine common principles of education including: schools should help students learn to use their minds well, teaching and learning should be personalized, and students should graduate only after successfully demonstrating that essential skills and knowledge have been mastered. **Purpose:** To help redesign schools for better student learning and achievement. **Activities:** Conducts ongoing research on teaching, learning, and assessment. Local centers support teachers and administrators in networks of CES schools around the country. Coordinates workshops, and other professional development institutes; facilitates exchange of ideas among members; and publishes a journal, *Horace.* **Contact:** Carrie Holden, Membership Coordinator • Coalition of Essential Schools, Brown University, PO Box 1969, Providence, RI 02912 • Phone: (401) 863-3384 • Fax: (401) 863-2045 • E-mail: carrie_holden@ ces.uu.holonet.net • URL: http://home.aisr. brown.edu/ces

Education Trust, Inc. Description: A national organization supporting collaboration between the K-12 system and the broader community. **Purpose:** To promote high academic achievement for students at all levels, kindergarten through college. Focuses on schools and colleges serving low-income, Latino, and African-American students. **Activities:** Works side-by-side with policy makers, parents, education professionals, and community and business leaders in cities and towns across the country who are working to implement standards-based reforms. Uses lessons learned in these schools, colleges, and communities to lobby for policy changes at the federal level. Hosts conferences and publishes books, manuals, and a quarterly newsletter, *Thinking K-16.* **Contact:** Kati Haycock, Director • Education Trust, Inc., 1725 K Street NW, Suite 200, Washington, DC 20006 • Phone: (202) 293-1217 • Fax: (202) 293-2605 • E-mail: khaycock@edtrust.org

ProTech, Boston, MA

Los Angeles Educational Alliance for Restructuring Now (LEARN) Description: A nonprofit coalition of civic and business leaders, educators, parents, and other community representatives who joined together in 1991 to put forward a community-generated vision for restructuring the Los Angeles Unified School District. The LEARN plan is currently being implemented in nearly 300 schools in Los Angeles. **Purpose:** To raise student achievement for every child by restructuring the city's school system, developing local leadership, and supporting the development of collaborative school cultures responsive to student and teacher needs. **Activities:** Mobilizes community support and helps school and community representatives build consensus around reform issues, such as shifting decision making and budget authority to the school sites. Provides professional development for teachers, administrators, and parents to develop local school leadership, promote school-wide collaboration, and strengthen instructional practice around clear goals for student achievement. **Contact:** Pamela Rubin, Director of Programming and Planning • Los Angeles Educational Alliance for Restructuring Now, 300 South Grand Avenue, Suite 1160, Los Angeles, CA 90071 • Phone: (213) 255-3276 • Fax: (213) 626-5830 • E-mail: LEARNLA@aol.com

Education Commission of the States (ECS)

Description: A national, nonpartisan membership organization of policy makers and education leaders from 49 states and four U.S. territories. **Purpose:** To promote policies that are supportive of systemic education reform. **Activities:** Monitors legislation related to education and works on initiatives with governors, state legislators, and education leaders at all levels. Conducts policy research and surveys and maintains an information clearinghouse with a computerized database of education issues and trends. Sponsors networks, meetings, and conferences; provides technical assistance to member states; and publishes reports, newsletters, and video materials. **Contact:** Arleen Arnsparger, Director of Communications • Education Commission of the States, 707 17th Street, Suite 2700, Denver, CO 80202 • Phone: (303) 299-3600 • Fax: (303) 296-8332 • E-mail: ecs@ecs.org • URL: http://www.ecs.org

Institute for Educational Leadership, Inc. (IEL)

Description: A 30-year-old nonprofit educational organization. **Purpose:** To support programs and policies that encourage leaders to work together to improve education for our nation's youth. **Activities:** Helps foster collaboration between educational institutions and health and human services agencies, advocacy groups, foundations, corporations, and all levels of government. Hosts conferences and seminars for private and public sector officials designed to develop leadership skills. Conducts research, publishes reports, and disseminates information about emerging trends and issues in education. **Contact:** Michael Usdan, President • Institute for Educational Leadership, Inc., 1001 Connecticut Avenue NW, Suite 310, Washington, DC 20036 • Phone: (202) 822-8405 • Fax: (202) 872-4050 • E-mail: iel@iel.org

<blockquote>
"The main lesson we have learned in our years of helping others rethink schooling is that smaller is better. If your staff can't sit around in a circle where everyone can be heard, and if staff don't know each other or the students, then your school is too big."

Paul Schwarz,[6] Co-Director, Central Park East Secondary School, New York City Community School District 4
</blockquote>

Los Angeles Educational Partnership (LAEP) Description: Nonprofit educational partnership founded in 1984 by a group of Los Angeles business, community, and education leaders. **Purpose:** To develop a high-quality education system for the children of Los Angeles through initiatives that involve teachers in reforming curriculum, instruction, and assessment; improving access and delivery of health and social services for children and families; and planning and implementing effective strategies for school-wide change. **Activities:** Offers professional development and leadership training and facilitates collaboration among educators. Provides grants for school reform. Supports development and implementation of curricular programs such as Humanitas, an interdisciplinary humanities program. Promotes access to integrated, school-linked health and social services. Supports comprehensive school reform through the Los Angeles Learning Center and the Learning Community Program. Also provides low-cost Internet access, training, and on-line content for educators. **Contact:** Peggy Funkhouser, President and Executive Director • Los Angeles Educational Partnership, 315 West Ninth Street, Suite 1110, Los Angeles, CA 90015 • Phone: (213) 622-5237 • Fax: (213) 629-5288 • E-mail: pfunkhou@laep.lalc.k12.ca.us • URL: http://www.lalc.k12.ca.us

Shorecrest High School, Shoreline, WA

National Association of Secondary School Principals (NASSP) Description: Membership association of more than 41,000 principals and assistant principals from middle schools and high schools. Also open to other educators and school leaders. **Purpose:** To serve the needs of middle and high school administrators and others. **Activities:** Brings school leaders and experts together through conferences and conventions. Sponsors recognition programs for administrators and students. Administers a host of programs including the National Association of Student Councils and the National Alliance of High Schools. Offers professional development programs and provides legal support and counsel to members. Produces electronic resources and publishes numerous print materials. **Contact:** Timothy J. Dyer, Executive Director • National Association of Secondary School Principals, 1904 Association Drive, Reston, VA 22091 • Phone: (703) 860-0200 • Fax: (703) 476-5432 • E-mail: nassp@nassp.org • URL: http://www.nassp.org

National Center for the Accelerated Schools Project Description: A leadership organization for the Accelerated Schools Project. Based on the ideas of Henry Levin, this comprehensive approach to school reform maintains that students who have fallen behind in school benefit more from a challenging curriculum than from remediation. **Purpose:** To narrow the gap between high and low achievers, helping all students perform at appropriate levels by the end of elementary school. **Activities:** Assists schools and districts across the country in implementing Accelerated Schools' principles including: developing collaborative decision making skills and accountability, working toward a common set of goals, and building on strengths of students. Serves as an information clearinghouse. Conducts research, provides training, publishes research reports, books, and a newsletter, *Accelerated Schools*. **Contact:** Claudette Sprague, Administrative Associate • National Center for the Accelerated Schools Project, Stanford University, CERAS 109, Stanford, CA 94305 • Phone: (415) 725-1676 • Fax: (415) 725-6140 • URL: http://www-leland.stanford.edu/group/ASP

National Policy Board for Educational Administration (NPBEA) Description: A board comprised of nine national professional associations representing school administrators, professors of educational administration, and state policy organizations. **Purpose:** To advance professional standards and quality of educational administration and leadership. **Activities:** Focuses on establishing high-level certification standards for principals, developing new accreditation standards for programs in educational administration, and strengthening the professional development of school leaders. Hosts national meetings on innovative programs to prepare educational leaders. Publishes *DESIGN for Leadership,* a quarterly newsletter. **Contact:** Patrick Forsyth, Corporate Secretary • National Policy Board for Educational Administration, University of Missouri-Columbia, 205 Hill Hall, Columbia, MO 65211 • Phone: (573) 884-8300 • Fax: (573) 884-8302 • URL: http://www.npbea.org

Alice Carlson Applied Learning Center, Fort Worth, TX

Panasonic Foundation Partnership Program
Description: A partnership program focusing on systemic restructuring with a small number of school districts and state departments of education. **Purpose:** To promote systemic K-12 educational reform around the country, particularly in districts with a large proportion of disadvantaged children. **Activities:** Assists in the development and implementation of district restructuring plans. Supports schools and districts by forming long-term partnerships. Offers technical assistance on systemic restructuring, including workshops, retreats, and community forums to increase public support for educational reform. Publishes two newsletters: *Panasonic Partnership Program (P³)* on school-level restructuring; and *Strategies,* on district-level restructuring. **Contact:** Sophie Sa, Executive Director • Panasonic Foundation Partnership Program, Panasonic Foundation, Inc., Two Panasonic Way, 7G7-A, Secaucus, NJ 07094 • Phone: (201) 392-4132 • Fax: (201) 392-4126 • E-mail: foundation@panasonic.com

New American Schools (NAS) Description: A private, nonprofit organization established by corporate and foundation leaders committed to system-wide reform of the nation's K-12 schools. **Purpose:** To help schools raise student achievement through the implementation of high-quality school improvement models. **Activities:** NAS has invested in the development and testing of seven "break-the-mold" design blueprints for school excellence. They are: ATLAS Communities, Audrey Cohen College, CoNECT Schools, Expeditionary Learning Outward Bound, Modern Red Schoolhouse, National Alliance for Restructuring Education, and Roots & Wings. Implementation is based on these frameworks, but tailored for each individual school. NAS is making its designs available to communities throughout the country, mounting public education and engagement campaigns, and providing technical assistance to participating schools and districts. NAS is also funding a comprehensive study of its efforts by the RAND Corporation. **Contact:** Mary Anne Schmitt, Director of Communications • New American Schools, 1000 Wilson Boulevard, Suite 2710, Arlington, VA 22209 • Phone: (703) 908-9500 • Fax: (703) 908-0622 • E-mail: mschmitt@nasdc.org • URL: http://www.naschools.org/home.htm

Public Education Network (PEN) Description: A national association of 100 community-based school reform organizations nationwide. **Purpose:** To assist local education funds and other organizations in helping their communities build systems of public schools that result in high achievement for every child. Its work is based on the belief that independent, community-based organizations are key to achieving fundamental school reforms. **Activities:** Manages initiatives in specific school reform policy areas run by local education funds in their communities. Convenes workshops, regional meetings, institutes, and conferences to provide local education funds and communities with information and training on systemic public school reform. Serves as a clearinghouse on education policy. Publishes newsletters, *Connections* and *Policy Updates,* and occasional papers. **Contact:** Howie Schaffer, Communications Associate • Public Education Network, 601 13th Street NW, Suite 290N, Washington, DC 20005 • Phone: (202) 628-7460 • Fax: (202) 628-1893 • E-mail: hbschaffer@aol.com • URL: http://www.PEFNET.org/PEN

"We will only succeed if we rebuild schools around a single proposition—to honor children's needs above those of all others. We have to constantly ask ourselves what best serves our children as learners."

Terry Roberts,[7] Director, National Paideia Center, University of North Carolina at Chapel Hill

Quality Education for Minorities Network (QEM)
Description: A nonprofit education and advocacy organization. **Purpose:** To improve education for minorities. **Activities:** Through outreach programs and leadership development, QEM helps communities ensure that minority students will benefit from educational restructuring efforts. Sponsors a mathematics and science teacher leadership corps; organizes student internship and apprenticeship programs; and disseminates information about policy and projects pertinent to education for minorities. **Contact:** Shirley McBay, President • Quality Education for Minorities Network, 1818 N Street NW, Suite 350, Washington, DC 20036 • Phone: (202) 659-1818 • Fax: (202) 659-5408 • E-mail: smmcbay@qem.org • URL: http://qemnetwork.qem.org/

Southern Regional Education Board (SREB) Description: An organization of educational and governmental leaders in 15 southern states working together to improve education in the region. Member states are Alabama, Arkansas, Florida, Georgia, Kentucky, Louisiana, Maryland, Mississippi, North Carolina, Oklahoma, South Carolina, Tennessee, Texas, Virginia, and West Virginia. **Purpose:** To help state leaders make informed decisions about education policies and practices. **Activities:** Serves as a clearinghouse for education-related information and publishes numerous reports and papers. Works with school districts and superintendents to improve the achievement of students in vocational classes through its High Schools that Work program. Also works with business partners to sponsor a Leadership Academy for educators. Other projects include a Ph.D. program for minority students and an educational technology initiative focused on expanding the effective use of technology in classrooms. **Contact:** Beth Giddens, Publications Editor • Southern Regional Education Board, 592 Tenth Street NW, Atlanta, GA 30318 • Phone: (404) 875-9211 • Fax: (404) 872-1477 • E-mail: beth.giddens@sreb.org • URL: http://www.peach.net/sreb

Periodicals

The American School Board Journal Description: Monthly magazine for school administrators and board members. **Focus:** Features articles on a range of school- and district-related issues, such as classrooms of the future and setting high standards. A periodic supplement, *Electronic School,* presents news and ideas about educational technology. **Publisher:** National School Boards Association, Alexandria, VA • Phone: (703) 838-6722.

Education Week Description: Weekly newspaper for educators, administrators, and policy makers. **Focus:** Furnishes comprehensive coverage of education-related news throughout the year. Also includes guest commentaries, special reports, and resource information. **Publisher:** Editorial Projects in Education, Washington, DC • Phone: (800) 347-6969.

"In order for schools to meet the needs of the 21st century, time, people, space, knowledge, and technology need to be organized in different ways. We must ensure that each student has work that is engaging to them and which results in their learning those things that parents, communities, and the society at large judge to be of most worth."

Phillip Schlechty,[8] President and CEO, Center for Leadership in School Reform, "The Schlechty Group"

Alice Carlson Applied Learning Center, Fort Worth, TX

Educational Leadership Description: A theme-based journal for educators and school leaders. **Focus:** Articles by practitioners, researchers, and other experts address issues such as how technology is transforming teaching, the challenges of higher standards, and improvements in assessment. **Publisher:** Association for Supervision and Curriculum Development, Alexandria, VA • Phone: (800) 933-2723.

The Harvard Education Letter Description: A bimonthly newsletter. **Focus:** Features in-depth examinations of various educational issues, synopses of research, and lists of resources. **Publisher:** Harvard University Graduate School of Education, Cambridge, MA • Phone: (800) 422-2681.

Educational Researcher Description: An academic newsletter. **Focus:** Provides articles, commentaries, resources, and book reviews on numerous educational issues. **Publisher:** American Educational Research Association, Washington, DC • Phone: (202) 223-9485.

Learning and Leading with Technology Description: A journal for technology-using educators. **Focus:** Explores the integration of technology in teaching and learning, including issues such as distance learning, software selection, and the benefits and obstacles of using technology to assist restructuring. **Publisher:** International Society for Technology in Education, Eugene, OR • Phone: (800) 336-5191.

Phi Delta Kappan Description: A journal for educators and others interested in education. **Focus:** Covers topical issues through articles, commentaries, special reports, and book reviews. **Publisher:** Phi Delta Kappa, Bloomington, IN • Phone: (812) 339-1156.

Teachers College Record Description: Quarterly research journal. **Focus:** Features articles, essays, original research, and book reviews on various aspects of education reform and teaching and learning. **Publisher:** Columbia University, Teachers College, New York, NY • Phone: (212) 678-3719.

> *"Teachers are besieged by well-intentioned initiatives from districts, states, businesses, and parents. These players could help much more if they focused directly on the intellectual quality of students' and teachers' work, instead of on procedures, and if they maintained support for promising initiatives over the long term."*
>
> Fred Newmann,[9] Professor of Curriculum and Instruction, University of Wisconsin at Madison

Rethinking Schools: An Urban Educational Journal Description: A quarterly newspaper for educators, parents, and community members. **Focus:** Articles written by teachers, activists, and parents promote educational equity and improved education, provide critical analysis of educational trends and policies, and present classroom teaching ideas. **Publisher:** Rethinking Schools, Ltd., Milwaukee, WI • Phone: (414) 964-9646.

Readings

Bodilly, Susan, Susanna Purnell, Kimberly Ramsey, et al. **Designing New American Schools: Baseline Observations on Nine Design Teams.** *Institute on Education and Training, RAND Corporation: Santa Monica, CA, 1995.* Phone: (310) 451-7002. ● Examines the initial efforts of nine design teams funded by New American Schools Development Corporation to develop "break-the-mold" schools.

Fullan, Michael G. **Change Forces: Probing the Depths of Educational Reform.** *Falmer Press: Bristol, PA, 1993.* Phone: (215) 785-5800. ● Examines the dynamics of practices such as site-based management and decision making in the context of a changing school environment. Identifies strategies teachers should learn to become agents of change.

Danzberger, Jacqueline P., Michael W. Kirst, and Michael D. Usdan. **Governing Public Schools: New Times, New Requirements.** *Institute for Educational Leadership: Washington, DC, 1992.* Phone: (202) 822-8405. ● The authors argue that the roles and responsibilities of local school boards need to be fundamentally changed to reflect decentralized decision making and other elements of systemic education reform.

Boyer, Ernest L. **The Basic School: A Community for Learning.** *Carnegie Foundation for the Advancement of Teaching: Princeton, NJ, 1995.* Phone: (800) 777-4726. ● Presents a new model for elementary education called the "Basic School," a composite of best practices such as: a curriculum that emphasizes literacy; a focus on relationships; effective teaching and learning strategies; ethical values; and a sense of civic responsibility.

Conley, David T. **Roadmap to Restructuring: Policies, Practices, and the Emerging Visions of Schooling.** *ERIC Clearinghouse on Educational Management: Eugene, OR, 1993.* Phone: (503) 346-5043. ● A synthesis of research, knowledge, and ideas about restructuring the educational system, including discussions of curriculum, assessment, scheduling, technology, and the roles and relationships of educators. Also presents strategies for planning and implementing reforms.

David, Jane L. **Transforming State Education Agencies to Support Education Reform.** *National Governors' Association: Washington, DC, 1994.* Phone: (301) 498-3738. ● One of a series of reports on professional development and systemic reform. In this volume, the author gives an overview of restructuring requirements and looks at the roles of governors and state education agencies.

"The major challenge to transforming our schools is that traditional school practices are deeply ingrained among families, teachers, and even students. We need to break out of these patterns and create a new culture of schools based upon stimulating activities and powerful learning situations for all."

Henry M. Levin,[10] David Jacks Professor of Higher Education and Economics, Stanford University

Education Commission of the States. **Bridging the Gap: School Reform and Student Achievement.** *ECS: Denver, CO, 1995.* Phone: (303) 299-3600. ● This report documents the gap between student performance and the demands of the modern workplace, profiles a range of state reform efforts, examines public perceptions of the education system, and summarizes research on education reform.

Glickman, Carl D. **Renewing America's Schools: A Guide for School-Based Action.** *Jossey-Bass: San Francisco, CA, 1993.* Phone: (800) 956-7739. ● Since the stated goal of public schools is to prepare students to become productive citizens of our democracy, the author argues, reform efforts should be geared to helping schools become democratic, moral, and purposeful.

Fuhrman, Susan H., and Jennifer A. O'Day, eds. **Rewards and Reform: Creating Educational Incentives that Work.** *Jossey-Bass: San Francisco, CA, 1996.* Phone: (800) 956-7739. ● Experts in the fields of educational policy, practice, and research examine incentive initiatives created to achieve lasting reform in K-12 education. Looks at incentive policies for students, teachers, and organizations and argues that motivation to reform is as complex an issue as reform itself.

Alice Carlson Applied Learning Center, Fort Worth, TX • Photo by Paul Moseley

Higginbotham, Marla, ed. **What Governors Need to Know About Education Reform.** *Center for Policy Research, Education Policy Studies Division, National Governors' Association: Washington, DC, 1995.* Phone: (301) 498-3738. ● A compilation of essays from diverse contributors including educators, parents, community leaders, and policy makers addressing issues such as poverty, standards, and leadership.

Fuhrman, Susan H., ed. **Designing Coherent Education Policy: Improving the System.** *Jossey-Bass: San Francisco, CA, 1993.* Phone: (800) 956-7739. ● In this collection, a variety of authors argue that a common set of goals and a unified purpose are needed to improve education policy making at the local, state, and federal levels.

Hallett, Anne C., ed. **Reinventing Central Office: A Primer for Successful Schools.** *Cross City Campaign for Urban Reform: Chicago, IL, 1995.* Phone: (312) 322-4880. ● Looks at issues of governance, budgets, curriculum and instruction, personnel, facilities, and accountability in urban school districts. The authors share a belief that decision making authority should be shifted from the central office to school sites.

Johnson, Jean, and John Immerwahr. **First Things First: What Americans Expect from the Public Schools.** *Public Agenda: New York, NY, 1994.* Phone: (212) 686-6610. ● This report, based on surveys of the American public, reveals that safety, discipline, and a focus on the basics are their primary concerns for today's schools. At the same time, it finds support among the public for innovations designed to help prepare students for the 21st century.

Sizer, Theodore R. **Horace's Hope: What Works for the American High School.** *Houghton Mifflin: New York, NY, 1996.* Phone: (800) 225-3362. ● Third in a trilogy that views education and reform through the eyes of Horace, a composite character representing the American high school teacher. This volume stresses the importance of relationships between teachers and students and provides insight into changes needed for fundamental reform.

Dzantik'i Heeni Middle School, Juneau, AK

Means, Barbara, and Kerry Olson. **Technology's Role in Education Reform: Findings from a National Study of Innovating Schools.** *SRI International: Menlo Park, CA, 1995.* Phone: (415) 859-5109. ● A research report on how technology can support education reforms, with an emphasis on project-based teaching and learning. Examines effects on students and teachers, as well as implications for leadership and policy. Includes case studies, a review of the literature, resources, and suggested strategies for technology implementation.

"With the new technologies, changes race ahead. Our schools lag far behind and need to catch up."

Ted Sizer,[11] Chairman, Coalition of Essential Schools, Brown University

Means, Barbara and Kerry Olson. **Restructuring School with Technology: Challenges and Strategies.** *SRI International: Menlo Park, CA, 1995.* Phone: (415) 859-5109. ● Presents case studies from nine schools that have integrated technology in teaching and learning. Analyzes and offers strategies for addressing issues such as the lack of equal access and inadequate teacher support.

Mehlinger, Howard. **School Reform in the Information Age.** *Center for Excellence in Education, Indiana University: Bloomington, IN, 1995.* Phone: (800) 523-5948. ● For decision makers and others interested in education reform, this report presents a vision of a future in which technology serves as an impetus for and an instrument of change.

Meier, Deborah. **The Power of Their Ideas: Lessons for America from a Small School in Harlem.** *Beacon Press: Boston, MA, 1995.* Phone: (617) 742-2110 ext. 596. ● Through journal entries and narrative, the author tells stories from Central Park East, a small elementary school in Harlem that is often held up as a model for reforming inner city schools. The author was a chief architect of the innovative elementary school and its offshoot, Central Park East Secondary School.

National Association of Secondary School Principals. **Breaking Ranks: Changing an American Institution.** *NASSP: Reston, VA, 1996.* Phone: (703) 860-0200. ● Principals, educators, and students offer ideas for improving high schools. Among the topics addressed are: connecting curriculum to the real world, integrating technology, organizing schools into small units, rethinking schedules, and providing students with adult advocates.

National Education Commission on Time and Learning. **Prisoners of Time: Schools and Programs Making Time Work for Students and Teachers.** *National Education Commission on Time and Learning: Washington, DC, 1994.* Phone: (212) 512-1800. ● A report of a two-year study on how scheduling and other time issues affect teaching and learning in the nation's schools. The commission offers eight recommendations, including: keeping schools open longer to meet the needs of students and the community, giving teachers the time they need, and investing in technology.

Newmann, Fred M., and Gary G. Wehlage. **Successful School Restructuring: A Report to the Public and Educators by the Center on Organization and Restructuring of Schools.** *Center on Organization and Restructuring of Schools, University of Wisconsin at Madison: Madison, WI, 1995.* Phone: (608) 263-7575. ● After examining school restructuring efforts in 44 schools around the country, the authors conclude that reforms to organizational structures and methods work only if they focus on improving student learning.

Ravitch, Diane, and Maris A. Vinovskis, eds. **Learning from the Past: What History Teaches Us About School Reform.** *The Johns Hopkins University Press: Baltimore, MD, 1995.* Phone: (410) 516-6900. ● This compilation of essays by prominent education reformers puts current issues into a historical context. Organized into four parts: "Changes in Education Over Time," "Equity and Multiculturalism," "Recent Strategies for Reforming the Schools," and "The Six National Goals."

Shorecrest High School, Shoreline, WA

Reigeluth, Charles M., and Robert J. Garfinkle, eds. **Systemic Change in Education.** *Educational Technology Publications: Englewood Cliffs, NJ, 1994.* Phone: (800) 952-2665. ● The thesis of this book is that piecemeal changes to the school system will not bring about needed reforms; rather, what is needed is a comprehensive, systemic approach to transforming education. Various authors address topics such as putting technology to work for school reform, school finance in a transformed education system, and the change process in practice.

Thornburg, David D. **Education in the Communication Age.** *Starsong Publications: San Carlos, CA, 1994.* Phone: (415) 508-0314. ● This book explains how rapid changes brought about by advances in technology require a corresponding transformation in the education system. Presents strategies for implementing reforms and integrating technology, as well as practical information on hardware and software. Includes a CD-ROM with software and reference materials.

Wilson, Kenneth, and Bennett Davis. **Redesigning Education.** *Henry Holt and Company: New York, NY, 1994.* Phone: (800) 488-5233. ● Argues for redesigning the entire education system due to changes in society and the economy that result from advances in technology and information.

Schlechty, Phillip C. **Schools for the 21st Century: Leadership Imperatives for Educational Reform.** *Jossey-Bass: San Francisco, CA, 1990.* Phone: (800) 956-7739. ● The author reasons that restructuring efforts should be based on a clearly understood purpose of schooling and specifies the need for creative education leaders to promote and sustain change.

Waddock, Sandra A. **Not By Schools Alone: Sharing Responsibility for America's Education Reform.** *Praeger Publishers: Westport, CT, 1995.* Phone: (203) 226-3571. ● Changing the education system to ensure that all children learn at a high level, the author posits, will require collaboration and shared responsibility among all stakeholders, including educators, families, employees of governmental and social service agencies, and business, community, and religious groups.

Education Week. **"Quality Counts: A Report Card on the Condition of Public Education in the 50 States."** A supplement to *Vol. XVI, January 22, 1997. Editorial Projects in Education: Washington, DC.* Phone: (800) 346-1834. ● A comprehensive study prepared in collaboration with The Pew Charitable Trusts. Evaluates each state using 75 specific measures, from class size to teacher qualifications to total funds allocated.

Contact Information

[1] **Linda Roberts** Director •
Office of Educational Technology,
U.S. Department of Education,
600 Independence Avenue SW,
Room 6223, Washington, DC 20202 •
Phone: (202) 401-1444 •
Fax: (202) 401-3093 •
E-mail: lroberts@ed.gov

[2] **Robert S. Peterkin** Director •
Urban Superintendents' Program,
Graduate School of Education,
Harvard University,
469 Gutman Library, Appian Way,
Cambridge, MA 02138 •
Phone: (617) 496-4827 •
Fax: (617) 496-3095 •
E-mail: usppeterkin@connectinc.com

[3] **Jayne John** Teacher-Director (retired) •
Alice Carlson Applied Learning Center,
Ft. Worth Independent School District,
3320 West Cantey Street,
Ft. Worth, TX 76109 •
Phone: (817) 922-6525 •
Fax: (817) 922-6528 •
E-mail: c.wms@tenet.edu

[4] **Jane L. David** Director •
Bay Area Research Group,
3144 David Avenue,
Palo Alto, CA 94303 •
Phone: (415) 493-4425 •
Fax: (415) 493-0574 •
E-mail: jdavid2@aol.com

[5] **Susan H. Fuhrman** Chair,
Management Committee • Consortium
for Policy Research in Education,
Graduate School of Education,
University of Pennsylvania,
3700 Walnut Street,
Philadelphia, PA 19104 •
Phone: (215) 898-7014 •
Fax: (215) 573-2032 •
E-mail: susanf@nwfs.gse.upenn.edu

[6] **Paul Schwarz** Co-Director •
Central Park East Secondary School,
New York City Community School
District 4, 1573 Madison Avenue,
New York, NY 10029 •
Phone: (212) 427-6230 •
Fax: (212) 876-3494

[7] **Terry Roberts** Director •
National Paideia Center,
University of North Carolina at
Chapel Hill, Campus Box 8045,
Chapel Hill, NC 27599 •
Phone: (919) 962-7380 •
Fax: (919) 962-7381 •
E-mail: troberts@email.unc.edu

[8] **Phillip Schlechty** President and CEO •
Center for Leadership in School Reform,
"The Schlechty Group," 950 Breckenridge
Lane, Suite 200, Louisville, KY 40207 •
Phone: (502) 895-1942 •
Fax: (502) 895-7901 •
E-mail: clsr@aol.com

[9] **Fred Newmann** Professor of
Curriculum and Instruction •
University of Wisconsin at Madison,
1025 West Johnson Street, Room 663,
Madison, WI 53706 •
Phone: (608) 263-1811 •
Fax: (608) 263-6448 •
E-mail: fnewmann@macc.wisc.edu

[10] **Henry M. Levin** David Jacks Professor of
Higher Education and Economics •
Stanford University, CERAS 109,
Stanford, CA 94305 •
Phone: (415) 723-0840 •
Fax: (415) 725-6140 •
E-mail: KA.HML@forsythe.stanford.edu

[11] **Ted Sizer** Chairman •
Coalition of Essential Schools,
Brown University, Box 1969,
Providence, RI 02912 •
Phone: (401) 863-3384 •
Fax: (401) 863-1290

Chapter 9
Places for Learning

A basic principle of architecture is that people build buildings, then buildings build people. The idea is that the **environments** in which we work, play, learn, and live shape us in many subtle but significant ways. The spaces we create **demonstrate** what we value, communicate expectations, and influence behavior.

Traditional school **buildings** represent an approach to education that emphasizes teachers as lecturers and students as listeners. Standard-sized classrooms were designed to hold groups of 30 or so **children,** who sit at desks facing a teacher standing at a blackboard. They were intended to contain young people, rather than expose them to the outside world. They emphasize uniformity and utilitarianism over diversity and **discovery.**

Even as our understanding of how people learn has become more **sophisticated** and we've developed innovative technologies and techniques to help children achieve, most schools still reflect an outmoded model of education. Eighty percent of current schools, for example, were built before the advent of personal **computers.** Most weren't designed with such innovative instructional practices as cooperative learning or project-based education in mind. Such out-of-date facilities present both **physical** and psychological barriers to **change.**

In this chapter, we focus on facilities as an **essential** element of educational improvement. In a growing number of communities around the country, educators and others are **collaborating** to integrate form and function in the places where students learn and teachers work. **Design** teams include not only administrators and architects, but the people who will actually use the schools—teachers, students, parents, and community members. They are working together to create **versatile** educational environments that feature varied spaces for **diverse** types of learning, from large-group presentations to small-group work, and from hands-on projects to individualized instruction.

From the first **planning** stages, these schools are constructed or remodeled around the principles of flexibility and the capacity to accommodate change. Electronic **infrastructures** are being designed to be easily updated as technologies evolve. Local-area and wide-area computer **networks** and distance learning are slowly becoming as common in schools as cafeterias and gyms.

The uses for school facilities are expanding. School buildings, for example, are increasingly being recognized as **teaching tools** in and of themselves, with both man-made structures and the surrounding natural environments offering rich **opportunities** for students to learn such subjects as math, science, and design. More and more, school facilities are being conceived of as **multipurpose** buildings that make better use of a community's investment by serving not only students, but also other residents. They are being created to stay open longer hours and throughout the summer as centers where **young and old** can take classes, participate in sports and recreational activities, attend plays and performances, and hold meetings and events.

As the following entries detail, schools can be more than just buildings—they can be places that encourage and **inspire** learning. ●

Imagine the Possibilities

BY ANNE P. TAYLOR

BUILDINGS *that*

The art of school design is taking a leap forward into the 21st century, resulting in the creation of multisensory, interactive, functionally well-designed, and aesthetically beautiful learning environments that are radically different from what we now traditionally think of as "schools." The architecture of these facilities is a vibrant interaction of the physical, technical, cultural, and natural environments. It recognizes that the way a school is designed and used can contribute to apathy or, conversely, can inspire a spirit of profound creativity. A growing number of communities across the country are building schools for the next century, incorporating some of the elements described below into facilities in which the architecture, landscape, and interiors are inextricably linked to learning.

The Indoor Learning Environment In state-of-the-art learning environments, classrooms with straight rows of desks and a teacher lecturing in the front are gone. Instead, the indoor spaces of the school are carefully planned to encourage learning and support the developmental needs of the whole person. They consist of places for students to engage in applied hands-on inquiry, problem solving, group work, discussions, presentations, and reflection.

The school building itself is carefully designed to stimulate curiosity and serve as an instructional tool. The architecture embodies concepts of math, science, social studies, and art that used to be found only in textbooks. Mechanical equipment for the heating and cooling systems of the school is visible, so students can study how it works. Exposed structural elements such as beams, trusses, and columns demonstrate principles of geometry, physics, and design. Walls, floors, and furnishings feature large-scale maps, murals, and timelines that prompt wonder among younger children and reinforce learning for older students. Hallways are no longer barren corridors, but display artifacts, cultural objects, student artwork, and scientific inventions. The "eatery" is a place where nutritious foods—some grown on school grounds—are served family-style, promoting communication between adults and children.

Classrooms are now studios, workstations, and laboratories for learning, with teachers serving as guides and mentors for students as they undertake discovery experiences using a variety of technologies. The areas are homelike: soft, color-coordinated, sound-attenuated, and inviting. Some older schools that exemplify the monumental symbolic power of classical architecture have been remodeled on the inside for simplicity and technical functionality. Students in these settings have been involved in the study of such sites and have experienced the value of historic preservation and the updating and recycling of old buildings.

The typical learning center is a large studio with a computer-managed network of workstations that gives students and teachers access to—and control of—applications and information. The network allows students to work on real-world problems in areas such as robotics, ecology, hydroponics, superconductivity, biotechnology,

Anne P. Taylor[1] is a professor of architecture and the director of the Institute for Environmental Education at the School of Architecture and Planning, University of New Mexico.

TEACH

laser optics, design, and architecture. The total volume of space, not just the floor, is used for learning. Walls, ceilings, and windows are systematically designed by teams of engineers, architects, scientists, and students to meet principles of modularity, deployability, and retractability. Everything in the room is on wheels, pulleys, and brakes. Some walls contain drop-down tables and pullout shelves. Some parts of the floors are also retractable or can be elevated to form amphitheaters and stages for readings, dances, or performances, which allow students to demonstrate their understanding of knowledge and learning processes in a variety of ways. These "high-tech, high-touch" studios are the heart of the learning environment, facilitating student-centered, experiential learning and promoting creativity, innovation, and collaboration.

Adjacent to the larger studios are niches for different activities, including a child-scaled cooking area for learning nutrition, science, and math; an art studio for three-dimensional work, such as building models of items designed on the computer; music studios for practicing; dance studios; a small theater; and private quiet areas for reading, contemplation, small group discussions, and social interaction. Teachers are trained to be space planners, space managers, and facilitators of environmental learning.

The Outdoor Learning Environment The landscape design of the school includes community gardens, root cellars, nature and jogging trails, pathways, and areas for growing plants, including food. The landscape maintenance crew includes students who maintain a healthy, functional, and beautiful area surrounding each learning community. Students are thus able to experience land stewardship, botany, eco-literacy, organic farming, and environmental aesthetics. In congested urban settings, rooftop gardens, greenhouses, and container gardens serve the same purpose. Because students are learning to nourish and care for their environment, there is no destructive graffiti.

Wind generators produce electricity so students can learn to track how much it costs to produce energy as part of their integrated studies in business and science. Where possible, solar power is used to heat the building. Windows are designed to help students track angles of the sun and to bring in natural light to all spaces.

Schools are a theatrical set designed for learning. Some, in benign or sunny climates, have canopies of retractable shade structures over outdoor amphitheaters with strings of tiny lights to act as dazzling displays under the night sky during outdoor performances. Landscape and buildings are interwoven and complement each other, incorporating a variety of design principles. Examples of symmetry, asymmetry, order, hierarchy, balance, and harmony abound. These concepts are imbedded in traditional and abstract geometry, vibrant and subdued color palettes, curvilinear and rectilinear forms, and cable and tensile structures. There is functionality to the design of these learning centers, but there is also the magical commodity of delight which motivates the community to want to be there, to want to be lifelong participants in the learning process.

The way a school is designed and used can contribute to apathy or, conversely, can inspire a spirit of profound creativity.

School is More Than a Place Today's state-of-the-art learning environments are no longer confined to one building or area. Learning takes place in labs, businesses, hospitals, museums, government offices, and homes. Students move throughout the community gathering resources to study different topics and themes in a variety of learning environments with an assortment of adult mentors.

Community service and internships are becoming more a part of education so that applied, real-life learning is possible. Students of all ages take part in city planning projects, neighborhood improvement plans, tree planting initiatives, soil conservation efforts, and water quality study programs—both on and off campus. Older students are matched with community mentors who provide learning experiences in banks, law offices, city halls, farms, stores, and other businesses. These experiences foster excitement about learning

and encourage students to take innovative, entrepreneurial approaches to their education.

More and more schools also serve as hubs for electronic learning networks linking students, staff, parents, and the broader community. Everyone on the network can contribute their expertise to learning, and anyone can use the network to further their own education. These networks link any area—urban, suburban, or rural—with the global community, so users can establish relationships with other students and adults around the world.

Centers of Lifelong Learning Schools are becoming multigenerational learning communities, open 12 months of the year, meeting a wide spectrum of community and cultural needs. Campuses include museums, libraries, daycare facilities, student-run businesses, conference centers, and fitness centers—all of which are used by students, staff, and community residents. These shared

facilities, along with parks, playgrounds, and swimming pools, serve as a center for community life and help break down the invisible barriers that formerly existed between schools and their surroundings. In fact, more and more adults are going back to their local schools to continue their own educations, especially to keep up with changing technology.

To ensure these schools play a central role in community life, every segment of the population served participates in the planning process. Teachers play a large part in design decisions, since they are responsible for creating the curriculum and the learning experiences that will occur on the site. Students are also involved, since an important goal is to build a place that is comfortable and enticing for children and young people. Parents and other community members give input on particular features of community life that can be incorporated into the school and on the services they would like to see available at the school site. These partners in the design process work with architects, developers, and consultants who understand, or who are willing to learn about, the developmental needs of students and about the manifestation of curriculum in architecture, building engineering, and landscape design.

Schools also serve as hubs for electronic learning networks linking students, staff, parents, and the broader community.

Throughout the planning process, everyone is conscious of the need to plan for unforeseen uses and technological advances. Flexibility is a byword: no one wants to repeat the mistakes of the 1970s and '80s when even newly constructed schools needed major overhauls to accommodate new learning techniques and technologies. It is no longer acceptable for learning to be constrained by facilities; instead, facilities are designed to serve the varied and ever-changing needs of the next century's citizens. ●

From the Front Lines

BY K. JOHN JONES

designing a dream

More than a thousand people filled the gymnasium of the recently opened Henry M. Jackson High School in Mill Creek, Wash. After three-plus years of planning and construction, the first new secondary school in 30 years in the Everett School District (which includes Mill Creek) was about to be dedicated. Machine-generated smoke created a hazy backdrop for a big red ribbon traced in the air by students with lasers. Using an oversized pair of scissors, principal Rolynn Anderson symbolically cut the bow of light and the crowd cheered.

That moment in November 1994 was the realization of a dream for hundreds of teachers, students, parents, administrators, community leaders, contractors, and architects who'd worked together to design and build Jackson High. The project began when the school district found itself faced with too many kids, not enough classrooms or teachers, and the feeling that its schools were in danger of being outpaced by rapidly changing technology. They decided to build a new facility and set goals that were lofty—"state-of-the-art," "dedicated to lifelong learning," "a school for the 21st century"— but lacking in specifics. When my firm, The Dykeman Architects, was chosen to design the

building, it felt like one of those times when you walk into a room, everyone gets quiet, turns to look at you, and the only thing you can do is to blurt out "What?!" The whole community was looking to us to help them through the process of making the dream come true.

The first order of business was to organize an Education Specifications committee to set the parameters of the project—what architects call "programming." Since this was the District's most important initiative in decades, they pulled out all the stops, forming a task force of more than 120 people, including administrative staff, teachers, students, parents, and other community representatives. As the project manager, I saw this as a potential nightmare of competing priorities, but my fears proved groundless as committee members organized into smaller groups, focusing on the needs of different academic disciplines, community use, maintenance, and other design questions.

The majority of committee members were teachers and administrators, handpicked for their openness to change. They helped think through how to translate innovative educational practices into bricks and mortar and pushed us to create a variety of kinds of spaces for learning, from large rooms for mass meetings to smaller, more intimate spaces for group work. They were particularly interested in promoting a project-based, interdisciplinary curriculum that would better prepare students for the workplace by taking their individual needs and interests into account. Community members helped define how the school would be used after hours, leading to designs that ensured areas like the library and auditorium would be accessible to the public without creating traffic through the rest of the school. Students were especially interested in technologies that would help prepare them for their future careers.

With the program in hand, design work started. Using a combination of computer-aided design and drafting software and manual technologies (architects just can't give up sketching on napkins), we went through several versions of the building plan. Much discussion occurred over how spatial relationships between classrooms could facilitate an integrated approach to teaching as well as ensuring flexibility to update the building in the future. The final result was a three-inch binder full of concepts and design specifics—the blueprint for our shared dream.

Today, the dream is a reality. The product of our collaboration is a two-story building that is arranged in three wings with room for 1,500 students. The first wing consists of a core of science and technology labs on both levels, surrounded by general-purpose classrooms on the perimeter; this relationship was chosen to make it easier to conduct interdisciplinary activities. The second

studio with closed-circuit capabilities, and several technology labs with specialized equipment. Students and teachers use all of this technology in myriad ways. Jackson students, for example, have worked with University of Washington's Human Interface Technology Lab to explore virtual reality. They designed a three-dimensional model of Washington State that teaches geography by letting computer users take a simulated journey through the state's terrain.

Projects like this are an integral part of the new curriculum Jackson implemented in conjunction with opening the facility. The school now has longer classes, and teachers teach in teams. All students are required to take courses necessary for college admission, and, of course, the curriculum

Photo courtesy of The Dykeman Architects

wing houses administrative offices and an area that, due to lack of funds to build separate facilities, serves as a combination auditorium, lecture hall, commons, and cafeteria. Students gather there for lunch and other activities, but on special occasions it can be converted to a fully functional auditorium. The area has acoustically articulated walls and ceilings, full theater lighting and sound systems, a raised proscenium stage, and a flat floor in the seating area. Fully upholstered theater seats are built on telescopic platforms that can be deployed or retracted with the flip of a switch. The third wing houses a 3,000-seat gym and other physical education facilities.

All areas of the school are outfitted with fiber optic cables to allow for networking of computers in all general-purpose classrooms and science labs. Some areas are even more technologically enriched, including a distance learning classroom that features interactive video conferencing, a TV production

emphasizes technology and the use of informational resources, including new networked relationships with other schools, public and private agencies, and data sources. These changes have not come without controversy. The teaching staff invested a great deal of effort to develop the new curriculum, but some parents were concerned about having their children venture into unfamiliar territory and transferred them to other schools.

As for the facility, it is performing up to the community's lofty expectations. I'm proudest of the fact that it's designed to handle change—it can easily accommodate new technologies and teaching techniques, even ones that haven't yet been imagined. It should well serve the needs of students, educators, and the community for many years to come. ●

K. John Jones[2] is a principal of The Dykeman Architects.

Snapshots

Butler Did It

The new Benjamin Franklin Butler Middle School of Technology in Lowell, Mass., replaced a facility built in 1882. "It was a brick building like one you'd visualize in a scene created by Charles Dickens," says principal Harry Kouloheras. "The new facility has moved us from the 19th century into the 21st century."

A group of teachers, parents, administrators, university professors, community members, and architects collaborated to design this inner city school which serves 560 students. The group wanted the building's design to support their vision of teaching

Photo courtesy of Benjamin Franklin Butler Middle School of Technology

and learning. They embraced ideas such as: all students can learn; they learn best when they work together in mixed groups; students can learn more by initiating, designing, and producing than by just sitting and listening; and teachers are managers of information rather than disseminators of facts.

The finished facility, opened in 1992, features a video and data

"The new facility has moved us from the 19th century into the 21st century."

network that carries resources to every classroom. "I taught at the old school for 27 years," says life science teacher Bill Gianoulis. "Students could only get information from my lectures and demonstrations or the textbook. Moving to the new school was like I'd died and gone to heaven." ●

Benjamin Franklin Butler Middle School of Technology
Lowell Public Schools, 1140 Gorham Street, Lowell, MA 01852 **Contact:** Harry D. Kouloheras, Principal • Phone: (508) 937-8973 • Fax: (508) 937-2819 • E-mail: sweeneym@tiac.net • URL: http://www.lowell.k12.ma.us/Butler/Butler.html

Moving Ahead in Hammond

When the School City of Hammond in Indiana embarked on a 14-year plan to upgrade its 24 schools, "We began by creating a vision of what schools should be," says Bob Flach, the district's business manager. The first schools targeted were the district's most dilapidated elementary facilities—Maywood, Thomas A. Edison, and Oliver P. Morton. A committee of educators, administrators, architects, business people, and community members reviewed the schools' current problems and projected future needs based on demographic trends, reports on school reform, and local businesses' future plans. The group concluded that each school should serve about 500 students and support such innovations as cooperative learning and technology to "bring the world to student desktops."

"We began by creating a vision of what schools should be."

The School City of Hammond
41 Williams Street • Hammond, IN 46320 **Contact:** David O. Dickson, Superintendent • Phone: (219) 933-2400 • Fax: (219) 933-2495 • E-mail: dicksond@hammond.k12.in.us

Under the supervision of local site committees, the new Morton and Edison schools were finished in 1992. Maywood, due to soil contaminants found on the original site, opened two years later. Like the two other new schools, every area in Maywood is designed to be multipurpose. Whereas Maywood's old classrooms were set up for just one instructional method—students sitting in rows listening and working as a large group—the new rooms are almost twice the size, with foldable walls, conference space, and common areas that accommodate a variety of teaching and learning activities. A media center in the building serves as the hub for electronic resources available in every classroom. The school also has office space for community service agencies, making them more accessible for working families. ●

Building on Local Traditions

The rich cultural traditions of the local community are reflected throughout Coyote Canyon Elementary School in Rancho Cucamonga, Calif. "All the classrooms in the school are built around courtyards, each of which has a theme to teach students about a different part of the history of our area," Melanie Sowa, the school's principal, explains. The Native American courtyard, for example, features a simulated dry riverbed running past a mock Indian village that includes a wickiup (a grass hut). Wolff/Lang/Christopher, the architects who designed the school, paid for the metal frame for the wickiup and arranged for a group of Native Americans to come show students how to weave cattail reeds to create the shelter. The Spanish-Mexican courtyard centers on a small Aztec-style pyramid kids can climb on. The Rancho Mission courtyard boasts a mission bell and an authentic wagon wheel. The Vineyard courtyard contains trellises covered with grape vines, a grape press, and cask head. "These areas allow children to feel a connection with their culture and history," Sowa says. "Every classroom opens up to one of the courtyards, and the outdoors is a natural part of our students' learning environment. Parent volunteers can bring students into the courtyards and do a variety of activities outside, while still being supervised by the teacher who can see them through the window."

Despite its emphasis on history and culture, the 700-student K–4 school, which opened in 1992, is technologically advanced. A school-wide network provides video and data to every classroom, allowing students to work on real-world projects such as a Monday morning news show called "Good Morning Coyote Canyon." "The most important thing about a school, of course, is the people inside," Sowa says. "The nice thing about Coyote Canyon is that we have an incredible staff that cares about—and has high expectations for—students, as well as a gorgeous facility that raises the pride and morale of the teachers and students." ●

Photo of Coyote Canyon Elementary School courtesy of Gaylaird Christopher

Coyote Canyon Elementary School Central Elementary School District, 7889 Elm Avenue, Rancho Cucamonga, CA 91730 **Contact:** Melanie Sowa, Principal • Phone: (909) 980-4743 • Fax: (909) 980-1596 • E-mail: coyote@cyberg8t.com • URL: http://www.geocities.com/Athens/1051

Historic Decisions

"Crow Island Elementary School is one of the earliest examples of a building that reflects what children want and value," principal Elizabeth Hebert says. The 430-student, K–5 school in the Chicago suburb of Winnetka, Ill., opened in 1940 and was named a National Historic Landmark in 1990. The product of a collaboration between the famed Finnish architects Eliel and Eero Saarinen and the local firm of Perkins, Wheeler, and Will, Crow Island was among the first schools in America to reflect concepts of progressive education in its construction. "The building is philosophy in brick," Hebert says. "Rather than the high ceilings that were standard for the time it was built, it has lower ones, creating a feeling of intimacy for children. Every classroom has a wall of windows with seats for kids to be able to look out into the world and enjoy it as part of their education. The benches in the auditorium are graded in size—from the smallest in front to the largest in the rear—so that every little one's feet touch the floor. Door handles, light switches, and plumbing are all on a child's level.

Crow Island's classrooms are large and L-shaped with separate areas for group discussions and for projects. Each has its own lavatory and an entrance to a courtyard for outside learning. The Pioneer Room is a log cabin within the school where the social studies and literature curricula are linked to play activity. "The thoughtfulness that went into designing the building is so pervasive," Hebert says. "It sends the message to kids that this building was built for them." ●

Crow Island Elementary School Winnetka Public Schools, 1112 Willow Road, Winnetka, IL 60093 **Contact:** Elizabeth A. Hebert, Principal • Phone: (847) 446-0353 • Fax: (847) 446-9021

It Takes A Village

The Perry Community Educational Village is the heart of Perry Township, a rural area in northwest Ohio with 8,000 residents. "The complex's name reaffirms that schools are the focal point of the Perry community," Perry High School principal, Bob Geisler, says. "That has historically been true here, and this new facility is designed to allow student learning and community educational development to take place hand-in-hand."

The Educational Village serves 1,900 kindergarten through 12th-grade students and consists of two areas. The West Campus, which opened in 1993, houses the high school and a community fitness center; the East Campus, opened in 1995, contains the elementary and middle schools. Although each school functions independently, they share common areas such as the auditorium, natatorium, and field house. "The campuses are connected through a local area computer network," Geisler says. "From servers, students can call up about 30 different pieces of software and all sorts of reference materials." The schools also feature video networks that offer programming via a 35-inch monitor in each classroom. "Our facility and technology are designed to support an educational philosophy of students as self-directed learners with the world as their classroom," Geisler says.

Perry Community Educational Village Perry Public Schools, 3961 Main Street, Perry, OH 44081 **Contact:** Scott Howard, Superintendent • Phone: (216) 259-3881 • Fax: (216) 259-3607 • E-mail: pe_howard@lgca.ohio.gov

After school hours, the complex serves the community in various ways. The state-of-the-art theater hosts events almost every day, the athletic facilities serve as a fitness club open to the public, and the school is a branch campus for classes offered by Lakeland Community College. "We've tried to create an educational center that will serve children and the community for the next 50 years," Geisler says. ●

Back to the Drawing Board

On the drawing board, Sandy Creek High School in Tyrone, Ga., seemed to have all the amenities of a new high school—wide hallways with recessed lockers, carpeted classrooms, a large gym, an auditorium, and a dining commons lit naturally with skylights. But, as principal Wayne Robinson pointed out to the architects, there were no plans for classroom technology or a network infrastructure. "We made changes that included accommodating a school-wide video system and worked a deal with Apple Computer to install computers and telecommunications technologies and make us one of their demonstration sites," Robinson says.

Today, Sandy Creek is a model of technology use for education. Each classroom in the 1,235-student school has a "teacher-productivity station," a networked computer with office software and e-mail. Rolling carts equipped with multimedia computers, scanners, digital cameras, and software

Sandy Creek High School
Fayette County Board of Education, 360 Jenkins Road, Tyrone, GA 30290 **Contact:** Wayne Robinson, Principal • Phone: (770) 969-2840 • Fax: (770) 969-2838 • E-mail: schs@mindspring.com • URL: http://www.mindspring.com/ ~apatriot/schs.html

are used for student projects and presentations. "These kinds of technologies support our philosophy that students need to be active in the classroom and involved in the learning process," Robinson says. "Most kids are visual learners these days and

computers help make education more hands-on and fun."

Using the Internet, for example, Sandy Creek students set up an import-export business with Wellington School in Glasgow, Scotland. Sandy Creek, which is just south of Atlanta, shipped 1996 Olympics t-shirts to be sold overseas while their partners sent Scottish souvenirs to be marketed in the U.S. Students at the school have become such technical whizzes that Robinson sends them—rather than teachers—to do presentations about educational technology to groups such as the Georgia state legislature. "Students feel pretty special because of the aesthetic environment and the technology," Robinson says. "All that makes them feel good about going to school here." ●

A Building to Brag About

If you're going to invest in a new high school, do it right. That's exactly what Modesto City Schools in California did with P.W. Johansen High School, which opened in 1992 and serves more than 2,000 students. "Sometimes when communities build a big, expensive new school they get embarrassed," says principal Chris Flesuras. "To show they're being responsible with money they cut back on things like having a good-sized gym. Then they have to go back years later and replace what they left out of the original building, often at much greater cost. Modesto, though, made a commitment that this school would be a community center with great facilities, and held to it."

Johansen High is a two-story brick complex with three self-contained clusters focusing on the humanities (English, social studies, and foreign language); science, math, and business; and fine arts and vocational education. It includes a three-acre working farm, where students study such subjects as aquaponics and animal husbandry; a Shakespearean theater-style courtyard; a 500-seat theater; and an on-campus television studio. The building is networked to offer students and teachers e-mail, Internet access, and other electronic resources. Among the school's athletic facilities are a 7,000-seat stadium, a 3,000-seat gym, and an Olympic-size swimming pool. "The school is used extensively by the community," Flesuras says. "There's enough space so we can have four different functions on the same night and not have them interfere with each other."

Johansen offers evening and weekend adult classes on topics ranging from computer technology to parenting. "This is the first school I've worked in where there's been a good gym, stadium, pool, and theater because the community made a decision not to scrimp," concludes Flesuras. "They built a building that people can be proud of. When our kids visit other schools they recognize they go to school someplace special. Mostly, though, they try not to brag." ●

Photo of P.W. Johansen High School courtesy of Jon Sousa Photography

"There's enough space so we can have four different functions on the same night and not have them interfere with each other."

Peter W. Johansen High School
Modesto City Schools, 641 Norseman Drive, Modesto, CA 95357 **Contact:** Chris Flesuras, Principal • Phone: (209) 576-4960 • Fax: (209) 576-4752 • E-mail: chris_flesuras@ monet.stan-co.k12.ca.us

Inspiring Community Pride

"Poor, run-down facilities tend to discourage community support for schools," observes Edward Westfall, principal of Roane County High School in Spencer, W.V. "In some rural areas, people aren't willing to do much for education, but our new school has inspired a sense of pride around here. People can see that their money is well spent, and that increases involvement in our schools."

Opened in 1993 to serve 1,000 students, Roane County High is a two-story building perched atop a hill. "The whole front of the school is windows overlooking a valley," Westfall says. "The natural environment is an important part of our school." The school boasts its own barn and greenhouses.

To counterbalance its rural isolation, Roane County employs the latest in high-tech tools. Networked computers offer Internet access, and

Roane County High School Roane County School District, 702 Charleston Road, Spencer, WV 25276 **Contact:** Edward Westfall, Principal • Phone: (304) 927-6420 • Fax: (304) 927-6404 • E-mail: aodle@access.k12.wv.us

students and community members can take college-level classes via interactive video in the school's library. "We believe it's important for students in a rural school not to be at a great disadvantage when it comes to learning. Technology helps bridge the gap between our building and outside resources," Westfall says. "This is a technologically and architecturally outstanding structure. People driving through the West Virginia countryside happen upon our school and are astonished by it." ●

Organizations

Children's Environments Research Group

Description: A university-based research and development center. **Purpose:** To help educators and facility planners apply research on environments and children. **Activities:** Provides assistance in planning children's learning environments, works on policy issues with municipal and federal agencies, and offers expertise in designing settings for children with special needs. **Contact:** Selim Iltus or Roger Hart, Co-Directors • Children's Environments Research Group, Center for Human Environments, The Graduate School, City University of New York, 33 West 42nd Street, Room 611N, New York, NY 10036 • Phone: (212) 642-2970 • Fax: (212) 642-2971 • E-mail: siltus@email.gc.cuny.edu or rhart@email.gc.cuny.edu

"Ongoing evaluation of facilities after they are in use is essential to making schools better environments for learning."

Wolfgang F. E. Preiser,[3] Professor of Architecture, College of Design, Architecture, Art and Planning, University of Cincinnati

Committee on Architecture for Education

Description: An American Institute of Architects' professional interest area and membership organization for architects, educators, and facility planners. **Purpose:** To serve as a network for people involved with planning and building educational facilities. **Activities:** Publishes a semiannual newsletter, *Committee on Architecture for Education,* and hosts regular forums for professionals involved with creating educational facilities. **Contact:** David Roccosalva, Director • Committee on Architecture for Education, American Institute of Architects, 1735 New York Avenue NW, Washington, DC 20006 • Phone: (202) 626-7300 • Fax: (202) 626-7518 • URL: http://www.aia.org/pia/cae/home.htm

Children's Environments Research and Design Group Description: A university-based research and development organization. **Purpose:** To improve children's environments by applying research to the design of schools, childcare centers, and outdoor playgrounds. **Activities:** Services to K-12 schools include planning assistance, design consulting, and evaluation of design and use. **Contact:** Gary T. Moore, Director • Children's Environments Research and Design Group, Center for Architecture and Urban Planning Research, University of Wisconsin Milwaukee, 2728 North Summit Avenue, Milwaukee, WI 53211 • Phone: (414) 229-5940 • Fax: (414) 229-6976 • E-mail: gtmoore@csd.uwm.edu

Photo of Maywood Elementary courtesy of The School City of Hammond

The Council of Educational Facility Planners International (CEFPI) Description: Membership organization of school administrators, architects, construction program managers, consultants, university professors, manufacturers, and suppliers. **Purpose:** To promote creative and responsible planning, design, construction, and renovation of facilities for the best possible learning environments. **Activities:** Offers a number of publications on school facilities, including *Educational Facility Planner,* a bimonthly journal. **Contact:** Deborah P. Moore, Director of Administration • The Council of Educational Facility Planners International, 8687 East Via de Ventura, Suite 311, Scottsdale, AZ 85258 • Phone: (602) 948-2337 • Fax: (602) 948-4420 • E-mail: cefpi@cefpi.com • URL: http://www.cefpi.com/cefpi

Environmental Design Research Association (EDRA) Description: Membership organization of design professionals, social scientists, educators, and environmental managers. **Purpose:** To promote understanding of the interrelationships between people and their built and natural surroundings. **Activities:** Publishes a quarterly newsletter, *Design Research News.* Sponsors an annual conference as well as committees and networks that focus on projects in areas of interest to planners of K–12 facilities. **Contact:** Janet Singer, Executive Director • Environmental Design Research Association, PO Box 7146, Edmond, OK 73083 • Phone: (405) 330-4863 • Fax: (405) 330-4150 • E-mail: amsedra@aol.com • URL: http://www.acs.ohio-state.edu/edra26/leadin.html

School Zone Institute Description: Advocacy organization and research institute. **Purpose:** To assist preschool through 12th-grade educators in developing indoor and outdoor environments that support learning. **Activities:** Offers teacher training, curriculum workshops, and consulting on new school design, school remodeling, and technology integration. Publishes a curriculum and teacher's guide on architecture for children. **Contact:** Anne P. Taylor, Director • School Zone Institute, 2709 Pan American Freeway NW, Suite G, Albuquerque, NM 87107 • Phone: (505) 345-5067 • Fax: (505) 345-4795 • E-mail: aetaylor@unm.edu

New American School Design Project Description: A research and design group serving educators and architects. **Purpose:** To improve K-12 school facilities. **Activities:** Publishes reports, creates designs for model schools, does consulting work with school systems, and hosts conferences. **Contact:** Roy Strickland, Associate Professor of Architecture • New American School Design Project, Department of Architecture, Massachusetts Institute of Technology, 77 Massachusetts Avenue, Room 10-471M, Cambridge, MA 02139 • Phone: (617) 253-7334 • Fax: (617) 253-9407 • E-mail: gargoyle@mit.edu

> *"Involving teachers, students, and the community in designing a new school poses some real challenges. But the synergistic effect generated by all of the people involved is sort of like an ongoing 'barn raising' event that helps to bring the community closer together."*
>
> Steven Bingler,[4] President, Concordia Architects

Institute for Environmental Education Description: A university-based nonprofit education organization. **Purpose:** To design learning environments of the future and teach students of architecture and education to recognize relationships between physical environments, learning, and design education. **Activities:** Sponsors outreach programs for K-12 schools in which university students share strategies for teaching math and science using architecture and design principles. **Contact:** Anne P. Taylor, Director, or Tina Patel, Assistant Director • Institute for Environmental Education, School of Architecture and Planning, University of New Mexico, 2414 Central Avenue SE, Albuquerque, NM 87131 • Phone: (505) 277-5058 • Fax: (505) 277-7113 • E-mail: aetaylor@unm.edu

Periodicals

Children's Environments Description: A quarterly journal for urban planners, policy makers, educators, and scholars. **Focus:** Presents research, articles, and book reviews on a host of issues related to children, urban planning, and school and playground design. **Publisher:** Chapman & Hall, New York, NY • Phone: (800) 552-5866.

Design Research News Description: A quarterly newsletter of the Environmental Design Research Association (EDRA). **Focus:** Provides information about EDRA members, conferences, publications, and other activities. Also covers current research and design applications. **Publisher:** Environmental Design Research Association, Edmond, OK • Phone: (405) 330-4863.

West Des Moines Community School District, West Des Moines, IA

New Designs for the Comprehensive High School Description: An annual newsletter for educators and architects. **Focus:** Updates research, professional practice, and lessons learned from the implementation of design concepts, all geared to designing high schools for the 21st century. **Publisher:** National Center for Research in Vocational Education, University of Minnesota, St. Paul, MN • Phone: (612) 624-1705.

The Educational Facility Planner Description: A bimonthly publication targeted to an international readership of educators, administrators, architects, and others. **Focus:** Themed issues provide articles, references, photos, and other information designed to advance knowledge of educational facilities planning and design. **Publisher:** The Council for Educational Facility Planners International, Scottsdale, AZ • Phone: (602) 948-2337.

Readings

American Association of School Administrators. **Schoolhouse in the Red: A National Study of School Facilities and Energy Use.** *AASA: Arlington, VA, 1992.* Phone: (888) 782-2272. ● Summarizes findings of a study of public school facilities. Provides information on building conditions, financial issues, and school energy consumption.

Educational Technology Office. **Building the Future: K-12 Network Technology Planning Guide.** *California Department of Education: Sacramento, CA, 1994.* Phone: (916) 445-1260. ● Discusses the technical issues involved in planning and implementing electronic networks in schools. Includes profiles of model schools and suggestions for staff development.

> "Schools should provide large and small spaces for activities from classroom learning to private counseling and from school-wide gatherings to informal one-on-one meetings. A good school building is similar to a good house—it has rooms for privacy and introspection as well as for group socialization and ritual."
>
> Roy Strickland,[6] Associate Professor of Architecture, Department of Architecture, Massachusetts Institute of Technology

Graves, Ben E. **School Ways: The Planning and Design of America's Schools.** *Architectural Record/McGraw-Hill Professional Book Group: New York, NY, 1993.* Phone: (800) 722-4726. ● Explores historical perspectives, design considerations, and future trends related to school facilities. Illustrated with many useful photographs and drawings.

Hawkins, Harold L., and H. Edward Lilley. **Guide for School Facility Appraisal.** *The Council of Educational Facility Planners International: Scottsdale, AZ, 1992.* Phone: (602) 948-2337. ● A tool for appraising school facilities, this guide focuses on six areas: school location, structural and mechanical features, building maintenance, school building safety and security, the adequacy of a building as a teaching and learning environment, and school aesthetics.

Hebert, Elizabeth, and Anne Meek, eds. **Children, Learning and School Design: A First National Invitational Conference for Architects and Educators.** *Winnetka Public Schools: Winnetka, IL, 1992.* Phone: (847) 446-0353. ● A summary of the discussions that occurred at the 1990 "Children, Learning and School Design Conference." Topics covered include the relationships between learning and school environments; collaboration between architects, educators, and community members; and descriptions of Crow Island Elementary School, a model facility where part of the conference was held.

> "The school building should not only be aesthetically pleasing, it should also be an integral part of the educational program, so students can explore the building structures, heating and cooling systems, and scale and proportion."
>
> Gaylaird Christopher,[5] Principal, Perkins & Will.

Cohen, Uriel, Jeffrey Beer, Elizabeth Kidera, et al. **Mainstreaming the Handicapped: A Design Guide.** *The Center for Architecture and Urban Planning Research, University of Wisconsin: Milwaukee, WI, 1994.* Phone: (414) 229-2878. ● Intended for planners and architects, this book provides school design principles that address the needs of children with disabilities. Covers topics such as building access, workspace design, and furniture adaptability.

Photo of Coyote Canyon Elementary School courtesy of Gaylaird Christopher

Lackney, Jeffrey A. **Educational Facilities: The Impact and Role of the Physical Environment of the School on Teaching, Learning and Educational Outcomes.** *The Center for Architecture and Urban Planning Research, University of Wisconsin: Milwaukee, WI, 1994.* Phone: (414) 229-2878. ● The author presents a framework for evaluating school learning environments and summarizes current ideas on facilities as an integral part of the educational experience.

Meek, Anne, ed. **Designing Places for Learning.** *Association for Supervision and Curriculum Development: Alexandria, VA, 1995.* Phone: (800) 933-2723. ● Explores issues of school design that reflect innovative approaches to teaching and learning such as cooperative group work, real-world activities, and technology integration. Includes photographs and diagrams of model sites.

Moore, Gary T., and Jeffrey A. Lackney. **Educational Facilities for the Twenty-First Century: Research Analysis and Design Patterns.** *The Center for Architecture and Urban Planning Research, University of Wisconsin: Milwaukee, WI, 1994.* Phone: (414) 229-2878. ● Summarizes research on the relationship between building design and education. Offers design ideas supportive of educational strategies, such as team teaching, flexible grouping, and community use.

Taylor, Anne P., and George Vlastos. **School Zone: Learning Environments for Children.** *School Zone: Albuquerque, NM, 1983.* Phone: (505) 266-3431. ● Provides ideas for designing learning environments based on the needs of the users. Includes diagrams and photographs of innovative indoor and outdoor spaces.

Photo of Perry High School courtesy of Ed Goodwin/Burgess & Niple Architects

Public Education Association, The Architectural League of New York, and Princeton Architectural Press. **New Schools for New York: Plans and Precedents for Small Schools.** *Princeton Architectural Press: New York, NY, 1992.* Phone: (800) 722-6657. ● This book presents arguments and plans for the renovation and construction of small schools to replace the large schools typical of New York City and other urban areas.

Stuebing, Susan, Elisabeth Martin, Anton Wolfshorndl, et al. **The Seattle Public Schools: School Design Notebook.** *Department of Architecture and Building Science, New Jersey Institute of Technology: Newark, NJ, 1992.* Phone: (201) 596-3097. ● A guide for parents, educators, and architects that presents a variety of innovative K-12 school building designs that foster teaching, learning, and the integration of technology.

"The school is both the microcosm and macrocosm of the entire community. Its primary focus should be on expanding the link between people and the world through its learning spaces and technologies."

Richard Fleischman,[7] Senior Partner, Richard Fleischman Architects Inc.

Moore, Deborah, ed. **Guide for Planning Educational Facilities, 1996 Edition.** *The Council of Educational Facility Planners International: Scottsdale, AZ, 1996.* Phone: (602) 948-2337. ● A newly updated edition of a guide that details the steps involved in creating a new school, from planning and financing through evaluating the completed facility. Useful for architects, administrators, and facility planning committees.

"The school building does not merely house the educational program—it is a part of the program."

Harold L. Hawkins,[8] Professor Emeritus, Department of Educational Administration, Texas A&M University

Contact Information

[1] **Anne P. Taylor** Director and Professor • Institute for Environmental Education, School of Architecture and Planning, University of New Mexico, 2414 Central Avenue SE, Albuquerque, NM 87131 • Phone: (505) 277-5058 • Fax: (505) 277-7113 • E-mail: aetaylor@unm.edu

[2] **K. John Jones** Principal • The Dykeman Architects, 1716 West Marine View Drive, Second Floor, Everett, WA 98201 • Phone: (206) 259-3161 • Fax: (206) 621-1831 E-mail: myggmark@whidbey.net

[3] **Wolfgang F.E. Preiser** Professor of Architecture • College of Design, Architecture, Art and Planning, University of Cincinnati, PO Box 210016, Cincinnati, OH 45221 • Phone: (513) 556-6743 • Fax: (513) 556-3288 • E-mail: linda.kocher@uc.edu

[4] **Steven Bingler** President • Concordia Architects, 201 St. Charles Avenue, Suite 4314, New Orleans, LA 70170 • Phone: (504) 569-1818 • Fax: (504) 569-1820 • E-mail: stevenbin@aol.com

[5] **Gaylaird Christopher** Principal • Perkins & Will, 234 East Colorado Boulevard #600, Pasadena, CA 91101 • Phone: (818) 683-9455 • Fax: (818) 683-5717 • E-mail: gw143754@eee.org

[6] **Roy Strickland** Associate Professor of Architecture • Department of Architecture, Massachusetts Institute of Technology, 10-471M, 77 Massachusetts Avenue, Cambridge, MA 02139 • Phone: (617) 253-7334 • Fax: (617) 253-9407 • E-mail: gargoyle@mit.edu

[7] **Richard Fleischman,** Senior Partner • Richard Fleischman Architects Inc., 1025 Huron Road, Cleveland, OH 44115 • Phone: (216) 771-0090 • Fax: (216) 771-6687 • E-mail: RFARCHI@aol.com

"The physical environments of schools, both natural and built, influence the attitudes, values, and response to learning of those who study and teach in them."

Henry M. Halsted III,[9] Vice President Emeritus, Johnson Foundation

[8] **Harold L. Hawkins** Professor Emeritus • Department of Educational Administration, Texas A&M University, College Station, TX 77843 • Phone: (409) 845-0284 • Fax: (409) 862-4347

[9] **Henry M. Halsted III** Vice President Emeritus • Johnson Foundation, 3147 Red Berry Road, Racine, WI 53406 • Phone: (414) 886-0504 • Fax: (414) 886-0504 • E-mail: winkh@aol.com

Chapter 10
Technology

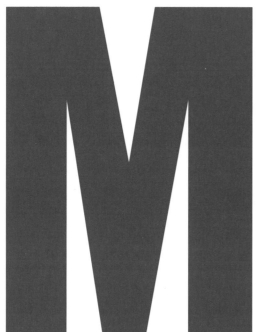

Many of the ideas for improving teaching and learning found in this book are **common sense**—they are based on the ways humans have learned throughout history and have a long track record of being used **effectively** in innovative schools around the world. What is different today is the availability of technologies that make it easier for these ideas to be put into practice on a wide scale. Technologies like computers, **telecommunications** networks, and virtual reality have the potential to **transform** education as profoundly as trains, planes, and automobiles have revolutionized transportation.

Effective learning requires access to good **information** and avenues for interaction. For students in the not-too-distant past, that meant the contents of textbooks, the **knowledge** possessed by their teachers, and the limited selections in their school library. Today's students, by contrast, have access to far **richer** and more current sources of information from digital devices accessed via local or wide area networks. As more primary source material gets digitized and put on the **Internet,** students are able to develop new knowledge from original **research.** Instead of reading about World War II in a textbook, they can see documentary footage from the war, listen to speeches by leaders on both sides, and read the full texts of the terms of surrender. If a student becomes curious about a particular aspect of the war—say the first black fighter squadron—he can search out **experts** and even communicate with actual airmen or their relatives through e-mail. Suddenly, learning can be more **exciting** and immediate than watching television.

Having this information and expertise **frees** teachers from always being the main dispensers of information. They can use their time instead to **plan** more ambitious activities and to **work** with individuals or small groups of students as they tackle each new challenge.

Technology is also giving educators the power to offer more **experiential** learning—the kind of learning that has taught all of us most of what we know. Schools have been hamstrung in providing **hands-on** learning, aside from sports, for example, by the limitations of resources and the logistics of taking students off-site. Through realistic computer **simulations** of real-world environments, jobs, and problems, students are able to have rich and rewarding learning experiences. They are traveling to distant parts of the world via the World Wide Web, **investigating** ocean bottoms, and learning to fly airplanes without leaving the classroom.

This chapter shows some of the ways technology is being used to help students develop a deeper **understanding** of the things they are learning and to keep them **motivated**. It describes how **assistive technologies** can give people with disabilities the chance to participate in learning in ways never before possible. It also raises some of the issues that are critical to the successful **integration** of technology in education, showing how different schools have handled the problems of acquiring the resources and developing the expertise needed to use technology effectively.

Technology is not a cure-all for America's schools; it's a **tool** that is only as useful as the decisions we make about how to use it. But, in the hands of creative teachers and inspired students, technology makes **possible** classrooms in which all students are working to their full potential. ●

Imagine the Possibilities

BY JAN HAWKINS

the world at your

Our schools have only just begun to explore the potential of information and communication technologies. They lag far behind businesses in using tools like computers and the Internet in their daily work. But there are already plenty of examples of how various electronic media can help students achieve more. This can be seen most dramatically in the ways that assistive technologies empower students with disabilities, allowing them to contribute in ways never before possible. It is increasingly clear that all students can benefit when technology is used intelligently to provide meaningful content and powerful tools for learning.

Students are conducting original research on the weather, for instance, using some of the same tools as professional scientists, then sharing their data and results with others all over the globe. Astronauts on the space shuttle and explorers in the jungles of Peru have involved students in the excitement of their discoveries as they happen. Using computer simulations, students are learning what it would be like to work in a particular career field, such as banking or hotel management, without leaving their classrooms.

Experiences like these help to prepare young people for a rapidly changing, highly technological world. In many jobs today, people use technology for communication, information gathering, and problem solving. Outside of work, growing numbers of people use electronic resources like the Internet to keep in touch with friends, do their banking, play interactive games, conduct research, and participate in on-line discussions. Since the power-price ratio of microchips continues to double every two years, it is likely that technology will play a ubiquitous role in as-yet unimagined ways throughout the lives of our nation's children and teachers.

Interactive multimedia and telecommunications technologies can be powerful tools for educational improvement—but they're only tools. Like screwdrivers or space shuttles, high-tech hardware and software are most useful when used for clearly defined purposes. Their power can only be unleashed if we also pay sustained attention to curriculum, school organization, educational philosophies, instructional practices, family and community involvement, and the other components of successful schools.

Instead of asking, "Should schools have computers?" we need to focus on a more productive

Jan Hawkins[1] is the director of the Center for Children and Technology at the Education Development Center, Inc.

213

fingertips

question: "How are technologies best used in education to help students achieve and prepare for the world outside of school?" In the rest of this essay, we'll explore three of the many facets of this question—how interactive technology can offer richer materials for learning, affect the way time is used in schools, and support ongoing professional development for teachers.

Richer Materials for Learning Traditional schools have long operated with fairly impoverished learning materials. In these schools, the primary sources of information are textbooks and the teacher's knowledge of the subject matter. While textbooks have a role to play, they are criticized rightly for often over-simplifying material and presenting it in bite-size packages that have little relation to each other. Additionally, they often provide outdated information. Teachers, in turn, should not be expected to be the main source of information, regardless of how deeply they understand their disciplines.

Technology brings into the classroom more interesting and diverse materials than ever before possible. Multimedia technologies and the Internet—which come together in the World Wide Web—are evolving rapidly and promise to offer easy access to everything from historical documents to breaking news. Hundreds of libraries and museums, including the Library of Congress and the Smithsonian, have already recorded parts of their collections in digital form and distribute these resources through electronic media. Science students are witnessing exciting astronomy discoveries as they unfold thanks to technologies that allow them to view images from the Hubble telescope.

Computer-based tools allow students to learn in a deeper and more immediate way. In a project called CoVis, for example, participants learn about science using some of the same research tools and data sets used by scientists in the field. Using

sophisticated software, the students collect and examine data on the weather—temperature, barometric pressure, and atmospheric chemistry—and are able to display and view the information in color-coded maps and graphs that aid in understanding.

Using Time Differently Ask any teacher and she'll tell you that one of the biggest obstacles to learning is the press of time. Given enough time and attention, any child can learn. But when a teacher is responsible for delivering instruction to a class with 30 or more students, she can rarely afford to give any individual substantial attention.

Using technology can change the dynamics of time in schools. By helping students work more independently, it gives teachers more time to work one-on-one or with small groups of students. With digital record keeping, phones in the classroom, and access to local networks to communicate with parents, administrators, and colleagues, teachers can spend more time teaching and less on paperwork.

By the same token, since it doesn't take as long for students to find information, they can spend their time evaluating, analyzing, and using it. Those with computers at home can continue to work on projects in much the same way as they would in school. By connecting to their school network or carrying their work home on a small disk, students can extend their learning. (The value of more time for learning at home is so great that some states and school districts are now loaning computers to families who do not already have them.)

More time for learning gives students the opportunity to wrestle with complex, real-life problems instead of being moved through material at a predetermined pace. They can develop useful skills while collaborating with other children around the world. I*EARN and the National Geographic Kids Network are examples of programs that connect students so they can work together on projects over an extended period of time. Through telecommunications technologies, I*EARN participants share their knowledge and experiences and, at the same time, they make contributions to the health and welfare of others. During one project, students helped collect food and clothing for victims of Hurricane Andrew in Florida. Through the Kids Network, students work collaboratively to examine scientific issues, such as the effects of acid rain on vegetation in their area. This is just one area in a science and geography curriculum facilitated by the Kids Network. It gives students first-hand, investigative experience and broadens their knowledge of the world around them.

True knowledge—understanding—develops through exploration, rumination, interpretation, judgment, and the application of information. Thoughtful work on projects and problems requires roaming through complex resources, seeking inspiration, messing around, making missteps and mistakes, and experiencing serendipitous discoveries. This kind of student learning and the in-depth interactions with teachers that it entails requires time. The intelligent use of technology can help to provide that time.

Professional Development As educators strive to guide students to meet higher standards and gain deeper understanding, teachers need to become expert with a new set of skills and knowledge. The lecture and drill methods many learned in college are no longer adequate to attain these goals. Professional development in new practices and in the technological tools they require need to be merged. Technology can assist with each of the four components I consider essential for professional development:

● Intensive sessions where teachers are able to explore new ideas and materials;

● Follow-up support over an extended period of time with mentors when teachers return to the classroom and try to implement new practices;

● Ongoing, reflective conversations with colleagues doing the same job and trying to make similar changes; and

● Observation of other teachers in their classrooms, both for exemplary practice and observing the process of change.

As teachers begin learning a new practice or idea, they can use technology in the same ways their students would. Teachers who plan to use computers with cooperative groups, for instance, need to experience what it's like working together around a computer. They can then see the kinds of issues that are likely to arise and be more prepared to deal with them in their own classrooms.

Follow-up assistance, after teachers return to the classroom, is an essential part of professional development often skipped because of the expense. With telecommunications technologies, however, the experts or mentors don't need to be physically on site. They can answer questions, conduct seminars, and offer support via e-mail, teleconferencing, or other on-line forums.

Technology enables learning to be limited by only one thing—imagination.

Telecommunications can also help colleagues talk over the issues that arise when they are making changes to their practice. Teachers are among the most isolated professionals in society, particularly if they teach specialized subjects, like physics or calculus. A number of networks, such as LabNet and Access Excellence, have sprung up to address this need. LabNet connects almost a thousand science and math teachers who solve problems together, share resources, and engage in collective professional development. Access Excellence connects several hundred of the nation's physics teachers with each other and with scientists at Genentech, Inc., a California biotechnology firm.

Finally, videotaping has created a new and more convenient way for teachers to observe other teachers—or themselves. A number of teacher preparation and professional development programs now use videotaped case studies to analyze specific classroom practices and situations.

Technology is a powerful tool that gives teachers, students, and others new ways to address problems like chronic shortages of time, materials, and professional development. Used in the context of intelligent decisions about other aspects of education, technology enables learning to be limited by only one thing—imagination. ●

From the Front Lines

BY JOHN McSWEENEY

technology in action

It's School Report Night at Cabot School, one of the few remaining schools in Vermont serving all grades from pre-kindergarten through high school. Everyone in our community—about a thousand people—has been invited to see an exhibition of work by our students. Parents, children, and their neighbors wander through the school gym as I furiously scramble to connect what seems like miles of cable to computers, monitors, modems, VCRs, and other high-tech equipment that many students are using in their presentations.

At one display, visitors click a mouse to navigate through stories written, illustrated, and recorded by primary students using multimedia tools. At another, a ninth grader, whose grandfather was one of the Japanese-Americans imprisoned in California during World War II, shows a

documentary he produced by combining photographs of the Manzanar Internment Camp with narration drawn from his own historical research. As I watch the kids excitedly drag their mothers and fathers by the hand to show them the projects they've created, I'm struck by the marvelous creativity and love of learning that technology has helped unleash within them.

In 1993, I had just completed a post-graduate certification program and had been offered a teaching position in a self-contained, fifth-grade classroom. I happened to see a classified ad for a "Technologist" at a nearby school. I was intrigued enough to apply, and my life has been anything but ordinary since.

I'd read a great deal about Cabot. Despite its rural setting, it had recently gained attention for its cutting-edge use of educational technology, thanks to the donation of a truckload of desktop computers, laptops, and other equipment by Apple Computer.

Other transformations were also well underway by the time I was hired. Members of the school community were redefining standards for the skills and knowledge they wanted students to acquire. A new mission statement and action plans promised continual professional development and improvement of the instructional program. The school was developing a project-based curriculum that focuses on learning by doing. (I understood the power of this instructional approach, because hands-on problem solving was the way I had learned my previous occupation, carpentry.) Technology had a role to play in the school's improvement efforts, but the focus would always be on sound curriculum and assessment.

My newly created job was to lead and assist the students, staff, and community in the infusion of technology. The job description included many specifics ranging from curriculum integration to equipment maintenance, but, as expected, it has evolved as the needs of the school have changed.

Today I support a wide spectrum of innovative and integrated technology use. Teachers routinely employ computers for instruction, communication, and to increase their own productivity. Students help me teach an Introduction to Computers course for local residents. High school seniors take Advanced Placement English via satellite. An exchange student from the Dominican Republic gets his hometown news daily from the World Wide Web. Art students develop new skills and talents with complex painting and graphics programs. My electronic journalism class produces both the yearbook and a monthly newspaper, using desktop publishing tools.

Working closely with teachers to plan and implement units, I look for ways to seamlessly incorporate technology into classroom learning. Our third graders, for instance, are engrossed when they use a software program like the Great Solar System Rescue. They argue about what to do next to retrieve lost space explorers, citing facts from their research using the program's electronic database, and pointing out visual clues from a companion video disk. I've helped older students apply scientific theory to the study of water in our local streams. They use computers to sort information, graph data, and discern patterns. These kinds of activities are powerful in part because they allow kids with different learning styles to work together. They also help students develop thinking and communications skills, and increase their confidence that they can tackle challenging problems.

The power is not in the machine; it is in how it is used.

Information access is another essential piece of effective educational technology use at Cabot. I've worked extensively with our library media specialist to establish reliable, low-cost Internet links, so students can access a wealth of on-line resources as they do research. Transforming this information into knowledge means making sense of data. Our sixth graders, for instance, use computerized image-processing software to learn about structure and scale by analyzing and manipulating digital photographs from sources like NASA and the National Weather Service.

While I consider myself primarily an educator, much of my time is devoted to technical support. With over 100 computers and assorted peripherals, it is rather like maintaining a fleet of vehicles. Along with a student tech team, I continue to learn the art of troubleshooting. Everyone jokes about the clutter in my tech studio—CPUs, monitors, and printers are in various states of repair, and boxes of cables, cords, and adapters are waiting for the moment when the right connection makes all the difference. We swap components and solder connections to jump-start our fleet. The number of technical glitches that crop up is directly proportional to the success of a technology-intensive program. It means the equipment is being used.

We continue to work together to learn new ways to do things. Students witness a good model of teachers as learners. I encourage teachers and students to use each other as resources to solve problems. I struggle to stay current by reading technology magazines and educational journals, going on-line, and attending conferences.

My biggest frustration is that we're always bumping the ceiling of what we can do with the hardware we have. Technology changes so quickly that it's a constant struggle to keep current. It's all worth it, though, when I witness the dramatic effect technology can have on education. Every day, I see students exploring, learning, and communicating, with purpose and creativity, using our hardware and software.

I began my journey as a teacher in early childhood education where work, play, and learning were synonymous. I marvel at first-grade students as they fearlessly point, click, and explore. They build their knowledge base and have fun, too. The power is not in the machine; it is in how it is used. The same fearless exploration, inquiring investigation, and joy for learning is possible for all students. ●

John McSweeney[2] is the technologist for Cabot School.

Snapshots

On the Frontier of Technology

Designing a new curriculum—and a new school building—from the ground up allowed the residents of Juneau, Alaska, to create a showplace for the uses of the latest technologies to support teaching

Dzantik'i Heeni Middle School Juneau School District, 10014 Crazy Horse Drive, Juneau, AK 99801 **Contact:** Charla Wright, Principal • Phone: (907) 463-1899 • Fax: (907) 463-1877 • E-mail: wrightc@jsd.k12.ak.us • URL: http://jsd.k12.ak.us

and learning. Dzantik'i Heeni Middle School is the result of a collaboration among educators and community members who created a curriculum that is challenging, project-based, and exciting. At each step along the way, the planning teams considered how technology could be used to further their goals. They also worked closely with the architects designing the school to make sure that the building itself supported the new curriculum. Every learning

area, for instance, has connections to computer and school-wide video networks.

The ubiquitous technology allows the school's 700 sixth, seventh, and eighth graders to work on projects that integrate academics with learning about the real world. In one project at the school, students helped to preserve regional history by chronicling the lives of local heroes. They created video documentaries with companion still photographs and written testimonials, then arranged a celebration where they presented their work to community members and those heroes who were still living.

One of the school's best-known projects resulted from a teacher asking his class to come up with ideas for dispelling myths about their home state. The class responded by creating Alaska On-Line, an award-winning project on the World Wide Web that

offers information about the state's history and folklore as well as guides to such Juneau-area attractions as the Mendenhall Glacier. (URL: http://jsd.k12.ak.us/ WWW/AKonline/AKhome.html)

"Community involvement in schools is strongest when the public can see that students are doing real work."

In 1994 the school joined Co-NECT, a consortium of schools with a common vision of education focused on project-based learning, strong community support, and the appropriate use of the best technologies. Observes Charla Wright, Dzantik'i Heeni's principal, "Community involvement in schools is strongest when the public can see that students are doing real work." ●

Technology Isn't Enough

"What makes us different from other districts is that our schools have a long-range vision for the integration of technology with teaching and learning," says Dennis McIntyre, director of Media and Instructional Technology Services for the Westside Community Schools in Omaha, Neb. "We recognize that technology isn't enough. Training, technical assistance, and ongoing support are key elements for success." To support the integration of technology in the curriculum, the district offers technology training classes for its more than 400 teachers and funds a technology expert at each of its 13 schools. The result is that teachers at every grade level have assistance in putting what they've learned about technology into practice.

Students at four elementary schools recently participated in a three-month, on-line learning adventure. While investigating the causes of the collapse of ancient Mayan civilization, they used e-mail and the World Wide Web to follow a research team traveling through Belize, Guatemala, Honduras, and Mexico.

At another school in the district, Westside Middle School, a class studied human rights by using the Internet to electronically search library resources and news reports as well as to contact foreign governments across the globe about their policies and practices. They identified countries that were violating human rights, created multimedia projects, and mailed them to the governments with the aim of getting them to undertake reforms. ●

"We recognize that technology isn't enough. Training, technical assistance, and ongoing support are key elements for success."

Westside Community Schools 909 South 76th Street, Omaha, NE 68114 **Contact:** Dennis McIntyre, Director of Media & Instructional Technology Services • Phone: (402) 390-2148 • Fax: (402) 390-2136 • E-mail: dennis_mcintyre@ internet.esu3.k12.ne.us • URL: http://www.wst.esu3.k12.ne.us

On-ramp to the Internet

When the Mendocino Unified School District decided to connect classrooms in each of its five schools to the Internet, this rural, coastal town in California faced the same obstacle that prevents many other small districts from

Mendocino Unified School District PO Box 1154, Mendocino, CA 95460 **Contact:** Mitchell Sprague, Teacher • Phone: (707) 937-5868 • Fax: (707) 937-0714 • E-mail: mitch@mcn.org • URL: http://www.mcn.org/ed

using the latest technology: insufficient funding. So the District decided to raise revenue by becoming an Internet service provider for the local community. It built the infrastructure by setting up partnerships to obtain hardware, software, and technical support. NASA, for example, provided the initial Internet connection. In exchange, the District agreed to develop an Internet-infused curriculum spanning the academic disciplines, which is distributed to educators nationwide on its World Wide Web site.

After the network infrastructure was in place, the District launched the Mendocino Community Network (MCN), which offers district teachers free access to electronic mail, the World Wide Web, and other Internet

services. More than 750 community members pay monthly subscriptions to use the service. Local businesses also pay a fee to the district to maintain World Wide Web pages advertising their wares. The revenues from MCN cover the cost of maintaining the district's electronic network and any surplus goes into the District's general fund. The District has been selected as a model site for Pacific Bell's Education First program, an initiative that aims to connect all of the state's classrooms to the Internet. ●

Cross-Country Collaboration

Juarez-Lincoln Accelerated School Chula Vista Elementary School District, 849 Twining Avenue, San Diego, CA 92154 **Contact:** Connie Smith, Principal • Phone: (619) 690-9222 • Fax: (619) 662-9679 • E-mail: gbonilla@ jlincoln.cvesd.k12.ca.us • URL: http://www.jlincoln.cvesd.k12.ca.us

"Teleconferencing is a powerful way for students to 'visit' each other. It allows a lot of social and racial barriers to be broken."

Juarez-Lincoln Accelerated School, in San Diego, Calif., and P.S. 92 in Queens, N.Y., couldn't be much farther apart geographically or culturally. Yet, through teleconferencing technology, students at the two schools got together to collaborate on a story for PBS's *Ghostwriter* television series, which is aimed at building literacy skills. Classes on each coast divided up responsibility for composing different parts of a mystery, shared ideas via e-mail, then used a video hookup to critique each other's work and create a final version that was presented for review to one of the program's writers.

"Teleconferencing is a powerful way for students to 'visit' each other," says George Bonilla, Juarez-Lincoln's community school specialist and network systems technologist. "It allows a lot of social and racial barriers to be broken. Adults won't say anything about the differences they see among people and that leads to misunderstandings and stereotyping, but kids talk about their observations and get it over with."

Juarez-Lincoln is a year-round, K-6 school serving 600 students. To fund its five teleconferencing sites, Internet connections in each classroom, and other technological tools, the school obtained grants and set up partnerships with other schools, corporations, and telecommunications providers. ●

On-line in Shoreline

Shorecrest High School, Shoreline, WA

Shoreline School District borders Seattle's Lake Washington near technology giants Microsoft Corp. and Boeing Corp., so it's no wonder that the District's 16 schools benefit from extensive community support for technology in the classroom. Bond measures provide $3 million per year in funding for computers and telecommunications technologies that are used throughout the curriculum.

"These students are doing things that business people think are only happening at the college level," says Al Morasch, team director. Tenth-grade students at Shorecrest High School, for example, used their skills in 3-D computer-aided design to create plans for interactive information kiosks at Seattle's Space Needle. The Space Needle Corporation decided to use the students' work in remodeling the tourist attraction's interior—rewarding Shorecrest with matching funds toward the purchase of advanced graphics-rendering hardware and software. "One of the executives on the project told me that the business community needs to recognize the level of accomplishment in K–12 students," Morasch says.

Each teacher in Shoreline has a computer issued by the District and can dial up from home to retrieve e-mail and get announcements on community bulletin boards. Even though Shoreline would be considered state-of-the-art by other districts, "our efforts are ongoing. We'll never be 'done,'" says superintendent Mary Ann Kendall-Mitchell. ● ★ FILM

Shoreline School District 18560 1st Avenue NE, Shoreline, WA 98155 **Contact:** Al Morasch, Team Director of Instructional Services • Phone: (206) 367-6111 • Fax: (206) 368-4116 • E-mail: amorasch@ slc.shorelin.wednet.edu • URL: http://www.shorelin.wednet.edu

Technology to Stay

Once teachers get a taste of technology, most take the knowledge and run with it. Starting in 1992, the 18,000-student Sioux Falls School District in South Dakota issued each of its 1,500 teachers a laptop computer. "Teachers were initially leery of this technology, but now they're saying 'How did we ever live without it?'" says fifth-grade teacher Cindy Nelson. "I find the technology indispensable for keeping grades, communicating, writing lesson plans, and creating assessments."

Teachers are also asking "What's next?" The answer is a fiber and coaxial network that will provide a fast, wide-bandwidth connection between all 37 buildings in the District. The network will allow students and staff to share resources, transfer files, communicate via e-mail, connect to the Internet, and more effectively administer the day-to-day operations of the District.

As teachers have become more comfortable with technology, they have sought out more information. A group of 63 Sioux Falls teachers joined together to pursue master's degrees in instructional technology at Augustana College. Rather than write formal theses, they conducted case studies using their own classrooms and students to investigate what works and what doesn't in educational technology.

Sioux Falls educators and Augustana College also collaborate on an annual summer institute called Tech Camp for educators and others. The camp features workshops and classes on integrating technology with learning. Summarizing the impact of educational technology on the district, Nelson says: "Technology helps create an environment where teachers and students are constantly learning." ●

"Teachers were initially leery of this technology, but now they're saying 'How did we ever live without it?'"

Sioux Falls School District 49-5
201 East 38th Street, Sioux Falls, SD 57117 **Contact:** John J. Keegan, Jr., Superintendent • Phone: (605) 367-7920 • Fax: (605) 367-4637 • E-mail: Ray.Christensen@YEBB.com

Teachers as Technology Experts

Each of the 50 teachers at the Webster School in St. Augustine, Fla., has become an expert in one area of technology, such as integrating it into the curriculum or software copyright laws. "Once one of our teachers learns about some aspect of technology," says Scarlet Harriss, the school's technology coordinator, "they are like grown-up kids—proud to be recognized as experts and eager to help their colleagues."

Webster, a school that serves 815 students, mostly in pre-K through fifth grade, developed the "teacher-expert" model under a state-funded program designed to encourage model technology sites. Its teachers have since served as trainers in the rest of the District and participated in a statewide technology infusion program.

At their own school, the teachers' knowledge and leadership has led to the widespread integration of interactive multimedia and telecommunications technologies throughout the curriculum. School-wide e-mail increases communication among the staff, while voice mail offers parents an easy way to connect with teachers. A closed-circuit television network with cable access is used to broadcast school news, announcements, and presentations. ●

The Webster School St. Johns County School District, 420 North Orange Street, St. Augustine, FL 32095 **Contact:** Scarlet Harriss, Educational Technology Specialist • Phone: (904) 824-2955 • Fax: (904) 829-5958 • E-mail: harriss@firn. mail.edu • URL: http://webster.stjohns.k12.fl.us

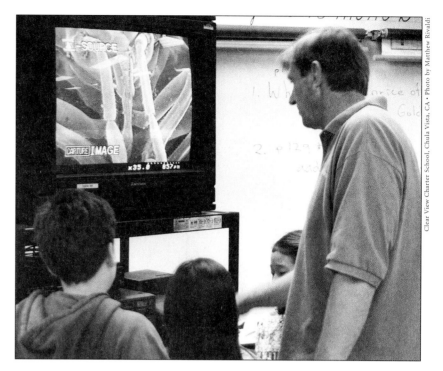

Clear View Charter School, Chula Vista, CA • Photo by Matthew Rivaldi

Turning Around a Troubled School

A few years ago, the Union City School District was in chaos, operating under threat of a takeover by the state of New Jersey for lack of performance and high transfer and drop-out rates. Now it boasts one of the most technologically advanced schools in the nation, Christopher Columbus School.

As part of an effort to revive the District, Bell Atlantic, a telephone and telecommunications company, agreed to make Columbus a test site to find out how educational telecommunications technology affects academic performance. The company provided this inner city school with hardware, software, and personnel to wire it for Internet access, e-mail, and video conferencing. It also provided computers, modems, and productivity software such as word processors and spreadsheets for use in the homes of a test group of seventh- and eighth-grade students. These tools allowed students to complete homework assignments by searching the Internet for information and encouraged parents to communicate with teachers by connecting to the school's network.

In partnership with the Education Development Center in New York City, Columbus also redesigned its curriculum to emphasize cooperative group work, interdisciplinary learning, and critical thinking, while taking full advantage of the new technology. Since the project began, student performance and attendance have improved dramatically, while transfer rates are the lowest in the district. ●

Christopher Columbus School
Union City School District, 3912 Bergen Turnpike, Union City, NJ 07087 **Contact:** Frank M. Vaccarino, Assistant Superintendent • Phone: (201) 348-5850 • Fax: (201) 348-5866 • E-mail: F.Vaccarino_@_ucboe@edc.org

On the Cutting Edge

"People here don't believe me when I tell them that our schools are on the cutting edge of technology," says Gary Day, technology coordinator for the Rogers School District in Arkansas. Every school district in the state has access to the Internet via the Arkansas Public School Computer Network (APSCN), but because it was set up primarily as a financial and student-management system, not many schools have tapped it as a learning tool. The Rogers School District, which consists of 16 schools serving almost 10,000 students, is an exception. It is leading the way in bringing classrooms direct, live connections to such Internet features as e-mail, bulletin boards, file transfers, and the World Wide Web.

"APSCN has allowed Arkansas to take a dramatic lead in worldwide resource accessibility for students, faculty, and administrators," says Day. Students in Rogers schools browse the World Wide Web to research papers, work on projects, and create supporting documents for activities like the Model United Nations. "E-mail

> *"E-mail has dramatically changed the efficiency of the faculty and administration."*

has dramatically changed the efficiency of the faculty and administration—their words, not mine," says Day. "People who for years would not touch a computer are now typing away (some very, very slowly) doing e-mail and some word processing."

The District's efforts to build its network have been enthusiastically supported by the community. Tax initiatives passed by the public generate roughly $450,000 a year for technology, and local businesses regularly donate time, knowledge, and equipment to the schools. "We're making slow, steady progress in applying technology to student learning," says Day. "Most teachers I work with are just now getting some idea of what it can do. Right now, that mainly means better access to information, but we will begin to incorporate other tools—more word processing, more manipulation software such as computer-aided design and art packages. It takes time to move an entire faculty from one point to another." ●

Rogers School District 220 South 5th Street, Rogers, AR 72756 **Contact:** Roland Smith, Superintendent • Phone: (501) 636-3910 • Fax: (501) 631-3504 • E-mail: rsmith@admin. nwsc.k12.ar.us • URL: http://rps.nwsc.k12.ar.us

Shorecrest High School, Shoreline, WA

Organizations

Alliance for Technology Access (ATA) Description: A network of technology vendors, consumer groups, family members, and others that offers hardware and software solutions for children and adults with disabilities. **Purpose:** To promote widespread use of technologies that can enable people with disabilities to become more independent and productive. **Activities:** Supports a growing national network of community-based computer resource centers and technology vendors that provide information about obtaining and using technology for children and adults with disabilities. **Contact:** Mary Lester, Associate Director • Alliance for Technology Access, 2175 East Francisco Boulevard, Suite L, San Rafael, CA 94901 • Phone: (415) 455-4575 • Fax: (415) 455-0654 • E-mail: atafta@aol.com • URL: http://marin.org/ata/

Association for Educational Communications and Technology (AECT)

Description: Association of instructional technology professionals and educators. **Purpose:** To help improve teaching and learning through the use of technology. **Activities:** Sponsors an annual conference and a trade exposition. Publishes *Tech Trends,* a magazine about the integration of technology and learning, and *Educational Technology Research and Development,* a quarterly journal devoted to research on educational technology and its uses in instruction. **Contact:** Stan Zenor, Executive Director • Association for Educational Communications and Technology, 1025 Vermont Avenue NW, Suite 820, Washington, DC 20005 • Phone: (202) 347-7834 • Fax: (202) 347-7839 • E-mail: aect@aect.org • URL: http://www.aect.org

Association for the Advancement of Computing in Education (AACE)

Description: An international organization of researchers, software developers, educators, and technology coordinators representing all disciplines and levels of education. **Purpose:** To encourage scholarly inquiry into computing in education. **Activities:** Disseminates research results and implementation strategies through publications and conferences. **Contact:** Gary H. Marks, Executive Director • Association for the Advancement of Computing in Education, PO Box 2966, Charlottesville, VA 22902 • Phone: (804) 973-3987 • Fax: (804) 978-7449 • E-mail: aace@virginia.edu • URL: http://curry.edschool.virginia.EDU/AACE/

Alice Carlson Applied Learning Center, Fort Worth, TX • Photo by Paul Moseley

Center for Interactive Educational Technology (CIET) Description: A research center based at George Mason University's Graduate School of Education. **Purpose:** To enhance the use of technology to improve teaching, learning, and school management. **Activities:** Conducts research, development, and evaluation projects that focus on the design of inquiry-based multimedia products and the evolution of learning-related technologies. **Contact:** Sunil Hazari, Director • Center for Interactive Educational Technology, Graduate School of Education (MSN 4B3), George Mason University, 4400 University Drive, Fairfax, VA 22030 • Phone: (703) 993-2143 • Fax: (703) 993-2013 • E-mail: shazari@gmu.edu • URL: http://www.gse.gmu.edu

Center for Applied Special Technology (CAST)

Description: A nonprofit research and development organization. **Purpose:** To help schools use innovative computer technologies to ensure that no child is excluded from education because of inaccessible teaching and learning materials. **Activities:** Engages in an active program of applied research and development in which multimedia technologies are used to help expand opportunities for individuals with disabilities. **Contact:** Anne Meyer or David Rose, Co-Executive Directors • Center for Applied Special Technology, 39 Cross Street, Peabody, MA 01960 • Phone: (508) 531-8555 • Fax: (508) 531-0192 • TTY: (508) 538-3110 • E-mail: cast@cast.org • URL: http://www.cast.org

Co-NECT Description: A school design model developed by BBN Corporation. **Purpose:** To help school districts create and implement an active learning environment structured around five key concepts: systemic school-based design, high standards for all, project-based learning, a strong professional community, and use of the best available technology. Drawing upon current cognitive research, networking technologies, and software development, the Co-NECT design provides a framework for setting performance goals, measuring progress, and reporting results to the local community. **Activities:** Provides consulting services to member schools, including professional development, technology planning, field support, access to the Internet, membership in the Co-NECT exchange (an on-line information service), and Critical Friends, an informal, school-to-school evaluation program. **Contact:** Lisa St. George, Project Administrator • Co-NECT, BBN Corporation, 70 Fawcett Street, Cambridge, MA 02138 • Phone: (617) 873-3069 • Fax: (617) 873-2455 • E-mail: info@co-nect.bbn.com • URL: http://co-nect.bbn.com

Computer Learning Foundation™ Description: Nonprofit educational foundation. **Purpose:** To improve education and the preparation of youth for the workplace through technology. **Activities:** Serves as a clearinghouse of information on using technology effectively. Sponsors Computer Learning Month (each October), an effort to increase national awareness of technology in education through competitions that encourage people to explore new ways of using technology with children. Also provides funding to schools through its Technology for Education Program and offers lesson plans, resource guides, and workshops for teachers and families. **Contact:** Sally Bowman Alden, Executive Director • Computer Learning Foundation,™ PO Box 60007, Palo Alto, CA 94306 • Phone: (415) 327-3347 • Fax: (415) 327-3349 • E-mail: clf@legal.com • URL: http://www.computerlearning.org

Consortium for School Networking (CoSN) Description: A membership association open to individuals as well as educational, institutional, and commercial organizations interested in all aspects of school networking. **Purpose:** To stimulate new ideas for more effective use of computer network technologies in K–12 education. **Activities:** Develops and disseminates network-based resources for educators and students designed to increase productivity and professional competence, and provides opportunities for learning and collaborative work. Also hosts conferences and lobbies for policy changes. **Contact:** William Wright, Executive Director • Consortium for School Networking, 1555 Connecticut Avenue NW, Suite 200, Washington, DC 20036 • Phone: (202) 466-6296 ext. 15 • Fax: (202) 462-9043 • E-mail: info@cosn.org • URL: http://www.cosn.org

Clear View Charter School, Chula Vista, CA

Educational Products Information Exchange Institute (EPIE) Description: A nonprofit consumer-oriented organization. **Purpose:** To provide educators with reliable evaluations of pre-K through college educational software. **Activities:** Developed and distributes TESS, The Educational Software Selector, a searchable electronic database of information about preschool to college software. Sponsors the States Consortium for Improving Software Selection, which provides member states with TESS. Offers curriculum analysis services to school districts. **Contact:** Ken Komoski, Executive Director • Educational Products Information Exchange Institute • 103-3 West Montauk Highway • Hampton Bays, NY 11946 • Phone: (516) 728-9100 • Fax: (516) 728-9228 • E-mail: EPIEInst@aol.com

Epistemology and Learning Group Description: A division of the Massachusetts Institute of Technology Media Laboratory. **Purpose:** To explore how technology can help learners develop new ideas while engaged in creating tangible objects that they can think about, talk about, and share with others. **Activities:** Develops technological tools to support children as designers of their own simulations, games, and robots. Other projects explore how new media technologies change relationships within real-world communities while developing new communities over networks. **Contact:** Mitchel Resnick, Associate Professor • Epistemology and Learning Group, Massachusetts Institute of Technology, 20 Ames Street, Room E15-318, Cambridge, MA 02139 • Phone: (617) 253-0330 • Fax: (617) 253-6215 • E-mail: el-info@media.mit.edu • URL: http://el.www.media.mit.edu/groups/el/

> *"Technology's power is in joining student and teacher as collaborators in the process of discovery and learning."*
>
> Barbara C. Sampson,[6] President and CEO, TERC

> *"Through imaginative and innovative applications of technology, teachers and parents are completely changing the educational landscape for students with disabilities."*
>
> Jacquelyn Brand,[7] Founder, Alliance for Technology Access

Institute for the Transfer of Technology to Education (ITTE) Description: A program of the National School Boards Association. **Purpose:** To encourage local school districts and their boards to study and employ communications and information technologies that improve teaching and learning, streamline administration, and enhance community and student services. **Activities:** Educates policy makers, administrators, educators, and business leaders about the potential of technology in schools through study panels and site visits. Supports the Technology Leadership Network, a national consortium of school districts using technology. Also sponsors national conferences and publishes *Insider's Letter,* a newsletter. **Contact:** Cheryl S. Williams, Director • Institute for the Transfer of Technology to Education, National School Boards Association, 1680 Duke Street, Alexandria, VA 22314 • Phone: (703) 838-6213 • Fax: (703) 548-5560 • E-mail: itte@nsba.org • URL: http://www.nsba.org/itte

Internet Society Description: An international organization of Internet users, including individuals, corporations, nonprofit organizations, and government agencies. **Purpose:** To advocate global cooperation and coordination for the Internet and its technologies and applications. **Activities:** Encourages the exploration of new Internet applications in academic, scientific, governmental, and industrial settings through its annual international conference, workshops, publications, and policy activities. **Contact:** Donald M. Heath, President and CEO • Internet Society • 12020 Sunrise Valley Drive, Suite 210 • Reston, VA 22091 • Phone: (703) 648-9888 • Fax: (703) 648-9887 • E-mail: isoc@isoc.org • URL: http://www.isoc.org

International Society for Technology in Education (ISTE) Description: The largest nonprofit organization serving computer-using educators. **Purpose:** To improve education through the integration of technology. **Activities:** Offers journals for special interest groups of educators using technology. Helps them network with peers through annual conferences, meetings, and graduate-level independent study courses. In addition, fosters partnerships between schools, businesses, and communities through its Private Sector Council. **Contact:** Maia S. Howes, Executive Secretary • International Society for Technology in Education • 1787 Agate Street, Eugene, OR 97403 • Phone: (541) 346-4414 • Fax: (541) 346-5890 • E-mail: iste@oregon.uoregon.edu • URL: http://isteonline.uoregon.edu

Global SchoolNet Foundation (GSN)

Description: Nonprofit foundation supported by educational and business institutions. **Purpose:** To support low-cost, community-based electronic networks so that all citizens can obtain equitable access to networked information and telecommunications. **Activities:** Serves as a centralized information resource for on-line learning projects in which students and teachers can network with others around the world to share project ideas. Supports collaborative partnerships among all segments of the community (schools, universities, businesses, and government organizations) to encourage lifelong learning. **Contact:** Al Rogers, Director • Global SchoolNet Foundation, PO Box 243, Bonita, CA 91908 • Phone: (619) 475-4852 • Fax: (619) 472-0735 • E-mail: helper@gsn.org • URL: http://www.gsn.org

Learning Technology Center Description: A research center at Vanderbilt University's Peabody College of Education with a multidisciplinary group of educators, researchers, and designers. **Purpose:** To investigate how interactive multimedia technologies can best be used in schools. **Activities:** Researches the uses of technologies in laboratory and field-based settings in areas such as mathematics, science, and literacy. Creates interactive learning environments that enhance K–12 classroom teaching, learning, and assessment. **Contact:** Faapio Po'e, Receptionist • Learning Technology Center, Peabody College at Vanderbilt University, PO Box 45, Nashville, TN 37203 • Phone: (615) 322-8070 • Fax: (615) 343-7556 • E-mail: poeft@ctrvax.vanderbilt.edu • URL: http://peabody.vanderbilt.edu/ltc/general/

Learning Through Collaborative Visualization (CoVis) Description: A Northwestern University project developed and funded by the National Science Foundation and the Illinois State Board of Education. **Purpose:** To create improved approaches to science education using high-bandwidth communications and visualization software. **Activities:** Works collaboratively with teachers at more than 40 schools to make classroom learning more like the practice of science. The project helps develop curricula, visualization tools, video conferencing, and other communication tools. Provides professional development and Internet access for collaborating partners. **Contact:** Susan Rand, Administrative Assistant • Learning Through Collaborative Visualization, School of Education and Social Policy, Northwestern University, 2115 North Campus Drive, Evanston, IL 60208 • Phone: (847) 467-2226 • Fax: (847) 467-1930 • E-mail: info@covis.nwu.edu • URL: http://www.covis.nwu.edu

The LINCT Coalition Description: A nonprofit education and advocacy organization. **Purpose:** To help communities develop locally run, cooperative telecomputing networks and achieve equitable access to computer technology, training, information, and lifelong learning. **Activities:** LINCT's Business for Equity through Telecomputing program is a partnership of local and regional businesses that helps communities acquire hardware and software. Learn-and-Earn Technology is run by volunteers who train members of the community in the use of computers. All members earn ComNet credit, a tax-exempt currency that converts volunteer time and effort into equipment and training or can be exchanged for other services such as childcare or eldercare, transportation, or housework. **Contact:** Ken Komoski, Executive Director • The LINCT Coalition, The Hamlet Green, Suite 3, 103-3 West Montauk Highway, Hampton Bays, NY 11946 • Phone: (516) 728-9100 • Fax: (516) 728-9228 • E-mail: komoski@aurora.liunet.edu • URL: http://www.interhelp.com/linct/linct.htm

Massachusetts Corporation for Educational Telecommunications (MCET) Description: Established by the Commonwealth of Massachusetts, MCET serves a broad base of educational institutions, nonprofit agencies, government services, and businesses. **Purpose:** To deliver distance learning educational resources to K–12 schools, universities, and community organizations. **Activities:** Developed and operates MassLearnPike, an educational satellite network supplying live, interactive distance learning programs based on various curriculum frameworks to schools in 28 states. Provides Internet access to all schools in Massachusetts through the Mass Ed OnLine LearnNet computer network. **Contact:** Beverly Simon, Senior Communications Specialist • Massachusetts Corporation for Educational Telecommunications, One Kendall Square, Building 1500, Cambridge, MA 02139 • Phone: (617) 252-5700 • Fax: (617) 252-5718 • E-mail: help@meol.mass.edu • URL: http://www.mcet.edu

"How can any teacher not be inspired to develop new and exciting ways to bring learning to life for her students through new technologies that provide tools for learning and connect the classroom with a whole world of knowledge?"

Dee Dickinson,[8] Chief Executive Officer, New Horizons for Learning

Periodicals

Consortium for School Networking News

Description: A quarterly newsletter for educators, business people, policy makers, and others interested in telecommunications. **Focus:** Articles address topics relating to the implementation and use of telecommunications technologies in the classroom. Provides updates on relevant legislation and information about useful education-related Internet resources. **Publisher:** Consortium for School Networking, Washington, DC • Phone: (202) 466-6296 ext. 15.

Educational Technology

Description: A bimonthly magazine for educators. **Focus:** Researchers, educators, and consultants write articles addressing the issues of technology in K–12 and higher education. **Publisher:** Educational Technology Publications, Englewood Cliffs, NJ • Phone: (800) 952-2665.

Alice Carlson Applied Learning Center, Fort Worth, TX

Electronic Learning Description: A magazine for educators published six times during the school year. **Focus:** Presents resources, articles, news, and research summaries on using technology in teaching and learning. Includes reviews of hardware and software as well as advice on set-up, maintenance, and equipment use. **Publisher:** Scholastic, Jefferson City, MO • Phone: (800) 544-2917.

MultiMedia Schools Description: A magazine for educators published five times per year. **Focus:** Offers how-to articles, reviews, and columns relating to using the Internet, multimedia technologies, and computer software and hardware in K–12 education. **Publisher:** OnLine, Wilton, CT • Phone: (800) 248-8466.

TECHNOS Description: Quarterly publication aimed at educators, business people, and the general public. **Focus:** Articles and interviews are a forum for the discussion of educational technology with a focus on school reform. Issues range from pedagogy to transforming schools through the use of networking technologies. **Publisher:** Agency for Instructional Technology, Bloomington, IN • Phone: (812) 339-2203.

T.H.E. Journal Description: A magazine for educators published monthly, except in July. **Focus:** Educators, researchers, and policy makers discuss the use of computing and networking technologies in all areas of education. **Publisher:** T.H.E. Journal, Tustin, CA • Phone: (714) 730-4011.

> *"At the heart of most technological advances are new forms of communication amplifying ideas across time and over distances. Rather than learn about this technology, it is far more important for students to develop the necessary interpersonal and evaluative skills to use it effectively."*
>
> Margaret Riel,[9] Education Program Consultant, InterLearn

Readings

Alliance for Technology Access. **Computer Resources for People with Disabilities: A Guide to Exploring Today's Assistive Technology, 2nd Edition.** *Hunter House: Alameda, CA, 1996.* Phone: (415) 455-4575. ● Offers practical information for people with disabilities including examples of the uses of assistive technologies and pointers to available resources.

Fisher, Charles, David C. Dwyer, and Keith Yocam, eds. **Educational Technology: Reflections on Computing in Classrooms.** *Jossey-Bass: San Francisco, CA, 1996.* Phone: (800) 956-7739. ● The Apple Classrooms of Tomorrow (ACOT) program was established to investigate how teachers and children could best use technology for classroom learning. Writers offer insights into technology intergration and educational change since 1985, when the ACOT program was first established.

Brock, Patricia Ann. **Educational Technology in the Classroom.** *Educational Technology Publications: Englewood Cliffs, NJ, 1994.* Phone: (800) 952-2665. ● A novice's guide that describes computers, multimedia, and on-line communication, and how they are used in today's classrooms.

> *"We have entered a new era of communication enhanced by electronic networks. The impact of this revolution is changing how we live, work, and learn. Educators need to understand the power of this transformation and apply it to creating schools that meet the needs of today's learners.*
>
> David Thornburg, Director,[10]
> Thornburg Center for Professional Development

Jones, Beau Fly, Gilbert Valdez, Jeri Nowakowski et al. **Designing Learning and Technology for Eduational Reform.** *North Central Regional Educational Laboratory: Oak Brook, IL, 1994.* Phone: (708) 571-4700. ● This report summarizes research and examines the costs and benefits of technology use for learning and education reform. Offers a framework for assessing technology's impact and makes policy recommendations.

Cradler, John, and Elizabeth Bridgforth. **Telecommunications Technology and Education: What Have We Learned from Research and Experience?** *Far West Laboratory for Educational Research and Development: San Francisco, CA, 1996.* Phone: (415) 565-3000. ● This report examines the state of telecommunications technologies and potential developments in networking resources. Offers advice to teachers, administrators, and policy makers about the technical assistance and staff development needed to integrate these resources into the schoools.

U.S. Congress, Office of Technology Assessment (OTA). **Education and Technology: Future Visions.** *GPO: Washington, DC, 1995.* Phone: (202) 512-1800. ● Presents papers commissioned by OTA for a 1995 workshop on the future of education. Includes a summary of workshop discussions on issues such as the potential of technology for education, improving curriculum and assessment, and new roles for educators.

Jones, Sue. **The Key Elements of Effective State Planning for Educational Technology.** *Southern Regional Education Board: Atlanta, GA, 1993.* Phone: (404) 875-9211. ● A reference guide designed to help state policy makers research, write, and evaluate statewide educational technology plans. Includes insights from educators and pointers to useful resources.

Sheingold, Karen, Linda G. Roberts, and Shirley M. Malcom, eds. **Technology for Teaching and Learning: Papers from the 1991 AAAS Forum for School Science.** *American Association for the Advancement of Science: Washington, DC, 1991.* Phone: (800) 222-7809. ● In this collection of papers, educators and researchers offer case histories to show how technology can accelerate learning in science and math for upper-elementary through high school age students.

Educational Research Service. **Internet Roadmap for Educators.** *ERS: Arlington, VA, 1996.* Phone: (703) 243-2100. ● For Internet novices and experienced users alike, this book provides tips for classroom use, resources, and examples of projects. Includes a glossary of technology terms.

Papert, Seymour. **The Children's Machine: Rethinking School in the Age of the Computer.** *BasicBooks: New York, NY, 1993.* Phone: (800) 331-3761. ● The author presents an argument for fundamental change in the institution of schooling and looks at the power and potential of computers for learning.

Lazarus, Wendy, and Laurie Lipper. **America's Children and the Information Superhighway: A Briefing Book and National Action Agenda.** *The Children's Partnership: Santa Monica, CA, 1994.* Phone: (310) 260-1220. ● This report describes recent developments in telecommunications technologies and recommends policies and activities that ensure all children have access to the educational benefits of the Internet. 1996 update available.

Garmer, Amy Korzick, and Charles M. Firestone. **Creating a Learning Society: Initiatives for Education and Technology.** *The Aspen Institute: Washington, DC, 1996.* Phone: (410) 820-5326. ● Identifies ways business, government, and nonprofits can collaborate on providing technology access in the classroom, training teachers, and creating a society that values lifelong learning.

Sivin-Kachala, Jay and Ellen R. Bialo. **Report on the Effectiveness of Technology in Schools, '95–'96.** *Software Publishers Association: Washington, DC, 1995.* Phone: (202) 452-1600. ● Presents research findings on the effects of technology on the learning process. Focuses on the relationships between technology and student achievement, attitudes toward learning, and classroom interactions.

Schofield, Janet Ward. **Computers and Classroom Culture.** *Cambridge University Press: New York, NY, 1995.* Phone: (800) 873-7423. ● Examines social and educational implications of computer use, with observations based on various urban high school classrooms and interviews with students and teachers. The author identifies how computers affect a school's culture and, in turn, how the school's culture determines computer use.

> *"Genuine computer literacy is not about learning to use tools like a word processor or spreadsheet, but about learning a new language of events, processes, and dynamic relationships that will help make the world and its ideas more understandable, more communicable, and more civilized."*
>
> Alan Kay,[11] Disney Fellow, Walt Disney Imagineering

U.S. Department of Education. **Getting America's Students Ready for the 21st Century: Meeting the Technology Literacy Challenge.** *GPO Washington, DC, 1996.* Phone: (800) 872-5327. ● This report lays out a plan for effectively integrating technology in schools and outlines federal, state, and local roles. It discusses the benefits of technology and associated costs.

Tinker, Robert F., and Peggy M. Kapisovsky, eds. **Prospects for Educational Telecomputing: Selected Readings.** *TERC: Cambridge, MA, 1993.* Phone: (617) 547-0430. ● These papers were commissioned by TERC to introduce concepts and ideas about school change at a 1991 conference on educational telecomputing. Contributors include researchers, policy makers, and educators.

Contact Information

[1] **Jan Hawkins** Director •
Center for Children and Technology, Education Development Center Inc., 96 Morton Street 7th Floor, New York, NY 10014 •
Phone: (202) 807-4251 •
Fax: (202) 633-8804 •
E-mail: jhawkins@edc.org

[2] **John McSweeney** Technologist •
Cabot School, Cabot School District, PO Box 98, Cabot, VT 05647 •
Phone: (802) 563-2289 •
Fax: (802) 563-2022 •
E-mail: juanmvt@aol.com

[3] **Connie Stout** Director •
Texas Education Network, J.J. Pickle Research Campus, University of Texas at Austin, Commons Building, Mail Code R8700, 10100 Burnet Road, Austin, TX 78758 •
Phone: (512) 475-9420 •
Fax: (512) 475-9445 •
E-mail: cstout@tenet.edu

[4] **David Dwyer** Vice President •
Advanced Learning Technology, Computer Curriculum Corporation, 1287 Lawrence Station Road, Sunnyvale, CA 94089 •
Phone: (408) 541-3967 •
Fax: (408) 745-6009 •
E-mail: ddwyer@cccpp.com

[5] **John Seely Brown** Director •
Xerox Palo Alto Research Center, 3333 Coyote Hill Road, Palo Alto, CA 94304 •
Phone: (415) 812-4341 •
Fax: (415) 812-4037 •
E-mail: jsb@parc.xerox.com

[6] **Barbara C. Sampson** President and CEO • TERC, 2067 Massachusetts Avenue, Cambridge, MA 02140 •
Phone: (617) 547-0430 •
Fax: (617) 349-3535 •
E-mail: Barbara_Sampson@TERC.edu

[7] **Jacquelyn Brand** Founder •
Alliance for Technology Access, 2175 East Francisco Boulevard, Suite L, San Rafael, CA 94901 •
Phone: (415) 455-4575 •
Fax: (415) 455-0654 •
E-mail: atafta@aol.com

[8] **Dee Dickinson** Chief Executive Officer • New Horizons for Learning, PO Box 15329, Seattle, WA 98115 •
Phone: (206) 547-7936 •
Fax: (206) 547-0328 •
E-mail: building@newhorizons.org

[9] **Margaret Riel** Education Program Consultant • InterLearn, 943 San Dieguito Drive, Encinitas, CA 92024 •
Phone: (619) 943-1314 •
Fax: (619) 943-1314 ext. 23 •
E-mail: mriel@iearn.org

[10] **David Thornburg** Director •
Thornburg Center for Professional Development, 3332 Brittan #17, San Carlos, CA 94070 •
Phone: (415) 508-0314 •
Fax: (415) 508-0315 •
E-mail: DThornburg@aol.com

[11] **Alan Kay** Disney Fellow •
Walt Disney Imagineering, 1401 Flower Street, Glendale, CA 94221 •
Phone: (818) 544-4700 •
Fax: (818) 544-4544 •
E-mail: alank@wdi.disney.com

Glossary

A Vocabulary of Reform Certain terms are central to the vision of the educational system we describe. We thought it would be helpful to provide some insight into how we used the terms throughout the book and accompanying documentary film.

accountability: Refers to strategies for holding educators responsible for results. Demands by policy makers, the business community, and the general public for accountability have increased as states and school districts shift more decision making authority to school sites. Though many systems are based on standardized test scores, we are talking about a broader system, based on clearly defined standards and more comprehensive measures of what students are learning.

assistive technologies: Throughout this book, we have described how new technologies can be used as powerful tools to help all students learn. Perhaps no group stands to benefit as much as students with disabilities. Using assistive technologies such as chin pointers, scanners, and speech synthesizers, people with disabilities are empowered to learn and live in ways that would otherwise be impossible.

alternative assessment: This term is defined differently by nearly everyone who uses it. We use it as an umbrella term that encompasses all alternatives to traditional standardized tests. Thus, it includes teacher observation, as well as portfolios, authentic assessments, and performance assessments. Alternative assessments provide better information about individual students than traditional tests and, unlike one-shot exams, can be used repeatedly to provide continuous feedback to the learner.

benchmarks: Carefully chosen examples of student work characterizing specific levels of achievement over time. They are typically ranked on a scale ranging from novice to expert and give students, teachers, parents, and the general public a clear picture of different levels of understanding and performance.

charter school: Special type of public school designed to promote innovation by giving educators latitude to operate outside of most local and state regulations. While the specifics vary from state to state, a limited number of charters are typically granted to groups of parents and educators with a particular plan or vision. In order to keep its charter, a school must meet agreed-upon targets for student achievement.

cognitive science: Scientists have only recently begun to uncover the mysteries of how people think, remember, reason, and learn. The work of developmental psychologists, neurologists, and other researchers is providing hard evidence for many of the practices in innovative schools. It also explains why traditional education practices such as lectures and rote learning are ineffective for many students.

constructivism: This theory of learning proposes that individuals make sense of new information and experiences by creating connections to their own past understanding and knowledge. In classrooms where this theory is implemented, teachers are facilitators, mentors, coaches, and guides. Students develop strategies, talk about ideas, and, in general, learn to be more self-directed.

coordinated services: A partnership among public and private agencies to provide more efficient and effective educational, health, and social services to children and families. These partnerships are based on the recognition that children have difficulty learning when their basic needs are not met. Since children spend a good deal of time at schools, these efforts are often located or coordinated at the school site.

cooperative learning: A strategy for grouping students together for learning with the aim of completing a task or project. Cooperative learning lessons are carefully structured to require students to pool their strengths, share their knowledge, and divide work equitably. This strategy has been shown to be effective in teaching students both academic and social skills.

individual learning plan: A written document that sets out learning goals and strategies for each student based on his unique needs and interests. The most effective plans are developed in collaboration with parents, teachers, counselors, students, and others interested in a child's success.

interactive multimedia: Technology that allows users to work with any combination of video, audio, animation, text, and graphics. Well-designed multimedia programs connect students to rich content and engage their interests by involving more of their senses in learning. When students have access to multimedia tools, they can create their own programs and express their ideas in new ways.

interdisciplinary curriculum: A course of study that blends several academic disciplines, often organized around a theme. Interdisciplinary work helps students use knowledge and skills from various disciplines and see the connections among different subjects.

Internet: A worldwide network of computer networks. Originally used primarily by scientists and engineers until the advent of user-friendly hardware and software. The most popular educational applications of the Internet include the World Wide Web and e-mail, which allow users convenient and inexpensive ways to access information and communicate with people around the world.

performance assessment: Any assessment that requires students to demonstrate their ability to use knowledge and skills rather than supplying predetermined answers. With performance assessments, students have a clear understanding of the goals, and may be evaluated on their ability to develop effective approaches to a task as well as on their actual demonstration of what they know and are able to do.

portfolio: A purposeful collection of student work that shows achievement over time, much like those used by artists and writers to document their work history. Portfolios often include thoughtful statements from the student about the criteria she used for selection and some form of self-evaluation. To ensure greater reliability when used for assessment purposes, individual pieces or the entire portfolio may be scored by a number of trained evaluators.

professional development school: A collaboration between a public school and a college or university that pursues several goals: to educate student teachers, provide continuing learning experiences for certified teachers, and conduct research on effective approaches to teaching and learning.

project-based learning: Sometimes called "experiential learning," this approach to education engages students in meaningful tasks as they learn. Students are often required to use skills and knowledge from various disciplines to create a product or propose solutions to a complex, real-world problem.

restructuring: The process of fundamentally changing or redesigning the public school system. As we use the term, restructuring includes efforts such as defining standards, decentralizing governance, improving assessments, professionalizing teaching, integrating technology, and fostering cooperation among all stakeholders in the education system.

rubric: A description of the criteria used to guide evaluation of student work. Rubrics help ensure that students and evaluators understand the standards against which work will be measured.

school-to-career program: A systematic effort to prepare students for the world of work. These programs help students acquire work experience as well as the high levels of academic skills and technological literacy needed to succeed in the modern workplace.

simulation software: The adage that "experience is the best teacher" is true. But it is not easy to provide students with many of the experiences they need to truly understand the material they are studying. Simulation software offers a way to allow students to work on tasks or projects that would otherwise be impractical, dangerous, or prohibitively expensive.

site-based management: A decentralized system of school governance that shifts decision making power from state and district offices to school sites. In many schools, site-based management is the responsibility of school councils composed of administrators, teachers, students, parents, and other community members. These councils typically have authority over issues ranging from personnel to resource allocation.

stakeholder: Individuals or groups who have an interest in the success of an endeavor. In education, stakeholders include students, educators, parents, the business community, policy makers, the media, and the general public.

standardized tests: Assessments that are designed to allow comparisons among students, schools, programs, and districts by requiring all test-takers to answer similar questions under similar conditions. Standardized tests have traditionally used multiple-choice questions because they are easy to score. Many efforts are underway to broaden the types of assessments that can be standardized so they provide a more accurate picture of what students have learned.

standards: As we use the term, these are formal, agreed-upon goals or definitions of excellence. There are two types of standards in education: content and performance. Content standards define what students should be expected to learn, and performance standards indicate acceptable levels of achievement.

telecommunications: This term encompasses all forms of communication carried out over computer networks. They are not limited to text and may include still pictures, video, and sound, as in a video conference. Telecommunications allow teachers and students to access information and communicate with experts and peers all over the world.

World Wide Web (WWW): An application available on the Internet that is easy to use and can accommodate graphics, sound, and video. Information on the Web is stored in what are known as "pages," based on the analogy of book pages, except that each Web page can be linked to many others around the world. Users can simply click on highlighted words or pictures to access more information. Addresses for pages on the Web are known as Universal Resource Locators, or URLs.

Electronic Resources

Using this list of electronic resources

Existing on-line libraries, mailing lists, World Wide Web pages, and e-mail addresses offer a rich array of resources for anyone using the Internet. No printed list can accurately describe what's out there. Sites become more sophisticated, change addresses, go "under construction," and appear or disappear daily. To cope with this, a periodically updated set of these links is kept at our Web site at **http://glef.org.**

Search Engines have been indispensable tools for putting this list together. If you are looking for information on a specific topic or group, a good search engine is often the best place to begin. As useful as search engines are, though, they are not perfect. No indexing system is complete or subtle enough to uncover all existing references and possibilities.

This list of educational resource sites and links to significant organizations and programs is intended to supplement the information in the body of this book. Because the Web is itself a collection of interconnected links, we offer several **Starting Points**—strong sites that also have rich and varied links. These provide a good sampling of the educational resources available on the Internet.

The rest of the links are divided into the following six sections. The first is **Labs & Centers,** which are in the business of researching and disseminating information about educational innovations and reforms. Links of special interest to teachers and administrators are listed as **Links for Educators.** The category of **Museums, Libraries & Clearinghouses** includes resources that provide documents, lessons, and other useful information on-line. **Organizations, Schools & Programs** is a collection of links to programs not included in the body of this book that are worth exploring. The rapidly growing world of educational projects that use the Internet to bring students, teachers, and ideas together is represented by **Student Projects.** Finally, networks and advocacy organizations promoting the integration of technology in education can be found under **Technology-Related Links.**

Search Engines

Alta Vista is one of the fastest and most comprehensive search engines currently available. It hunts through hundreds of thousands of servers, mailing lists, and newsgroups, usually reporting back in seconds. **URL: http://www.altavista.digital.com**

Excite offers a fast and comprehensive search engine as well as a variety of specialized subject areas, Web site reviews, and news feeds. Some subject areas contain weekly columns that are hotlinked to other relevant Web sites. **URL: http://www.excite.com**

HotBot is capable of indexing and searching every word on the World Wide Web. As a result, users can conduct more complex searches. **URL: http://www.hotbot.com**

Lycos indexes millions of sites. Not quite as comprehensive or fast as some, but turns up resources sometimes not available through other searchers. Also maintains an extensive list of education home pages with brief descriptions, evaluations, and links to related sites. **URL: http://www.lycos.com**

Magellan is best for broad subject-specific searches. Magellan is updated weekly and rates content based on quality and its fitness for children. **URL: http://www.mckinley.com**

WebCrawler is an easy to use search engine that maintains a detailed list of education-related links. **URL: http://www.webcrawler.com**

Yahoo! offers subject and phrase-specific searches and screens the sites it lists for quality. Maintains a list of K-12 education sites, making it a good starting place for a survey of available resources. **URL: http://www.yahoo.com**

Yahooligans! is the children's version of Yahoo! Designed to be easy for kids ages 8 to 14 to use and understand. All sites are screened for appropriateness. **URL: http://www.yahooligans.com**

Starting Points

AskERIC is part of the Educational Resources Information Center (ERIC), an information service sponsored by the federal government that searches for and makes available education articles, lesson plans, and books. ERIC covers a broad range of education-related issues through 16 subject-specific clearinghouses. **URL: http://ericir.syr.edu**

Council for Educational Development and Research (CEDaR) explores practical solutions to today's educational problems. CEDaR promotes the use of technology in education and has links to the federally funded regional educational labs. **URL: http://www.cedar.org • E-mail: dgstoner@cedar.org**

EdWeb, Exploring Technology and School Reform is a practical guide to Internet-related issues as well as to educational resources on the Web. Sponsored by the Corporation for Public Broadcasting.
URL: http://k12.cnidr.org:90/resource.cntnts.html • E-mail: acarvin@k12.cnidr.org

Eisenhower National Clearinghouse is a centralized collection of multimedia lessons, electronic resources, and links to publications and useful sites for math and science educators. Includes a sophisticated search engine.
URL: http://info@enc.org • E-mail: web@enc.org

Library of Congress maintains an on-line catalog, keeps information on local and state governments, makes available collections of historical documents, and has links to Internet resources. **URL: http://www.loc.gov • E-mail: lcweb@loc.gov**

NASA K-12 Internet Initiative supports educators and students with links to current NASA research, scientists, and suggestions on how to use NASA curriculum and World Wide Web resources effectively. **URL: http://quest.arc.nasa.gov • E-mail: M_Leon@qmgate.arc.nasa.gov**

North Central Regional Educational Laboratory (NCREL) is a federally sponsored lab that researches topics such as technology use in education and serves a region encompassing Illinois, Indiana, Iowa, Michigan, Minnesota, Ohio, and Wisconsin. Its World Wide Web site includes the *Pathways to School Improvement* page, a collection of resources on school governance, school-to-career programs, and curriculum reform.
URL: http://www.ncrel.org • E-mail: info@ncrel.org

Researcher's Guide to the U.S. Department of Education has links to most major sites on the Web of interest to anyone doing research on schools and learning. Includes links to all federally funded regional educational labs and many of the centers.
URL: http://www.ed.gov/pubs/ResearchersGuide/

School Reform Networks at a Glance provides a guide to dozens of school reform organizations. Includes detailed profiles and contact information. **URL: http://www.care.panam.edu/CENTER/SRN/SRNINTRODUCTION**

Web 66 uses the metaphor of the famed Route 66 to link schools to lesson plans, student work, collaborative projects, and a list of schools on the Web. Sponsored by the University of Minnesota. **URL: http://web66.coled.umn.edu • E-mail: WebMaster@web66.coled.umn.edu**

Labs & Centers

Appalachia Educational Laboratory, Inc. (AEL) is one of the 10 federally sponsored regional research labs. It supports education initiatives in Kentucky, Tennessee, Virginia, and West Virginia. **URL: http://www.ael.org/ael.htm • E-mail: aelinfo@ael.org**

Center for Networked Information Discovery and Retrieval (CNIDR) promotes and supports networked software applications such as the World Wide Web. CNIDR disseminates information about these applications and helps to build consensus among developers and users to ensure compatibility. **URL: http://www.cnidr.org • E-mail: nrn@cnidr.org**

Center for Research on the Education of Students Placed at Risk (CRESPAR) is a federally funded center that focuses on early intervention for disadvantaged students to ensure success through improved partnerships between schools, families, and communities.
URL: http://www.ed.gov/offices/OERI/At-Risk/howhop1.html • E-mail: reneek@jhu.edu

Mid-Atlantic Laboratory for Student Success (LSS) is based at Temple University and supports the revitalization and reform of education in Delaware, Maryland, New Jersey, Pennsylvania, and the District of Columbia. Funded by the federal government.
URL: http://www.temple.edu/departments/LSS/ • E-mail: lss@vm.temple.edu

Mid-continent Regional Educational Laboratory (McREL) explores the development of K-12 curriculum as part of its mission as one of the federal research labs. It provides direct services to schools and districts in Colorado, Kansas, Missouri, Nebraska, North Dakota, South Dakota, and Wyoming. **URL: http://www.mcrel.org • E-mail: info@mcrel.org**

National Center for Education Statistics (NCES) is a federal organization with a Congressional mandate to collect information and report on the condition of education. This site includes data from their reports *Digest of Education Statistics* and the *Condition of American Education.* **URL: http://www.ed.gov/NCES •**
E-mail: NCESwebmaster@ed.gov

National Center on Adult Literacy (NCAL) seeks to improve adult literacy by publishing reports, sponsoring conferences, and promoting the use of technology. Co-sponsored by the U.S. Departments of Labor and Health and Human Services. **URL: http://litserver.literacy.upenn.edu •**
E-mail: ncal@literacy.upenn.edu

National Center on Education in the Inner Cities (CEIC) conducts research on families, schools, and communities with the goal of helping to improve education for youth in urban areas. Funded by the federal government. **URL: http://www.ed.gov/offices/OERI/At-Risk/temple1.html**

National Center on Educational Outcomes (NCEO) looks at the achievement of students and schools. The center does research, works with government agencies, and participates in efforts to set national educational standards. **URL: http://www.coled.umn.edu/NCEO •**
E-mail: ysseloo1@maroon.tc.umn.edu

National Center on the Educational Quality of the Workforce is a federally sponsored research center that looks at ways to strengthen the relationship between education and career preparation. **URL: http://www.stw.ed.gov/RFI/nceqw.htm •**
E-mail: eqw-requests@irhe.upenn.edu

National Center to Improve Practice in Special Education Through Technology, Media and Materials (NCIP) focuses on the use of assistive technologies to enhance learning for students with disabilities. Targeting educators, technology specialists, school administrators, and others, activities include: NCIPnet, a series of on-line forums; the NCIP Library; and a collection of video profiles illustrating the benefits of assistive technologies. **URL: http://www.edc.org/FSC/NCIP/ • E-mail: NCIP@edc.org**

National Clearinghouse for Bilingual Education (NCBE) collects and distributes information on how to effectively educate individuals with a wide range of linguistic and cultural backgrounds. Their Web site includes an archive of success stories from the field. **URL: http://www.ncbe.gwu.edu •**
E-mail: bsilcox@ncbe.gwu.edu

National Research Center on the Gifted and Talented focuses on providing information about educational programs for students with special talents. The center also seeks ways to identify gifted students not commonly detected by standard tests and programs. **URL: http://www.ed.gov/offices/OERI/At-Risk/javitctr.html**

Northeast and Islands Regional Educational Laboratory is a federal regional lab serving Connecticut, Maine, Massachusetts, New Hampshire, New York, Rhode Island, Vermont, Puerto Rico, and the Virgin Islands. The lab supports collaborative, systemic reform efforts and hosts the Policy and Information Center, which identifies legislation, guidelines, and strategies that promote lasting school change. **URL: http://www.lab.brown.edu • E-mail: LAB@brown.edu**

Northwest Regional Educational Laboratory (NWREL) investigates and reports on topics such as school improvement. NWREL is federally funded and provides technical support to selected educational programs in Alaska, Idaho, Montana, and Washington. **URL: http://www.nwrel.org • E-mail: info@nwrel.org**

Pacific Region Educational Laboratory (PREL) is federally sponsored and studies topics such as math and science education in its region, which includes Hawaii, the Commonwealth of Northern Mariana Islands, American Samoa, Guam, the Republic of Palau, the Republic of the Marshall Islands, and the Federated States of Micronesia. **URL: http://prel.hawaii.edu •**
E-mail: webmaster@prel.hawaii.edu

Southeastern Regional Vision for Education (SERVE), funded by the federal government, examines topics such as early childhood education and serves the states of Alabama, Florida, Georgia, Mississippi, North Carolina, and South Carolina. **URL: http://www.serve.org • E-mail: webmaster@serve.org**

Southwest Educational Development Laboratory (SEDL) researches topics such as K-12 science and math and is federally funded. Works towards increased family and community involvement in education. Provides direct assistance to schools and districts in Arkansas, Louisiana, New Mexico, Oklahoma, and Texas. **URL: http://www.sedl.org:80/sedl/brief.html • E-mail: pkronkos@sedl.org**

WestEd is a federal regional lab serving Arizona, California, Nevada, and Utah that focuses on curriculum, assessment, and accountability. **URL: http://www.Wested.org**

Links for Educators

AgentSheets Remote Explorium stocks a series of interactive science, math, and art applications that can be downloaded for use in the classroom. **URL: http://www. cs.colorado.edu/~l3d/systems/remote-explorium/ • E-mail: corrina@cs.colorado.edu**

American Association of School Administrators is a professional organization for educational leaders that publishes reports, holds conferences, and advocates for the public schools. **URL: http://www.aasa.org • E-mail: webmaster@aasa.org**

American Journal of Education publishes a mix of peer-reviewed research and reviews of literature on learning and teaching. **URL: http://www.journals.uchicago.edu/AJE/home.html**

Argonne National Laboratory, Division of Educational Programs (ANL-DEP) provides resources for classroom teachers that help promote educational change at all levels. Includes an on-line conference that allows students to ask working scientists about the mysteries of the universe. **URL: http://www.newton.dep.anl.gov • E-mail: enc-support@kiwi.dep.anl.gov**

Armadillo's K-12 WWW Resources offers a vast array of subject-specific resources for educators as well as links to on-line museums, virtual field trips, and Web sites just for kids. **URL: http://chico.rice.edu/armadillo/Rice/K12resources.html • E-mail: skumari@rice.edu** or **dperkins@tenet.edu**

ARTSEDGE connects working artists, art educators, and other art professionals. Sponsored by the Kennedy Center for the Performing Arts, this site includes archives of art-related information, search tools, and K-12 curriculum materials. **URL: http://artsedge.kennedy-center.org • E-mail: editor@artsedge.Kennedy-center.org**

ArtsEdNet is sponsored by The Getty Education Institute for the Arts and offers numerous links to the latest information about arts education, professional development opportunities, and many other useful resources. **URL: http://www.artsednet.getty.edu • E-mail: artsednet@getty.edu**

Assessment Training Institute provides educators, policy makers, and others with practical information about integrating assessment with teaching and learning. They offer workshops, conferences, and training materials at the local, regional, and national levels. **E-mail: 73704.2432@compuserve.com**

Association for Supervision and Curriculum Development, Network on Authentic Assessment links educators and organizations to promote discussions of improved assessment practices. The network also publishes a newsletter, conducts workshops, and provides consulting services to educators. **E-mail: alvestad@mail.ameritel.net**

Bread Loaf Rural Teachers Network connects teachers of writing and literature through an electronic mailing list and local meetings. **URL: http://www.breadloaf.middlebury.edu • E-mail: info@breadnet.middlebury.edu**

California Subject Matter Projects is a network of 65,000 teachers organized into subject-specific groups who share a dedication to improving the teaching of academic disciplines. **URL: http://www.ucop.edu/acadady/ace/csmp/csmp.html • E-mail: robert.polkinghorn@ucop.edu**

Center for Innovation in Instruction assists schools in North Dakota with the integration of technology in teaching and learning. Offers professional development programs for educators. Web site provides links to upcoming technology-related events. **URL: http://www.cii.k12.nd.us • E-mail: rross@sendit.nodak**

Center for Research on Educational Accountability and Teacher Evaluation (CREATE) looks at ways to improve the evaluation of teachers, administrators, and schools. CREATE sponsors a National Joint Committee that helps set standards for evaluation in education. **URL: http://www.wmich.edu/evalctr • E-mail: arlen.gullickson@wmich.edu**

Center for the Future of Teaching & Learning brings together California educators to develop collaborative projects to strengthen teaching practices. The Center supports initiatives that respond to needs and challenges identified by teachers, researchers, and the public. **URL: http://www.ksagroup.com/thecenter • E-mail: harveyhunt@aol.com**

Center for Media Literacy promotes the development of media literacy—the understanding of how media such as movies, television, and advertising convey messages and affect the lives of children and adults. Provides links to an array of resources for media literacy education. **URL: http://websites.earthlink.net/~cml/ • E-mail: cml@earthlink.net**

Children's Literature Web Guide lists hundreds of children's books, furnishes information on publishers, and supplies resources for writers and teachers. **URL: http://www.ucalgary.ca/~dkbrown/ • E-mail: dkbrown@acs.ucalgary.ca**

Cisco Education Archives (CEARCH) links educators to lesson plans, projects, and colleagues to create a "virtual schoolhouse." Includes a search engine. **URL: http://sunsite.unc.edu/cisco/edu-arch.html • E-mail: cearch@sunsite.unc.edu**

Classline is an initiative of *USA TODAY* that integrates topical news and events with existing lesson plans in 6th- through 12th-grade classrooms. Newpapers are delivered to the classroom up to five days a week along with the teaching guide, *Classline TODAY,* to help educators effectively structure work around current issues. **URL: http://classline.usatoday.com**

Collaboratives for Humanities and Arts Teaching (CHART) has worked since 1985 to improve instruction in these subjects at all grade levels. **E-mail: dennis@info.csd.org**

Curricular Resources and Networking Projects is a service of the U.S. Department of Education with links to innovative networked projects for teachers and students at all levels. **URL: http://inet.ed.gov/EdRes/EdCurric.html**

Curriculum Web is a collection of K-12 lesson plans, activities, and other resources including connections to on-line projects, K-12 schools, colleges and universities, and federal and state government departments. **URL: http://www.curriculumweb.com/curriculumweb/ • E-mail: dblanch@cyberramp.net or rbourdage@bizdesign.com**

Daily Report Card offers an on-line summary of news in K-12 education. Includes information about the implementation of the national educational goals. **URL: http://www.utopia.com/mailings/reportcard/index.html**

Developing Educational Standards provides hundreds of well-catalogued links to educational standards, resources, and tips on Internet use. **URL: http://putwest.boces.org/standards**

Educators for Social Responsibility helps kids learn to settle disputes and work towards non-violent solutions to personal and global issues. Includes links to conflict resolution resources. **URL: http://www.benjerry.com/esr/about-esr.html**

Electronic Archives for Teaching American Literature is a resource of on-line texts, discussions, and bibliographies for teachers. **URL: http://www.georgetown.edu/tamlit/tamlit-home.html • E-mail: tamlit@guvax.georgetown.edu**

GLOBE Program is a collaborative classroom project comprised of kindergarten through 12th-grade students, teachers, and scientists worldwide studying the environment. Site provides program information through its on-line tour. Also serves as the forum where participants post findings and observations related to the activities. **URL: http://www.globe.gov • E-mail: info@globe.gov**

History of the United States is a comprehensive set of resources for teachers and students, categorized by topics such as immigration and industrialization. **URL: http://www.msstate.edu/Archives/History/USA/usa.html • E-mail: djm1@ra.msstate.edu**

Incredible Art Department is dedicated solely to art and art curriculum. Profiles K-12 art classes at various schools, offers lesson ideas, and provides links to K-12 and college-level art departments as well as to other art sites. **URL: http://www.in.net/~kenroar/ • E-mail: kenroar@in.net**

K-12 Resources for Music Educators includes hundreds of links to resources for teachers and students. Assembled and maintained by a Minnesota classroom teacher.
URL: http://www.isd77.k12.mn.us/resources/staffpages/shirk/k12.music.html •
E-mail: cshirk1@dakota.isd77.k12.mn.us

Kathy Schrock's Guide for Educators offers an extensive list of Internet sites, from curriculum resources to grant information to professional development links.
URL: http://www.capecod.net/Wixon/wixon.htm •
E-mail: kschrock@capecod.net

LabNet is a forum for kindergarten through 12th-grade science and math teachers to collaborate on curriculum. On-line discussion groups provide access to working scientists and experienced educators for students who research questions they generate. URL: http://labnet.terc.edu/labnet/

Leonard Berstein Center for Education Through the Arts promotes an arts-based multidisciplinary curriculum that encourages hands-on learning. Member schools are connected through the National School Network, and teachers participate in professional development workshops.
URL: http://www.bernstein.org •
E-mail: Kathy_Earnst@bernstein.org

Louisiana Collaborative for Excellence in the Preparation of Teachers (LaCEPT) is a statewide reform effort to improve the preservice education of math and science teachers in kindergarten through higher education. Their site provides information about programs and a calendar of upcoming events.
URL: http://webserv.regents.state.la.us/laceptho.htm

Mayerson Academy for Human Resource Development offers professional development opportunities for educators and supports the use of technology in the Cincinnati Public Schools. URL: http://www.mayacad.org •
E-mail: Dean.William@Mayacad.org

Mega Math uses interactive on-line exhibits to bring important mathematical ideas such as mapping, knots, and graphing to elementary-level students. Sponsored by the Los Alamos National Laboratory. URL: http://www.c3.lanl.gov/mega-math/

MiddleWeb focuses on the reform of middle grades through on-line publications, links to other sites, and connections with educators. URL: http://www.middleweb.com •
E-mail: MiddleWeb@middleweb.com

My Virtual Reference Desk provides links to newspapers, international news feeds, the weather, a virtual encyclopedia, and a variety of other humorous and interesting sites.
URL: http://www.refdesk.com/main.html •
E-mail: rbdrudge@www.refdesk.com

NASA Weather, Maps, Environment presents current satellite weather maps of the world that students and teachers can access to enhance the study of meteorology and related topics.
URL: http://metro.turnpike.net/adorn/nasa.html

National Assembly of Local Arts Agencies (NALAA) is a professional organization for administrators of arts agencies. Connects members, profiles innovative arts programs, and works to strengthen funding for and public awareness of the arts. URL: http://artsnet.heinz.cmu.edu/artsed/cs.nalaa.html

National Association of Elementary School Principals (NAESP) is the largest group of school administrators in the nation. NAESP connects administrators nationwide through its conferences and publications.
URL: http://naesp.org/naesp.htm • E-mail: naesp@naesp.org

National Association of State Boards of Education works to strengthen state leadership and build support for public education. URL: http://www.nasbe.org •
E-mail: boards@nasbe.org

National Council for Geographic Education links geography educators together to share materials, ideas, and resources. The Council publishes a journal, holds an annual conference, and sponsors a variety of student and teacher awards programs.
URL: http://multimedia2.freac.fsu.edu/ncge/index-ns.html •
E-mail: dmay@freac.fsu.edu

National Council for the Social Studies (NCSS) promotes the improvement of social studies education by building a network of teachers, researchers, curriculum designers, and college professors who share information and other resources. NCSS holds conferences and also publishes a newsletter.
URL: http://www.ncss.org • E-mail: publications@ncss.org

National Council of Teachers of English (NCTE) is an organization of teachers of literature and composition. Holds conferences, publishes a newsletter, and works to improve the teaching of English. URL: http://www.ncte.org

National Council of Teachers of Mathematics (NCTM) is the largest organization of mathematics educators in the United States. Develops standards and supports the improvement of mathematics education through networking, publications, and conferences. **URL: http://www.nctm.org/index.htm • E-mail: nctm@nctm.org**

National Geographic Online offers a variety of fun and educational features for both adults and children, including artricles from current issues of *National Geographic* magazine and an on-line edition of *World,* a magazine specifically for children. Links to the Geography Education Program, which includes a national network of geography teachers and university professors as well as resources such as lesson plans and links to professional organizations. **URL: http://nationalgeographic.com**

National Public Radio (NPR) Science Friday provides lessons, discussions, and background articles that supplement the content of this weekly radio show. **URL: http://www.npr.org/sfkids/index.html • E-mail: www@pbs.org**

National School Boards Association brings together thousands of individuals active with local school boards across the nation to share information about policy development and education reform. **URL: http://www. nsba.org**

National Science Teachers Association (NSTA) is the largest science education organization in America. It holds conferences, publishes a journal, and sponsors student projects. **URL: http://www.nsta.org • E-mail: alex.mondale@nsta.org**

NetTeach News Online offers a variety of resources to help navigate the Internet and understand how to use it as a teaching tool. Highlights include the *NetTeach News* newsletter and the NetTeach Cyberlounge, providing links to teacher training and professional development information as well as professional education associations. **URL: http://www.chaos.com/netteach • E-mail: netteach@chaos.com**

NickNacks provides comprehensive information on collaborative on-line projects. Gives educators lesson plans, examples of successful projects, and links to additional resources. **URL: http://www1.minn.net:80/~schubert/NickNacks.html • E-mail: schubert@minn.net**

North American Association of Environmental Education (NAAEE) provides membership information, a directory of publications, and links to other resources for this national group of environmental educators. **URL: http://www.edu.uleth.ca/ciccte/naceer.pgs/naaee.htm • E-mail: woodtj02@hg.uleth.ca**

North Dakota ICICLE Project, also known as the **Internet Comprehensive Instructional and Curricular Library for Educators** provides links to K-12 curricular materials. Sites are divided by academic subject matter and also connect to Gopher, Telnet, and UseNet groups. **URL: http://calvin.cc.ndsu.nodak.edu/wayne/icicle.html • E-mail: syvinski@sendit.sendit.nodak.edu**

Office of Educational Research and Information (OERI) collects and distributes statistical information on the status and progress of American education. OERI also conducts research and funds demonstration projects to improve education. Includes links to federally sponsored educational research centers and labs. **URL: http://www.ed.gov/offices/OERI/**

Public Broadcasting Service (PBS) On-line offers teaching resources, extensive background information, and discussion related to its educational television programming. **URL: http://www.pbs.org • E-mail: www@pbs.org**

Schoolhouse provides a comprehensive collection of lesson plans, papers, projects, links, and information on various education-related topics, such as integrating technology in the classroom and grant resources. **URL: http://ericir.syr.edu/schoolhouse/ • E-mail: deash@aol.com**

Sites for Educators is a subject-by-subject set of hundreds of resource links put together by an Oregon classroom teacher. **URL: http://www.mtjeff.com/~bodenst/page5.html • E-mail: bodenst@mtjeff.com**

Skill Standards and Certification is sponsored jointly by the Departments of Labor and Education and has links to information about legislation, standards, and activities related to career preparation. **URL: http://www.ttrc.doleta.gov/skillstd.html • E-mail: ttrc@ttrc.doleta.gov**

Spacelink provides status reports on NASA projects, information on outer space, and lesson plans. **URL: http://spacelink.msfc.nasa.gov • E-mail: comments@spacelink.msfc.nasa.gov**

Teacher's Edition On-line (TeachNet) includes lesson plans, classroom-management suggestions, and links to sites useful for teachers. The site also serves as the headquarters for an on-line newsletter. **URL: http://www.teachnet.com** •
E-mail: staff@teachnet.com

Teacher Talk Home Page is the on-line version of *Teacher Talk,* which provides a forum for teachers to share ideas, discuss their roles, and stay informed.
URL: http://education.indiana.edu/cas/tt/tthmpg.html •
E-mail: ttalk@indiana.edu

Teacher's Guide to the U.S. Department of Education is a centralized collection of information by and about the Department that relates to teachers and teaching. Includes guides to resources and services.
URL: http://www.ed.gov/pubs/TeachersGuide/

Theory of Multiple Intelligences provides links to resources that explore the educational implications of Howard Gardner's theory that human intelligence takes many forms.
URL: http://k12.cnidr.org:90/edref.mi.intro.html •
E-mail: acarvin@k12.cnidr.org

Transforming Schools Consortium (TSC) is a group of schools, districts, and individuals that encourages educators to incorporate technology into the classroom and share resources and ideas to improve schools and teaching.
URL: http://www.anoka.k12.mn.us/Transform/Transform.html •
E-mail: tsc@Mr.Net

21st Century Teachers is sponsored by several leading national education organizations to support educators who are using the latest technologies in innovative ways with their students and peers. Their Web site provides links to projects, networks, and other information. **URL: http://www.21ct.org** •
E-mail: 21st@21ct.org

Virtual Cave recreates a visit to the inside of an "ideal cave" compiled from images of subterranean chambers around the world. Allows students to investigate minerals found in caves, and has links to other resources as well as digital pictures. Assembled by an earth scientist.
URL: http://www.vol.it/MIRROR2/EN/CAVE/virtcave.html •
E-mail: djuna@earthsci.ucsc.edu

Windows to the Universe is a guide about earth and space sciences. Includes documents, movies, and data to illuminate the links between the study of the heavens and human history.
URL: http://www.windows.umich.edu

Museums, Libraries & Clearinghouses

American Library Association (ALA) is the oldest and largest library association in the world. ALA promotes the idea that information should be free and readily available and encourages public participation through programs and conferences.
URL: http://www.ala.org • **E-mail: rcarlson@ala.org**

Argus Clearinghouse identifies and evaluates resources on the Internet focusing on subjects such as education, science, and the humanities. **URL: http://www.clearinghouse.net**

City Links uses the San Francisco Public Library as a central point for contacting city services, tutoring programs, city officials, and schools. **URL: http://sfpl.lib.ca.us** •
E-mail: mikeh@sfpl.lib.ca.us

Distance Education Clearinghouse provides information on the use of technologies like satellite communications and video conferencing that allow learning to take place simultaneously at different locations.
URL: http://www.uwex.edu/disted/home.html •
E-mail: webmaster@ics.uwex.edu

ERIC Clearinghouse for Reading, English, and Communications (ERIC/REC) collects and disseminates articles, lesson plans, and research for educators, parents, and others. Includes contact lists and links to other relevant sites.
URL: http://www.indiana.edu:80/~eric_rec •
E-mail: ericcs@indiana.edu

ERIC Clearinghouse for Science, Mathematics, and Environmental Education (ERIC/CSMEE) includes lesson plans, articles, an index of journal articles, and a list of relevant organizations. **URL: http://www.ericse.org** •
E-mail: ericse@osu.edu

ERIC Clearinghouse for Social Studies/Social Science Education (ERIC/ChESS) monitors and reports on issues related to history, economics, and other social sciences. Provides access to materials such as curriculum guides, journal articles, and research reports.
URL: http://www.indiana.edu/~ssdc/eric-chess.html •
E-mail: downey@indiana.edu

ERIC Clearinghouse on Adult and Vocational Education (ERIC/CACVE) provides access to resources on adult literacy, career preparation, and family involvement programs.
Gopher: ericir.syr.edu:70/11/Clearinghouses/16houses/CACVE

ERIC Clearinghouse on Disabilities and Gifted Education (ERIC/EC) tracks articles and books about educating people who have special needs because they are gifted and/or have a disability. Includes information about prevention, identification and assessment, intervention, and support.
Gopher: ericir.syr.edu:70/11/Clearinghouses/16houses/ERIC_EC •
E-mail: ericec@inet.ed.gov

ERIC Clearinghouse on Elementary and Early Childhood Education (ERIC/EECE) collects and distributes information on child development and education from birth to early adolescence as well as information relating to parenting and family life. **URL: http://ericps.ed.uiuc.edu** •
E-mail: eeceweb@ericps.ed.uiuc.edu

ERIC Clearinghouse on Educational Management (ERIC/CEM) indexes thousands of documents, papers, and articles on educational management. In addition, CEM produces books, monographs, and papers on topics of interest to educational policy makers, school administrators, researchers, and other school personnel.
URL: http://darkwing.uoregon.edu:80/~ericcem/home.html •
E-mail: linda_lumsden@ccmail.uoregon.edu

ERIC Clearinghouse on Information and Technology (ERIC/IT) maintains a collection of articles and other resources about the use of technology in the fields of education and library and information sciences.
Gopher: ericir.syr.edu:70/11/Clearinghouses/16houses/CIT • **E-mail: eric@ericir.syr.edu**

ERIC Clearinghouse on Language and Linguistics (ERIC/CLL) provides a wide range of resource materials and services for language educators.
URL: http://www.cal.org/ericcll • **E-mail: eric@cal.org**

Getty Information Institute furnishes an ambitious array of art resources in a searchable database.
URL: http://www.gii.getty.edu • **E-mail: gii-info@getty.edu**

Library of Congress Congressional Server provides access to current Congressional bills, historical documents, an explanation of how laws are made, and connections to government sites. **URL: http://thomas.loc.gov** •
E-mail: thomas@loc.gov

Library of Congress Learning Page for the National Digital Library Program supplies students and educators of American history with primary source text, pictures, and video and audio clips. **URL: http://lcweb2.loc.gov/ammem/ndlpedu/** •
E-mail: ndlpedu@loc.gov

National Parent Information Network (NPIN) offers information for parents and those who work with families. Sponsored by the ERIC Clearinghouse on Urban Education and the ERIC Clearinghouse on Elementary and Early Childhood Education. **URL: http://ericps.ed.uiuc.edu:80/npin/** •
E-mail: npinweb@ericps.ed.uiuc.edu

On-line Exhibitions and Images links to a variety of museums and exhibits around the world that relate to natural history and biology. Sponsored by the Australian National Museum. **URL: http://155.187.10.12/fun/exhibits.html** •
E-mail: jrc@anbg.gov.au

Science Learning Network is an on-line group of museums, schools, and students dedicated to developing inquiry-based lessons and exhibitions through the World Wide Web. Participants include San Francisco's Exploratorium, the Franklin Institute Science Museum and Planetarium in Philadelphia, and the Science Museum of Minnesota. Sponsored by Unisys and the National Science Foundation.
URL: http://sln2.fi.edu/org/behind.html

Smithsonian Office of Elementary and Secondary Education provides information about the Smithsonian Institution's education-related programs and materials.
URL: http://www.si.edu/intro.html •
E-mail: eseem010@sivm.si.edu

Thinking Fountain Science Education Museum of Minnesota is an interactive postcard that serves as a launching point for science lessons and links on a wide variety of topics. For example, a fountain might include an image of a snowman on grass that links to a site on the nature of snow and weather. **URL: http://www.sci.mus.mn.us/sln/tf/**

WebMuseum Network, Paris links to art museums around the world. Has extensive exhibitions of famous painters.
URL: http://mistral.enst.fr/wm/net/

Organizations, Schools & Programs

Academy for Educational Development (AED) sponsors national and international programs on career preparation, the use of technology in education, and community support for schools. **URL: http://www.aed.org •**
E-mail: Admindny@aed.org

Americorps is a national community service program open to Americans of all ages. Among other benefits, participants receive tuition assistance for continued education. Service projects include renovating homes, helping with immunization programs, and developing educational programs.
URL: http://www.cns.gov/americorps.html •
E-mail: listserv@american.edu

Autodesk Foundation develops model programs and strategies for improving public schools. Programs share an emphasis on project-based learning using computers.
URL: http://www.autodesk.com/compinfo/found/found.htm •
E-mail: AFInfo@autodesk.com

BankAmerica Foundation supports nonprofit community-based groups working to improve education and foster economic development. **URL: http://www.bankamerica.com/ community/comm_devov.html • E-mail: russbank@aol.com**

BellSouth Foundation makes grants to programs in southern states to improve their educational systems. Grantees often emphasize the integration of technology into education or provide educational services to underserved groups.
URL: http://www.bellsouth.corp.com/bsf •
E-mail: Steed.Noah@bsc.bls.com

Benton Foundation promotes equitable access to the Internet to advance the public interest, including free or low-cost connections for libraries, schools, and hospitals. Links to descriptions of initiatives, publications, and discussions of Internet access issues. **URL: http://www.benton.org •**
E-mail: benton@benton.org

Blackstock Junior High School is actively working to integrate technology in the curriculum. Uses multimedia technology in a variety of ways to further learning. **URL: http://www.huensd. k12.ca.us/blackstock/html/index/htm •**
E-mail: scarr@huensd.k12.ca.us

Boeing Company provides paid time off for employees involved with schools. The company also develops partnerships with school districts around the country where it has operations to support mentoring programs, encourage employees to volunteer in schools, and promote school change.
URL: http://www.boeing.com

California Academic Partnership Project is a cooperative effort between schools and business to help better prepare students for college and careers. Their programs, called "Partnerships Academies," combine exposure to the world of work with academics. **Telnet: nis.calstate.edu • Login: capp • Password: (leave blank)**

Cambridge Rindge & Latin School is a comprehensive high school; the Web page describes the school's programs and the philosophy. One program, the Rindge School of Technical Arts, plays an important role in developing school-to-career programs by integrating academics with vocational education.
URL: http://snafu.mit.edu/crls/index.html •
E-mail: liyan@us1.channel1.com

Center for Family, School and Community is an organization that builds family and community support for education reform. Projects focus on serving young children, children with disabilities, and other underserved groups.
URL: http://www.edc.org/FSC/ • E-mail: NancyA@edc.org

Center for Media Education educates policy makers and the general public about media-related policy issues, with a particular focus on those that affect children.
URL: http://www.cme.org/org • E-mail: cme@access.digex.net

Center for the Study of Human Resources includes research updates and links that focus on the relationships between training, education, and work.
URL: http://www.utexas.edu/research/cshr/ •
E-mail: cshr@www.utexas.edu

Center on Education and Work provides access to school-to-career resources, including conference information and chat sessions. **URL: http://www.cew.wisc.edu •**
E-mail: cewmail@soemadison.wisc.edu

Children Now is a nonprofit public policy and advocacy organization. Their site includes links to other children's organizations, access to publications, and alerts about issues being considered by various policy making bodies.
URL: http://www.dnai.com/~children/ •
E-mail: children@dnai.com

Children, Youth, & Environments Network links design professionals, educators, and students interested in the relationships between young people and their physical environment. Includes discussions of both natural surroundings and designed facilities.**URL: http://www.cedar.univie.ac.at/arch/ eia/95apr/maillist.html#00037** •
E-mail: CYE-L-request@cunyvms1.gc.cuny.edu

Children's Defense Fund (CDF) is a nonprofit child-advocacy organization. Through lobbying efforts, community action, and publications, CDF works to educate the public about children's needs and to marshal government and private-sector support for health and education programs.
URL: http://www.tmn.com/cdf/index.html •
E-mail: cdf@tmn.com

Coalition for America's Children is a network of 350 local, state, and national nonprofit organizations working on behalf of children. Through their publications and advertising campaigns, they help ensure that children's needs maintain a prominent place on the nation's public policy agenda.
URL: http://www.usakids.org •
E-mail: cac-comments@cdinet.com

Committee for Economic Development (CED) serves as a forum where business leaders and public officials exchange ideas about issues such as education, training for careers, and improving the connections between businesses and schools.
URL: http://www.ced.org • **E-mail: cfeurey@aol.com**

Community Update is the digitized version of a newsletter sponsored by the U.S. Department of Education that connects readers to resources, publications, and services helping schools and communities work together.
URL: http://www.ed.gov/G2K/community/ •
E-mail: joy_belin@ed.gov

Council of Great City Schools is a membership organization of representatives from the nation's largest urban public school systems. The group lobbies on behalf of urban education, holds conferences, publishes reports, and disseminates information. **URL: http://www.cgcs.org** •
E-mail: webmaster@cgcs.org

Council for Basic Education promotes high academic standards for all students by supporting efforts to strengthen the curriculum in traditional academic subjects.
URL: http://www.c-b-e.org • **E-mail: info@c-b-e.org**

Craftsmanship 2000 is a three-year school-to-career program in Tulsa, Okla. that combines academics, an emphasis on education beyond high school, and paid apprenticeships in machining and metal work.
URL: http://www.tulsachamber.com/edc2000.htm

Cross City Campaign for Urban School Reform works nationally to improve urban education by promoting school decentralization. They build partnerships between community organizations and schools to support local, site-based control of education. **E-mail: 102534,1723@compuserve.com**

Edison Electric Institute (EEI) On-line helps keep employees of Edison Electric and the public informed about education reform and promotes partnerships between the utility company and schools in the eastern United States.
URL: http://www.eei.org • **E-mail: ecionline@eei.org**

Family Involvement Partnership for Learning is a program of the U.S. Department of Education that offers support and resources for improving parental involvement in education.
URL: http://www.ed.gov/Family/schools.html

Foundation Center is a comprehensive collection of information on where, how, and when to apply for grants and other types of funding. **URL: http://fdncenter.org** •
E-mail: mfn@fdncenter.org

Harvard Family Research Project was created to develop policies and programs that support the involvement of families and communities in education. Their newsletter, *The Evaluation Exchange: Emerging Strategies in Evaluating Child and Family Services,* is available on-line.
URL: http://hugse1.harvard.edu/~hfrp/hfrpeval2.html •
E-mail: hfrp@hugse1.harvard.edu

Health and Human Development Programs work in partnership with health care, criminal justice, and human services agencies to promote physical, mental, and emotional health for people of all ages. Operated by the Education Development Center. **URL: http://www.edc.org/HHD/** •
E-mail: CherylV@edc.org

Hewlett Packard (HP) makes grants to support elementary and secondary schools in communities near the company's facilities, with a particular focus on math and science literacy and teacher professional development.
URL: http://www.hp.com

InformED helps disseminate information about teacher preparation programs. The site is sponsored by the American Association for Information Officers for Colleges of Education.
URL: http://www.vpds.wsu.edu/informed/ •
E-mail: InformED@listproc.wsu.edu

Institute for Education and the Economy (IEE) conducts research on the way changes in the economy influence training and career preparation.
URL: http://www.stw.ed.gov/rfi/iee.htm •
E-mail: iee@columbia.edu

Institute on Education and Training (IET), part of the Rand Corporation, conducts research on educational technology, assessment, and the social and economic effects of school change. **URL:** http://www.rand.org/centers/iet/ •
E-mail: Kathleen_Shizuru@rand.org

KidsCampaign is a 10-year effort of the Advertising Council, the Benton Foundation, the Coalition for America's Children, and AT&T to raise national awareness about the needs of children. The site links to hundreds of national efforts to help children, includes an extensive search engine, provides the latest statistics about kids, and supplies updates on public policies affecting children. **URL:** http://www.kidscampaigns.org

MCI Foundation provides educational and technological support for low-income groups. MCI projects have helped develop community networks and provided computer training and equipment to individuals who could otherwise not afford them. **URL:** http://www.cerritos.edu/cerritos/development/funders_mci.html • **E-mail:** Kristinat@cerritos.edu

Metropolitan Center (the MET) is a secondary school in Providence, R.I., that integrates academic and technical skills to better prepare students for the world of work.
URL: http://met.state.K12.ri.us
E-mail: info@met.state.K12.ri.us

Michigan Association of Community and Adult Education (MACAE) promotes lifelong learning for all members of the community. Its services include workshops, a newsletter, and training. **E-mail:** MACAE@aol.com

Minnesota Center for Arts Education is a residential public school that uses its Web page to provide news of regional developments in the arts and links to dance, music, theater, and visual arts resources on the Internet. **URL:** http://www.mcae.k12.mn.us • **E-mail:** jengel@mcae.k12.mn.us

National Academy of Sciences (NAS) advises the federal government on scientific and technical matters. NAS carries out its mission by doing research, publishing reports, and holding conferences. Their information is also useful to educators working to set standards and develop curriculum.
URL: http://www2.nas.edu/nas • **E-mail:** news@nas.edu

National Assessment Governing Board (NAGB) was created by the U.S. Congress. It sets policy for the National Assessment of Educational Progress (NAEP), a group that reports on student skills and achievement across the nation. Their site lists board members, activities, and links to NAGB publications and other assessment resources.
URL: http://www.nagb.org • **E-mail:** nagb@arols.com

National Business Education Association (NBEA) identifies resources for business-school partnerships and links to programs around the country.
URL: http://www.thomson.com/partners/nbea/default.html

National Center for Fathering conducts research and provides information and other resources aimed at strengthening support for single fathers. **URL:** http://www.fathers.com •
E-mail: ncf@aol.com

National Conference of State Legislatures (NCSL) assists state legislators and their staffs with critical public policy issues, including education. Tracks legislation and provides information in areas such as education finance, school-to-career programs, standards, and charter schools.
URL: http://www.ncsl.org • **E-mail:** Doug.Sacarto@NCSL.ORG

National Council of La Raza (NCLR) created the Center for Community Educational Excellence (C2E2) to help Hispanic families become more involved in their children's education, to develop school-community partnerships, and to help improve the quality of education for Hispanic youth.
URL: http:www//nclr.org • **E-mail:** mfisher@nclr.org

National Educator Awards Program recognizes outstanding educators and promotes the benefits of technology use in education. Sponsored by the Milken Family Foundation. **URL: http://www.mijcf.org/Resource/edguide/toc.html** • **E-mail: info@mijcf.org**

National Governors' Association (NGA) is a membership organization consisting of the governors of the U.S. states and territories. NGA has devoted a considerable portion of its energies over the past decade to school reform, including providing support for the national education summits and efforts to create national standards. **URL: http://www.social.com/health/nhic/data/hr1600/hr1612.html**

New Horizons for Learning uses the metaphor of a building to hold information about innovative approaches to education, facilities, and programs that support learning, as well as resources for educators. **URL: http://www.newhorizons.org** • **E-mail: building@newhorizons.org**

Pacific Bell Foundation provides grants for systemic reform of teaching and learning, with an emphasis on integrating technology in education. **URL: http://www.pactel.com/found/home.html** • **E-mail: webmaster@pactel.com**

Parents for Educational Excellence serves Latino youth and their families through workshops, seminars, and publications. The program's sponsor, ASPIRA, also promotes demonstration projects to explore Latino community involvement in education. **E-mail: aspira1@aol.com**

Parents Helping Parents is a grassroots effort that connects parents of children with special needs to share information and resources. **URL: http://www.php.com** • **E-mail: sysop@php.com**

Pew Charitable Trusts makes grants to groups working to change the education system by raising standards and improving student performance. The Trusts focus on efforts that serve disadvantaged students. Their site includes application information and profiles of current and former grantees. **URL: http://www.pewtrusts.com**

Public/Private Ventures promotes programs to help young people from low-income communities increase their academic and career skills. **URL: http://www.stw.ed.gov/rfi/ppv.htm** • **E-mail: PPVKids@aol.com**

Public School Forum of North Carolina researches the social and educational effects of the state's efforts to integrate technology with education. **URL: http://www.ncforum.org** • **E-mail: jdcran@ncforum.org**

Ralph Bunche School is an elementary school in New York City with a specialized academy dedicated to teaching kids computer and telecommunications skills. The school also has a student-produced video news program, *Kid Witness News.* **URL: http://mac94.ralphbunche.rbs.edu** • **E-mail: hamidoud@ralphbunche.rbs.edu**

School & Main is an organization that supports community efforts to better prepare urban youth to be productive citizens. Its programs provide guidance, academic tutoring, college preparation, and the opportunity to explore career possibilities. **URL: http://www.stw.ed.gov/rfi/main.htm** • **E-mail: jamie.coats@es.nemc.org**

School-to-Work Partnership of Broome and Tioga Counties combines apprenticeships in manufacturing, robotics, and other industries with academics to help high school students in upstate New York understand the connections between school, work, and higher education. **URL: http://www.tier.net/schools/stw** • **E-mail: lcasey@spectra.net**

Strong Families Strong Schools provides links to articles and books that focus on encouraging active family involvement in schools. Based on the book of the same name written for the U.S. Education Department's Initiative on Families. **URL: http://eric-web.tc.columbia.edu/families/strong/** • **E-mail: dg119@columbia.edu**

Teach for America recruits and trains recent college graduates to teach in inner cities and rural areas. **URL: http://www.teachforamerica.org** • **E-mail: farecnat@aol.com**

Triangle Coalition promotes and supports real scientific work experiences for teachers, providing them with insights into the work environments and the skills necessary for student success after graduation, examples to make instruction more relevant, and connections to a larger professional community. **URL: http://emf.net/~iisme/swepnet/triangle.html** • **E-mail: tricoal@triangle.mste.org**

21st Century Education Initiative is a coalition of business, education, and community leaders devoted to improving education in California's Silicon Valley through technology and networking in schools and the community.
E-mail: jvsvoffice@aol.com

Urban Education Web contains manuals, research, and bibliographies on issues such as school reform, safety, and the problems of minority families living in the inner city.
URL: http://eric-web.tc.columbia.edu •
E-mail: lry2@columbia.edu

U.S. Conference of Mayors represents over 1,000 mayors in the nation's largest cities. A recently adopted plan supports mayors as key figures in mobilizing community resources for schools, strengthening the ties between education and business, establishing schools as safe places, increasing parental involvement, and improving student performance.
URL: http://www.usmayors.org/uscm/ •
E-mail: jrichard@cais.com

U.S. Department of Education offers materials for teachers, educational researchers, and others. An on-line library has funding information, policy updates, information for teachers, a researcher's guide, and a page of statistical information on American education. Includes a search engine.
URL: http://www.ed.gov

Student Projects

Academy One is an international site for kindergarten through 12th-grade students and teachers to share resources, find keypals, and collaborate on projects.
URL: http://www.nptn.org:80/cyber.serv/AOneP/ •
E-mail: info@nptn.org

Adventure On-line links kids to on-line expeditions to distant places such as Mayan ruins and the Nile. Includes an on-line quiz and discussion area. URL: http://www.adventureonline.com •
E-mail: oylerl@freenet.msp.mn.us

Cyberspace Middle School is targeted to sixth, seventh, and eighth graders and their teachers who are integrating the World Wide Web in classroom activities. Lists fun and educational sites for kids, as well as links to science and math-oriented projects and educational resources for educators.
URL: http://www.scri.fsu.edu/~dennisl/CMS.html •
E-mail: larry@fsulcd.physics.fsu.edu

Gallery of Interactive Geometry allows students to explore interesting areas of mathematics through interactive exhibits. URL: http://www.geom.umn.edu/apps/ •
E-mail: webmaster@geom.umn.edu

GlobaLearn is a series of interactive virtual trips to interesting places around the world like the Black Sea. Includes archives and ways for students to communicate with one another.
URL: http://www.globalearn.org •
E-mail: Webmaster@globalearn.com

I*EARN links students from around the world to work collaboratively in solving real problems and to share their understandings about each others' cultures and their visions for the future. URL: http://www.learn.org/learn •
E-mail: hgp@copenfund.igc.apc.org

Intercultural E-mail Classroom Connections helps kids from different nations connect with one another to collaborate on projects that enhance international understanding.
URL: http://www.stolaf.edu/network/iecc/ •
E-mail: cdr@stolaf.edu

Internet Projects Registry keeps a central monthly calendar of Internet-based school projects. Includes projects sponsored by Global SchoolNet, I*EARN, NASA, GLOBE, Academy One, TIES, TENET, TERC, and several universities.
URL: http://199.106.67.200/GSN/proj/index.html •
E-mail: yvonne@gsn.org

KIDLINK is a global, multilingual network for 10-15 year olds. The group also coordinates curriculum projects through KIDPROJ.
URL: http://www.kidlink.org • E-mail: kidlink-info@kidlink.org

Kidspace is a virtual meeting space for children from around the world to share ideas, drawings, and personal experiences.
URL: http://plaza.interport.net/kids_space/

Learning By Design helps kindergarten through 12th-grade students better understand the factors that influence their physical surroundings. Students look at the designs of towns, schools, and public buildings. Sponsored by the American Institute of Architecture.
URL: http://www.aia.org/srcebook.htm •
E-mail: webmaster@aia.org

National Geographic Kids Network presents science and geography projects that groups of students around the country can work on simultaneously, sharing their data and comments over the Internet.
URL: http://www.gii-awards.com/nicampgn/28ba.htm

Passport to Knowledge is a series of interactive electronic field trips to remote locations such as the Arctic or the middle of the ocean. Learning materials are made available through the Internet as well as through broadcast television and videotape. Sponsored by NASA.
URL: http://quest.arc.nasa.gov/hst/aboutptk.html •
E-mail: traicoff@quest.arc.nasa.gov

ThinkQuest® an annual contest for students ages 12-18, is designed to help them use the Internet as an interactive teaching tool. With teachers and experts as their coaches, students build on-line projects in their favorite subjects. Winners receive $25,000 scholarships; coaches can get up to $5,000, with another $5,000 going to their school or institution. Winning projects are available on-line.
URL: http://www.advanced.org/ThinkQuest/index.html

Ultimate Children's Internet Sites is an extensive compilation of fun and educational Web sites for kids sorted by school-age group. Also offers a variety of informative sites for parents and educators. URL: http://www.vividus.com/ucis.html#ucis

Whale Times includes interesting facts about whales, links to students' studying whales, and environmental tips.
URL: http://www.whaletimes.org •
E-mail: whaletimes@whaletimes.org

Why Files, a project of the National Institute for Science Education, features articles and information relating to current science topics in the news. Designed for both educators and students as an enhancement to science classroom activities.
URL: http://whyfiles.news.wisc.edu •
E-mail: staff@whyfiles.news.wisc.edu

You Can with Beakman and Jax encourages kids to ask questions about the world around them and explore science and math through a variety of hands-on activities. Their site ties into the *Beakman's World* television show.
URL: http://www.nbn.com/youcan/index.html

Technology-Related Links

AT&T Learning Network is helping to get America's schools connected to the Information Superhighway by the year 2000. Program components include: AT&T WorldNet℠ Service, dial-up Internet access free to schools for five months; technology guides for schools and communities; and the *AskLN℠* program, offering on-line mentoring to assist educators in navigating the Internet and incorporating it in classroom activities.
URL: http://www.att.com/learning_network/ •
E-mail: LearningNet@attmail.com

Bell Atlantic World School is a project that connects more than 700 West Virginia schools to the Internet. Schools share electronic lessons and collaborate on projects. The site also offers a resource page for parents.
URL: http://www.bell-atl.com/wschool/ •
E-mail: wschool@citynet.net

Big Sky Telegraph offers hundreds of educational and health and social service links. Also serves as the gateway to a well-attended electronic conferencing network for Western Montana.
URL: http://macsky.bigsky.dillon.mt.us •
E-mail: franko@bigsky.dillon.mt.us

California Instructional Technology Clearinghouse (CITC) works with teachers to evaluate electronic resources and provides information on-line about recommended products. Is comprised of the California Instructional Video Clearinghouse and the California Software Clearinghouse.
URL: http://tic.stan-co.k12.ca.us •
E-mail: jvaille@stan-co.k12.ca.us

Center for Children and Technology collaborates with schools and universities to develop new ways to use technology to support learning. URL: http://www.edc.org/CCT/ •
E-mail: cct@edc.org

Center for Educational Leadership & Technology (CELT) promotes the integration of multimedia technology consistent with current educational reforms and research. CELT also helps organizations and schools develop networking plans to make it easier to use and acquire new technology.
URL: http://www.celt.org • E-mail: webmaster@celt.org

Center for Learning, Teaching, & Technology works with teachers, administrators, and policy makers to improve literacy, math proficiency, and understanding of science and technology. **URL: http://www.edc.org/LTT/ltthome/** • **E-mail: Humphrys@edc.org**

Center for Technology in Learning (CTL) develops multimedia tools to support learning and assess achievement, examines technology-related educational policy, and provides technical support to selected school districts. Affiliated with the Stanford Research Institute. **URL: http://www.sri.com** • **E-mail: Inquiry_Line@sri.com**

Charlotte's Web is a community-based network that provides access to technology for residents in and around Charlotte, N.C. Links to city government, job listings, and schools. **URL: http://www.charweb.org/home.html** • **E-mail: shsnow@charweb.org**

Cleveland Freenet offers links to agencies, libraries, and community information. This is one of the oldest and largest community-based networks in the country. **Telnet: freenet-in-a.cwru.edu**

Community Technology Centers' Network (CTCNet) supports the goal of equitable access to computers and technology. The network is composed of more than 65 sites at locations ranging from museums to job training centers to shelters. Each is designed to provide community members with the opportunity to learn and use computers, software, and related technologies such as the Internet. **URL: http://www.ctcnet.org** • **E-mail: ctcnet@edc.org**

Computer Professionals for Social Responsibility (CPSR) is an alliance of computer scientists and others interested in the impact of technology on society. CPSR keeps the public informed about critical issues raised by advances in computing. **URL: http://www.cpsr.org/dox/home.html** • **E-mail: mwoodbury@cpsr.org**

Computers for School Program is a project of the Detwiler Foundation, a nonprofit group working to develop an efficient system for encouraging donations of used computer equipment, providing needed repairs and upgrades, and placing them in schools. **URL: http://www.detwiler.org** • **E-mail: diana@detwiler.org**

ConnecTen is part of an effort to connect all K-12 schools in Tennessee to the Internet. The project is sponsored by a partnership between the state and several corporate donors. **URL: http://www.state.tn.us/education** • **E-mail: jshrago@tbr.state.tn.us**

ConnSense Bulletin brings together information on technology and programs for students with special needs. **URL: http://www.ucc.uconn.edu/~wwwpcse/CSBull.html** • **E-mail: Rucker@UConnvm.UConn.edu**

CyberEd Van is an 18-wheel truck outfitted as a state-of-the-art technology classroom on wheels. The truck moves from city to city, providing teachers, students, and others with hands-on activities and highlighting the importance of educational technology and partnerships between schools and businesses. **URL: http://ustc.org/CyberEd/rig.htm** • **E-mail: cybered@ustc.org**

Directory of Public Access Networks links to networks that provide free access as well as community-based networks around the country. A linked map makes it easier for users to find networks in a particular region. **URL: http://www.morino.org/pandhome.html** • **E-mail: feedback@morino.org**

Educom is an alliance of universities and corporations that seeks to integrate technology in education. Educom publishes two newsletters. **URL: http://www.educom.edu** • **E-mail: info@educom.edu**

Florida Information Resources Network (FIRN) connects this state's public school educators in a single network. Teachers use FIRN to share telecommunications-based lesson plans, news, and ideas. **URL: http://www.firn.edu** • **E-mail: webmaster@mail.firn.edu**

Free-Nets & Community Networks links to scores of free and community-based networks around the world. Compiled by a Canadian librarian. **URL: http://duke.usask.ca/~scottp/free.html** • **E-mail: scottp@moondog.usask.ca**

From Now On is an electronic educational journal that focuses on technology-related issues such as professional development and planning for effective technology integration. **URL: http://www.pacificrim.net/~mckenzie/** • **E-mail: mckenzie@pacificrim.net**

Goals 2000/Louisiana Networking Infrastructure for Education Project (Goals 2000/LaNIE), funded by a U.S. Department of Education Challenge Grant, is developing pilot sites at K-12 schools to integrate technology in the curriculum and a state educational technology plan. Provides detailed information about the mission, goals, and strategies of the project. **URL: http://www.lasip.state.la.us/lanie.htm** • **E-mail: dwest@regents.state.la.us**

Harvard Educational Technology Center (ETC) develops and studies ways to use computers and other emerging technologies to improve education. The Center publishes and distributes a wide variety of books, software, curriculum materials, and videotapes. **URL: http://edetc1.harvard.edu** • **E-mail: hayeskr@hugse1.harvard.edu**

Hawaii Education and Resource Network (HERN) ties this island state together through projects that encourage schools, colleges, and community organizations to collaborate. **URL: http://www.hern.hawaii.edu/hern/about.html** • **E-mail: hern@hawaii.edu**

Highway 1 helps members of Congress and other government leaders understand and use new information technologies. The Center acts as a clearinghouse for research, educational information, and community organizations involved in promoting computer networking. **URL: http://www.highway1.org** • **E-mail: info@highway1.org**

Institute for Learning Technologies (ILT) collects and distributes readings, texts, and journals to promote discussion of the role of multimedia in education. Links to hundreds of projects across the country. **URL: http://www.ilt.columbia.edu/projects/index.html** • **E-mail: webmaster@ilt.columbia.edu**

Institute for the Learning Sciences (ILS) is a research and development center creating innovative educational software for practical applications in businesses, schools, government agencies, and the community. ILS draws together faculty and students from the fields of computer science, psychology, cognitive science, and education. **URL: http://www.ils.nwu.edu** • **E-mail: schank@ils.nwu.edu**

iowa.net™ is a nonprofit network with links to organizations, schools, and companies throughout the state. The network keeps a statewide calendar of events. **URL: http://www.iowa.net** • **E-mail: webmaster@iowa.net**

Kickstart Initiative is a federally sponsored effort to help local leaders develop electronic networks in their communities. **URL: http://www.benton.org/KickStart/** • **E-Mail: Benton@Benton.org**

Kidsphere is a mailing list for teachers interested in using the Internet for educational purposes. **E-mail: Kidsphere@vms.cis.pitt.edu**

Living Schoolbook Project makes video and text materials more readily available to students by working to improve the software and the network distribution process. **URL: http://www.npac.syr.edu/projects/ltb/overview.html** • **E-mail: kim@npac.syr.edu**

Media Lab New and Noteworthy is home to visionary projects on the Internet such as the Media Moo, a state-of-the-art virtual meeting place/discussion group. Sponsored by the Massachusetts Institute of Technology. **Telnet: purple-crayon.media.mit.edu:8888/**

Missouri Research and Education Network (MOREnet) creates projects designed to provide communities with Internet connectivity. Also works with the Missouri Department of Elementary and Secondary Education to link K-12 schools to the Internet. **URL: http://www.more.net** • **E-mail: infomgr@more.net**

Multimedia in Education is a German site that has hundreds of links to information on the effects of multimedia technology on learning. **URL: http://www.uni-sb.de/sonstige/ mefis/emlink01.htm** • **E-mail: Mefis@Mefis.uni-sb.de**

National School Network Testbed is an electronic network that links schools across the country to work on collaborative projects. Compiled by BBN Corp., one of the architects of the Internet. **URL: http://copernicus.bbn.com/testbed2/TBdocs/ TB1July94Report.html**

National Telecommunications and Information Administration (NTIA) furnishes grant information and descriptions of promising community and educational projects that promote the use of the Internet and other electronic resources. **URL: http://www.ntia.doc.gov** • **E-mail: webmaster@ntia.doc.gov**

Network Montana Project provides access to and promotes the use of telecommunications technologies in K-12 and higher education programs statewide. Assists schools with planning and implementing networks as well as curriculum and program development. **URL:** http://www.nmp.umt.edu • **E-mail:** morarre@selway.umt.edu

Networking Infrastructure for Education funds proposals from schools and organizations to increase their capacity to use new technologies in education. Previous grantees have improved electronic libraries and evaluated existing networks. **URL:** http://141.142.3.130/General/PIO/NCSAInfo-Press-Netwk.html

New Jersey Networking Infrastructure in Education combines resources, science information, and Internet lessons with a network that links schools and community organizations throughout the state. **URL:** http://njnie.dl.stevens-tech.edu/new/new.html • **E-mail:** caddison@njnie.dl.stevens-tech.edu

North Carolina Information Highway (NCIH) connects schools, health care organizations, law enforcement, and government offices. NCIH provides low-cost access to the network so all residents can benefit. **URL:** http://www.ncih.net • **E-mail:** mark.cooke@ncih.net

Ohio SchoolNet provides computers and networking assistance to schools. The site is linked to information about wiring standards and other networking resources. **URL:** http://www.ode.ohio.gov/www/schoolnet/schnet.html • **E-mail:** ims_best@ode.ohio.gov

Online Internet Institute is a cooperative project with 400 teachers and an array of experts from higher education, industry, and schools to help educators make better use of the Internet in the classroom. The Institute also sponsors a summer workshop. **URL:** http://oii.org • **E-mail:** OII-request@prism.prs.k12.nj.us

Plugged In brings technology to kids in the low-income community of East Palo Alto, Calif., through training and activities such as a virtual trip across America with a school in New Haven, Conn. The site offers connections to communities around the world. **URL:** http://www.pluggedin.org • **E-mail:** info@pluggedin.org

Reinventing Education is sponsored by the IBM Corporation to help integrate technology and improve student performance in K-12 schools around the country. Their partnerships with school districts and states focus on changes within the educational system. **URL:** http://www.ibm.com/IBM/IBMGives/k12ed/k-12init.htm • **E-mail:** ibmgives@vnet.ibm.com

ShareNet is a nonprofit partnership of school districts, universities, businesses, and community organizations, encompassing 10 counties in Kansas and Missouri. It provides members with access to the Internet as well as to a variety of electronic resources. **URL:** http://www.ed.gov/pubs/EdReformStudies/EdTech/sharenet.html • **E-mail:** joanw@cyclops.pei.edu

Software Publishers Association (SPA) is a trade association for the industry. Publishes resource guides, tracks legislation, organizes conferences, and offers on-line lesson plans. **URL:** http://www.spa.org • **E-mail:** webmaster@spa.org

Sparkman Center, a project of TCI, offers technology training to educators and the general public. **URL:** http://www.tcinc.com/sparkman.html

Teacher Technology Center helps teachers develop subject-specific curriculum that takes advantage of new technologies. **URL:** http://www.lacoe.edu/doc/ttc/ttc.html • **E-mail:** Chun_Thomas@ttc.lacoe.edu

TEAMS Distance Learning is a national distance learning consortium administered by the Los Angeles County Office of Education. Site provides information about the TEAMS project as well as program schedules, class projects, and links to a variety of education-related resources. **URL:** http://teams.lacoe.edu • **E-mail:** gperry@teams.lacoe.edu

Telelearning Project funded by the Louisiana Board of Elementary and Secondary Education, offers students in rural communities opportunities to participate for credit in courses that are not offered by their schools. Participants use computers, microphones, electronic blackboards, and graphics pads to communicate between sites. Courses include foreign languages, fine arts, advanced mathematics, computer science, and physics. **URL:** http://www.lsma.edu/telelearning • **E-mail:** loftin@alpha.nsula.edu

TENET electronically connects educators across Texas. This site uses a train metaphor to link schools, education resources, and museums around the world. **URL: http://www.tenet.edu •
E-mail: web-master@tenet.edu**

U.S. Department of Education Technology Initiatives

highlights grant opportunities, noteworthy programs, federal guidelines, and workshops that promote the integration of technology in education.
URL: http://www.ed.gov/Technology

Utah Education Network is a collection of resources for educators, parents, students, and the Utah community. Comprised of KUED (the statewide PBS affiliate providing instructional television programming), KULC (Utah's Learning Channel, offering telecourses for credit), EDNET (an interactive, closed-circuit television network linking K-12 schools with colleges and universities), and UtahLink (giving schools and universities access to the Internet as well as a vast array of education-related links). **URL: http://www.uen.org/index.html •
E-mail: webmaster@uen.org**

Virginia Public Education Network (VaPEN) connects educators and the residents of Virginia through an electronic network that provides lesson plans and other educational information. **URL: http://pen.k12.va.us •
E-mail: jaulino@pen.k12.va.us**

Index

About This Index

In our effort to provide you with a comprehensive index, items can be accessed in a variety of ways. We hope readers will seek information from many perspectives. If you can't find what you're looking for the first time, think about it in a different way. Here are some helpful hints:

The index is alphabetized in **letter-by-letter** order, in which all spaces and punctuation are ignored up to the comma at the end of a heading, or up to the comma after the first part of an inverted heading (e.g., up to the comma following "Lucas" in "Lucas, George"). In other words, entries are alphabetized as if all their letters were run together as one word. For example, "School boards" and "Schoolhouse" precede entries for "Schools," while "School-to-career programs" and "School Zone Institute" follow "Schools."

Each chapter of the book contains organizational, periodical, and reading resources. Under some main headings readers will find subheadings for these resources listed as **organizations for, periodicals for, and readings on.** The electronic resources section located at the back of the book contains only e-mail and World Wide Web addresses. Under many main headings readers will find a subheading for these resources listed as **electronic resources for.**

Each state and U.S. foreign territory's main heading includes subheadings for specific schools, programs, and organizations identified within the body of the book. Following these entries, you will find a city location in parentheses **(City)**. Each state's subheadings also include the electronic resources from the section at the back of the book, which are noted by an **(Internet)** designation. Additionally, under the main headings **K–8, K–12, Elementary Schools, Middle Schools,** and **High Schools, (State)** or **(Internet)** designations follow appropriate entries.

A

Academy for Educational Development, 243

Academy One, 247

Accelerated Schools Project, 183

Access Excellence, 91, 215

Accountability
  defined, 231
  electronic resources for, 237
  of schools and districts, 14, 43, 45, 169–170
  standards and, 14
  of teachers, 14, 97, 170
  See also Responsibility

Accreditation
  of administrator education programs, 184
  of teacher education programs, 96

ACT Academy, 72, 80

Adams, John Truslow, 6

Adler, Louise, 139

Adler, Mortimer, 26, 32

Administrators
  assessment of, 237
  assessment of students and, 41, 47, 49
  business partnership programs and, 147
  curriculum development and, 178
  electronic resources for, 237, 242, 249
  local control and accountability by, 169–170
  minority students and, 119
  mission and goals definition and, 3, 169
  national policy for, 184

Administrators *(continued)*
  organizations for, 137, 184, 237
  periodicals for, 185
  professional development of, 184
  responsibility of, 4, 171
  school design teams and, 192, 198, 200
  site-based management and, 113, 114, 173
  teachers and, 69, 72
  technology and, 171, 221, 223, 224, 226, 229
  See also Budgeting; Financing; Governors; Local policy; Mayors; National policy; Policy makers; Principals; School boards; State policy; Superintendents

Adult education
  community learning centers and, 113, 117, 125, 127, 128–129, 132, 133, 134, 135, 137, 138, 139, 197, 202, 203
  electronic resources for, 236, 242, 245
  importance of, 111
  See also Distance learning; Lifelong learning

Adult literacy, 117, 236, 242

Adventure On-line, 247

Advocates, 3, 65

African-American students and families.
  See Minority students and families

Age groups. *See* Multi-ability groups; Multi-age groups

AgentSheets Remote Explorium, 237

Agents of Change (Wentworth), 158

Alabama
  Southeastern Regional Vision for Education (Internet), 237
  Southern Regional Education Board (Atlanta, GA), 185

Alaska
  Alaska On-Line (Internet), 218
  Dzantik'i Heeni Middle School (Juneau), 218
  North Star Elementary School (Nikiski), 50
  Northwest Regional Educational Laboratory, 52 (Portland, OR), 55 (Portland, OR), 236 (Internet)

Alice Carlson Applied Learning Center, 172–173, 175, 190

Alliance for Technology Access, 224, 228, 230

Alta Vista, 234

Alternative assessment, defined, 231.
  See also Assessment (alternative/authentic/performance)

Alverno College of Education, 91, 98

Ambassadors, teachers as, 65

Ambrosh, Karen, 96, 98

American Association for the Advancement of Science, 30, 38

American Association of Colleges for Teacher Education, 94

American Association of School
Administrators, 206, 237

American Educational Research Association, 30

American Educator, 78

American Federation of Teachers, 76, 78, 80

American Journal of Education, 237

American Library Association, 241

American Samoa, Pacific Region Educational
Laboratory (Internet), 236

American School Board Journal, The, 185

American Youth Policy Forum, 154, 158

*America's Children and the Information
Superhighway* (Lazarus and Lipper), 229

America's Choice (The Commission on the Skills
of the American Workforce), 156, 157

Americorps, 243

Anderson, Ronald D., 35

Annie E. Casey Foundation, 136

Appalachia Educational Laboratory, Inc., 235

Apple Computer, Inc., 29, 174, 202, 216, 228

Apple Classrooms of Tomorrow, 151

Apprenticeships, student, 143, 147, 151, 157,
185. *See also* School-to-career programs

Architects, 198–199, 200, 201, 204, 205, 208

Architecture. *See* Schools, physical design of

Argonne National Laboratory, Division of
Educational Programs, 237

Argus Clearinghouse, 241

Arizona
assessment in, 55

Council of Educational Facility Planners
International, The (Scottsdale), 204

WestEd (Internet), 237

Arkansas
Rogers School District (Rogers), 223

Southern Regional Education Board
(Atlanta, GA), 185

Southwest Educational Development
Laboratory (Internet), 237

Armadillo's K-12 WWW Resources, 237

Arts, 245
architecture of schools and, 195, 196

assessing, 49, 50

curriculum, 238, 239

dance, 28, 245

distance learning of, 251

drama, 26, 245

electronic resources for, 237, 238, 239, 242,
245, 251

hands-on learning and, 24, 31

Arts *(continued)*
interdisciplinary curriculum
emphasizing, 28, 94, 239

mathematics and, 46

music, 24, 26, 28, 49, 196, 238, 245

organizational resources for, 31

teacher education and professional
development in, 237, 239

technology and, 217, 223

ARTSEDGE, 237

ArtsEdNet, 237

ASCD Curriculum/Technology Quarterly, 34

Ashlawn Elementary School, 70–71

Asian Family-School Partnership Project,
National, 119, 122

AskERIC, 235

Assessing Student Performance (Wiggins), 56

Assessment (alternative/authentic/
performance), 40–56

of administrators, 237

administrators and, 41, 47, 49

alternative assessment defined, 231

of art learning, 49, 50

auditing methods of, 45, 49

authentic assessment, 37, 43–45, 54, 55,
231, 237

benchmarks and, 37, 44, 45, 49, 231

business people and, 45, 47, 146

college admissions officers and, 4, 41, 45, 47

community and, 21, 45, 47, 49, 50, 51, 54, 170

critique circles for, 46–47

databases and, 44, 45, 53, 54

defined, 231, 232

of districts, 43, 45

electronic resources for, 52, 53, 236, 237, 245

expectations clearly established and, 39,
43, 45, 46, 175

feedback for, 44, 46, 53

graduation by exhibition, 51

legal issues, 55

letter grades for, 40, 45, 47

local councils and, 169

longitudinal, 45, 55

of mathematics learning, 49, 50

motivation and, 55

multimedia and, 20, 41, 44, 52, 146, 216

note-taking by teachers for, 44

organizational resources for, 52–54

overview of, 20–21, 40–41, 43–45, 49

parents and, 21, 41, 47, 50

Assessment *(continued)*
by peers
for students, 17, 19, 28, 44, 46, 47, 50, 51

for teachers, 75, 77, 91, 170

performance assessment defined, 232

periodicals on, 54, 78

personalized, 44–45, 46

policy makers and, 43, 45, 47, 53, 54, 55,
171, 245

portfolios and. *See* Portfolios

purpose of, 43, 232

of reading comprehension, 48

readings on, 36, 37, 54–55, 79, 80

real-world learning and, 40, 44, 47, 49, 50, 55

research on, 52–54, 56, 245

of schools, 43, 45, 80, 145, 236, 237

of science learning, 48

self-. *See* Self-assessment

of special-needs students, 242

standards and. *See* Standards, assessment and

of states, 43, 45, 189

of teachers, 75, 77, 87, 91, 96, 170, 237

teachers and. *See* Teachers, assessment
of students and

technology and, 41, 44, 54, 221

test scores and, 21, 40–41, 43, 50.
See also Standardized tests

training in, 237

of writing skills, 48, 49, 50

Assessment and Accountability Program, 52

Assessment Training Institute, 56, 237

Assistive technologies, 211, 213, 224, 226,
228, 231, 236, 249

Association for Educational Communications
and Technology, 224

Association for Supervision and Curriculum
Development, 38, 180

Association for Supervision and Curriculum
Development, Network on
Authentic Assessment, 237

Association for the Advancement of
Computing in Education, 224

AT&T
AT&T Learning Network, 248

KidsCampaign, 245

partnership with, 113

ATLAS Communities, 31, 33

At-risk students
business partnership programs and, 150

community learning centers and, 127–128

At-risk students (*continued*)

    research organizations for, 38, 235

    site-based management and, 112–113

    See also Low-income students and families;
        Minority students and families

Atwell, Nancie, 78, 80

Auditing assessment methods, 45, 49

Authentic assessment. *See* Assessment
    (alternative/authentic/performance)

Authentic Assessment in Practice
    (Darling-Hammond et al.), 54

Authority

    of community members, 170

    of parents, 110, 170

    of principals, 170

    of teachers, 4–5, 60, 64, 68, 69, 72, 167, 170

Autodesk Foundation, 243

Awards, 56, 246

B

Bailey, Thomas, 157

Baker, Eva L., 54, 56

Ballard, Robert, 27

BankAmerica Foundation, 243

Bank Street College of Education, 80

Barr, Camille C., 30, 38

Basic School, The (Boyer), 186

Bay Area Research Group, 190

Bay Area Writing Project, 93

Bayside Middle School for the Arts and
    Creative Technology, 38

Beacons Initiative, 138

Beakman's World, 248

Beane, James A., 35

Bell Atlantic, 222

    Bell Atlantic World School, 248

BellSouth Foundation, 243

Benchmarks, 37, 44, 45, 49, 231

Benjamin Franklin Butler Middle School
    of Technology, 200

Benton Foundation, 243

Berla, Nancy, 121

Bialo, Ellen R., 229

Big Sky Telegraph, 248

Bilingual education, 236

Bingler, Steven, 205, 208

Biology, 18–20, 21, 71, 91, 97, 242

Blackstock Junior High School, 243

Blank, Martin, 138, 140

Bloomfield, William, 154, 158

Board on Biology, 97

Boards of education, 239. *See also* Departments
    of education; School boards

Bodilly, Susan, 186

Bodily-kinesthetic intelligence, 21, 28

Boeing Company, The, 158, 243

Boston College, Center for the Study of Testing,
    Evaluation, & Educational Policy, 56

Boyer, Ernest L., 186

Bracey, Bonnie, 70–71, 80

Brand, Jacquelyn, 226, 230

Bread Loaf Rural Teachers Network, 237

Breaking Ranks (National Association of
    Secondary School Principals), 188

"Break-the-mold" school design.
    See New American Schools

Bridgforth, Elizabeth, 229

Bridging the Gap (Education Commission
    of the States), 187

Brighton High School, 148–149, 158

Brock, Patricia Ann, 229

Brooks, Jacqueline Grennon, 35

Brooks, Martin G., 35

Brown Barge Middle School, 26, 38

Brown, John Seely, 225, 230

Brown, Rexford, 10, 38

Bruer, John T., 36

Bruner, Charles, 139

Bruner, Jerome, 35

Buddy System Project, The, 116

Budgeting

    business partnership programs and, 147

    local councils and, 169

    personnel and, 179

    readings on, 187

    site-based management and, 171

    teachers and, 65, 72

    See also Financing

Building the Future (Educational
    Technology Office), 206

Business, 142–158

    assessment and, 45, 47, 146

    community learning centers and, 128, 131,
        133, 135, 136

    curriculum development and, 142

    employee participation in schools
        encouraged by, 110, 115, 118, 122,
        143, 147, 158, 243

    future competencies required by, 158

Business (*continued*)

    mission and goals definition and, 3, 14,
        17–18, 166–167, 169

    overview of, 142–143

    partnership programs

        administrators and, 147

        apprenticeships, 143, 147, 151, 157, 185

        contacts for, 158

        electronic resources for, 243, 244, 245,
            247, 248

        health care field, 148–149, 150, 153

        higher education and, 143, 146, 148,
            152, 153

        importance of, 102

        Internet and, 113, 138, 147, 149, 202

        internships, 143, 147, 148, 149, 152,
            153, 155, 158, 185, 197

        job shadowing, 152, 153

        knowledge transfer and, 147

        low-income students and, 148–149, 153

        mentoring, 147, 149, 152, 153, 243, 248

        minority students and, 148–149, 153

        organizational resources for, 154–156

        overview of, 142

        periodicals on, 156

        policy makers and, 154, 155, 156, 158

        readings on, 157–158

        real-world learning and, 143, 146, 147,
            149, 150–158

        role of, 146–147

        school restructuring assistance and,
            147, 184, 200, 223

        school-to-career programs, 143, 147,
            148–158, 233, 235, 236, 243, 244,
            245, 246

        science field, 150, 153

        teachers and, 65, 69, 143, 147

        technology and, 113, 138, 146–147, 149,
            152, 156, 227, 229, 248, 249

        value of, 147, 197

    site-based management and, 113, 172–173

    standards and, 49, 56, 145–146, 148, 150,
        154, 156, 157, 158, 170, 187

    student modeling of, 29, 75

    student-run, 197

    technology and, 113, 138, 143, 145,
        146–147, 149, 152, 156, 213, 220,
        223, 226, 227, 228, 248, 249

    See also Employment; Experts; *specific*
        companies

Business and the Schools (Council for Aid
to Education), 157
Business Coalition for Education Reform, 154
*Business Leader's Guide to Setting Academic
Standards, A* (The Business Round-
table), 157
Business Roundtable Participation Guide, The
(National Alliance of Business and
The Business Roundtable), 157
Business Roundtable, The, 154, 157
Byck Family Resource Center, 130–131, 140

C

Cabot School, 174, 216–217, 230
Cahill, Michele, 127–129, 140
Calendar. *See* Scheduling.
California
Access Excellence (South San Francisco),
91, 215
Alliance for Technology Access
(San Rafael), 224, 228, 230
Apple Classrooms of Tomorrow
(Cupertino), 151
assessment in, 46–47, 53, 54, 55, 56
Bay Area Research Group (Palo Alto), 190
Bay Area Writing Project (Berkeley), 93
Bayside Middle School for the Arts and
Creative Technology (San Mateo), 38
Blackstock Junior High School (Internet), 243
Center for Civic Education (Calabasas), 39
Center for Collaboration for Children
(Fullerton), 136, 140
Center for Research on Education, Diversity
and Excellence (Santa Cruz), 32
Center for Research on the Context
of Teaching (Stanford), 76, 80
Center for the Future of Teaching &
Learning (Internet), 237
Center for the Study of Parent
Involvement (Orinda), 118
Child Development Project (Oakland), 31
City Links (Internet), 241
Clear View Charter School
(Chula Vista), *ix*, 178
Computer Curriculum Corporation
(Sunnyvale), 230
Computer Learning Foundation™
(Palo Alto), 225

California *(continued)*
Computer-Using Educators, Inc.
(Alameda), 76
Coyote Canyon Elementary School
(Rancho Cucamonga), 201
Developmental Studies Center (Oakland), 31
El Cerrito High School (El Cerrito), 98
EQUALS (Berkeley), 31
Exploratorium, The, 31 (San Francisco),
242 (Internet)
Family Support Services Center
(San Diego), 133
Galef Institute, The (Los Angeles), 78, 94
Global SchoolNet Foundation,
226 (Bonita), 247 (Internet)
Institute for Research on Learning
(Menlo Park), 32
InterLearn (Encinitas), 230
Internet connection for all classrooms in, 219
Juarez-Lincoln Accelerated School
(San Diego), 220
KidsVoice Alert (San Rafael), 121
Los Angeles Educational Alliance for Restruc-
turing Now (Los Angeles), 182
Los Angeles Educational Partnership
(Los Angeles), 183
Mendocino Unified School District
(Mendocino), 219
National Center for Research in Vocational
Education (Berkeley), 155, 158
National Center for Research on Evaluation,
Standards, and Student Testing, The
(Los Angeles), 53, 56
National Center for the Accelerated
Schools Project (Stanford), 183
O'Farrell Community School (San Diego),
46–47, 56, 133
Open Charter School (Los Angeles), 29
Parent Institute for Quality Education
(San Diego), 119
Parents' Educational Resource Center
(San Mateo), 120
Pasadena Partnership Academies
(Pasadena), 150
Perkins & Will architects (Pasadena), 208
Peter W. Johansen High School
(Modesto), 203
Plugged In (Internet), 251
Silicon Valley programs, 138 (Santa Clara),
247 (Internet)

California *(continued)*
Smart Valley, Inc. (Santa Clara), 138
Stanford University School of Education
(Stanford), 56
TEAMS Distance Learning
(Internet), 251
Thornburg Center for Professional
Development (San Carlos), 230
Turnbull Learning Academy
(San Mateo), 115
Urban Village program (San Fernando), 134
Vaughn Family Center (San Fernando),
134, 140
Vaughn Next Century Learning Center
(San Fernando), 134, 140
Walt Disney Imagineering (Glendale), 230
WestEd (Internet), 237
Xerox Palo Alto Research Center
(Palo Alto), 230
California Academic Partnership Project, 243
California Instructional Technology
Clearinghouse, 248
California Subject Matter Project, 237
Calloway County Middle School, 80, 176
Cambridge Rindge & Latin School, 243
Career assistance. *See* Business, partnership
programs; Employment
Carnegie Corporation of New York, 35
Carnegie Corporation Task Force
on Teaching as a Profession, 4, 77
Carnegie Council on Adolescent
Development, 139
Carrero, Alexis, 22–23, 38
Carroll County Public Schools, 48
Carver, George Washington, 70
Cawelti, Gordon, 35
Center for Applied Special Technology, 224
Center for Career Development, 152
Center for Children and Technology, 230, 248
Center for Civic Education, 30
Center for Collaboration for Children, 136, 140
Center for Collaborative Education, 38
Center for Community Partnerships, 132
Center for Educational Leadership &
Technology, 248
Center for Educational Renewal, 94
Center for Family, School and Community, 243
Center for Innovation in Instruction, 237
Center for Interactive Educational
Technology, 224

Center for Law and Education, 122

Center for Leadership in School Reform, "The Schlechty Group", 180, 190

Center for Learning, Teaching, & Technology, 249

Center for Media Education, 243

Center for Media Literacy, 238

Center for Networked Information Discovery and Retrieval, 235

Center for Performance Assessment, 52, 56

Center for Research on Educational Account-ability and Teacher Evaluation, 238

Center for Research on Education, Diversity and Excellence, 32

Center for Research on the Context of Teaching, 76, 80

Center for Research on the Education of Students Placed at Risk, 38, 235

Center for Teaching and Learning, 76, 80

Center for Technology in Learning, 249

Center for the Future of Teaching & Learning, 238

Center for the Study of Human Resources, 243

Center for the Study of Parent Involvement, 118

Center for the Study of Testing, Evaluation, & Educational Policy, 56

Center on Education and Work, 243

Center on Families, Communities, Schools and Children's Learning, 122

Center on Learning, Assessment, and School Structure, 52, 56

Center on School, Family, and Community Partnerships, 119, 120, 122

Centers, electronic resources for national, 234, 235–237

Center Work, 156

Central Park East, 22, 23, 188

Central Park East Secondary School, 22–23, 179, 188, 190

Certifying
  principals, 184
  students, 153, 156, 157, 179, 240
  teachers, 77, 94, 240

Challenge of Change, The (National Alliance of Business), 157

Change Forces (Fullan), 186

Changing Contexts of Teaching, The (Lieberman), 79

Charlotte's Web, 249

Charter schools, *ix*, 10, 29, 38, 170, 178, 231, 245

Charting a Course (Bruner et al.), 139

Chattanooga School for the Arts and Sciences, 26

Chavkin, Nancy F., 121

Cheltenham Elementary School, 133

Cherkasky-Davis, Lynn, 88–89, 98

Child and Family Policy Center, 136

Childcare
  at community learning centers, 113, 128–129, 130, 131, 132, 133, 134, 137, 138, 139, 197
  design of centers for, 204
  at schools, 110, 125

Child development, 35, 73. *See also* Early childhood education

Child Development Project, 31

Children at the Center (Miller), 37

Children, Learning and School Design (Hebert and Meek), 206

Children Now, 244

Children's Defense Fund, 244

Children's Environment, 205

Children's Environments Research and Design Group, 204

Children's Environments Research Group, 204

Children's Literature Web Guide, 238

Children's Machine, The (Papert), 229

Children's School of Rochester, The, 72

Children's Software Revue, 120

Children, Youth, & Environment Network, 244

Christopher, Gaylaird, 206, 208

Christopher Columbus School, 222

Cisco Education Archives, 238

City Links, 241

Civic responsibility
  community learning centers and, 127, 129, 134, 138
  electronic resource for, 241
  preparing students for, 1, 2, 30, 68
  See also Democracy

Civics. *See* History/Social science

Classline, 238

Classroom Connect, 78

Classrooms
  design of, 195–196, 198, 200, 201, 205
  telephones in, 72, 106, 113
  See also Schools, physical design of

Clearinghouses, 52, 53, 94, 185, 225, 234, 235, 236, 241–242, 248

Clear View Charter School, *ix*, 178

Cleveland Freenet, 249

Coaches, teachers as, 20, 26, 43, 64

Coal Creek Elementary School, 74

Coalition for America's Children, 244

Coalition of Essential Schools, 53, 179, 181, 190

Cobb, Nina, 35

Cognition. *See* Learning theories; Metacognition; Understanding

Cognitive science, defined, 231

Cohen, Uriel, 206

Collaboratives for Humanities and Arts Teaching, 238

College professors
  architecture of schools and, 200
  community education association for, 137
  of education, 38, 80, 82–83, 98, 184, 190
  standards and, 45
  teacher relationship with, 69

Colleges, community learning centers and, 132. *See also* Colleges of education; Higher education; Schools of educa-tion; *specific colleges and universities*

Colleges of education
  Alverno College of Education (Wisconsin), 91, 98
  Bank Street College of Education (New York), 80
  Florida Atlantic University (Florida), 140
  Michigan State University (Michigan), 80
  organizational resources for, 94
  University of Nevada, (Nevada), 98
  University of Southern Maine, (Maine), 92
  See also Schools of education

Colón, Mary D., 112–113, 122

Colorado
  Cheltenham Elementary School (Denver), 133
  Coal Creek Elementary School (Louisville), 74
  Education Commission of the States (Denver), 182, 187
  Family Resource Schools (Denver), 133
  Mid-continent Regional Educational Laboratory, 56 (Aurora), 236 (Internet)
  Peakview Elementary School (Aurora), 175

Comer, James P., 109–111, 117, 121, 122

Commission on Life Sciences, 97

Commission on the Skills of the American Workforce, The, 156, 157

Committee for Economic Development, 244

Committee on Architecture for Education, 204

Committee on Biology Teacher Inservice Programs, 97

Commonwealth of North Mariana Islands, Pacific Region Educational Laboratory (Internet), 236

Communities in Schools, Inc., 136

Community, 124–140

assessment and, 21, 45, 47, 49, 50, 51, 54, 170

authority of, 170

contributing to, 1, 2, 125, 132. *See also* Community learning centers; Community service programs

cross-grade teams and, 175

curriculum development and, 3, 124–125

electronic resources for, 237, 243, 244, 245, 246, 247

hands-on learning and, 24, 25

importance of involvement of, 124–125, 127–129, 140

local councils and, 114, 169

mentoring and, 125, 128, 197

mission and goals definition and, 3, 14, 166–167, 169, 170

multipurpose nature of schools and, 124, 125, 127–129

networking with schools, 125, 135, 139, 197, 249

overview of, 17–18, 100–102, 124–125

parental involvement in, 107, 110, 115, 117, 120, 127, 129

periodical for community members, 186

project-based learning and, 24, 25, 218

public access networks, 249

real-world learning and, 124–125

research on, 120, 121, 136

school facilities design and, 135, 193, 197, 198, 200, 205

school restructuring and, 135, 170, 172, 181, 182, 183, 184, 197

site-based management and, 170, 172

standards and, 49, 124, 170

student relationship to, 20, 28, 132

student service to. *See* Community service programs

teachers and, 65, 69

Community *(continued)*

technology and, 125, 138, 226, 249

learning how to use, 217, 225, 227

town meetings, *xiii*, 169, 170

volunteers, 135

See also Adult education; Business; Community learning centers; Early childhood education; Health and social services; Higher education; School boards

Community learning centers, 124–140

architecture of schools and, 135, 193, 200

business and, 128, 131, 133, 135, 136

childcare at, 113, 128–129, 130, 131, 132, 133, 134, 137, 138, 139, 197

civic responsibility and, 127, 129, 134, 138

contacts for, 140

design of, 135, 193, 197, 198

employment assistance and, 128–129, 132, 133, 134, 135, 137, 138

examples of, 130–135, 178, 202

gang prevention and, 127, 133, 134

health and social services and, 113, 124, 127, 129, 130–140

low-income students and families and, 124, 130–140

minority students and families and, 124, 130–140

organizational resources for, 136–138

overview of, 124–125, 127–131, 197

parents and, 113, 127–129, 130–140

periodicals on, 138

policy makers and, 135

readings on, 139–140

recreational activities at, 127–128, 131, 132, 134, 138, 197

services offered by, 113, 124, 125, 127–131, 132, 133

social activities at, 127–128, 129, 131

students and, 127–128, 129, 130–140

teachers and, 129, 133

technology and, 129, 133, 134, 135, 138, 139

teen programs, 125, 129, 134

See also Adult education; Lifelong learning

Community service programs, 125, 127, 133, 134, 138, 139, 197, 215, 243

Community Technology Center Review, 138

Community Technology Centers' Network, 249

Community Updates, 244

Computer Curriculum Corporation, 230

Computer Learning Foundation™, 225

Computer Professionals for Social Responsibility, 249

Computer Resources for People with Disabilities (Alliance for Technology Access), 228

Computers. *See* E-mail; Internet; Laptop computers; Networking; Technology; Telecommunications; World Wide Web (WWW)

Computers and Classroom Culture (Schofield), 229

Computers for School Program, 249

Computer-Using Educators, Inc., 76

Concordia Architects, 208

Cone, Joan, 95, 98

Co-NECT, 218, 225

Conflict-mediation programs, 30, 172, 238

Conley, David T., 186

Connected Family, The (Papert), 122

ConnecTen, 249

Connecticut

Exemplars (Westport), 56

Northeast and Islands Regional Educational Laboratory (Internet), 236

School Development Program (New Haven), 120, 121, 122

Schools of the 21st Century (New Haven), 138

Connecting Students to a Changing World (Research and Policy Committee), 36

ConnSense Bulletin, 249

Consensus, school governance and, 172, 173, 175, 182

Consortium for Policy Research in Education, 180, 190

Consortium for School Networking, 225

Consortium for School Networking News, 228

Constructivism

defined, 232

theory of, 35, 36

Constructivism (Fosnot), 36

Consulting teachers, 5, 75

Contacts

assessment, 56

business partnership programs, 158

community learning centers, 140

learning, 38

parents, 122, 140

school facilities, 208

school restructuring, 190

Contacts *(continued)*
 teacher education and professional
  development, 98
 teacher role, 80
 technology, 230
Content of the Curriculum (Glatthorn), 37
Content Knowledge (Kendall and Marzano), 37
Content standards. *See* Standards
*Contexts That Matter for Teaching and
 Learning* (McLaughlin and Talbert), 79
Cooperative groups. *See* Consensus;
  Cooperative learning
Cooperative learning
 defined, 232
 hands-on learning and, 24
 mathematics and, 31, 46
 organizational resources for, 30, 38
 readings on, 36, 37, 207
 research by students and, 17
 science and, 176
 teacher education and professional
  development in, 30
 value of, 15, 20, 35, 37, 46
 See also Multi-ability groups;
  Multi-age groups
Cooperative Learning Center, 30, 38
Coordinated services, defined, 232.
  See also Health and social services
Corcoran, Thomas C., 97
Cornell University, Cornell Youth and Work
 Program, 158
Corporations. *See* Business
Cothran, Shirley, 60, 80
Council for Aid to Education, 157
Council for Basic Education, 158, 244
Council for Educational Development and
 Research, 235
Council of Chief State School Officers, 181
Council of Educational Facility Planners
 International, The, 204
Council of Great City Schools, 244
Counselors, teachers as, 68, 179
Countee Cullen Community Center, 134
Cousins, Emily, 36
Coyote Canyon Elementary School, 201
Cradler, John, 229
Craftsmanship 2000, 244
Creating a Learning Society (Garmer and
 Firestone), 229

Creating Family/School Partnerships
 (Rutherford), 121
Creating Learning Communities (Komoski
 and Priest), 139
CRESST. *See* National Center for Research
 on Evaluation, Standards, and Student
 Testing, The
CRESST Line, The, 54
Critical thinking. *See* Thinking
Cross City Campaign for Urban School
 Reform, 244
Cross-grade teams. *See* Multi-ability groups;
  Multi-age groups
Crossroads, 156
Crow Island Elementary School, 201, 206
C. S. Mott Foundation, 137, 140
Cultural activities
 at community learning centers, 127–128, 129
 at schools, 125
Culture of Education, The (Bruner), 35
Curricular Resources and Networking
 Projects, 238
Curriculum
 developing
  administrators and, 178
  business and, 142
  community and, 3, 124–125
  electronic resources for, 236
  frameworks for, 3, 35, 79
  lesson plans, 72, 225, 235, 238, 240, 241,
   249, 251, 252
  locally, 3
  mission and goals and, 3
  organizational resources for, 30–32, 52,
   53, 180
  parents and, 17, 26, 110, 115, 116, 117, 178
  periodicals on, 78
  readings on, 35, 36, 37, 79, 80
  standards and. *See* Standards
  teachers and, 60, 65, 72, 73, 80, 173,
   178, 179, 183
  team teaching and, 173, 178, 179
  themes and, 19, 37
  universal questions and, 19
 electronic resources for, 235, 236, 238,
  240, 250
 interdisciplinary curriculum defined, 232.
  See also Interdisciplinary project-
  based learning; Project-based learning
 motivation and, 15

Curriculum *(continued)*
 multimedia. *See* Multimedia
 readings on, 35, 36, 37, 79, 80
 technology and, 20, 32, 33, 78, 199,
  216–223, 225, 251. *See also*
  Technology, integrating
 traditional, *v*, 14–15
 See also Arts; Assessment (alternative/
  authentic/performance); History/
  social science; Humanities;
  Language arts; Mathematics;
  Physical education; Science
Curriculum Designers, Inc., 38
Curriculum Web, 238
Curry School of Education, 90
CyberEd Van, 249
Cyberspace Middle School, 247

D

Dade Academy for the Teaching Arts, 73
Daggett, Willard R., 36
Daily Report Card, 238
Dance. *See* Arts.
Danzberger, Jacqueline P., 186
Darling-Hammond, Linda, 54, 85–87, 97, 98
Daro, Phil, 53, 56
Databases
 assessment and, 44, 45, 53, 54
 of education issues and trends, 182
 of instructional strategies, 78
 of parent and community resources, 173
 for schools and social service providers,
  133, 135
 student research and, 20
 work-based learning and, 146
 See also Electronic resources
David, Jane L., 180, 187, 190
Davidson, Neil, 36
Davies, Don, 102
Davis, Bennett, 189
Daycare. *See* Childcare
Decentralization. *See* Site-based management
Decker, Larry E., 140
Defining Excellence for American Schools
 (Daggett), 36
Delaware
 Hodgson Vo-Tech High School
  (Newark), 150

Delaware *(continued)*
  Mid-Atlantic Laboratory for Student
    Success (Internet), 235
Democracy, *v, ix*, 30, 169, 187. *See also* Civic
  responsibility
Department of Labor. *See* U.S. Department
  of Labor
Departments of education, 181.
    See also Policy makers; State policy;
    U.S. Department of Education
Design, of schools. *See* Schools, organizational
  design of; Schools, physical design of
Designing Coherent Education Policy
  (Fuhrman), 187
*Designing Learning and Technology for
  Educational Reform* (Jones et al.), 229
Designing New American Schools
  (Bodilly et al.), 186
Designing Places for Learning (Meek), 207
Design Research News, 205
Designs for Change, 181
Designs for Learning, 137, 140
Developing Educational Standards, 238
Developmental Studies Center, 31
Dewey, John, 2, 85
Dickinson, Dee, 227, 230
Different Kind of Classroom, A (Marzano), 79
Different Ways of Knowing
  (The Galef Institute), 94
Digital portfolios, 17, 41, 44, 47, 50, 111
Directory of Public Access Networks, 249
Disabilities, students with
  assessment of, 242
  assistive technologies for, 211, 213, 224,
    226, 228, 231, 236, 249
  electronic resources for, 236, 242, 243, 249
  learning disabilities, 25, 120, 236, 246
  mainstreaming, 206
  parents of, 120, 246
  school design principles for, 206
  science and math program for, 30
Distance Education Clearinghouse, 241
Distance learning, 95, 111, 186, 193, 199, 227,
  241, 251
District of Columbia. *See* Washington, D.C.
Districts
  assessment of, 43, 45. *See also*
    Schools, assessment of
  responsiblity of, 171

Districts *(continued)*
  See also Administrators; Local policy;
    Policy makers; School boards;
    Superintendents; *specific school
    districts*
Diversity
  educational research and, 32, 33
  readings on, 80
  of student body, 26
  of teachers, 92, 96, 98
  of technology, 214
  teleconferencing and, 220
  See also Immigrant families; Low-income
    students and families; Minority stu-
    dents and families; Multi-ability
    groups; Multi-age groups
Diversity in the Classroom (Shulman and
  Mesa-Bains), 80
Documentary film, *Learn & Live™,vi, ix, xi,* 231
Drama. *See* Arts
Dryfoos, Joy G., 139
DuSable High School, 114
Dwyer, David, 225, 230
Dykeman Architects, The, 198–199, 208
Dzantik'i Heeni Middle School, 218

E

Early childhood education, 118, 130–131,
  138, 236, 242
Early Literacy Portfolio, 48
Earth science. *See* Science
Economics education.
    See History/social science
Edison Electric Institute On-line, 244
Edmonds, Ron, 171
Education
  democracy and,*v, ix,* 169, 187
  purposes of, *ix,* 1, 2, 3, 4, 6, 30, 68
  statistics on, 236, 240, 247
  See also Public education
Educational Assessment, 54
Educational Facilities (Lackney), 206
*Educational Facilities for the Twenty-First
  Century* (Moore and Lackney), 207
Educational Facility Planner, The, 205
Educational Leadership, 54, 185
Educational Measurement, 54
Educational Products Information
  Exchange, 225

Educational Renewal (Goodlad), 97
Educational Researcher, 185
Educational Research Service, 229
Educational Resource Information Center.
    See entries beginning with ERIC
Educational Technology (Fisher et al.), 228
Educational Technology (periodical), 228
Educational Technology in the Classroom
  (Brock), 229
Educational Technology Office, 206
Educational Testing Service, Center for
  Performance Assessment, 52, 56
Education and Technology (Office
  of Technology Assessment), 229
Education Commission of the States, 182, 187
Education Development Center, Inc., 31
Education First program, 219
Education in the Communication Age, 189
Education Today, 120
Education Trust, Inc., 178, 182
Education Week, 185, 189
Educators for Social Responsibility, 238
Educom, 249
Edwards, Pat, 137, 140
EdWeb, Exploring Technology and School
  Reform, 235
Eisenhower National Clearinghouse, 235
El Cerrito High School, 98
Electronic Archives for Teaching American
  Literature, 238
Electronic Learning, 228
Electronic resources, 234–252
  administrators, 237, 242, 249
  adult education, 236, 242, 245
  assessment, 52, 53, 236, 237, 245
  at-risk students, 235
  business partnership programs, 243, 244,
    245, 247, 248
  clearinghouses, 52, 53, 94, 185, 225, 234,
    235, 236, 241–242, 248
  community, 237, 243, 244, 245, 246, 247
  curriculum development, 236
  educator links, 234, 237–241
  on equal access, 243, 245, 249, 251
  on financing, 230, 238, 243, 244, 245, 247
  George Lucas Educational Foundation,
    The, *xi,* 234
  gifted and talented students, 236, 242
  health and social services, 244, 248, 251
  labs and centers, 234, 235–237

Electronic resources *(continued)*

legislation, 236, 240, 242, 245, 251

libraries, 234, 235, 241–242

low-income students and families, 236, 245, 246, 247, 251

minority students and families, 236, 245, 246, 247

for multimedia, 235, 243, 249, 250

museums, 234, 237, 241–242, 249, 252

news, 238, 239, 246

organizations, schools, and programs, 234, 236, 237, 239, 243–247. *See also* Elementary schools; High schools; K-8 schools; K-12 schools; Middle schools; Organizations

overview of, 234

parents, 237, 242, 243, 244, 246, 248

policy makers, 239, 240, 242, 243, 244, 245, 247, 249

readings on, 79

search engines, 234

site-based management, 235, 242, 244

special-needs students, 236, 242, 243, 249

standards, 236, 238, 240, 244, 245, 246

starting points, 234, 235

student projects, 234, 237, 238, 243–248

teachers, 77, 94, 234, 236, 237–241, 242, 243, 245, 248

technology, 234, 235, 237, 240, 241, 242, 245, 246, 247, 248–252

See also Databases; Internet; World Wide Web (WWW)

Elementary schools

Alice Carlson Applied Learning Center (Texas), 172–173, 175, 190

Ashlawn Elementary School (Virginia), 70–71

Central Park East (New York), 22, 23, 188

Cheltenham Elementary School (Colorado), 133

Child Development Project (California), 31

Children's School of Rochester, The (New York), 72

Clear View Charter School (California), *ix*, 178

Coal Creek Elementary School (Colorado), 74

Coyote Canyon Elementary School (California), 201

Elementary Schools *(continued)*

Crow Island Elementary School (Illinois), 201, 206

Emma E. Booker Elementary School (Florida), 117

ERIC Clearinghouse on Elementary and Early Childhood Education, 242 (Internet)

Fienberg-Fisher Elementary School (Florida), 117

Gardendale Elementary Magnet School (Florida), 75

Hemingway Elementary School (Idaho), 24–25, 38

Isaac Dickson Elementary School (North Carolina), 73

Juarez-Lincoln Accelerated School (California), 220

Morristown Elementary School (Vermont), 49

National Association of Elementary School Principals, 239

North Star Elementary School (Alaska), 50

Open Charter School (California), 29

Peakview Elementary School (Colorado), 175

P.S. 1 Charter School (Colorado), 38

Ralph Bunche School (Internet), 246

School City of Hammond, The (Indiana), 200

Shutesbury Elementary School (Massachusetts), 28

Turnbull Learning Academy (California), 115

Vaughn Next Century Learning Center (California), 134, 140

Webster School, The (Florida), 222

Ysleta Elementary School (Texas), 178

See also K-8 schools; K-12 schools

El Paso Collaborative, 178

E-mail

administrators and, 223

community learning centers and, 129

community-school communication and, 125

school design teams and, 173

students and, 177, 223, 247

teacher-parent communication and, 107, 111, 116

teachers and, 220, 222, 223

value of, 232

Emma E. Booker Elementary School, 117

Emotional development, of students, 109

Emotional Intelligence (Goleman), 37

Employment

community learning centers and, 128–129, 132, 133, 134, 135, 137, 138

preparing students for, 1–2, 45, 134, 137, 138, 145–146, 147, 148–153, 242, 245

See also Business

English, 217, 239, 241. *See also* Literature; Reading; Writing

English-limited students, 117, 148, 178. *See also* Bilingual education

Enhancing Thinking Through Cooperative Learning (Davidson and Worsham), 36

Environmental Design Research Association, 204

Environmental science. *See* Science

Environments Network, 244

Epistemology and Learning Group, 226

Epstein, Joyce, 119, 122

Equal access

electronic resources for, 243, 245, 249, 251

to Internet, 135, 226, 227, 229, 243, 245, 249, 251

organizational resources for, 94, 180

periodical on, 186

policy makers and, 171

to technology, 111, 116, 131, 135, 138, 224, 226, 227, 229, 243, 245, 249, 251

EQUALS, 31

Equity

for minority students, 119

in testing, 53

ERIC Clearinghouse for Reading, English, and Communications, 241

ERIC Clearinghouse for Science, Mathematics, and Environmental Education, 241

ERIC Clearinghouse for Social Studies/Social Science Education, 241

ERIC Clearinghouse on Adult and Vocational Education, 242

ERIC Clearinghouse on Assessment and Evaluation, 52

ERIC Clearinghouse on Disabilities and Gifted Education, 242

ERIC Clearinghouse on Educational Management, 242

ERIC Clearinghouse on Elementary and Early Childhood Education, 242

ERIC Clearinghouse on Information and Technology, 242

ERIC Clearinghouse on Language and Linguistics, 242

ERIC Clearinghouse on Teaching and Teacher Education, 94, 242

ERIC online information service, 235

ERIC Review, The
"Performance-Based Assessment", 55
"Professional Development", 97

Evaluation. *See* Assessment (alternative/authentic/performance)

Examinations. *See* Written examinations

Exceptional Parent, 120

Excite, 234

Exemplars, 56

Expanding Student Assessment (Perrone), 55

Expectations, establishing clear, 43, 45, 46, 49, 175, 182

Expeditionary Learning Outward Bound® approach, 34, 36

Experiential learning. *See* Hands-on learning; Project-based learning; Real-world learning

Experts
adult education and, 129
business partnership programs and, 143, 147
student interaction with, ix, 20, 25, 27, 64–65, 70, 146, 170, 178, 199, 210, 213, 233, 237, 239
teacher-experts in technology, 219, 222
teacher interaction with, 91, 170, 215, 233

Exploratorium, The, 31, 242

Extended Teacher Education Program, 92

F

Facilitators, teachers as, 68, 70–71, 196

FairTest, 53

Families and Schools in a Pluralistic Society (Chavkin), 121

Family. *See* Parents

Family Involvement Partnership for Learning, 244

FAMILY MATH, 31

Family PC, 121

Family resource centers. *See* Community learning centers

Family Resource Coalition, 137

Family Resource Schools, 133

Family Resource/Youth Services Centers, 137

Family Support Services Center, 133

Federal policy. *See* Government; Legislation; National policy; Policy makers; *entries beginning with* U.S.

Federated States of Micronesia, Pacific Region Educational Laboratory (Internet), 236

Feedback, to students, 44, 46, 53

Female students, science and math and, 30, 31

Fiber optics, 178, 199, 221

Field trips, virtual, 237, 241, 247, 248, 251

Fieldwork (Cousin and Rodgers), 36

Fienberg-Fisher Elementary School, 117

Film. *See* Documentary film

Financing
electronic resources for, 230, 238, 243, 244, 245, 247
research on, 180
of school facilities, 207, 219, 220, 223
of school restructuring, 179, 180, 184, 207
of technology, 76, 219, 220, 225, 227, 245, 250, 251, 252
in a transformed system, 189
See also Budgeting

Firestone, Charles M., 229

First Things First (Johnson and Immerwahr), 188

Fisher, Charles, 228

Flambeau School District, 116

Fleischman, Richard, 207, 208

Flexibility
in design of schools, 47, 171, 193, 197, 198, 199
in scheduling. *See* Scheduling

Florida
Brown Barge Middle School (Pensacola), 26, 38
Dade Academy for the Teaching Arts (Miami Beach), 73
Emma E. Booker Elementary School (Sarasota), 117
Fienberg-Fisher Elementary School (Miami Beach), 117
Florida Atlantic University College of Education (Boca Raton), 140
Florida Information Resources Network (Internet), 249
Full Service Schools (Santa Rosa County), 135

Florida *(continued)*
Gardendale Elementary Magnet School (Merritt Island), 75
Referral and Information Network (Miami Beach), 117
School Development Program (Sarasota), 117
Southeastern Regional Vision for Education (Internet), 237
Southern Regional Education Board (Atlanta, GA), 185
Webster School, The (St. Augustine), 222

Florida Atlantic University College of Education, 140

Florida Information Resources Network, 249

Foreign languages, 26, 28, 236, 251.
See also English-limited students

Fort Worth Project C³, 152

Fosnot, Catherine T., 36

Foundation Center, 244

Foundations School, The, 89, 98

Four Seasons Network, 53

Foxfire Fund, Inc., 53, 73, 76

Franklin Institute Science Museum and Planetarium, 242

Frederiksen, John, 56

Free-Nets & Community Networks, 249

From Now On, 249

Fuhrman, Susan H., 181, 187, 190

Fullan, Michael G., 186

Full-Service Schools (Dryfoos), 139

Full Service Schools (Florida), 135

Fund for the City of New York, 140

Funding. *See* Financing

Future of Children, The, 138

Future of Education, The (Cobb), 35

G

Galef Institute, The, 78, 94

Gallery of Interactive Geometry, 247

Gang prevention, 127, 133, 134

Gardendale Elementary Magnet School, 75

Gardner, Howard, 17–21, 28, 36, 38, 86, 241

Gardner, Sidney, 139, 140

Garfinkle, Robert J., 189

Garmer, Amy Korzick, 229

Geiger, Keith, 79, 80

Gender issues, periodical on, 96.
See also Female students

Genentech, Inc., Access Excellence, 91, 215

Geography. *See* Science

Geology. *See* Science

George Lucas Educational Foundation, The, *vi*, 234

Georgia

    Foxfire Fund, Inc. (Mountain City), 53, 73, 76

    High Schools that Work (Atlanta), 154

    Sandy Creek High School (Tyrone), 202

    Southeastern Regional Vision for Education (Internet), 237

    Southern Regional Education Board (Atlanta), 185

Getting America's Students Ready for the 21st Century (U.S. Department of Education), 230

Getty Information Institute, 242

Gifted and talented students, 25, 236, 242

Girls, science and math and, 30, 31

Glatthorn, Alan A., 37

Glickman, Carl D., 187

Global access to information, 20, 71, 167, 170, 178, 197, 213, 223, 226, 233, 247

GlobaLearn, 247

Global SchoolNet Foundation, 226, 247

GLOBE Program, 238, 247

Glossary, 231–233

Goals 2000/Louisiana Networking Infrastructure for Education Project, 250

Goals

    defining, 3, 14, 17–18, 166–167, 169, 170

    national, 189, 238

    See also Standards

Goldberger, Susan, 157

Gold, Lawrence, 158

Goleman, Daniel, 37

Goodlad, John, 94, 97

Gorham School Department, 74

Governance, school

    conflict-mediation programs, 30, 172, 238

    consensus and, 172, 173, 175, 182

    principles of, 170

    readings on, 186, 187

    See also Administrators; Boards of education; Departments of education; School boards; Site-based management

Governing Public Schools (Danzberger), 186

Government, technology implementation and, 226, 227, 229, 250. *See also* Legislation; National policy; Policy makers; *entries beginning with* U.S.

Governors, resources for, 182, 185, 187, 246. *See also* Policy makers; State policy

Grades, letter, 40, 45, 47

Graham & Parks Alternative Public School, 114

Graves, Ben E., 206

Great Transitions (Carnegie Council on Adolescent Development), 139

Group governance. *See* Site-based management

Group work. *See* Cooperative learning

Guam, Pacific Region Educational Laboratory (Internet), 236

Guardians. *See* Parents

Guide for Planning Educational Facilities (Moore), 207

Guide for School Facility Appraisal (Hawkins and Lilley), 206

Guides, teachers as, 15, 43, 64–65, 68, 70–71, 79, 179, 195

Guide to Authentic Instruction and Assessment, A (Newmann et al.), 55

H

Hallett, Anne C., 187

Halperin, Samuel, 154, 158

Halsted, Henry M., III, 208

Hamilton, Steven F., 157, 158

Hancock, Vicki, 33, 38

Handbook of Research on Improving Student Achievement (Cawelti), 35

Hand in Hand, 118

Hands-on learning

    architecture of schools and, 196

    art and, 24, 31

    business internships and, 148

    community and, 24, 25

    cooperative learning and, 24

    electronic resources for, 239

    family and community support of, 24

    mathematics and, 24, 31, 248

    motivation of students and, 71

    parents and, 24, 25

    project-based learning and, 24–25, 33

    real-world learning and, 24, 25, 29, 34, 36, 150

Hands-on learning *(continued)*

    research by students and, 24

    science and, 24–25, 31, 33, 48, 150, 248

    teacher development of, 73, 76

    technology and, 24, 31, 211

    See also Project-based learning; Real-world learning

Harvard Education Letter, The, 185

Harvard Family Research Project, 121, 244

Harvard Project Zero, 33, 53

Harvard Educational Technology Center, 250

Harvard University

    Graduate School of Education, 38, 190

    Performance Assessment Collaboratives for Education, 54, 56

    Project on Effective Interventions, 140

Haselkorn, David, 94, 98

Hawaii

    Hawaii Education and Resource Network (Internet), 250

    Pacific Region Educational Laboratory (Internet), 236

Hawaii Education and Resource Network, 250

Hawkins, Harold L., 206, 207, 208

Hawkins, Jan, 213–215, 230

Haynes, Norris M., 109–111, 122

Health and Human Development Programs, 244

Health and social services

    community learning centers and, 113, 124, 127, 129, 130–140

    coordinated services defined, 232

    electronic resources for, 244, 248, 251

    minority students and families and, 119

    policy makers and, 137

    schools and, 65, 112, 113, 117, 124, 127, 137, 183, 200

    site-based management and, 112–113

Health care field, school-to-career program in, 148–149, 150, 153

Hebert, Elizabeth, 206

Hemingway Elementary School, 24–25, 38

Henderson, Anne T., 121, 122

Henry M. Jackson High School, 198–199

Herman, Joan, 55

Heterogeneous age groups. *See* Multi-ability groups; Multi-age groups

Hewlett Packard, 245

Higginbotham, Marla, 187

Higher education, business partnerships and, 143, 146, 148, 152, 153. *See also entries beginning with* College

High schools

Brighton High School (Massachusetts), 148–149, 158

Cambridge Rindge & Latin School (Internet), 243

Central Park East Secondary School (New York), 22–23, 179, 188, 190

Dade Academy for the Teaching Arts (Florida), 73

design periodical for, 205

DuSable High School (Illinois), 114

El Cerrito High School (California), 98

Henry M. Jackson High School (Washington), 198–199

Hodgson Vo-Tech High School (Delaware), 150

Holt Senior High School (Michigan), 93

Illinois Mathematics and Science Academy (Illinois), 27

Metropolitan Center (Internet), 245

parents as students in, 114

Peter W. Johansen High School (California), 203

principals of, 183

Roane County High School (West Virginia), 203

Roosevelt Renaissance 2000 (Oregon), 153

Sandy Creek High School (Georgia), 202

Shorecrest High School (Washington), *ix*

University Heights High School (New York), 51

Walden III Middle/High School (Wisconsin), 51

Wood River Middle/High School (Idaho), 38

See also K-12 schools

High Schools that Work, 154

Highway I, 250

Hill, Nana, 76, 80

Hispanic Policy Development Project, 118, 122

Hispanic students and families. *See* Minority students and families

History/Social science

architecture of schools and, 195, 201

civics, 30

curriculum, 239, 241

economics, 241

electronic resources for, 238, 239, 241, 242

History/Social science *(continued)*

hands-on learning and, 24

project-based learning and, 18, 22–23, 24, 174, 218, 219

See also Civic Responsibility

History of the United States, 238

Hodgson Vo-Tech High School, 150

Hollingsworth, Sandra, 79

Holmes, Oliver Wendell, 4

Holmes Group, The, 97

Holt Senior High School, 93

Home, technology in the, 25, 107, 111, 113, 114, 116, 121, 131, 139, 222

Home Environment and School Learning, The (Kellaghan et al.), 121

Home Instruction Program for Preschool Youngsters USA, 118

Hoover, Stephany, 130–131, 140

Horace's Hope (Sizer), 188

HotBot, 234

Humanities, 238, 241. *See also* History/Social science; Language arts

Human Services Policy Center, 137

I

IBM, 178, 251

Idaho

Hemingway Elementary School (Ketchum), 24–25, 38

Northwest Regional Educational Laboratory, 52 (Portland, OR), 55 (Portland, OR), 236 (Internet)

Wood River Middle/High School (Hailey), 38

I*EARN, 214–215, 247

IEE Brief, 156

Illinois

Crow Island Elementary School (Winnetka), 201, 206

Designs for Change (Chicago), 181

DuSable High School (Chicago), 114

Family Resource Coalition (Chicago), 137

Foundations School, The (Chicago), 89, 98

Illinois Mathematics and Science Academy (Aurora), 27

Learning Through Collaborative Visualization (Evanston), 227

National PTA, The (Chicago), 119

Illinois *(continued)*

North Central Regional Educational Laboratory (Internet), 235

Parent Academic Success Service (Chicago), 114

Quest Center (Chicago), 77

White Career Academy (Chicago), 122

Illinois Mathematics and Science Academy, 27

Immerwahr, John, 188

Immigrant families, resources for, 119, 120, 122. *See also* Low-income students and families; Minority students and families

Impact II—The Teachers Network, 77, 79

Incredible Art Department, 238

Indiana

Buddy System Project, The (Indianapolis), 116

Key Renaissance School (Indianapolis), 28

School City of Hammond, The (Hammond), 200

Individual differences of students. *See* Students, individual differences of

Individual learning plans, 107, 177, 232

Individual relationships with students, by teachers, 64, 68, 71, 86, 167, 170, 179, 214

Information

global access to, 20, 71, 167, 170, 178, 197, 213, 223, 226, 233, 247

learning and, 210, 214, 217

InformED, 245

Inner city students. *See* Low-income students and families; Minority students and families

Innovations In Parent & Family Involvement (Rioux and Berla), 121

Innovative Assessment (Northwest Regional Educational Laboratory), 55

In Search of Understanding (Brooks and Brooks), 35

Institute for Educational Leadership, Inc., 140, 182

Institute for Education and the Economy, 245

Institute for Environmental Education, 205, 208

Institute for Learning Technologies, 250

Institute for Research on Learning, 32

Institute for Responsive Education, 118, 122

Institute for the Learning Sciences, 250

Institute for the Transfer of Technology to Education, 226

Institute on Education and Training, 245

Instructional strategies

organizational resources for, 30–32, 76–78

periodicals on, 34, 78

readings on, 35, 36, 37, 79–80

See also Cooperative learning; Hands-on
learning; Multi-ability groups;
Multi-age groups; Project-based
learning; Real-world learning;
Student-directed learning; Team
teaching; Work-based learning

Intelligence

bodily-kinesthetic, 21, 28

emotional, 37

interpersonal, 20, 21

intra-personal, 21

linguistic, 21, 28

logical-mathematical, 21, 28

multiple, 21, 28, 36, 86, 225, 241

musical, 21, 28

research on, 33

spatial, 21

Interactive multimedia. *See* Multimedia

Intercultural E-mail Classroom
Connections, 247

Interdisciplinary curriculum, defined, 232.
See also Interdisciplinary project-based
learning; Project-based learning

Interdisciplinary Curriculum (Jacobs), 37

Interdisciplinary project-based learning

architecture of schools and, 198, 199

arts-infused, 28, 94, 239

examples of, 19, 21, 37

teacher creation of, 72

value of, 15, 19, 37, 198

See also Project-based learning

InterLearn, 230

Intermediate School 218, 132

International Society for Technology in
Education, 226

Internet

business partnership programs and, 113,
138, 147, 149, 202

community access via schools, 125, 135, 249

defined, 232

equal access to, 135, 226, 227, 229, 243,
245, 249, 251

interacting with experts via. *See* Experts

learning to use, 138, 240, 248, 249, 251

Internet *(continued)*

locally run, cooperative access providers,
219, 227

organizational resources for, 71, 226, 227

periodicals on, 228

projects registry for, 247

providing services on, 219

public access networks, 249

rapid evolution of, 214

readings on, 229

research and, 20, 64–65, 177, 210, 213,
214–215, 217, 219, 222, 223, 234,
235, 247–248

school restructuring and, 173, 177, 178,
197, 199, 202, 203, 222

science education and, *ix*, 20, 27, 70, 91,
178, 199, 213, 214, 215, 237, 239

students and, 20, 64–65, 138, 177, 210,
213, 214–215, 217, 219, 221, 222,
223, 226, 234, 235, 247–248

teachers and, 5, 64–65, 72, 74, 76, 78, 79,
211, 221, 223, 234, 237–241, 250, 251

value of, 5–6, 64–65, 71, 213, 214, 217

See also Electronic resources; E-mail;
Networking; Telecommunications;
World Wide Web (WWW)

Internet Comprehensive Instructional and
Curricular Library for Educators, 240

Internet Projects Registry, 247

Internet Roadmap for Educators
(Educational Research Service), 229

Internet Society, 226

Internships

student, 143, 147, 148, 149, 152, 153,
155, 158, 185, 197. *See also*
School-to-career programs

teacher, 86–87, 88, 90, 92, 93

Interpersonal intelligence, 20, 21

Interstate New Teacher Assessment and
Support Consortium, 94

Intra-personal intelligence, 21

Iowa

Child and Family Policy Center
(Des Moines), 136

Iowa.net (Internet), 250

Learning Resource Center, The
(West Des Moines), 140

North Central Regional Educational
Laboratory (Internet), 235

Iowa *(continued)*

West Des Moines Community School
District (West Des Moines), 135

Iowa.net, 250

Isaac Dickson Elementary School, 73

*Issues of Curriculum Reform in Science,
Mathematics and Higher Order
Thinking Across the Disciplines*
(Anderson et al.), 35

ITI (Kovalik and Olsen), 37

J

Jacobs, Heidi Hayes, 31, 37, 38

JASON Foundation for Education, 27

Jefferson, Thomas, 3, 70

Jennings, Wayne, 138, 140

Jobs for the Future, 154, 157

Job shadowing, 152, 153

Job training. *See* Employment

John, Jayne, 172–173, 190

Johns Hopkins University, The

Center for Research on the Education of
Students Placed at Risk, 38, 235

Center on Families, Communities, Schools
and Children's Learning, 122

Johnson, David, 30, 37

Johnson, Jean, 188

Johnson, Juliette, 148–149, 158

Johnson, Roger, 30, 35, 38

Johnson, Samuel, 5

Johnson, Susan Moore, 79

Johnson Foundation, 208

Jones, Beau Fly, 229

Jones, K. John, 198–199, 208

Jones, Roberts T., 145–147, 158

Jones, Sue, 229

Journal of Computing in Teacher Education, 96

Journal of Science Education and Technology, 34

Journal of Staff Development, 96

Journal of Teacher Education, 96

Journal of Technology and Teacher Education, 96

Juarez-Lincoln Accelerated School, 220

Junior high schools. *See* Middle schools

K

K-8 schools

Graham & Parks Alternative Public School
(Massachusetts), 114

Maplewood K-8 School (Washington), 115

MicroSociety®, Inc., schools
(multiple states), 29, 34

White Career Academy (Illinois), 122

Williston Central School (Vermont), 177

See also Elementary schools;
Middle schools

K-12 Resources for Music Educators, 239

K-12 schools

ACT Academy (Texas), 72, 80

Cabot School (Vermont), 174, 216–217, 230

Carroll County Public Schools
(Maryland), 48

Chattanooga School for the Arts and
Sciences (Tennessee), 26

Gorham School Department (Maine), 74

JASON Project and, 27

Mendocino Unified School District
(California), 219

Perry Community Educational Village
(Ohio), 202

Pittsburgh Public Schools (Pennsylvania), 49

Rogers School District (Arkansas), 223

Shoreline School District (Washington), 220

Sioux Falls School District 49-5
(South Dakota), 221

South Brunswick Public Schools
(New Jersey), 48

Upper Arlington City Schools (Ohio), 50

Westside Community Schools
(Nebraska), 219

See also Elementary schools; High schools;
Middle schools

Kagan, Sharon L., 139

Kallick, Bena, 52, 56

Kansas, ShareNet (Internet), 251

Kapisovsky, Peggy M., 230

Kathy Schrock's Guide for Educators, 239

Kay, Alan, 230

Kellaghan, Thomas, 121

Kendall, John S., 37

Kentucky

Appalachia Educational Laboratory, Inc.
(Internet), 235

Byck Family Resource Center (Louisville),
130–131, 140

Kentucky *(continued)*

Calloway County Middle School
(Murray), 80, 176

Center for Leadership in School Reform,
"The Schlechty Group" (Louisville),
180, 190

Family Resource/Youth Services Centers
(Frankfort), 137

Partnership for Kentucky School Reform,
The (Lexington), 155

Southern Regional Education Board
(Atlanta, GA), 185

Kentucky Education Reform Act of 1990,
155, 176

*Key Elements of Effective State Planning for
Educational Technology, The* (Jones), 229

Key Renaissance School, 28

Kickstart Initiative, 250

KIDLINK, 247

KidsCampaign, 245

Kidspace, 247

Kidsphere, 250

KidsVoice Alert, 121

Kilbourne, Larry, 139

Koch, Melissa, 79

Komoski, P. Kenneth, 139

Kovalik, Susan, 37

Kruse, Sharon D., 80

L

LabNet, 215, 239

Labs and centers, electronic resources for,
234, 235–237. *See also entries
beginning with* Center

Lackney, Jeffrey A., 206, 207

Language arts, 24, 31, 36, 217, 242. *See also*
English; Foreign languages; Literature;
Reading; Writing

Lanier, Judith Taack, 67–69, 80

Laptop computers, 72, 221

Latino students and families. *See* Minority
students and families

Laws. *See* Legislation

Lazarus, Wendy, 229

Leadership

federal government and, 171

periodical on, 185

school restructuring and, 182, 184, 189

teachers and, 74, 75, 76, 77–78, 94, 95, 185

Leadership programs, community learning
centers and, 133, 137

Leadership teams, site-based management
and, 113

League of Schools Reaching Out, 118

Learning, 14–38

assessment of. *See* Assessment
(alternative/authentic/performance)

contacts for, 38

distance, 95, 111, 186, 193, 199, 227, 241, 251

in-depth, 18–19, 28, 179, 214

information and, 210, 214, 217

lifelong. *See* Adult education;
Lifelong learning

motivating. *See* Motivation

organizational resources for, 30–33, 76–78

overview of, 14–16

periodicals on, 34, 78

questions and, 19

readings on, 35–37, 79–80

research on, 30–32, 33, 34, 35–37, 186, 237

standards and, 14

to teach. *See* Teachers, learning to teach

teacher's role and, 68, 69

themes and, 19, 37

thinking and, 15, 35, 36

understanding and, 15, 18, 22, 33, 35, 36, 47

See also Cooperative learning; Curriculum;
Hands-on learning; Project-based
learning; Real-world learning;
Student-directed learning; Team
teaching; Work-based learning

Learning and Leading with Technology, 186

Learning by Design, 247

Learning-disabled students. *See* Disabilities,
students with

Learning from the Past
(Ravitch and Vinovskis), 189

Learning plans, individual, 107, 177, 232

Learning Research and Development Center, 32

Learning Resource Center, The, 140

Learning/Teaching Collaborative, The, 90

Learning Technology Center, 227

Learning theories, 21, 28, 35, 36, 232.
See also Multiple intelligences

Learning Through Collaborative
Visualization, 227

Learning Through Work (Goldberger et al.), 157

Legal Implications of High-Stakes Assessment
(Phillip), 55

Legislation
    electronic resources for, 236, 240, 242,
        245, 251
    Kentucky Education Reform Act of 1990,
        155, 176
    organizational resources for, 76, 119, 137, 155
    periodicals on, 156, 228
    school boards oversee compliance with, 171
    See also Policy makers
Leonard Bernstein Center for Education
        Through the Arts, 239
Levine, James A., 121
Levin, Henry M., 183, 187, 190
Levy, Frank, 37
Libraries, 197, 198, 203, 214, 217, 243
    electronic resources for, 234, 235, 241–242
Library of Congress, 214, 235, 242
License to Teach, A (Darling-Hammond
        et al.), 97
Licensing. *See* Certifying
Lieberman, Ann, 79, 97
Lifelong learning, 41, 111, 116, 127, 128–129,
        137, 139, 143, 155, 197, 225, 226, 227,
        245. *See also* Adult education
Life-skills workshops, 133
Lilley, H. Edward, 206
Lincoln, Abraham, 1
LINCT Coalition, The, 227
Linguistic intelligence, 21, 28
Linking Assessment with Reform (Sheingold
        and Frederiksen), 56
Lipper, Laurie, 229
Literacy
    adult, 117, 236, 242
    assessment of, 48
    improving student, 249
    media, 33, 238
    parental programs, 117
    technology use for, research on, 227
    teleconferencing project, 220
Literature, 23, 201, 237, 238, 239
Live Wire, 34
Living Schoolbook Project, 250
Lobbying, by parents, 113, 114
Local control and accountability, 169–170
Local councils, 17–18, 114, 169–170, 176
Local policy
    assessment and, 43, 45
    electronic resources for, 239, 247
    goal of, 3, 4, 169–170, 171, 187

Local policy *(continued)*
    local councils and, 114, 169–170, 176
    organizational resources for, 183, 239, 247
    overview of, 169–171
    readings on, 187, 188, 229, 230
    technology integration and, 188, 226,
        229, 230
    traditional approach to, 4
    workforce skills and, 156
    See also National policy; Policy makers;
        School boards; State policy
Logical-mathematical intelligence, 21, 28
Los Angeles Educational Alliance for
        Restructuring Now, 182
Los Angeles Educational Partnership, 183
Louisiana
    Concordia Architects (New Orleans), 208
    Goals 2000/Louisiana Networking
        Infrastructure for Education
        Project (Internet), 250
    Louisiana Collaborative for Excellence
        in the Preparation of Teachers
        (Internet), 239
    Southern Regional Education Board
        (Atlanta, GA), 185
    Southwest Educational Development
        Laboratory (Internet), 237
    Telelearning Project (Internet), 251
Louisiana Collaborative for Excellence
        in the Preparation of Teachers, 239
Low-income students and families
    business partnership programs and,
        148–149, 153
    community learning centers and, 124,
        130–140
    electronic resources for, 236, 245, 246,
        247, 251
    model schools for, 178, 200, 222
    organizational resources for, 38, 136, 182,
        184, 188, 235
    parental involvement and, 110, 117, 118,
        119, 130–135, 182
    preschooler preparation, 118, 130–131
    recruiting teachers for inner city schools, 246
    technology access and. *See* Equal access
    See also At-risk students; Diversity; Health
        and social services; Immigrant fam-
        ilies; Minority students and families

Lucas, George, *iv–v. See also* George Lucas
        Educational Foundation, The
Lycos, 234

M

Madaus, George, 52, 56
Maeroff, Gene I., 79
Magellan, 234
Maine
    Gorham School Department (Gorham), 74
    Maine Career Advantage
        (South Portland), 152
    Northeast and Islands Regional Educa-
        tional Laboratory (Internet), 236
    University of Southern Maine Extended
        Teacher Education Program
        (Gorham), 92
Maine Career Advantage, 152
Mainstreaming the Handicapped
        (Cohen et al.), 206
Malcom, Shirley, 36, 38
Management. *See* Administrators; Governance,
        school; Site-based management
Maplewood K-8 School, 115
Maryland
    Annie E. Casey Foundation (Baltimore), 136
    assessment in, 48, 55, 56
    Carroll County Public Schools
        (Westminster), 48
    Center for Research on the Education
        of Students Placed at Risk, 38
        (Baltimore), 235 (Internet)
    Center on Families, Communities, Schools
        and Children's Learning
        (Baltimore), 122
    Center on School, Family, and Community
        Partnerships (Baltimore),
        119, 120, 122
    Maryland Assessment Consortium
        (Ijamsville), 55, 56
    Mid-Atlantic Laboratory for Student
        Success (Internet), 235
    National Network of Partnership-2000
        Schools (Baltimore), 120
    Southern Regional Education Board
        (Atlanta, GA), 185
Maryland Assessment Consortium, 55, 56
Marzano, Robert J., 37, 54, 56, 79

Massachusetts
 Benjamin Franklin Butler Middle School
  of Technology (Lowell), 200
 Brighton High School (Brighton),
  148–149, 158
 Cambridge Rindge & Latin School
  (Internet), 243
 Center for Applied Special Technology
  (Peabody), 224
 Center for the Study of Testing,
  Evaluation, & Educational Policy
  (Chestnut Hill), 56
 Co-NECT (Cambridge), 218, 225
 Education Development Center, Inc.
  (Newton), 31
 Epistemology and Learning Group
  (Cambridge), 226
 Graham & Parks Alternative Public School
  (Cambridge), 114
 Harvard Family Research Project
  (Cambridge), 121
 Harvard Project Zero (Cambridge), 33, 53
 Harvard Technology Center (Internet), 250
 Harvard University Graduate School of
  Education (Cambridge), 38, 190
 Institute for Responsive Education
  (Boston), 118, 122
 JASON Foundation for Education
  (Waltham), 27
 Jobs for the Future (Boston), 154, 157
 League of Schools Reaching Out
  (Boston), 118
 Learning/Teaching Collaborative, The
  (Boston), 90
 Massachusetts Corporation for Educational
  Telecommunications
  (Cambridge), 227
 Massachusetts Field Center for Teaching
  and Learning (Boston), 95
 Massachusetts Institute of Technology
  Department of Architecture
  (Cambridge), 208
 Massachusetts Institute of Technology
  Media Lab New and Noteworthy
  (Internet), 250
 National Asian Family-School Partnership
  Project (Boston), 119, 122
 National Center for Fair & Open Testing
  (FairTest) (Cambridge), 53

Massachusetts (continued)
 New American School Design Project
  (Cambridge), 205
 Northeast and Islands Regional Educa-
  tional Laboratory (Internet), 236
 Performance Assessment Collaboratives
  for Education (Cambridge), 54, 56
 Pioneering Partners Foundation
  (Centerville), 156
 Private Industry Council (Boston), 148
 ProTech (Boston), 153
 Recruiting New Teachers, Inc.
  (Belmont), 96, 98
 School & Main, 158 (Boston),
  246 (Internet)
 Shutesbury Elementary School
  (Shutesbury), 28
 Tech Corps (Sudbury), 158
 TERC, 33 (Cambridge), 230 (Cambridge),
  247 (Internet)
Massachusetts Corporation for Educational
 Telecommunications, 227
Massachusetts Field Center for Teaching and
 Learning, 95
Massachusetts Institute of Technology
 Department of Architecture, 208
Massachusetts Institute of Technology Media
 Lab New and Noteworthy, 250
Mathematics
 architecture of schools and, 195, 196
 art and, 46
 assessment of, 49, 50
 business partnership programs and, 153
 community learning centers and, 133
 cooperative learning and, 31, 46
 critique circles and, 46–47
 curriculum, 20, 31, 32, 33, 239
 disabled students and, 30
 distance learning of, 251
 electronic resources for, 235, 236, 237, 239,
  241, 245, 247, 248, 249
 female students and, 30, 31
 grants for, 245
 hands-on learning and, 24, 31, 248
 minority students and, 30, 31, 185
 organizational resources for, 31
 parents and, 31
 project-based learning and, 23, 27
 readings on, 36
 standards, 36, 239

Mathematics (continued)
 teacher education and professional
  development in, 27, 30, 31, 33, 239
 teacher networking for, 215, 239
 teacher organization for, 239
 technology use for, research on, 227, 229
Mayerson Academy for Human Resource
 Development, 239
Mayors, 247. See also Local policy;
 Policy makers
McGuffey Project, The, 80
MCI Foundation, 245
McLaughlin, Milbrey, 79, 80
McSweeney, John, 216–217, 230
McTighe, Jay, 55, 56
Means, Barbara, 188
Measuring Up (Rothman), 55
Media
 assessment of schools and, 43
 literacy in, 33, 238
 parents and, 120
 policy issues, 243
 studies in, 18
Media Lab New and Noteworthy, 250
Meek, Anne, 206, 207
Mega Math, 239
Mehlinger, Howard, 188
Meier, Deborah, 188
Melaville, Atelia I., 140
Mendocino Unified School District, 219
Mental health services. See Health and
 social services
Mentoring
 by business people, 147, 149, 152, 153,
  243, 248
 by community members, 125, 128, 197
 by parents, 110
 by students, 73
 by teachers
  of students, 195
  of teachers, 69, 73, 74, 75, 83, 86, 87, 88,
   90, 92, 170, 195, 215, 236, 248
Merritt, Donna, 157
Mesa-Bains, Amalia, 80
Metacognition, 47
Meteorology. See Science
Metropolitan Center, 245
Michigan
 C. S. Mott Foundation (Flint), 137, 140
 Holt Senior High School (Holt), 93

Michigan *(continued)*

    Michigan Association of Community and
        Adult Education (Internet), 245

    Michigan State University College of
        Education (East Lansing), 80

    National Board for Professional Teaching
        Standards (Southfield), 77

    National Center for Community
        Education (Flint), 137

    National Center for Research on Teacher
        Learning (Lansing), 95

    North Central Regional Educational
        Laboratory (Internet), 235

Michigan Association of Community and
    Adult Education, 245

Michigan State University College of
    Education, 80

MicroSociety®, Inc., 29, 34, 75

Mid-Atlantic Laboratory for Student
    Success, 235

Mid-continent Regional Educational
    Laboratory, 56, 236 (Internet)

Middle School Curriculum (Beane), 35

Middle schools

    Bayside Middle School for the Arts and
        Creative Technology (California), 38

    Benjamin Franklin Butler Middle School
        of Technology (Massachusetts), 200

    Blackstock Junior High School
        (Internet), 243

    Brown Barge Middle School
        (Florida), 26, 38

    Calloway County Middle School
        (Kentucky), 80, 176

    Christopher Columbus School
        (New Jersey), 222

    Cyberspace Middle School (Internet), 247

    Dade Academy for the Teaching Arts
        (Florida), 73

    Dzantik'i Heeni Middle School (Alaska), 218

    Intermediate School 218 (New York), 132

    Key Renaissance School (Indiana), 28

    O'Farrell Community School
        (California), 46–47, 56, 133

    Turner Middle School (Pennsylvania), 132

    Walden III Middle/High School
        (Wisconsin), 51

    Wood River Middle/High School
        (Idaho), 38

Middle Schools *(continued)*

    See also K-8 schools; K-12 schools

MiddleWeb, 239

Miller, Bruce, 37

Miller, Lynne, 97

Minnesota

    Cooperative Learning Center
        (Minneapolis), 30, 38

    Designs for Learning (St. Paul), 137, 140

    Minnesota Center for Arts Education
        (Internet), 245

    North Central Regional Educational
        Laboratory (Internet), 235

    Redesign (Minneapolis), 112–113, 122

    Resource Centers (Hennepin County), 113

    Science Museum of Minnesota
        (Internet), 242

Minnesota Center for Arts Education, 245

Minority students and families

    African-American, 119, 182

    Asian, 119, 122

    business partnership programs and,
        148–149, 153

    community learning centers and, 124,
        130–140

    electronic resources for, 236, 245, 246, 247

    Hispanic/Latino, 118, 122, 133, 182, 246

    organizational resources for, 118, 119, 182,
        184, 185, 188, 246

    parental involvement and, 110, 117, 118,
        119, 130–135, 182

    science and math and, 30, 31, 48, 185

    social and economic equality for, 119

    technology access and. *See* Equal access

    See also At-risk students; Diversity;
        English-limited students;
        Immigrant families; Low-income
        students and families

Mission, defining, 1, 3, 14, 17–18, 107,
    166–167, 169, 170

Mississippi

    Parents for Public Schools, Inc.
        (Jackson), 120

    Southeastern Regional Vision for Education
        (Internet), 237

    Southern Regional Education Board
        (Atlanta, GA), 185

Missouri

    Missouri Research and Education
        Network (Internet), 250

Missouri *(continued)*

    National Policy Board for Educational
        Administration (Columbia), 184

    ShareNet (Internet), 251

Missouri Research and Education
    Network, 250

Mitchell, Ruth, 55

Mixed groups. *See* Multi-ability groups;
    Multi-age groups

Monitoring. *See* Assessment
    (alternative/authentic/performance)

Montana

    Big Sky Telegraph (Internet), 248

    Network Montana Project (Internet), 251

    Northwest Regional Educational
        Laboratory, 52 (Portland, OR), 55
        (Portland, OR), 236 (Internet)

Montessori, Maria, 85

Moore, Deborah, 207

Moore, Gary T., 207

Moral development, of students, 34, 109,
    187, 208

Morristown Elementary School, 49

Motivation

    assessment and, 55

    curriculum and, 15

    by learning environment, 25, 71, 146, 153,
        157, 193, 195, 196, 197, 201, 202,
        205, 206, 208

    of parents, 25

    by teachers, 25, 55, 68, 70–71, 78

    by technology, 210, 211, 216, 217, 222, 229

Multi-ability groups, 20, 69, 175

Multi-age groups, 20, 37, 69, 114, 117,
    175, 177

Multidisciplinary learning. *See* Interdisciplinary
    curriculum; Interdisciplinary project-
    based learning

Multimedia

    assessment and, 20, 41, 44, 52, 146, 216

    curriculum and, 177, 178, 219, 222

    defined, 232

    electronic resources for, 235, 243, 249, 250

    importance of, vi, 6, 64, 213, 214, 225, 250

    organizational resources for, 224, 227

    periodicals on, 228

    projects, 177, 178, 219

    readings on, 229

    research on, 227

Multimedia in Education, 250

MultiMedia Schools, 228

Multiple-choice tests, 23, 40–41, 43, 44, 49, 233

Multiple intelligences, 21, 28, 36, 86, 225, 241

Multiple Intelligences (Gardner), 36

Murnane, Richard J., 37

Museums, 31, 197, 214

    electronic resources for, 234, 237,
        241–242, 249, 252

Music. *See* Arts

Musical intelligence, 21, 28

My Virtual Reference Desk, 239

N

NASA

    electronic field trips, 248

    NASA K-12 Internet Initiative, 235

    NASA Weather, Maps, Environment, 239

    projects registry for, 247

    Spacelink, 240

National Academy Foundation, 155

National Academy of Sciences, 33, 245

National Alliance for Restructuring
    Education, 32, 174, 176

National Alliance of Business, 157, 158

National Asian Family-School Partnership
    Project, 119, 122

National Assembly of Local Arts Agencies, 239

National Assessment Governing Board, 245

National Assessment of Educational Progress,
    53, 245

National Association for Sport and Physical
    Education, The, 32

National Association of Elementary School
    Principals, 239

National Association of Partners in
    Education, Inc., 155

National Association of Secondary School
    Principals, 183, 188

National Association of State Boards of
    Education, 239

National Board for Professional Teaching
    Standards, 77

National Business Education Association, 245

National Center for Community Education, 138

National Center for Education Statistics, 236

National Center for Fair & Open Testing, 53

National Center for Fathering, 245

National Center for Research in Vocational
    Education, 155, 158

National Center for Research on Evaluation,
    Standards, and Student Testing, The,
    53, 56

National Center for Research on Teacher
    Learning, 95

National Center for Restructuring Education,
    Schools and Teaching, 53, 77, 85, 98

National Center for the Accelerated Schools
    Project, 183

National Center on Adult Literacy, 236

National Center on Educational Outcomes, 236

National Center on Education and the
    Economy, 174

National Center on Education in the Inner
    Cities, 236

National Center on the Educational Quality
    of the Workforce, 236

National Center to Improve Practice in Spe-
    cial Education Through Technology,
    Media and Materials, 236

National Clearinghouse for Bilingual
    Education, 236

National Coalition for Parent Involvement
    in Education, 119

National Commission on Teaching &
    America's Future, The, 97

National Community Education
    Association, 137

National Conference of State Legislatures, 245

National Council for Accreditation of
    Teacher Education, 96

National Council for Geographic
    Education, 239

National Council for the Social Studies, 239

National Council of La Raza, 245

National Council of Teachers of English, 239

National Council of Teachers of
    Mathematics, 240

National Education Association, 76, 80

National Education Commission on Time
    and Learning, 188

National Educator Awards Program, 246

National Forum on Assessment, 55

National Foundation for the Improvement of
    Education, 78

National Geographic Kids Network, 71,
    214–215, 248

National Geographic Online, 240

National goals, 189, 238

National Governors' Association, 246

National Infrastructure Information
    Advisory Council, 71

National Network of Partnership-2000
    Schools, 120

National Paideia Center, 32, 190. *See also*
    Paideia program

National Parent Information Network, 242

National policy

    administration and, 184

    assessment and, 43, 53, 170, 245

    electronic resources for, 245, 247

    goal of, 3, 4, 170, 171, 187

    readings on, 187, 229, 230

    state policy and, 181

    technology integration and, 229, 230

    traditional approach to, 4

    workforce skills and, 156

    See also Local policy; National goals;
        Policy makers; State policy

National Policy Board for Educational
    Administration, 184

National PTA, The, 119

National Public Radio Science Friday, 240

National Research Center on the Gifted and
    Talented, 236

National School Boards Association, 240

National School Network Testbed, 250

National School-to-Work Learning and
    Information Center, 155

National Science Resources Center, 33

National Science Teachers Association, 240

National Staff Development Council, 95, 98

*National Standards in American
    Education* (Ravitch), 37

National Telecommunications and
    Information Administration, 250

National Telemedia Council, 33

National Urban Alliance for Effective
    Education, 95

National Urban League, 119

National Writing Project, 93

Nation Prepared, A (Carnegie Corporation), 4

Nature education. *See* Science

Nebraska, Westside Community Schools
    (Omaha), 219

NetLearning (Serim and Koch), 79

NetTeach News Online, 240

Networking
    of community and schools, 125, 135, 139,
        197, 249
    locally run, cooperative, 219, 227
    organizational resources for, 95, 224–227
    of parents and teachers, 107, 111, 116,
        197, 222
    periodicals on, 228
    public access networks, 249
    readings on, 206, 228–229
    of schools, 135, 171, 193, 199, 202, 221,
        225, 248, 249, 250, 251, 252
    of students, 27, 170, 197, 214–215, 221,
        226, 238, 247, 248
    of teachers. *See* Teachers, networking of
    of workstations, 195–196, 199, 200, 201,
        202, 203, 206, 218
    See also Internet; World Wide Web (WWW)
Networking Infrastructure for Education, 251
Network Montana Project, 251
Nevada
    University of Nevada College of Education
        (Las Vegas), 98
    WestEd (Internet), 237
New American School Design Project, 205
New American Schools, 31, 32, 33, 174, 176,
    184, 186, 205
New Circles of Learning (Johnson et al.), 37
*New Designs for the Comprehensive High
    School*, 205
New Expectations (Levine and Pitt), 121
New Generation of Evidence, A (Henderson
    and Berla), 121
New Hampshire, Northeast and Islands
    Regional Educational Laboratory
    (Internet), 236
New Horizons for Learning, 230, 246
New Jersey
    Center for Performance Assessment
        (Princeton), 52, 56
    Center on Learning, Assessment, and
        School Structure (Princeton), 52, 56
    Christopher Columbus School
        (Union City), 222
    Mid-Atlantic Laboratory for Student Success
        (Internet), 235
    New Jersey Networking Infrastructure in
        Education (Internet), 251
    Panasonic Foundation Partnership Program
        (Secaucus), 184

New Jersey *(continued)*
    South Brunswick Public Schools
        (Monmouth), 48
New Jersey Networking Infrastructure in
    Education, 251
Newmann, Fred M., 55, 186, 189, 190
New Mexico
    Institute for Environmental Education
        (Albuquerque), 205, 208
    School Zone Institute (Albuquerque), 205
    Southwest Educational Development
        Laboratory (Internet), 237
New Professional Teacher project, 96
News, electronic resources for, 238, 239, 246
New Schools for New York (Public Education
    Association et al.), 207
New Standards, 32, 49, 53, 56, 174
New York
    Bank Street College of Education
        (New York City), 80
    Beacons Initiative (New York City), 138
    Carnegie Corporation of New York
        (New York City), 35
    Carnegie Council on Adolescent
        Development (New York City), 139
    Center for Children and Technology, 230
        (New York City), 248 (Internet)
    Center for Collaborative Education
        (New York City), 38
    Central Park East (New York City),
        22–23, 188
    Central Park East Secondary School
        (New York City), 22–23, 179, 188, 190
    Children's Environments Research Group
        (New York City), 204
    Children's School of Rochester, The
        (Rochester), 72
    Cornell Youth and Work Program
        (Ithaca), 158
    Countee Cullen Community Center
        (New York City), 134
    Curriculum Designers, Inc. (Rye), 38
    Educational Products Information
        Exchange (Hampton Bays), 225
    Four Seasons Network (New York City), 53
    Fund for the City of New York
        (New York City), 140
    Hispanic Policy Development Project
        (New York City), 118, 122

New York *(continued)*
    Home Instruction Program for Preschool
        Youngsters USA (New York City), 118
    Impact II—The Teachers Network
        (New York City), 77
    Intermediate School 218
        (New York City), 132
    LINCT Coalition, The (Hampton Bays), 227
    National Academy Foundation
        (New York City), 155
    National Center for Restructuring
        Education, Schools and Teaching
        (New York City), 53, 77, 85, 98
    National Urban Alliance for Effective
        Education (New York City), 95
    National Urban League
        (New York City), 119
    New Schools for New York (Public
        Education Association et al.), 207
    Northeast and Islands Regional Educa-
        tional Laboratory (Internet), 236
    Public School 194 (Internet), 134
    Ralph Bunche School (Internet), 246
    School-to-Work Partnership of Broome
        and Tioga Counties (Internet), 246
    University Heights High School
        (New York City), 51
NickNacks, 240
Nicolau, Siobhan, 122
North American Association of Environmental
    Education, 240
North Carolina
    Charlotte's Web (Internet), 249
    Isaac Dickson Elementary School
        (Asheville), 73
    National Paideia Center (Chapel Hill),
        32, 190
    North Carolina Information Highway
        (Internet), 251
    Public School Forum of North Carolina
        (Internet), 246
    Southeastern Regional Vision for
        Education (Internet), 237
    Southern Regional Education Board
        (Atlanta, GA), 185
North Carolina Information Highway, 251
North Central Regional Educational
    Laboratory, 235
North Dakota, North Dakota ICICLE Project
    (Internet), 240

Northeastern University, Institute for
Responsive Education, 118, 122
Northeast and Islands Regional Educational
Laboratory, 236
North Star Elementary School, 50
Northwest Regional Educational Laboratory,
52, 55, 236 (Internet)
Not By Schools Alone (Waddock), 189
Note-taking by teachers, 44

O

O'Day, Jennifer A., 187
O'Farrell Community School, 46–47, 56, 133
Office of Educational Research and
Information, 240
Office of Educational Technology, 190
Office of Technology Assessment, 80, 229
Ohio
Cleveland Freenet (Internet), 249
Mayerson Academy for Human Resource
Development (Internet), 239
National Staff Development Council
(Oxford), 95, 98
North Central Regional Educational
Laboratory (Internet), 235
Ohio Schoolnet (Internet), 251
Peer Assistance and Evaluation Program
(Cincinnati), 75
Perry Community Educational Village
(Perry), 202
Richard Fleischman Architects, Inc.
(Cleveland), 208
University of Cincinnati College of
Design, Architecture, Art and
Planning (Cincinnati), 208
Upper Arlington City Schools
(Columbus), 50
Ohio Schoolnet, 251
Oklahoma
Craftsmanship 2000 (Internet), 244
Environmental Design Research
Association (Edmond), 204
Southern Regional Education Board
(Atlanta, GA), 185
Southwest Educational Development
Laboratory (Internet), 237
Olsen, Karen, 37
Olson, Kerry, 188
On-line Exhibitions and Images, 242

Online Internet Institute, 71, 251
On-line services. *See* Electronic resources;
E-mail; Internet; Telecommunications;
World Wide Web (WWW)
On the Road Ahead!, 78
Open Charter School, 29
Open-door policies, 110, 113, 114–117
Oregon
Assessment and Accountability Program
(Portland), 52
Assessment Training Institute,
56 (Portland), 237 (Internet)
International Society for Technology in
Education (Eugene), 226
Northwest Regional Educational
Laboratory, 52 (Portland),
55 (Portland), 236 (Internet)
Roosevelt Renaissance 2000 (Portland), 153
teacher education in, 98
Organizational design. *See* Multi-ability
groups; Multi-age groups; Scheduling;
Schools, organizational design of;
Team teaching
Organizations
assessment, 52–54
business partnership programs, 154–156
community learning centers, 136–138
curriculum development, 30–32, 52, 53, 180
electronic resources for, 234, 243–247
instructional strategies, 30–32, 76–78
parent, 118–120, 136–138
policy maker, 30, 137, 181, 182, 184, 185
project-based learning, 30–32, 76–78
school facilities, 204–205
school restructuring, 76–78, 180–185
teacher education and professional development, 30–32, 76–78, 94–96, 180
teacher role, 76–78
team teaching, 77, 78, 94–96
technology, 30, 31, 32, 33, 224–227

P

Pace, Judy, 17–21, 38
Pacific Bell Education First program, 219
Pacific Bell Foundation, 246
Pacific Region Educational Laboratory, 236
Paideia program, 26, 32, 184, 190
Panasonic Foundation Partnership
Program, 184

Papert, Seymour, 122, 229
Paraprofessionals, 74, 96
Parent Academic Success Service, 114
Parent Cooperative Education Program, 115
Parent Institute for Quality Education, 119
Parents, 106–122
assessment and, 21, 41, 47, 50
authority of, 110, 170
career training for. *See* Employment,
community learning centers and
community involvement of, 107, 110, 115,
117, 120, 127, 129
community learning centers and, 113,
127–129, 130–140
contacts for, 122, 140
as coordinators, 113, 114
hands-on learning and, 24, 25
health and social services and. *See* Health
and social services
as high-school students, 114
importance of involvement of, 102, 106,
107, 109, 110, 111, 112–117, 118, 121
lifelong learning of. *See* Adult education;
Lifelong learning
lobbying by, 113, 114
mathematics learning and, 31
media and, 120
motivation of, 25
organizational resources for, 118–120,
136–138
overview of, 106–107
parenting skills classes, 113, 133, 134, 135,
137, 138, 203
parents helping other, 113, 115, 117, 246
periodicals for, 120–121, 138, 186
policy makers and, 110, 119, 120, 121
project-based learning and, 24, 25
readings for, 121–122, 139–140
real-world learning and, 110
single fathers, 245
of special-needs children, 120, 246
superintendents and, 120
teachers and schools and
collaboratively operated schools, 110,
114–117
communication between, 107, 111, 116,
197, 222
contacts for, 122
curriculum development and, 17, 26,
110, 115, 116, 117, 178

Parents *(continued)*

teachers and schools and *(continued)*

electronic resources for, 237, 242, 243, 244, 246, 248

e-mail and, 107, 111, 116

employer support of parental participation, 110, 115, 118, 122, 143, 147, 243

health and social services and, 65

immigrant parents, 119, 120, 122

learning plans and, 107

low-income parents, 110, 117, 118, 119, 130–135, 182

mentoring, 110

minority parents, 110, 117, 118, 119, 130–135, 182

mission and goals definition, 3, 17–18, 107, 166–167, 169

mutual respect between, 109, 110–111, 117

networking with teachers, 107, 111, 116, 197, 222

open-door policies, 110, 113, 114–117

organizational resources for, 118–120

parents as teachers, 106, 110, 115

parents as teacher's aides, 25, 110

parent-teacher organizations, 110, 119

periodicals on, 120–121

readings on, 121–122

required parental participation, 115, 173

research on, 118, 120, 121

roles of parents, 25, 106, 110–111, 114, 115, 116

school design teams and, 110, 114–117, 192–193, 197, 198, 200

site-based management and, 72, 107, 110, 112–113, 117, 169, 170, 172, 173

standards and, 49, 69, 170

technology and, 111, 113, 114, 116, 222

volunteering, 106, 111, 112, 113, 114, 117, 135

technology and, 25, 107, 111, 113, 114, 116, 121, 131, 139, 222

See also Childcare; Early childhood education

Parents' Educational Resource Center, 120

Parents for Educational Excellence, 246

Parents for Public Schools, Inc., 120

Parents Helping Parents, 246

Parents' Public School Handbook (Shore), 122

Partnership for Kentucky School Reform, The, 155

Pasadena Partnership Academies, 150

Passport to Knowledge, 248

Pathways, 96

PBS On-line, 240

P.E. *See* Physical education

Peakview Elementary School, 175

Peer Assistance and Evaluation Program, 75

Peers

assessment by

for students, 17, 19, 28, 44, 46, 47, 50, 51

for teachers, 75

of teachers, 65, 69, 71, 73, 74, 75, 77, 83, 87, 89, 91, 170, 215.

See also Teachers, networking of

Pennsylvania

Center for Community Partnerships (Philadelphia), 132

Consortium for Policy Research in Education (Philadelphia), 180, 190

Franklin Institute Science Museum and Planetarium (Internet), 242

Learning Research and Development Center (Pittsburgh), 32

MicroSociety®, Inc. (Philadelphia), 29, 34, 75

Mid-Atlantic Laboratory for Student Success (Internet), 235

Pittsburgh Public Schools (Pittsburgh), 49

Turner Middle School (Philadelphia), 132

Performance assessment. *See* Assessment (alternative/authentic/performance); Portfolios

"Performance Assessment, Using" (*Educational Leadership*), 54

Performance Assessment Collaboratives for Education, 54, 56

"Performance-Based Assessment" (*ERIC Review, The*), 55

Periodicals

assessment, 54, 78

business partnership programs, 156

community learning centers, 138

curriculum development, 78

general education, 34, 185, 186

instructional strategies, 34, 78

learning, 34, 78

parents, 120–121, 138, 186

policy makers, 96, 185, 205

Periodicals *(continued)*

project-based learning, 34, 78

school facilities, 205

school restructuring, 185–186

science, 34

software, 120, 121, 186, 228

teacher education and professional development, 96

teacher role, 78, 240

technology, 34, 96, 186, 228

Perkins & Will architects, 208

Perkins, Wheeler, and Will architects, 201

Perrone, Vito, 55

Perry Community Educational Village, 202

Personal life, leading a satisfying, 1, 2, 68

Peterkin, Robert S., 169–171, 190

Peter W. Johansen High School, 203

Pew Charitable Trusts, 189, 246

Phi Delta Kappan, 186

Phillips, S. E., 55

Physical design. *See* Schools, physical design of

Physical education, 32, 199, 202, 203

Physics. *See* Science

Piaget, Jean, 85

Pioneering Partners Foundation, 156

Pitt, Edward W., 121

Pittsburgh Public Schools, 49

Planning schools. *See* Schools, planning

Plugged In, 251

Policy makers

assessment and, 43, 45, 47, 53, 54, 55, 171, 245

business partnership programs and, 154, 155, 156, 158

community learning centers and, 135

curriculum on public policy making, 30

electronic resources for, 239, 240, 242, 243, 244, 245, 247, 249, 250

equal access and, 171

health and social services providers and, 137

low-income students and, 182

media-related policy issues, 243

minority students and, 119, 182

mission and goals definition and, 3, 14, 17–18, 166–167, 169, 170

organizations for, 30, 137, 181, 182, 184, 185

organizations influencing, 30, 76, 94–96, 180, 181, 182, 185, 204, 244

parents and, 110, 119, 120, 121

periodicals for, 96, 185, 205

Policy makers *(continued)*

quick fixes and, 167, 171, 189

readings for, 37, 186–188, 229, 230

research on policy, 32, 76, 180, 181, 182, 185

school-to-career programs and, 154

site-based management and, 4, 110

teachers and, 69, 76, 95

technology and, 226, 228, 229, 230, 249

See also Administrators; Boards of
education; Departments of
education; Government; Governors;
Legislation; Local policy; Mayors;
National policy; Principals; School
boards; Standards; State policy;
Superintendents; U.S. Congress

*Politics of Linking Schools and Social Services,
The* (Adler and Gardner), 139

Portfolios

for art, 49, 50

auditing of, 49

business assessment of, 45

college admission officer assessment of, 45

college professor assessment of, 45

community assessment of, 21, 45

defined, 41, 232

digital, 17, 41, 44, 47, 50, 111

early literacy, 48

examples of using, 17, 19, 23, 44, 45,
46–47, 49–51, 179

expectations clearly established and, 46, 49

for mathematics, 50

multimedia, 20, 41, 44, 52

for music, 49

organizational resources for, 52–54

parental assessment of, 21, 47, 50

personalized assessment and, 45, 46–47, 50

readings on, 54, 55

real-world learning and, 47

research on, 52–54

self-assessment and, 19, 41, 44, 45, 46–47,
49, 50

teacher, 77, 87

technology and, 20, 41, 44, 47

test scores and, 23, 49

value of, 23, 41, 45, 46–47, 49, 50

work-based learning and, 150

for writing, 49, 50

See also Assessment
(alternative/authentic/performance)

Power of Their Ideas, The (Meier), 188

Practical Guide to Alternative Assessment, A
(Herman et al.), 55

Preiser, Wolfgang F. E., 204, 208

Preparing Teachers to Involve Parents
(Shartrand et al.), 122

Preschool children, preparing for school,
118, 130–131, 138. *See also* Childcare;
Early childhood education

Preschools, 110, 174

Prevention Report, The, 138

Priest, W. Curtiss, 139

Principals

authority of, 170

certifying, 184

mission and goals definition and, 169

organizations for primary, 239

organization for secondary, 183, 188

school restructuring and, 188

site-based management and, 72, 113,
114, 173

teachers and, 30, 170, 173

See also Administrators

*Principles and Indicators for Student
Assessment Systems* (National Forum
on Assessment), 55

Prisoners of Time (National Education Commission on Time and Learning), 188

Private Industry Council, 148

Professional development. *See* Administrators,
professional development of;
Teachers, learning to teach;
Teachers, professional development of

Professional development schools, 93, 97, 232

"Professional Development"
(*The Eric Review*), 97

Professionalism and Community
(Seashore-Louis and Kruse), 80

Professionals. *See* Experts

Professors. *See* College professors

Project 2061, 30

Project-based learning

biology examples, 18–20, 21, 71

community and, 24, 25, 218

defined, 233

design of schools and, 194–198

electronic resources for, 243

hands-on learning and, 24–25, 33

history examples, 18, 22–23, 174, 218, 219

individual differences of students and,
5–6, 19, 25

Project-based learning *(continued)*

interdisciplinary, 19, 21, 28, 72, 94, 198,
199, 239

mathematics example, 23

media studies example, 18

multiple intelligences and, 28

organizational resources for, 30–32, 76–78

overview of, 18–20, 21

parents and, 24, 25

periodicals on, 34, 78

readings on, 35, 36, 37, 79–80

real-world learning and, 24, 25, 27, 29, 34,
75, 172, 173, 175

research by students and, 22, 28

schools and organizations using, 22–29,
30, 38, 46–51, 71–75, 172–179,
198–203, 216–223

science examples, 23, 24–25, 26, 27, 31, 33,
176, 217

self-assessment and, 19, 43, 44

teacher development of, 72, 73

technology and, 23, 24, 27, 29, 175, 176,
188, 225

value of, 18–20, 21, 24–25, 68, 211

work-based, 146, 148–149, 150–153

See also Hands-on learning;
Real-world learning

Project on Effective Interventions, 140

Prospects for Educational Telecomputing
(Tinker and Kapisovsky), 230

ProTech, 153

P.S. 1 Charter School, 38

P.S. 194. *See* Public School 194

PTA, 110, 119

Public Broadcasting Service On-line, 240

Public education

current state of, *ix*, 1, 189

democracy and, *v*, *ix*, 169, 187

importance of, *v*,

improving, *v–vi*, *ix–x*, 2–6

Lucas, George, on, *v*

problems with traditional, *v*

public opinion on, 188

purposes of, *ix*, 1, 2, 3, 4, 6, 30, 68

stakeholders in, 3, 21, 172, 233

statistics on, 236, 240, 247

Public Education Association, 207

Public Education Network, 184

Public/Private Ventures, 246

Public School 1 Charter School. *See* P.S. 1 Charter School
Public School 194, 134
Public School Forum of North Carolina, 246
Puerto Rico, Northeast and Islands Regional Educational Laboratory (Internet), 236
Putting Families First (Kagan and Weissbourd), 139

Q

Quality Counts (Education Week), 189
Quality Education for Minorities, 185
Quarterly, The, 34
Quest Center, 77

R

Raby, Marilyn, 158
Raising Our Future (Harvard Family Research Project), 121
Raising Standards, 78
Rallying the Whole Village (Comer et al.), 121
Ralph Bunche School, 246
Ravitch, Diane, 37, 189
Reading
    architecture of schools and, 196
    assessing, 48
    "buddies" for, 175
    business partnership programs and, 153
    community learning centers and, 133
    electronic resources for, 241
    family involvement and, 115
    hands-on learning and, 24
    parental training in, 117
Readings
    on assessment, 36, 37, 54–55, 79, 80
    on business partnership programs, 157–158
    on community learning centers, 139–140
    on curriculum, 35, 36, 37, 79, 80
    on diversity, 80
    on instructional strategies, 35, 36, 37, 79–80
    on learning, 35–37, 79–80
    for parents, 121–122, 139–140
    for policy makers, 37, 186–188, 229, 230
    on project-based learning, 35, 36, 37, 79–80
    on scheduling, 188

Readings *(continued)*
    on school facilities, 206–207
    on school restructuring, 186–189
    on teacher education and professional development, 98–99
    on teacher role, 79–80
    on technology, 79–80, 228–230
Real-world learning
    assessment and, 40, 44, 47, 49, 50, 55
    business partnership programs and, 143, 146, 147, 149, 150–158
    community and, 124–125
    electronic resources for, 247
    hands-on learning and, 24, 25, 29, 34, 36, 150
    importance of, 15, 18–19, 173, 227
    parents and, 110
    project-based learning and, 24, 25, 27, 29, 34, 75, 172, 173, 175
    simulations and. *See* Simulations
    technology and, 71, 116, 211, 214–215, 218, 224, 226
    See also Apprenticeships; Community service programs; Hands-on learning; Internships; Project-based learning
Reasoning. *See* Thinking
Rebuilding the Partnership for Public Education (Kilbourne et al.), 139
Recruiting New Teachers, Inc., 96, 98
Recruiting teachers, 92, 96, 98, 246
Redesign, 112–113, 122
Redesigning Education (Wilson and Davis), 189
Redwood, Kenyetta, 118, 122
Referral and Information Network, 117
Regional educational laboratories, 235, 236
Reigeluth, Charles M., 189
Reinventing Central Office (Hallett), 187
Reinventing Education, 251
Renewing America's Schools (Glickman), 187
Rényi, Judith, 97
Report on the Effectiveness of Technology in Schools (Sivin-Kachala and Bialo), 229
Republic of the Marshall Islands, Pacific Region Educational Laboratory (Internet), 236
Republic of Palau, Pacific Region Educational Laboratory (Internet), 236

Research
    on assessment, 52–54, 56, 245
    on communities and schools, 120, 121, 136
    on early childhood education, 138
    on families and schools, 118, 120, 121
    on learning, 30–32, 33, 34, 35–37, 186, 237
    on policy, 32, 76, 180, 181, 182, 185
    on school facilities, 204, 205, 207
    on school restructuring, 180–185, 186, 188, 189
    on school-to-career programs, 154, 155, 156, 157
    search engines for, 234
    state support of, 171
    by students
        cooperative learning and, 17
        hands-on learning and, 24
        Internet and, 20, 64–65, 177, 210, 213, 214–215, 217, 219, 222, 223, 234, 235, 247–248
        project-based learning and, 22, 27, 28
        teachers and, 25
    on teacher education and professional development, 76, 77, 94, 95, 96, 237
    on teacher role, 74, 76, 77, 79
    by teachers, 69, 74, 76, 77, 79, 235
    on technology, 222, 224, 227, 228, 229, 235, 246, 250
    translating into practice, 21, 32, 33, 92
Research and Policy Committee, 36
Researcher's Guide to the U.S. Department of Education, 235
Resource Centers, 113
Responsibility
    of school boards and administrators, 4, 171, 172–173
    of students, 15, 46, 47, 50, 175
    of teachers, 4–5, 60, 64, 68, 69, 72, 167, 170
    See also Accountability; Civic responsibility
Restructuring, defined, 233. *See also* Schools, organizational design of
Restructuring Schools with Technology (Means and Olson), 188
Rethinking America (Smith), 157
Rethinking Schools, 186
Rewards and Reform (Fuhrman and O'Day), 187
Rhode Island
    Coalition of Essential Schools (Providence), 53, 179, 181, 190
    Metropolitan Center (Internet), 245

Rhode Island *(continued)*
    Northeast and Islands Regional Educa-
        tional Laboratory (Internet), 236
Richard Fleischman Architects, Inc., 208
Richmond, George H., 29, 34
Riel, Margaret, 228, 230
Rigden, Diana W., 156, 158
Right of Passage Experience, 51
Rioux, J. William, 121
Roadmap to Restructuring (Conley), 186
Roane County High School, 203
Roberts, Linda, 162, 190
Roberts, Terry, 184, 190
Robinson, Ronn, 158
Rodgers, Melissa, 36
Rogers School District, 223
*Role of Scientists in the Professional
        Development of Science Teachers, The*
        (Committee on Biology Teacher
        Inservice Programs et al.), 97
Roosevelt Renaissance 2000, 153
Rothman, Robert, 55
Rubric, defined, 233
Rutherford, Barry, 121

S

Saarinen, Eliel and Eero, 201
Sakatani, Ken, 34, 38
Sampson, Barbara C., 226, 230
Sandy Creek High School, 202
San Francisco Public Library, 241
Scheduling
    beginning teachers and, 87
    block, 74, 170
    extended calendar, 93, 193
    extended hours of operation.
        See Community learning centers
    extended school days, 69, 188
    flexible business scheduling, 147
    flexible instructional periods, 69, 74, 87,
        93, 169, 170, 177, 188, 199
    professional development and, 87, 93
    readings on, 188
    technology and, 188, 214–215
    year-round, 69, 75, 175, 197
Schlechty, Phillip, 180, 185, 189, 190
Schofield, Janet Ward, 229
School & Main, 158, 246

School boards
    assessment and, 47
    electronic resources for, 239, 240
    periodicals for, 185
    readings for, 37, 186
    responsibility of, 4, 171, 172–173
    state boards of education, 239
    technology implementation and, 226
    See also Administrators; Local councils;
        Policy makers
School City of Hammond, The, 200
School Development Program (Connecticut),
        120, 121, 122
School Development Program (Florida), 117
School districts. *See* Districts
Schoolhouse, 240
Schoolhouse in the Red (American Association
        of School Administrators), 206
School Reform in the Information Age
        (Mehlinger), 188
School Reform Networks at a Glance, 235
Schools, 160–208
    accountability of, 14, 43, 45, 169–170
    assessment of, 43, 45, 80, 145, 236, 237
    business and. *See* Business
    charter, *ix*, 10, 29, 38, 170, 178, 231, 245
    childcare at. *See* Childcare
    community and. *See* Community;
        Community learning centers
    electronic resources for, 234, 243–247
    financial aspects of. *See* Budgeting;
        Financing
    health and social services and. *See* Health
        and social services
    lifelong learning and. *See* Adult education;
        Lifelong learning
    management of. *See* Administrators;
        Governance, school; Site-based
        management
    mission and goals of, 3, 14, 107, 166–167,
        169, 170
    networking of, 135, 171, 193, 199, 202,
        221, 225, 248, 249, 250, 251, 252
    open-door policies, 110, 113, 114–117
    organizational design of, 160–190
        accommodating change, 47, 171
        business assistance and, 147, 184, 223
        community and, 170, 172, 181, 182,
            183, 184, 197
        contacts for, 190

Schools *(continued)*
    organizational design of *(continued)*
        design teams for, 110, 173, 186
        electronic resources for, 236, 237
        examples of, 172–179, 184, 186
        financing, 179, 180, 184, 207
        for governance. *See* Site-based
            management
        as multipurpose facilities, 124, 125,
            127–129
        organizational resources for, 76–78,
            180–185
        overview of, 166–167, 169–171
        parents and, 110, 114–117
        periodicals on, 185–186
        principals and, 188
        professional development and, 93, 98
        readings on, 186–189
        research on, 180–185, 186, 188, 189
        restructuring defined, 233
        for scheduling. *See* Scheduling
        by students and teachers, 69, 89, 110, 188
        technology and, 174, 175, 177, 178,
            180, 188, 189, 195–196, 216–217,
            218, 222. *See also* Technology,
            integrating
        traditional, *v, vi*, 5, 67
        See also Multi-ability groups; Multi-age
            groups; Team teaching
    overview of, 160–162
    parents and. *See* Parents, teachers and
        schools and
    physical design of, 192–208
        accommodating change, 193, 197,
            198, 199
        by administrators, 192, 198, 200
        architects and, 198–199, 200, 201, 204,
            205, 208
        auditoriums, 198, 199, 201, 202, 203
        business assistance and, 200, 223
        cafeterias, 195, 199
        classrooms, 195–196, 198, 200, 201, 205
        community and, 135, 193, 197, 198,
            200, 205
        community learning centers and, 135,
            193, 197, 198
        conference centers, 197
        contacts for, 208
        current condition of, 206
        design teams for, 192–193, 197, 198, 200

Schools *(continued)*

  physical design of *(continued)*

    disabilities and, 206

    electronic resources for, 244, 247

    energy consumption of existing
        schools, 206

    examples of, 198–203

    farms, 203

    financing, 207, 219, 220, 223

    fitness centers, 197, 202, 203

    heating/cooling system, 195, 196

    indoor spaces, 195–196, 198, 200, 201, 205

    landscaping, 196, 197

    as multipurpose facilities, 193, 198,
        199, 200

    off-campus spaces, 197

    organizational resources for, 204–205

    outdoor environment, 196, 197, 201, 205

    overview of, 192–193, 194–196

    by parents, 192–193, 197, 198, 200

    periodicals on, 205

    playgrounds, 204, 205

    project-based learning and, 194–198

    readings on, 206–207

    research on, 204, 205, 207

    by students, 188, 192–193, 196, 197,
        198, 205

    by teachers, 192–193, 196, 197, 198, 205

    as teaching tool, 193, 195–197, 206, 207

    technology and, 72, 106, 195–196,
        197, 198, 199, 200–201, 202,
        207, 214, 216–217, 218.
            See also Technology, integrating

    theaters, 199, 202, 203

    traditional, 192, 195

    windows, 196, 201, 203

  planning, 110, 193, 197, 198–199, 204, 207

  preschools, 110, 174

  public opinion on, 188

  recreational activities at, 125

  small, 174, 179, 183, 188, 207

  technology and. *See* Technology

  See also Administrators; Elementary
      schools; High schools; K-8 schools;
      K-12 schools; Middle schools;
      Students; Teachers

Schools for the 21st Century (Schlechty), 189

Schools for Thought (Bruer), 36

Schools of education

  Harvard University (Massachusetts), 38, 190

Schools of education *(continued)*

  organizational resources for, 94

  Stanford University (California), 56, 190

  University of Virginia (Virginia), 90

  See also Colleges of education

Schools of the 21st Century, 138

School-to-career programs, 143, 147, 148–158,
    233, 235, 236, 243, 244, 245, 246

School to Work (Stern et al.), 157

School-to-Work Partnership of Broome and
    Tioga Counties, 246

*School-to-Work Transition and Youth Appren-
    ticeship, The* (Bailey and Merritt), 157

School Ways (Graves), 206

School Zone (Taylor and Vlastos), 207

School Zone Institute, 205

Schorr, Daniel, 140

Schorr, Lisbeth B., 137, 140

Schrock, Kathy, 238

Schwarz, Paul, 183, 190

Science

  architecture of schools and, 195, 196, 199

  assessment of, 48

  biology, 18–20, 21, 71, 91, 97, 242

  business partnership programs and, 150, 153

  cognitive, 231

  cooperative learning and, 176

  curriculum, 30, 32, 33, 48, 78, 156, 227,
      239, 245

  disabled students and, 30

  distance learning of, 251

  diversity and, 48

  earth science, 239, 241

  electronic resources for, 235, 236, 237, 239,
      240, 241, 242, 245, 247, 248, 249

  environmental science, 31, 196, 238, 239,
      240, 241, 248

  female students and, 30, 31

  geography, 24, 199, 215, 219, 239, 247, 248

  geology, 241

  hands-on learning and, 24–25, 31, 33, 48,
      150, 248

  interacting with experts in, *ix*, 20, 27, 70,
      178, 199, 213, 237, 239

  Internet and, *ix*, 20, 27, 70, 91, 178, 199,
      213, 214, 215, 237, 239

  meteorology, 239

  minority students and, 30, 31, 48, 185

  natural history, 242

Science *(continued)*

  organizational resources for, 30, 31, 38,
      240, 245

  periodicals on, 34

  physics, 215

  project-based learning and, 23, 24–25, 26,
      27, 31, 33, 176, 217

  readings on, 36, 97

  scientific expeditions and, 27

  space science, 235, 239, 240, 241

  standards, 36, 245

  teacher education and professional
      development in, 27, 30, 31, 33, 97,
      239, 246

  teacher networking for, 27, 215

  teacher organization for, 240

  technology use for, research on, 227, 229

  See also Technology

Science Learning Network, 242

Science Museum of Minnesota, 242

Search engines (Internet), 234

Seashore-Louis, Karen, 80

Seattle Public Schools, The (Stuebing), 207

Secondary schools. *See* High schools

Self-assessment

  expectations clearly established and, 45, 46

  portfolios and, 19, 41, 44, 45, 46–47, 49, 50

  project-based learning and, 19, 43, 44

  readings on, 55

SEQUALS, 31

Serim, Ferdi, 79

Shanker, Al, 78, 80

ShareNet, 251

Shartrand, Angela, 122

Shavelson, Richard J., 56

Sheingold, Karen, 56, 229

Shorecrest High School, *ix*

Shore, Kenneth, 122

Shoreline School District, *ix*, 220

Shulman, Judith H., 80

Shutesbury Elementary School, 28

Silicon Valley, 138, 247

Simulations, *vi*, 20, 44, 143, 146, 211, 213,
    226, 233

Sioux Falls School District 49-5, 221

Site-based management

  administrators and, 113, 173

  budgeting and, 171

  business and, 113, 172–173

  community and, 170, 172

Site-based management *(continued)*

competitive bid solicitation and, 171

conflict-mediation programs, 30, 172, 238

consensus and, 172, 173, 175, 182

defined, 233

electronic resources for, 235, 242, 244

health and social services and, 112–113

importance of, 4, 6, 169–170, 173

local councils and, 114, 169–170, 176

parents and, 72, 107, 110, 112–113, 117, 169, 170, 172, 173

policy makers and, 4, 110

principles of school governance, 170

readings on, 186, 187

school design teams and, 173

students and, 113, 172, 173

teachers and, 65, 72, 75, 170, 172, 173

See also Administrators

Sites for Educators, 240

Sivin-Kachala, Jay, 229

Sizer, Ted, 181, 188, 190

Skill Standards and Certification, 240

Slavin, Robert, 37, 38

Small schools, 174, 179, 183, 188, 207

Smart Valley, Inc., 138

Smith, Hedrick, 157

Smithsonian Institution, 33, 214

Smithsonian Office of Elementary and Secondary Education, 242

Social science. *See* History/Social science

Social services. *See* Health and social services

Social studies. *See* History/Social science

Sockett, Hugh, 79

Socratic method, 26, 169

Software

assistive, 224

evaluation of, 225, 248

periodicals on, 120, 121, 186, 228

readings on, 189

resources for, 225, 250, 251

student experts on, 172

types used in schools, 217, 220, 222, 223

See also Simulations

Software Publishers Association, 251

South Brunswick Public Schools, 48

South Carolina

South Carolina Center for the Advancement of Teaching and School Leadership (Columbia), 78

South Carolina *(continued)*

South Carolina Center for Teacher Recruitment (Rock Hill), 92

Southeastern Regional Vision for Education (Internet), 237

Southern Regional Education Board (Atlanta, GA), 185

South Carolina Center for the Advancement of Teaching and School Leadership, 78

South Carolina Center for Teacher Recruitment, 92

South Dakota, Sioux Falls School District 49-5 (Sioux Falls), 221

Southeastern Regional Vision for Education, 237

Southern Regional Education Board, 185

Southwest Educational Development Laboratory, 237

Spacelink, 240

Space science. *See* Science

Sparkman Center, 251

Sparks, Dennis, 98

Spatial intelligence, 21

Special-needs students. *See* At-risk students; Disabilities, students with; English-limited students; Equal access; Immigrant families; Low-income students and families; Minority students and families

Staff Development for Education in the 90's (Lieberman and Miller), 97

Stakeholders, 3, 21, 172, 233

Standardized tests, 40–41, 43, 44, 45, 50, 52, 53, 54, 55, 56, 69, 233

Standards

accountability and, 14

accreditation of teacher education programs and, 96

achieving, 170

assessment and, 32, 40–41, 43, 44–45, 49, 50, 53, 55, 56, 170, 171

business and, 49, 56, 145–146, 148, 150, 154, 156, 157, 158, 170, 187

civics, 30

college professors and, 45

community and, 49, 124, 170

content standards defined, 233

curriculum development and, 3

defined, 233

Standards *(continued)*

developing, 4, 5, 14, 32, 169, 170, 171, 236, 238

electronic resources for, 236, 238, 240, 244, 245, 246

language arts, 36

learning and, 14

local councils and, 169

mathematics, 36, 239

need for high, 145–146, 147, 244

organizational resources for, 53

parents and, 49, 69, 170

performance standards defined, 233

physical education, 32

readings on, 37

research on, 53

science, 36, 245

states and, 171

student understanding of, 45, 46, 49

for teachers, 77, 96, 97

teachers and, 44, 49, 170

See also New Standards

Stanford University

Center for Research on the Context of Teaching, 76, 80

School of Education, 56, 190

State Collaborative on Assessment and Student Standards, 54

State policy

assessment and, 43, 45, 53, 54, 170, 189

departments of education, 181

electronic resources for, 239, 245, 250

goal of, 3, 4, 170, 171, 187

national policy and, 181

organizational resources for, 181, 239, 245

readings for, 37, 187, 229, 230

technology integration and, 229, 230, 250

traditional approach to, 4, 170

workforce skills and, 156

See also Governors; Kentucky Education Reform Act of 1990; Local policy; National policy; Policy makers; School boards

States and Communities on the Move (Gold), 158

Statistics

on children, 245

on education, 236, 240, 247

Stern, David, 157

Stiggins, Richard J., 55, 56

Stirring the Chalkdust (Wasley), 80

Stout, Connie, 224, 230

Strickland, Roy, 206, 208

Strong Families, Strong Schools
    (Internet), 246

Strong Families, Strong Schools (U.S.
    Department of Education), 122, 246

Strudler, Neal, 95, 98

Student-Centered Classroom Assessment
    (Stiggins), 55

Student-directed learning, 5–6, 19, 25, 173, 196

Students, 7–56

    assessment of. *See* Assessment (alternative/
      authentic/performance)

    business and. *See* Business

    certifying, 153, 156, 157, 179, 240

    community learning centers and, 127–128,
      129, 130–140

    community relationship of, 20, 28, 132

    community service programs and,
      125, 127, 133, 134, 138, 139, 197,
      215, 243

    design of schools and, 188, 192–193, 196,
      197, 198, 205

    electronic resources for, 234, 237, 238,
      243–248

    e-mail and, 177, 223, 247

    emotional development of, 109

    employment preparation of, 1–2, 45, 134,
      137, 138, 145–146, 147, 148–153,
      242, 245. *See also* Business,
      partnership programs

    expectations clearly established for, 43, 45,
      46, 49, 175, 182

    feedback to, 44, 46, 53

    field trips (virtual), 237, 241, 247, 248, 251

    global access to information by, 20, 71,
      167, 170, 178, 197, 213, 223, 226,
      233, 247

    individual differences of

      cooperative learning and, 15, 20

      intelligence types and, 21

      interdisciplinary studies and, 19, 198

      project-based learning and, 5–6, 19,
        25, 198

      successful learning and accommodation
        of, 5, 17

      technology and, 5–6

      See also Cooperative learning; Multi-
        ability groups; Multi-age groups

Students *(continued)*

    individual learning plans for, 107, 177, 232

    individual relationship of teachers to, 64,
      68, 71, 86, 167, 170, 179, 214

    interacting with experts, *ix*, 20, 25, 27,
      64–65, 70, 146, 170, 178, 199, 210,
      213, 233, 237, 239

    Internet and. *See* Internet, students and

    learning and. *See* Learning

    on local councils, 169

    maximizing performance of all, 1, 2, 14,
      21, 26, 43, 48, 51, 68, 69, 71, 86,
      167, 170, 171, 176, 178, 182, 183,
      189, 225

    as mentors, 20, 73, 175

    mission and goals definition and,
      3, 17–18, 169

    moral development of, 34, 109, 187, 208

    motivation of. *See* Motivation

    needs of today's, 8–10, 14–15, 19

    networking of, 27, 170, 197, 214–215, 221,
      226, 238, 247, 248

    parents as high-school, 114

    research by. *See* Research, by students

    responsiblity of, 15, 46, 47, 50, 175

    site-based management and, 113, 172, 173

    standards as understood by, 45, 46, 49

    teachers as equal partners with, 20, 22,
      24–25, 32, 49, 64, 68–69, 70–71, 226

    technology and

      learning how to use, 138, 219, 225, 249

      organizational resources for, 156

      value of, *vi*, 5–6, 15, 20, 36, 64–65,
        68–69, 71, 175, 177, 178, 210,
        211, 213–215, 217, 226

      See also Technology

      See also Parents; Teachers

Students with disabilities. *See* Disabilities,
    students with

Student teachers, 86–87, 88–89, 90, 91

Stuebing, Susan, 207

Successful School Restructuring
    (Newmann and Wehlage), 189

Superintendents

    assessment and, 47

    contact for, 190

    organizational resources for, 137, 185

    parents and, 120

    school restructuring and, 172–173

    See also Administrators

Systemic Change in Education (Reigeluth
    and Garfinkle), 189

T

Talbert, Joan E., 79

Taylor, Anne P., 195–197, 207, 208

Te, Bouy, 120, 122

Teacher Cadet program, 92

Teacher Magazine, 78

Teacher Research and Educational Reform
    (Hollingsworth and Sockett), 79

Teachers, 57–98

    accountability of, 14, 97, 170

    administrators and, 69, 72

    aides for, 25, 110

    assessment of, 75, 77, 87, 91, 96, 170, 237

    assessment of students and, 41, 43–45,
      46, 47, 49, 50, 51, 52–56, 72, 80,
      179, 183

    authority and responsibility of, 4–5, 60,
      64, 68, 69, 72, 167, 170

    budgeting and, 65, 72

    business partnership programs and, 65,
      69, 143, 147

    certifying, 77, 94, 240

    community learning centers and, 129, 133

    design of schools and

      organizational, 69, 89, 110, 188

      physical, 192–193, 196, 197, 198, 205

    diversity of, 92, 96, 98

    electronic resources for, 77, 94, 234, 236,
      237–241, 242, 243, 245, 248

    e-mail and, 107, 111, 116, 220, 222, 223

    emotional development of students and, 109

    health and social services and, 65, 112

    interacting with experts, 91, 170, 215, 233

    Internet and. *See* Internet, teachers and

    learning to teach, 82–98

      accreditation of education programs, 96

      case studies and, 86, 90

      contacts for, 98

      electronic resources for, 94, 236, 242, 243

Teachers (continued)

learning to teach (continued)

fifth year of college, 86–87, 90, 92, 93

first four years of college, 85–86

internships, 86–87, 88, 90, 92, 93

mentoring and, 86, 87, 90, 92

organizational resources for, 94–96

overview of, 58–60, 82–83

periodicals on, 96

readings on, 97–98

student teachers, 86–87, 88–89, 90, 91

team teaching and, 87, 90

technology and, 90, 95, 96

See also Colleges of education;
Schools of education; Teachers,
professional development of

on local councils, 169, 170

minority, 92, 96, 98

mission and goals definition and, 3, 14,
17–18, 166–167, 169

moral development of students and,
34, 109

motivation by, 25, 55, 68, 70–71, 78

networking of

biology teachers, 91

electronic resources for, 237, 238, 239,
240, 249, 252

e-mail and, 220, 222, 223

geography teachers, 239

literature teachers, 237

mathematics teachers, 215, 239

mentoring and, 87, 215

organizational resources for, 76, 77,
94, 226

overview of uses for and value of,
5, 71, 72, 73, 74, 76, 77, 78, 79,
83, 170, 226

with parents, 107, 111, 116, 197, 222

periodicals on, 96

professional development and, 94–96, 215

readings on, 79, 80

school boards and, 171

science teachers, 27, 215

time saved by, 214

writing teachers, 237

parents and. See Parents, teachers and
schools and

parents as, 106, 110, 115

Teachers (continued)

peers and, 65, 69, 71, 73, 74, 75, 77, 83, 87,
89, 91, 170, 215. See also Mentoring,
of teachers; Teachers, networking of

policy makers and, 69, 76, 95

portfolios of, 77, 87

principals and, 30, 170, 173

professional development of, 82–98

in arts, 237, 239

in assessment, 237

beginning teachers, 87, 122

in civics, 30

co-learning with students and, 71

contacts for, 98

in cooperative learning, 30

electronic resources for, 94, 238, 239,
242, 243, 245

externships, 73

follow-up assistance for, 215

grants for, 245

importance of, 65, 82, 83, 87

in Internet use, 240, 251

in leadership, 74, 75, 76, 77–78, 94, 95, 185

lifelong nature of, 87, 88–89, 94, 96

in mathematics, 27, 30, 31, 33, 239

mentoring and, 69, 73, 74, 75, 83, 86, 87,
88, 90, 92, 170, 195, 215, 236, 248

networking and, 94–96, 215

organizational resources for, 30–32,
76–78, 94–96, 180

overview of, 4–5, 65

periodicals on, 96

in physical education, 32

readings on, 97–98

research on, 76, 77, 94, 95, 96, 237

research by teachers and, 74, 79

sabbaticals, 73, 74

scheduling and, 87, 93

school boards and, 171

school restructuring and, 93, 98

schools of, 93, 97, 232

in science, 27, 30, 31, 33, 97, 239, 246

self-directed, 83, 97

state education agencies and, 187

team teaching and, 65, 69

technology and, 80, 83, 89, 95, 96, 135,
151, 215, 221, 222, 227, 237, 250.
See also Teachers, technology
and, learning how to use

traditional, 4–5, 88

Teachers (continued)

professional development of (continued)

videotaping and, 89, 91, 215

See also Teachers, learning to teach

recruiting, 92, 96, 98, 246

research by, 69, 74, 76, 77, 79, 235

respect for, 67, 68, 72, 73, 77, 96, 109,
110–111, 117

role of, 64–80

advocates, 65

ambassadors, 65

coaches, 20, 26, 43, 64

consultants, 5, 75

contacts for, 80

counselors, 68, 179

curriculum developers, 60, 65, 72, 73,
80, 173, 178, 179, 183

electronic resources for, 240

equal partners with students, 20, 22,
24–25, 32, 49, 64, 68–69,
70–71, 226

facilitators, 68, 70–71, 196

guides, 15, 43, 64–65, 68, 70–71, 79,
179, 195

individual relationships with students,
64, 68, 71, 86, 167, 170, 179, 214

as information sources, 67, 68, 70,
210, 214

leadership, 74, 75, 76, 77–78, 94, 95, 185

learning and, 68, 69

management and budgeting, 65, 72, 75,
170, 172, 173

mentors of students, 195

mentors of teachers, 69, 73, 74, 75, 83,
86, 87, 88, 90, 92, 170, 195, 215,
236, 248

organizational resources for, 76–78

outside classroom, 65, 69

overview of, 58–60, 64–65, 127

periodicals on, 78, 240

readings on, 79–80

real-world learning and, 68

redefining, 64–65, 67–69

researching, 69, 74, 76, 77, 79, 235

teacher-directors, 173

team teaching and, 65, 69, 72

technology and, 64–65, 68–69, 79, 211

thinking and, 68–69

traditional, 26, 64, 67, 68, 69, 70, 79

Teachers (continued)

site-based management and, 65, 72, 75, 170, 172, 173

standards for, 77, 96, 97

standards for students and, 44, 49, 170

teams of. See Team teaching

technology and

database of instructional strategies, 78

laptop computers, 72, 221

learning how to use, 80, 83, 138, 219, 221, 222, 225, 229, 240, 248, 249, 251

learning to teach and, 90, 95, 96

organizational resources for, 76, 156, 224–227

parents and, 111, 113, 114, 116, 222

periodicals on, 78, 228

professional development and, 80, 83, 89, 95, 96, 135, 151, 215, 221, 222, 227, 237, 250

readings on, 79–80, 228–229

role redefinition and, 64–65, 68–69, 79, 211

teacher-experts, 219, 222

teacher relationship to technology, 31, 229

value of, vi, 5–6, 58–60, 64–65, 69, 71, 72, 95, 135, 175, 211, 214, 215, 217, 221, 226

See also Technology

See also Students

Teachers & Technology (Office of Technology Assessment), 80

Teachers at Work (Johnson), 79

Teachers College Record, 186

Teacher's Edition On-line, 241

Teachers Guide to Cyberspace (Impact II— The Teachers Network), 79

Teacher's Guide to the U.S. Department of Education, 241

Teachers Take Charge of Their Learning (Rényi), 97

Teacher Talk Home Page, 241

Teacher Technology Center, 251

Teacher-to-Teacher, 78

Teach for America, 246

Teaching and Change, 78

Teaching for Diversity (Villegas et al.), 98

Teaching the New Basic Skills (Murnane and Levy), 37

TeachNet, 77, 240

Team Building for School Changes (Maeroff), 79

Teams

cross-grade. See Multi-ability groups; Multi-age groups

school design, 110, 173, 186, 192–193, 197, 198, 200

See also Team teaching

TEAMS Distance Learning, 251

Team teaching

beginning teachers and, 87

curriculum development and, 173, 178, 179

defined, 69, 167, 170

examples of, 72, 175, 177, 178, 199

learning to teach and, 87, 90

organizational resources for, 77, 78, 94–96

readings on, 79

research and, 74

technology and, 175, 177

value of, 65, 69, 72, 167, 170

See also Multi-ability groups; Multi-age groups

Tech Corps, 156

Technology, 210–230

administrators and, 171, 221, 223, 224, 226, 229

art and, 217, 223

assessment and, 41, 44, 54, 221

assistive, 211, 213, 224, 226, 228, 231, 236, 249

business and, 113, 138, 143, 145, 146–147, 149, 152, 156, 213, 220, 223, 226, 227, 228, 248, 249

community and. See Community, technology and

community learning centers and, 129, 133, 134, 135, 138, 139

contacts for, 230

curriculum and, 20, 32, 33, 78, 199, 216–223, 225, 251.
See also Technology, integrating

distance learning and, 95, 111, 186, 193, 251

diversity of, 214

electronic resources for, 234, 235, 237, 240, 241, 242, 245, 246, 247, 248–252

equal access to. See Equal access

examples of using, 216–223

feedback and, 53

financing, 76, 219, 220, 225, 227, 245, 250, 251, 252

government leader understanding of, 250

Technology (continued)

hands-on learning and, 24, 31, 211

in the home, 25, 107, 111, 113, 114, 116, 121, 131, 139, 222

integrating, 73, 80, 96, 107, 151, 216–230, 234, 235, 237, 240, 241, 242, 243, 246, 248–252. See also Technology, school restructuring and

laptop computers for teachers, 72, 221

learning how to use

community members, 217, 225, 227

low-income groups, 245, 251

students, 138, 219, 225, 249

teachers, 80, 83, 138, 219, 221, 222, 225, 229, 240, 248, 249, 251

lending programs, 107, 111, 214, 222

local councils and, 169, 176

maintaining, 217

motivation by, 210, 211, 216, 217, 222, 229

organizational resources for, 30, 31, 32, 33, 224–227

overview of, 210–211, 213–215

parents and, 25, 107, 111, 113, 114, 116, 121, 131, 139, 222

parent-teacher communication and, 111, 113, 114, 116, 222

periodicals on, 34, 96, 186, 228

policy makers and, 226, 228, 229, 230, 249

portfolios and, 20, 41, 44, 47

project-based learning and, 23, 24, 27, 29, 175, 176, 188, 225

readings on, 79–80, 228–230

real-world learning and, 71, 211, 214–215, 218, 224, 226

research on, 222, 224, 227, 228, 229, 235, 246, 250

rural schools and, 174, 203, 216, 219, 251

scheduling and, 188, 214–215

school facilities and, 72, 106, 195–196, 197, 198, 199, 200–201, 202, 207, 214, 216–217, 218. See also Technology, integrating

school restructuring and, 174, 175, 177, 178, 180, 188, 189, 195–196, 216–217, 218, 222.
See also Technology, integrating

schools as hubs of, 125, 197

students and. See Students, technology and

teachers and. See Teachers, technology and

team teaching and, 175, 177

Technology (continued)

telephones in classrooms, 72, 106, 113, 214

television, 203, 222

time-saving nature of, 214–215, 223

used equipment donations, 249

value of. See Parents, technology and;
Students, technology and, value of;
Teachers, technology and, value of

video conferencing, 125, 147, 177, 199,
220, 222, 227, 233, 241

virtual reality, 147, 199, 210

voice mail, 222

See also Electronic resources; E-mail;
Internet; Multimedia; Networking;
Simulations; Software;
Telecommunications; World Wide
Web (WWW); specific companies

Technology & Learning, 34

Technology for Teaching and Learning
(Sheingold et al.), 229

Technology Leadership Network, 226

Technology's Role in Education Reform
(Mean and Olson), 188

TECHNOS, 228

Telecommunications

defined, 233

importance of, vi, 210–211, 213–215

research on teaching and learning and, 33

See also Electronic resources; E-mail;
Internet; Networking; Technology;
Video conferencing; World Wide
Web (WWW)

Telecommunications Technology and Education
(Cradler and Bridgforth), 229

Teleconferencing. See Video conferencing

Telelearning Project, 251

Telephones, in classrooms, 72, 106, 113, 214

Television, 203, 222

TENET, 72, 230, 247, 252

Tennessee

Appalachia Educational Laboratory, Inc.
(Internet), 235

Chattanooga School for the Arts and
Sciences (Chattanooga), 26

ConnecTen (Internet), 249

Learning Technology Center (Nashville), 227

Leonard Bernstein Center for Education
Through the Arts (Internet), 239

Southern Regional Education Board
(Atlanta, GA), 185

TERC, 33, 230, 247

Testing. See Assessment (alternative/authentic/
performance); Standardized tests;
Written examinations

Testing for Learning (Mitchell), 55

Texas

ACT Academy (McKinney), 72, 80

Alice Carlson Applied Learning Center
(Fort Worth), 172–173, 175, 190

El Paso Collaborative (El Paso), 178

Fort Worth Project C³ (Fort Worth), 152

Southern Regional Education Board
(Atlanta, GA), 185

Southwest Educational Development
Laboratory (Internet), 237

Texas A&M University Department
of Educational Administration
(College Station), 208

Texas Education Network (TENET),
72 (Austin), 230 (Austin),
247 (Internet), 252 (Internet)

Ysleta Elementary School (El Paso), 178

Texas A&M University Department
of Educational Administration, 208

Texas Education Network (TENET), 72, 230,
247, 252

Theater. See Arts

T.H.E. Journal, 228

Theory, translating into practice, 21, 32, 33,
92. See also Learning theories

Theory of Multiple Intelligences, 241.
See also Multiple intelligences

Thinking

curriculum development and, 15

hands-on learning and, 24

individual differences and, 48

learning and, 15, 35, 36

portfolios and, 41

readings on, 35

research on, 32

teacher's role and, 68–69

See also Understanding

Thinking Fountain Science Education
Museum of Minnesota, 242

ThinkQuest, 248

Thode, Brad, 32, 38

Thode, Terry, 24–25, 38

Thornburg, David D., 189, 229, 230

Thornburg Center for Professional
Development, 230

Time. See Scheduling

Tinker, Robert F., 230

Together We Can (Melaville et al.), 140

Tomorrow's Schools of Education
(The Holmes Group), 97

Totally for Teachers, 78

Toward a Coherent Curriculum (Beane), 35

Town meetings, xiii, 169, 170

Training. See Business, partnership
programs; Employment; Teachers,
learning to teach; Teachers,
professional development of

Transforming Professional Development for
Teachers (Corcoran), 97

Transforming Schools Consortium, 241

Transforming State Education Agencies to
Support Education Reform (David), 187

Trevino, Yoland, 136, 140

Triangle Coalition, 246

Turnbull Learning Academy, 115

Turner Middle School, 132

21st Century Education Initiative, 247

21st Century Teachers, 241

Tyson, Harriet, 98

U

Ultimate Children's Internet Sites, 248

Understanding

assessment of. See Assessment
(alternative/authentic/performance)

cooperative learning and, 20, 36

curriculum development and, 15

defined, 18

developing capacity for, 34

developing true, 215

learning and, 15, 18, 22, 33, 35, 36, 47

reading and, 48

research on, 32

simulations and, 44

writing and, 48

See also Thinking

Universities. See entries beginning with
College; specific universities

University of California Berkeley, National
Center for Research in Vocational
Education, 155, 158

University of California Los Angeles, National Center for Research on Evaluation, Standards, and Student Testing, The, 53, 56

University of Cincinnati, College of Design, Architecture, Art and Planning, 208

University Heights High School, 51

University of Minnesota, Cooperative Learning Center, 30, 38

University of Nevada, College of Education, 98

University of New Mexico, Institute for Environmental Education, 205, 208

University of Pennsylvania, Consortium for Policy Research in Education, 180, 190

University of Southern Maine, Extended Teacher Education Program, 92

University of Texas at Austin, Texas Education Network (TENET), 72, 230, 247, 252

University of Virginia, Curry School of Education, 90

University of Wisconsin at Madison, 190

Upper Arlington City Schools, 50

Urban Education Web, 247

Urban Learning Communities, Inc., 38

Urban Village program, 134

U.S. Conference of Mayors, 247

U.S. Congress
  Library of Congress Congressional Server, 242
  National Assessment Governing Board, 245
  Office of Technology Assessment, 80, 229
  technology use and, 250
  See also Legislation; Policy makers

U.S. Department of Education, 32, 122, 230, 250
  electronic resources for, 235, 238, 241, 244, 246, 247, 252
  Office of Educational Research and Information, 240
  Office of Educational Technology, 190

U.S. Department of Labor, Secretary's Commission on Achieving Necessary Skills, 158

Utah
  Utah Education Network (Internet), 252
  WestEd (Internet), 237

Utah Education Network, 252

V

Vaughn Family Center, 134, 140

Vaughn Next Century Learning Center, 134, 140

Vermont
  assessment in, 49, 55
  Cabot School (Cabot), 174, 216–217, 230
  Morristown Elementary School (Morrisville), 49
  Northeast and Islands Regional Educational Laboratory (Internet), 236
  Williston Central School (Williston), 177

Video conferencing, 125, 147, 177, 199, 220, 222, 227, 233, 241

Videos
  evaluation of, 248
  resource for, 250
  See also Documentary film

Videotaping, professional development and, 89, 91, 215

Villegas, Ana Maria, 98

Vinovskis, Maris A., 189

Virginia
  Appalachia Educational Laboratory, Inc. (Internet), 235
  Ashlawn Elementary School (Arlington), 70–71
  Association for Supervision and Curriculum Development, 38 (Alexandria), 180 (Alexandria), 237 (Internet)
  Association for the Advancement of Computing in Education (Charlottesville), 224
  Center for Interactive Educational Technology (Fairfax), 224
  Communities in Schools, Inc. (Alexandria), 136
  Institute for the Transfer of Technology to Education (Alexandria), 226
  Internet Society (Reston), 226
  National Association for Sport and Physical Education, The (Reston), 32
  National Association of Partners in Education, Inc. (Alexandria), 155
  National Association of Secondary School Principals (Reston), 183, 188
  National Community Education Association (Fairfax), 137
  New American Schools (Arlington), 31, 32, 33, 174. 176, 184, 186, 205

Virginia (continued)
  Southern Regional Education Board (Atlanta, GA), 185
  University of Virginia Curry School of Education (Charlottesville), 90
  Virginia Public Education Network (Internet), 252

Virginia Public Education Network, 252

Virgin Islands, Northeast and Islands Regional Educational Laboratory (Internet), 236

Virtual Cave, 241

Virtual encyclopedias, 239

Virtual field trips, 237, 241, 247, 248, 251

Virtual reality, 147, 199, 210

Visions, 156

Visual arts. See Arts

Vlastos, George, 207

Voice mail, 222

Volunteering, 106, 111, 112, 113, 114, 117, 135

Voting
  community learning centers and, 129, 134, 138
  preparing students for, 1, 2
  See also Civic responsibility

W

Waddock, Sandra A., 189

Walden III Middle/High School, 51

Walt Disney Imagineering, 230

Washington
  Boeing Company, The, 158 (Seattle), 243 (Internet)
  Center for Educational Renewal (Seattle), 94
  Dykeman Architects, The (Everett), 198–199, 208
  Henry M. Jackson High School (Mill Creek), 198–199
  Human Services Policy Center (Seattle), 137
  Maplewood K-8 School (Edmonds), 115
  New Horizons for Learning, 230 (Seattle), 246 (Internet)
  Northwest Regional Educational Laboratory, 52 (Portland, OR), 55 (Portland, OR), 236 (Internet)
  Parent Cooperative Education Program (Edmonds), 115
  Seattle Public Schools, The (Stuebing et al.), 207
  Shorecrest High School (Shoreline), ix

Washington *(continued)*
　Shoreline School District
　　(Shoreline), *ix,* 220
Washington, D.C.
　American Association for the Advancement
　　of Science, 30, 38
　American Association of Colleges for
　　Teacher Education, 94
　American Educational Research
　　Association, 30
　American Federation of Teachers, 76, 78, 80
　American Youth Policy Forum, 154, 158
　Association for Educational Communications
　　and Technology, 224
　Business Coalition for Education
　　Reform, 154
　Business Roundtable, The, 154, 157
　Center for Law and Education, 122
　Center for Teaching and Learning, 76, 80
　Committee on Architecture for
　　Education, 204
　Consortium for School Networking, 225
　Council for Basic Education, 158,
　　244 (Internet)
　Council of Chief State School Officers, 181
　Education Trust, Inc., 178, 182
　ERIC Clearinghouse on Assessment and
　　Evaluation, 52
　ERIC Clearinghouse on Teaching and
　　Teacher Education, 94
　Hand in Hand, 118
　Institute for Educational Leadership,
　　Inc., 140, 182
　Interstate New Teacher Assessment and
　　Support Consortium, 94
　McGuffey Project, The, 80
　Mid-Atlantic Laboratory for Student
　　Success, 235
　National Assessment of Educational
　　Progress, 53, 245 (Internet)
　National Coalition for Parent Involvement
　　in Education, 119
　National Council for Accreditation of
　　Teacher Education, 96
　National Education Association, 76, 80
　National Foundation for the Improvement
　　of Education, 78

Washington, D.C. *(continued)*
　National School-to-Work Learning and
　　Information Center, 155
　National Science Resources Center, 33
　New Standards, 32, 49, 53, 56, 174
　Project on Effective Interventions, 140
　Public Education Network, 184
　Quality Education for Minorities, 185
　State Collaborative on Assessment and
　　Student Standards, 54
　Workforce Skills Program, 156
　See also U.S. Congress; U.S. Department
　　of Education; U.S. Department
　　of Labor
Wasley, Patricia A., 80
Web. *See* World Wide Web (WWW)
Web, The, 34
Web 66, 235
WebCrawler, 234
WebMuseum Network, Paris, 242
Webster School, The, 222
Wehlage, Gary G., 189
Weissbourd, Bernice, 139
Wentworth, Eric, 158
West Des Moines Community School
　District, 135
WestEd, 237
Westside Community Schools, 219
West Virginia
　Appalachia Educational Laboratory, Inc.
　　(Internet), 235
　Bell Atlantic World School (Internet), 248
　Roane County High School (Spencer), 203
　Southern Regional Education Board
　　(Atlanta, GA), 185
Whale Times, 248
*What Governors Need to Know About Educa-
　tion Reform* (Higginbotham), 187
What Matters Most (The National Commission
　on Teaching & America's Future), 97
What Work Requires of Schools (U.S.
　Department of Labor), 158
White Career Academy, 122
Who Will Teach the Children? (Tyson), 98
Why Files, 248
Wiggins, Grant, 43–45, 56
Williston Central School, 177
Wilson, Kenneth, 189

Windows to the Universe, 241
Winston, Betty, 139, 140
Wisconsin
　Alverno College of Education
　　(Milwaukee), 91, 98
　Children's Environments Research and
　　Design Group (Milwaukee), 204
　Flambeau School District (Tony), 116
　Johnson Foundation (Racine), 208
　National Telemedia Council (Madison), 33
　North Central Regional Educational
　　Laboratory (Internet), 235
　University of Wisconsin (Madison), 190
　Walden III Middle/High School (Racine), 51
　Wisconsin Youth Apprenticeship Program
　　(Madison), 151
Wisconsin Youth Apprenticeship Program, 151
Within Our Reach (Schorr and Schorr), 140
Wolf, Dennie Palmer, 55, 56
Wolff/Lang/Christopher architects, 201
Wood River Middle/High School, 38
Work-based learning, 146, 148–149,
　150–153. *See also* Business,
　partnership programs; Employment
Workforce Skills Program, 156
World Wide Web (WWW)
　defined, 233
　search engines, 234
　value of, 211, 232
　See also Electronic resources; Internet
Worsham, Toni, 36
Writing
　assessing, 48, 49, 50
　business partnership programs and, 153
　electronic resources for, 237
　parental training in, 117
　teaching, 34, 88–89, 93, 237
　work-based learning and, 150
Written examinations
　multiple-choice, 23, 40–41, 43, 44, 49, 233
　performance assessment and, 21, 40–41,
　　43, 50
　portfolios and, 23, 49
　score focus of, 43, 45
　standardized. *See* Standardized tests
WWW. *See* World Wide Web (WWW)

X

Xerox Palo Alto Research Center, 230

Y

Yahoo!, 234

Yahooligans!, 234

Yale Child Study Center, School Development
Program, 120, 121, 122

Year-round scheduling, 69, 75, 175, 197

Years of Promise (Carnegie
Corporation of New York), 35

Yoshida, Clyde, 46–47, 56

You Can with Beakman and Jax, 248

Ysleta Elementary School, 178

Notes on Typography, Art & Production

Learn & Live™ was designed and art-directed by Thomas Ingalls and Caryl Gorska.

The text face is Minion, a digital font created by Robert Slimbach inspired by oldstyle typefaces of the late Renaissance. Named for one of the type sizes used in the early days of typefounding, Minion means "beloved servant," a reflection of the font's useful and unobtrusive qualities.

Display typography is set in Minion Display and Bureau Grotesque 37. Bureau Grotesque is a contemporary sans serif designed in 1989 by Jonathan Hoefler and David Berlow. Grotesques are so-called because they were considered ugly when they first came into use as display type in the 1830s. They were not widely used until their rediscovery by the Bauhaus movement in the early 20th century. Today the term grotesque is used synonymously with sans serif.

The index was created by Trisha Lamb Feuerstein. The software used to deliver and maintain the index, CINDEX™ for Macintosh, was donated by Indexing Research, Rochester, N.Y.

The book was printed by Anderson Lithograph, City of Commerce, Calif., on Multi Web, an acid-free archival paper manufactured by Repap Paper Company, Great Falls, Wis.

Full-color illustrations were created exclusively for this book by the following artists: George Abe (chapters 4, 8, 9); Kristen Funkhouser (cover art, chapters 1, 6); Robert Kopecky (chapters 2, 7); Marc Rosenthal (chapters 5, 10); and Mark Ulriksen (chapter 3). Max Seabaugh did the two-color spot illustrations that appear throughout the book.

Still photography was provided by Chris Church, Christopher Fitzgerald, Nancee Lewis, Paul Moseley, Matthew Rivaldi, Howard Roffman, and Brian Wallace. School building photography was graciously lent by Gaylaird Christopher (Wolff Lang Christopher), Ed Goodwin (Burgess & Niple), K. John Jones (Dykeman Architects), Jon Sousa, and the School City of Hammond. All other photographs were captured from footage shot for the documentary film.